D0202424

PUBLICATIONS

OF THE

NAVY RECORDS SOCIETY

VOL. 123

THE NAVY OF THE LANCASTRIAN KINGS

THE NAVY RECORDS SOCIETY was established in 1893 for the purpose of printing rare or unpublished works of naval interest.

Any person wishing to become a Member of the Society is requested to apply to the Hon. Secretary, c/o Royal Naval College, Greenwich, SE10 9NN. The annual subscription is £5.50, the payment of which entitles the Member to receive one copy of each work issued by the Society for that year, and to purchase back volumes at reduced prices. The subscription for Libraries and Institutions is £7.00.

Subscriptions and orders for back volumes should be sent to the Hon. Treasurer, c/o Barclays Bank, 54 Lombard St., London, EC3P 3AH.

THE COUNCIL of the NAVY RECORDS SOCIETY wish it to be clearly understood that they are not answerable for any opinions or observations that may appear in the Society's publications. For these the responsibility rests entirely with the Editors of the several works.

Folio no. 42 recto from vol. PLA/18 in the library of The National Maritime Museum, the Accounts and Inventories of William Soper. Reproduced by kind permission of the National Maritime Museum.

THE NAVY OF THE LANCASTRIAN KINGS

Accounts and Inventories of William Soper,
Keeper of the King's Ships, 1422–1427

Edited by
SUSAN ROSE

PUBLISHED BY GEORGE ALLEN & UNWIN
FOR THE NAVY RECORDS SOCIETY
1982

© The Navy Records Society, 1982.
This book is copyright under the Berne Convention. No
reproduction without permission. All rights reserved.

**George Allen & Unwin (Publishers) Ltd,
40 Museum Street, London, WC1A 1LU, UK**

George Allen & Unwin (Publishers) Ltd,
Park Lane, Hemel Hempstead, Herts HP2 4TE, UK

Allen & Unwin Inc.,
9 Winchester Terrace, Winchester, Mass 01890, USA

George Allen & Unwin Australia Pty Ltd,
8 Napier Street, North Sydney, NSW 2060, Australia

First published in 1982

British Library Cataloguing in Publication Data

The Navy of the Lancastrian kings: accounts and
inventories of William Soper, keeper of the
King's Ships, 1421–1427. – (Publications of the
Navy Records Society; v. 123)
1. Great Britain – Royal Navy – History – Sources
2. Great Britain – History, Naval – Sources
I. Rose, Susan   II. Series
359'.00941   DA80
ISBN 0–04–942175–1

Set in 10 on 12 Times by Grove Graphics, Tring
and printed in Great Britain
by William Clowes Limited, Beccles and London

THE COUNCIL
OF THE
NAVY RECORDS SOCIETY
1982

PATRON
H.R.H. THE PRINCE PHILIP, DUKE OF EDINBURGH, K.G., O.M., F.R.S.

PRESIDENT
THE RT HON. THE LORD CARRINGTON, P.C., K.C.M.G., M.C.

VICE PRESIDENTS
Capt. S. W. ROSKILL, C.B.E., D.S.C., Litt.D., F.B.A., M.A., R.N.
Sir John LANG, G.C.B.
Prof. C. C. LLOYD, M.A.
Richard OLLARD, F.R.S.L., M.A.
R. J. B. KNIGHT, M.A., Ph.D.
Capt. A. B. SAINSBURY, V.R.D., M.A., R.N.R.

COUNCILLORS
Prof. Peter NAILOR, M.A.
Mrs Susan ROSE, M.A., Ph.D.
E. K. TIMINGS, F.S.A., M.A.
J. GOOCH, B.A., Ph.D., F.R.Hist.S.
P. M. KENNEDY, M.A., D.Phil., F.R.Hist.S.
H. C. TOMLINSON, M.A., Ph.D., F.R.Hist.S.
P. M. H. BELL, B.A., B.Litt.
Prof. J. S. BROMLEY, M.A., F.R.Hist.S.
D. K. BROWN, M.Eng., C.Eng., F.R.I.N.A., R.C.N.C.
J. D. BROWN
Admiral Sir James EBERLE, G.C.B.
Lieut. J. V. P. GOLDRICK, B.A., R.A.N.
Prof. D. M. SCHURMAN, M.A., Ph.D.
Geoffrey TILL, M.A., Ph.D.
Cdr. A. R. WELLS, M.A., M.Sc., Ph.D., R.N.
Jonathan COAD, M.A.
Miss P. K. CRIMMIN, B.A., M.Phil.
C. I. HAMILTON, M.A., Ph.D.
Richard HOUGH
A. P. McGOWAN, M.A., Ph.D.
Capt. R. H. PARSONS, M.A., C.Eng., M.I.E.R.E., R.N.
Prof. B. McL. RANFT, M.A., D.Phil., F.R.Hist.S.
R. W. A. SUDDABY, M.A.

HON. GENERAL EDITOR
A. N. RYAN, M.A., F.R.Hist.S.

HON. SECRETARY
N. A. M. RODGER, M.A., D.Phil., F.R.Hist.S.

HON. TREASURER
H. U. A. LAMBERT, M.A.

For S

CONTENTS

PREFACE

This book has been in preparation for a long time and would never have been finished without the great kindness of many, both colleagues and members of my family.

The MS on which this volume is based is in the library of the National Maritime Museum at Greenwich and I have always been made welcome by all the staff there. I would particularly like to record my thanks to the late George Naish who gave me great encouragement at the very beginning of this project. Most of the supporting material comes from the Public Record Office where the staff has also been very helpful.

The finished work owes a great deal to the help of Dr Alwyn Ruddock, my supervisor at Birkbeck College. Anthony Ryan, the General Editor of the Navy Records Society, has given me much assistance in the final stages.

London   Susan Rose
May 1981

The Council of the Navy Records Society wishes to record its thanks to the Trustees of the National Maritime Museum and the Council of the Society for Nautical Research for their generosity in making grants towards the costs of publication.

LIST OF ABBREVIATIONS

P.R.O.	Public Record Office, London
C.P.R.	*Calendar of Patent Rolls*
C.C.R.	*Calendar of Close Rolls*
C.F.R.	*Calendar of Fine Rolls*
L.T.R.	Lord Treasurer's Remembrancer
K.R.	King's Remembrancer
M.M.	*Mariner's Mirror*
Proc. H.F.C.	*Papers and Proceedings of the Hampshire Field Club*
S.R. Soc.	Publications of the Southampton Record Society
S.R. Ser.	Southampton Record Series – continuing the work of the above Society under the auspices of the University of Southampton
Davies	*The History of Southampton* by J. Sylvester Davies
Blk. Bk.	*The Black Book of Southampton*, edited by A. B. Wallis Chapman, published by the Southampton Record Society
V.C.H.	*Victoria County History*

Introduction

GENERAL INTRODUCTION

Among the manuscripts in the library of the National Maritime Museum at Greenwich (numbered no. 4102) is a large folio volume of fifteenth-century naval accounts. These accounts were drawn up by authority of William Soper, the clerk of the King's ships, and refer to the years 1422–27; the period during which the navy built up by Henry V for the French war was largely dispersed by sale following his death.

The volume itself consists of a parchment book of 128 folios in a leather binding of the type usually associated with nineteenth-century libraries, probably dating from the time when the manuscript formed part of the collection of Thomas Phillipps, the well-known bibliophile and antiquarian. It came to Greenwich in 1946 with other naval items from the Phillipps collection through the munificence of Sir James Caird: a benefaction which formed the nucleus of the Department of Manuscripts at the Museum.

There is no doubt that the major part of the manuscript is the book of particulars mentioned in the account of William Soper in the enrolled Foreign Accounts of the Lord Treasurer's Remembrancer for the corresponding period. It should therefore form part of the class of Accounts Various (Exchequer) in the Public Record Office. However, while the enrolled accounts of the clerk of the King's ships form a series from 22 Richard II to 30 Henry VI, with relatively few gaps, all occurring in the period before the accession of Henry V, the corresponding particulars exist for only a small minority of the accounts. It is rare to find the particulars existing as a complete account book; most are bundles of indentures or short inventories stitched together and sometimes enclosed in a leather pouch. From the accession of Henry VI, also, when a *contrarotulator* was appointed, whose duties consisted of keeping a second book of particulars as a check upon the first, it should be possible to discover two sets of particulars for each accounting period. However, the duplicate set of books exists only for one period – 11–15 Henry VI (1432–7).[1] Moreover, these two accounts books are virtually identical and even seem to have been written by the same clerk. Exchequer clerks, therefore, did not regard the particulars as documents of much importance once the enrolled account had been made up. It is not known how the manuscript came to survive and enter the Phillipps collection as a rarity of antiquarian interest.

Soper's account occupies a total of 115 folios. Compared with the corresponding enrolled account the book of particulars contains much more information on matters of detail: the names of individual workmen; the purpose for which various items of naval stores were intended; the reasons for writing off ships as beyond repair. It is in the normal medieval form: first a list of sums of money received by Soper, divided into receipts from the Exchequer and receipts from other sources (foreign receipts), followed by a list of expenditure carefully itemised. The entries are further sub-divided, in this case, into those occurring before and after the appointment of Nicholas Banastre as *contrarotulator* in March 1423. The accounts also contain an elaborate inventory of all naval stores and equipment in the possession of the office of the King's ships. This is arranged under the name of the ship to which the equipment in question last belonged, whether or not that vessel was still in royal ownership at the date of the accounts or whether indeed it still existed at all. The equipment is first listed as received; a note then follows of what has been used up during the accounting period and of any additions purchased or transferred from other ships; finally a further list is made of everything still remaining in the possession of the office at the close of the accounting period. Throughout the manuscript there are marginal notes in a different contemporary hand, perhaps that of Soper himself, the main part of the accounts having probably been written by his clerk. These notes do not provide additional information, but show that the manuscript had been carefully checked. The remaining 13 folios are divided into two groups; one bound in at the beginning and the other at the end of the main part of the work. The group of five folios at the beginning (Appendix I) is not in good repair, being rubbed and worn with one or two holes and four folios have been cut short at the bottom so that between one and four lines of text are missing. It contains fragments of an account dating from the time of Henry V dealing with the wages of workmen, the cost of the carriage of materials and the cost of repairs to the *Jesus*. These folios are numbered in a contemporary hand. The larger group of eight folios at the end of Soper's account (Appendix II) is in better repair, although the folio headings have been erased and the entries have been cancelled with a line drawn down each sheet (the normal practice of the Exchequer clerks once the enrollment of an account had been completed). The entries refer to repairs carried out on various royal ships for the purpose of joining the Duke of Bedford's expedition which went to the relief of Harfleur in 1416. Numbering in a modern hand begins at the first folio of Soper's accounts for 1422–7 and continues to the end of the volume, including the folios referred to above. On the last folio is a note apparently in the same hand: 'Misplaced in binding see the beginning.' It seems likely that both these fragmentary accounts come from books of particulars now lost and were added to the Soper accounts because of the similarity of subject matter. There is no evidence of when this took place or who was responsible.

THE CAREER OF WILLIAM SOPER

William Soper, the compiler of the accounts, is probably as well known by name to students of the fifteenth century as any of the myriad collection of clerks, knights, yeomen of the chamber, squires, merchants and local workmen in general who crowd the pages of the calendars of the Patent, Close and Fine Rolls. They were men essential to the machinery of government: the floods of directives, of writs and commissions which poured from the Exchequer and the Chancery depended on their goodwill and efficiency for execution. Nevertheless, they remain a shadowy, colourless body of men; a mere catalogue of names and positions without even the prestige of high rank and illustrious family heritage which attached to the magnates of the time, whose careers are often similarly unillumined by information of a personal nature.

Largely because a substantial body of local material has survived in the City Archives of Southampton to supplement the records of the central government, a much more balanced picture of his life and background can be constructed in the case of Soper.

It is, therefore, proposed to devote the first part of this introduction to Soper and his life in Southampton while the second part will deal with the royal ships and the administrative machinery which enabled them to put to sea.

Soper's date of birth, his birthplace, and the origin of his family are obscure. In his Will he names his parents as Robert and Clemency Soper.[2] Following up a suggestion in Josiah C. Wedgwood's *History of Parliament* Barbara Carpenter-Turner asserts that his father, Robert, was a draper of Winchester.[3] A man of this name appears in the Ulnage Accounts for Winchester of 18 Richard II assessed for 48 cloths without grain: but does not appear in the next surviving account that for 21 Richard II. In view of the extremely unreliable nature of the Ulnage Accounts both as a source of economic information and as a source of names, it is unwise to place too much reliance on this mention particularly when there is no supporting material available from the Winchester City Records. The bequest of three shillings and fourpence to Winchester Cathedral, also made by Soper in his Will, which Mrs Carpenter-Turner cites as further evidence of a connection with Winchester was a purely conventional bequest to the mother church of the diocese, so common as to be almost standard practice in pre-Reformation Wills. For example, at the same period, Walter Fetplace, a Southampton burgess whose family came from North Denchworth in Berkshire left as much as forty shillings to the church of St Swithyn (the Cathedral) Winchester in his Will: [4] and Robert Florice, who had come to Southampton from Guernsey, left twenty pence for the building of the Cathedral Church of Winchester.[5] Later at the end of the century, William Gunter, who came originally from Andover left the Cathedral at Winchester twelve pence.[6] Certainly there was no old established Soper family in Southampton itself: William is the only person of that name mentioned in the City records.

He may possibly have come from Salisbury. He himself owned a house there in 1455 and a merchant named John Soper who could perhaps have been a relation was trading in Salisbury in the 1440's. Robert Aylward,[7] another contemporary Southampton merchant, also owned a house in Salisbury at the same date, but unfortunately there is no evidence to enable one to state conclusively whether these properties were investments, a convenient pied-à-terre for a business-man after the tiring overland journey from Southampton, or the last symbol of an attachment to their possible mutual place of origin.

There is the further possibility that Soper may have come as an apprentice from the West Country as William Nicholl[8] had probably done. A family by the name of Soper was living at about this period in the neighbourhood of Totnes, but no definite connection between them and William exists. It does seem reasonably certain that Soper first came to Southampton as a youth to be apprenticed to a merchant of the town. Industry in Southampton at this period was almost negligible and the leading citizens of the town were merchants to a man. Their trade was varied and growing, depending heavily on Southampton's position both in relation to the major wool producing and cloth manufacturing areas of western and central England and as a convenient outport for London, possessing both a good safe anchor-age and adequate communications with the capital by road, thus sparing ships' masters the difficult and time consuming passage round the North Foreland and up the Thames Estuary.

The port was crowded with coastal shipping and was, to an increas-ing extent, visited by the galleys and carracks of the Italians.[9] Ships also came regularly from Flanders, France, Portugal and Spain. Inland trade was equally flourishing, carts leaving through the Bargate for London, Salisbury, Devizes, even Coventry and many other places.

As in other medieval merchant communities those successful in trade were soon expected, and indeed, seem to have welcomed the opportunity to play a part in the government of the town. At this period Southampton's constitution, based on the charter of 1401, was the result of a fusion of functions between the ancient burgh government and the merchant guild and by convention the post of seneschal or steward,[16] originally the treasurer and vice-president of the guild, was the first usually held by rising young men of Southampton. The steward's powers had gradually declined but the office still entailed attendance at all meetings of the town courts and close attention to the finances of the town. It is, indeed, as steward that Soper first appears in the Southampton records, witnessing two deeds in October and November 1410.[11] From this point Soper's career might well have developed on lines similar to those of his contemporaries and colleagues such as Peter James and Walter Fetplace, in an unhindered progression from steward to bailiff to mayor of the town, coupled with increasing wealth reflected in the volume of trade recorded in his name in the Local Custom or Port Books and the Brokage Books of Southampton. He would occasionally be involved in property transactions inside and outside the town limits; occasionally squabble with fellow townsmen and taking them to court; occasionally assist the central government by serving on commissions of inquiry or those concerned with assessments to subsidies. Nor would such a life have been dull or limited. Southampton in the first half of the fifteenth century was in general prosperous and busy: a centre of overseas trade, her quays crowded with shipping sometimes laden with exotic merchandise; dates and other fruits, silks and damasks of various colours, grains of Paradise (a medicine), leopard skins, gold dust, vermilion. Her streets were thronged, sometimes with seamen and merchants from Flanders, Brittany, Spain, Portugal and Italy: sometimes with knights, men at arms, archers and foot soldiers waiting for passage across the Channel as fortunes fluctuated in the French wars.

Soper's career, however, was not destined to follow this relatively conventional pattern. In May 1413 he was returned to Parliament as the junior member for Southampton with the experienced Thomas Marleburgh.[12] It is reasonable to suppose that the Exchequer officials were on the look out for a young man of energy, intelligence and respectability from this part of the country to fill a position in the important administration of the customs. In the autumn of 1413, Soper was appointed with John Esgaston to collect tunnage and poundage (voted in the last Parliament for defence) at the usual rate of three shillings per tun of wine and 12d in the pound on all merchandise, imported and exported, with the exception of wool, hides, woolfells, corn, flour, fresh fish and beasts imported and ale exported to Calais.[13] Some two months later Soper was further appointed, again with John Esgaston, collector of the custom and subsidy on wool, hides and woolfells: the custom on woollen cloths made in England for export: and the petty custom of 3d in the pound value granted to Edward I by merchants alien.[14]

It has been suggested that it was his connection with the petition presented to the Parliament of 1414 by the mayor and burgesses of Southampton which first brought him to government attention but in view of the appointment above this is obviously not so.[15] This petition complaining of the financial straits to which the town had been reduced because of the falling away of the number of alien merchants visiting the port, was an unfortunate result of the expedition to the Mediterranean mounted in 1412 by a group of London merchants, principally Drew Barentyn, William Waldern and Walter Cotton. The Genoese were already disturbed by the increased Florentine interest in the English trade following their capture of Porto Pisano and reacted violently to the appearance of English ships in Genoa. The ships and merchandise were seized and the factors thrown into jail. The London merchants were granted letters of marque for £34,000 and all Italian goods at Southampton were arrested. Soper, who had already been a customer for a year by this date, would have had personal experience of the great fall in the amount of alien merchandise passing through the customs house at Southampton, and as a merchant would have had personal experience of the effect of the fall off in trade on his own business. He would, undoubtedly, have been closely involved with the discussions in Southampton which would have preceded the petition and because of his special experience may well have presented it. This incident occurring right at the start of his official career shows him combining both his public and official role and his private and business capacity. This duality is the keynote of his career and can never be ignored when considering any aspect of his life. Soper, the customer, the clerk of the king's ships, was always also Soper, the merchant and leading citizen of Southampton.

Medieval administration depended on the existence of such people trusted both by royal officials (in Soper's case those of the Exchequer) and by local people, forming an indispensable link between the Crown and the population at large. There is a problem though concerning Soper's position in the customs administration and his own business as a merchant. According to the strict letter of the law, as soon as he was appointed collector of customs at Southampton it was illegal for him to indulge in any trade whatsoever or to have any but the most formal and official relations with foreign merchants. A petition presented to the Parliament of 1390 had demanded: *Auxi soit ordeine que null custumer ne contre-rollour n'eient nulles Niefs de lour propres ne se medleront de Freght de Niefs*: also let it be ordered that no customer nor controller may have any ships of their own nor may involve themselves with the cargoes of ships – and this demand had met with a favourable response. Towards the end of Soper's career a much more detailed petition on the same lines resulted in the statute of 20 Henry VI Cap. 5. which declared that: 'no customer, controller of the custom, clerks, Deputies, Ministers, or Factors shall have any ships of their own or shall buy or sell by way or by colour of Merchandise nor shall they not meddle with Freighting of Ships or have or occupy any such wharfs or keys or shall hold any Hostries or Taverns nor shall be any Factors or Attorneys for any Merchant Denizen or Alien nor shall they be hosts to any Merchant Alien.' The purpose behind such legislation is obvious – to prevent the corruption of the officials of the Customs House by setting them apart from the merchant community. In Soper's case, however, although there is not a shred of evidence that he was corrupt it is clear that he traded throughout his active life. His normal description in official documents was William Soper, merchant and there is no reason to doubt that his considerable fortune was amassed through trade.

When one wishes to examine his position in more detail there is a curious lack of evidence. Before his appointment as customer in 1413, for the vital first years of the fifteenth century when he was establishing himself as a man of substance there are no local Port Books (records of the town customer) extant in Southampton. The royal customs records for the early part of the fifteenth century are equally unhelpful. The particulars of account which alone give the names of merchants exist for the period 4–6 Henry IV, but are lost for the succeeding years until 4 Henry VI. The particulars of Henry IV's reign do not mention Soper. The only evidence of merchant activity by Soper at this period is a charter party from 1412 between Soper, William Nicholl and Geoffrey of Flouille, master of the *St Gabriel of Brittany*, concerning the transport of 50 barrels of wine of La Rochelle from that port to Southampton.[16] When the series of local port books for Southampton covering the fifteenth century begins with that for 1426–7,[17] Soper's trade (even though he had at this date been customer for 13 years) does not differ markedly from that of his friends and associates Walter Fetplace, Peter James,[18] William Nicholl and Robert Aylward. In the Port Books that exist for subsequent years the contrast is very marked; Fetplace, James, Nicholl and Aylward are revealed as active traders dealing in considerable quantities of merchandise, but Soper (according to this evidence) deals in so little that one might well conclude that he had indeed given up trading. The evidence from the Brokage Books of Southampton – the records kept by the keeper of the Bargate in Southampton recording the amount paid in tolls by carts entering and leaving Southampton and thus providing useful evidence of the inland trade of the port – is equally emphatic. His four associates' names frequently appear and one can discern some development in their activities. Over the years Walter Fetplace is the largest trader increasingly specialising in the dispatch of dyestuff and mordants (principally woad and alum) to the cloth-making towns of Wessex, principally Salisbury: Peter James becomes more exclusively concerned in the inland wine trade. Soper, however, sends very little through the Bargate, and items which seem intended either for his own use or as gifts to friends rather tian real articles of trade. In March 1440 the two pipes of wine he sent to Salisbury were for the Dean of Salisbury.[19] Similarly the two pipes of wine and one barrel of malmsey sent to Guildford in December 1441 are noted in the margin as being 'resseyv of ye kyngs howse'.[20] In 1443 the goods he sent to London – a barrel of wine and a 'fardell' of unspecified content – are described as being 'pro hospicio'.[21] Another barrel of wine and one of oil which followed them in March may have had the same destination. Finally in 1447 he sent by way of Romsey 2,000 slates which are noted as being *pro tecte domys*[22] [sic]. It seems unlikely that these slates were for his own house – being just across Southampton Water transport by boat would have been more practical – but they may have been intended for the repair of the royal hunting lodge near Romsey which formed part of the responsibilities of the verderer of the New Forest – a post which Soper had just relinquished at this date.

Evidence from other sources, however, flatly contradicts the conclusion that Soper obeyed the law and gave up his activities as a merchant. This evidence mainly comes not from the usual economic sources but from the Patent Rolls and similar classes and the Early Chancery Proceedings. A group of four export licences indicates a considerable interest in trade with Italy: the earliest dating from 1417 shows the export of 113 sacks of wool to the port *de Pyse in Italia*.[23] The second in point of time, dating from 1420, permits Soper to ship 419 pockets of wool of Spain to foreign parts free of custom.[24] Because of the provisions that in this case the wool should not bear customs duty, the details of the operation of this licence are known. The total quantity of 419 pockets was exported over three years: 34 pockets in 1420, 373 in 1421, and 9 in 1422.[25]

In at least three instances the ships' masters concerned – Richard Rowe, William Cheke and George Mixtowe[26] – were also royal ship masters. The date of the third licence is uncertain, but it was granted in response to Soper's petition to the king that he *'merchant de vostre vile de Suthampton'*, should have leave to *'charger en le dit port de Suthampton C et VIII sakes de layne pour porter a port de pise en ytaille.'*[27] The final licence is on a more personal level and even in fact raises the possibility that Soper may have travelled to Italy himself. The licence – to export twenty sacks of wool – is granted to enable him to pay for the expenses of a pilgrimage to Lombardy.[28] There is also evidence that Soper had well-established trading links with Spain, probably mainly with Bilbao. His confidential servant, David

Savage, was employed as his factor there and at least on occasion he acted in partnership with Walter Fetplace and Peter James in the same area.[29] Thus David Savage, servant of William Soper of Southampton, was granted a general licence to trade with Spain in September 1424. Soper and Fetplace together received a further licence in April 1429 and another in June of the following year. By June 1432 Savage, although still Soper's factor, had perhaps also set up in business on his own as a vessel owned jointly by himself and John Clement of Southampton was granted a protection for trading voyages between Spain and England. Soper received a similar privilege for a vessel of his own on the same day.[30] Overseas trade at this date was full of pitfalls as Soper and his colleagues found to their cost that same year. As Soper, Fetplace and James explained in a petition to the Chancellor, 'Davy Savage servant and factor of ye seide bysechere' arrived at 'Bylbawe' with a barge the *Mary of Bilbao* laden with merchandise mainly cloth to the value of £500 under protection of a safe conduct. John de Tasse of Bilbao and Orion Sanchez with the aid of John Derblanche, Sanchez Deyr and Ochoa de Merkyn threw Savage into jail, went off with all the goods and then demanded a ransom of £200 for Savage's release. Fortunately Derblanche, Deyr and Merkyn came to London and the petitioners beg for them to be confined in the Fleet Jail until Savage is released and the goods returned.[31] Unfortunately the answer to their petition has not survived and there is no way of knowing the outcome of the affair, although it is perhaps significant that there are no further licences to trade with Spain in Soper's name. Nevertheless, this group of licences do reveal a serious attempt to establish regular trading relations with Bilbao: a very different enterprise from the casual solitary licence which Soper obtained with William Payn in 1426 to export wine and salt and import fresh salmon and hides from Ireland.[32]

Equally the evidence for Soper owning ships of his own does not come from the local port books, but from the records of a naval expedition. His barge the *Julian of Hampton* of 140 tons was among those ships arrested for the expedition led by the Earl of Arundel in 1418.[33] Although, as was the normal practice in the Southampton Port Books, the owner's name is not stated, a vessel named the *Gylyene* or *Julian* makes several appearances in the Port Books for 1426–7 – on one occasion having goods of Soper among others on board.[34] Her master was George Mixtow, a mariner whom we have already mentioned as assisting in the export of Soper's wool and who appears in the Phillipps manuscript Account Book as master of the royal vessel, the *Falcon*. It seems reasonable to suppose that she was still in Soper's ownership at this date. Equally, as already mentioned, an unnamed vessel belonging to Soper was granted a safe conduct to Spain in 1432.

Presumably Soper used his ships to transport both his own merchandise and the goods of others, receiving the usual freight charges for the goods so moved from port to port and thereby adding a new source to his income. There is a possibility that he may have obtained a special grant from King or Council, permitting him to own ships and engage in overseas trade in spite of the statutory prohibition of such activities to all customs officials. Such grants are occasionally found on the Close and Fine Rolls and even on the Treaty Rolls (or French Rolls) in the fifteenth and early sixteenth centuries, but an extensive search of these sources has failed to reveal any trace of such a grant having been made and enrolled in Soper's name.

There are two possible explanations for this apparent divergence of evidence. Either Soper ensured by some means that the full extent of his trading activities was not recorded in the customs accounts and local port books because of their dubious legality, or he turned increasingly to forms of business activity which left no trace on the classes of economic documents extant. In theory there is little doubt that the opportunity existed for him to conceal his merchant activities if he had so desired. As collector of the royal customs himself, there would have been no difficulty in omitting to record or pay the duties for which he himself was liable. Legislation such as that concerning the customers, in the absence of any form of police force at this date, depended on the laying of information by private citizens (rewarded by the moiety of any fines imposed) for enforcement. The career of one enthusiastic informer, George Whelplay, a haberdasher, has been traced for a later period during the reign of Henry VIII.[35] All his exertions met with an almost total lack of success and there is no reason to suppose that he would have been more successful a century earlier. It would have been a bold man who informed against Soper, taking into account his standing in the local community; and it is doubtful whether Soper would have been seriously concerned over the possibility. Turning to the local port dues, Soper was not obliged to pay them – as a burgess of Southampton he was exempt. However, the same privilege was enjoyed by his associates, by Fetplace, James, Nicholl and Aylward. It is possible to imagine that the water bailiff treated his merchandise differently from that of all other Southampton merchant burgesses but hardly likely. Goods of burgesses were entered in the port books even if they were free of custom and the lack of entries for Soper is most simply explained by a lack of goods.

We are left, therefore, with the possibility that Soper turned increasingly, though never exclusively, in the years after 1426 to forms of trade which fell outside the scope of the royal or local customs and toll records. Customs dues were paid on goods entering or leaving the country or goods entering or leaving the town. They were not concerned with goods changing hands within the confines of Southampton itself. Trade in the borough was reserved for burgesses of the town and could be extremely profitable, taking into account the opportunities to distribute the luxuries and more mundane articles entering the port from the Continent to traders from all over the western half of England and also the Midlands. The possibility that Soper may have been heavily involved in this middleman activity is enhanced by the fact that in 1433 he leased the Watergate of Southampton from the Corporation.[36] This gate led directly onto the town quay and the greater part of the merchants and their merchandise, newly arrived at the port, had perforce to pass through it. What better position could there be for the business premises of an aspiring middleman? Moreover in 1439, Soper erected on a vacant plot on the west side of the eastern tower of the gate what is specifically described in the deed as a *shoppa* – a shop – with a chamber over.[37]

There is one group of documents, however, which does give full details of how visiting foreign merchants disposed of their cargoes within the borough of Southampton. These are the Hosting Returns which the Mayors of the seaport towns had to send to the Exchequer following the Hosting Act of 1439.[38] This required all merchants alien to reside with a Host appointed by the Mayor and for all their business transactions, whether buying or selling, to be recorded by the Host for eventual transmission to the Exchequer. These detailed accounts exist for Southampton for 19–20 Henry VI (1440–41) for a Breton merchant, Yvonn Tanguy and for a group of Spaniards, Peter Kyrmewe, Martin Ochoa, Torald Gonsalve, Martyn Pagao and Ivon Jarr.[39] Yvonn Tanguy imported 116 tuns of La Rochelle wine the greater part of which was sold to Walter Fetplace with William Larke, John Emery, John Hosier, John Heriot and Laurence John taking between 8 and 1 tuns each. Of the Spaniards Peter Kyrmewe also imported wine – 41 tuns of which were sold to Cardinal Henry Beaufort, Bishop of Winchester, Robert Aylward, Gilbert Holben, Nicholas Bylot, John Allcock, John Canby and John Arblaster. He bought in the town, for export, cloth without grain from Walter Fetplace and Robert Aylward and soap from William Nicholl. Torald Gonsalve and Martyn Pagao imported only iron. Martin Ochoa imported iron and also 29 rolls of beaver, (sent to London for sale) 10 small balets of cumin, 5 balets of licorice, 140 kid skins and 20 tuns of wine. The iron, 257 tuns in all, was sold to a total of twenty merchants. Of these Robert Aylward, Walter Fetplace, William Nicholl and John Payn took the most: 38 tuns, 33 tuns, 31 tuns and 28 tuns respectively. William Soper bought only 15c 1 qua 25 lb valued at 53s 10½d. The wine was sold to Nicholas Bylot and John Clement. The Spaniards bought cloth as their return cargo: 60 cloths valued at £133 6s 8d were bought from Walter

Fetplace and Robert Aylward and 29 broad cloths valued at £81 from William Nicholl and John Payn. This evidence is not conclusive relating as it does to only one year and one small group of merchants, but it shows that the merchants who were prominent in the trade covered by the local custom and toll records were also the most important in trade within the town, and lends no support at all to the supposition that Soper became heavily involved as a middleman in the trade between merchants alien and merchants denizen in Southampton. This supposition is further undermined by the views of Hosts of the following two years which, while neither so detailed nor in such good repair as that already mentioned, show goods being sold by the alien merchants to many of the Southampton men already mentioned but not at all to Soper.[40]

There is, however, one field of business activity which Soper seems to have been unusually well placed to exploit – and which for reasons which will be made clear below would leave only scant traces in contemporary official documents. This is the field of financial management; broadly speaking, the beginnings of what is today the concern of the merchant banker.

The systematic use of money-lending and money-changing and the development of negotiable instruments was at this date largely the preserve of the so-called 'Lombards' – the merchants of Genoa, Lucca, Florence and Venice – the undoubted leaders of the commercial world of this period. Soper was fortunate in having unusually warm personal and business relationships with the members of Italian commercial firms who visited Southampton or who resided there, particularly those from Florence, which familiarised him with the paper financial instruments employed by them. This is demonstrated in striking fashion in the detailed log of his voyage kept by Luca di Maso degli Albizzi, Captain of the Florentine Galleys for the Flanders voyage of 1429–30, which contains a long and fascinating account of his visit to Soper and to Southampton.[41] Albizzi had arrived with the galleys from Sluys on Saturday 7 January 1430 and having had dinner at an inn went to visit William Overey (Guglielmo Aure) and his wife Agnes who had previously been married to Bartholomew Marmora, the former Florentine agent in Southampton.[42] On Monday he settled down to business, meeting the Mayor (Thomas Belle) and Aldermen of Southampton in a church and agreeing with them how best to control the crews of the galleys during their stay in the town. It seems more than likely that Soper was present at this meeting acting with the others with *molta carita et discretione* – as Albizzi states – and arranging that the Italians should not cause damage, climb on the town walls, carry offensive arms, or go about at night without a light. On 31 January he went with Soper to visit the king's great ships riding at anchor at Hamble. Albizzi thought the *Gracedieu* the largest and most beautiful vessel he had ever seen, and much enjoyed having dinner on board. The following Wednesday, 2 February, Albizzi and the patrons of the galleys went to visit Soper's house on the edge of the New Forest with Soper's fellow customer, John Asshefeld and another local worthy whose name is given as Roberto Arsaelse (perhaps Robert Aylward).[43] This impressed the Italian for the house was richly decorated on the exterior and surrounded by a moat. There were sufficient servants and horses and many dogs because the house was so near the Forest. After dinner the party went hunting, some on horseback and others on foot and Albizzi was made a present of the dog which brought down the deer killed that day. They then went home again for supper and later heard vespers in Soper's private chapel. By this time Albizzi was enjoying himself so much that he did not wish to leave (*et cosi ci fe tutte quelle cortesi et dimestichezze che dire se potessi non volendo ci partissimo*) but at last they re-embarked in their boats and sailed back to Southampton taking with them the deer 'which we could not leave behind' (*che lasciare no gli potemo*).[44]

The man who was thus entertained by Soper was widely travelled having been as far as Hungary and the Holy Land.[45] As Captain of the Galleys he occupied one of the highest paid posts in the Florentine public service and had set forth with a suite consisting of four squires (one a notary), two personal servants, a chaplain, a doctor and two trumpeters.[46] Perhaps more important for the development of Soper's business interests, however, was his close contact with Bartholomeo Martelli to whom he was host following the passage of the Hosting Act of 1439.[47] Martelli was a member of a family prominent in Florentine politics who had himself played an important part in the seizure of power by Cosimo de' Medici. His family bank had branches in Seville, Pisa and Venice and was also much involved in maritime affairs at Livorno. He himself was in Southampton as patron or as Captain of the Galleys in 1440, 1442, 1447, 1456 and (after Soper's death) 1462. In addition Soper had contacts with the Italians resident in Southampton, principally the Spinola and Cattanei from Genoa. One of his Southampton properties, indeed, was let to Lazzaro Cattaneo.[48] Two of his other properties had Italian tenants in 1454: Gabriel Corbet a Venetian by birth who had settled permanently in England taking out letters of denization rented a house in the parish of Holy Rood[49] and Soper's own former town house (*capitalis tenementum*) was let to Filippo Larcario.[50] There is no doubt that Soper had direct experience of the use of the letters of payment or inland bills used by the Italians. As the evidence we have on this point comes from the Local Port Books and the Stewards' Books of Southampton, this early form of negotiable instrument is first found being used for the benefit of both the Italians and the burgesses of Southampton in easing the collection of local customs and paying the fee farm due to the Crown from the proceeds. The total due from the Italians for a year was set down in a letter of payment drawn on the associates of the Southampton Italians in London and made out in favour of the burgess entrusted by the steward of the town with the payment of the fee farm at the Exchequer. The cash would be obtained in London by this individual without the dangers and problems of transporting large sums in specie from Southampton to London. The use of this early form of money transfer by civic officials is known only from Southampton at this period.

Soper was responsible for paying the fee farm in 1427, receiving letters of payment from Jacopo Spinola, Bartholomeo Cattaneo and Paolo Morelli: [51] in 1429 £150 was entrusted to him but no mention is made of the method: [52] in 1434, however, £7 15s 2d was entrusted to him, again in letters of payment, for this purpose. Furthermore, in this year Soper was bound by indentures with the Spinola, Cattanei, Paolo Morelli and others for payment of their customs dues to the steward by such letters of payment.[53] The letter of payment was also used by the corporation, drawn on the London agent of Cristoforo Cattaneo and Andrea Spinola in 1434, so that Soper might pay at the Exchequer the proceeds of the fifteenth and tenth due at that time, totalling £35 19s.[54] In 1436, Soper was again charged with paying £100 to the representatives of the Queen Mother Joan – to whom the farm of Southampton had been granted – in the same way.[55] No mention of a letter of credit is made in 1442 when Soper was entrusted with £200 for the fee farm as mentioned in the unpublished Steward's Book for 1441–2 but by this time the method would have lost its novelty and may have been taken for granted.

Moreover, it is certain that Soper acted on occasion to obtain actual loans of money on the town's behalf as well as using the Italians for money transfers. Again in 1442, he obtained several sums of money in London, 'for the townys nede', probably seeking help from associates of the Southampton Italians or their agents in London, since the money was repaid to Italian merchants in Southampton – £5 to Gregorio Cattaneo, £10 to Paolo Morelli and £8 to Gabriel Corbett.[56] It would be normal nowadays for the provision of such facilities for the transfer of money to be rewarded by the deduction of a commission and a straight financial loan to be negotiated at interest. Such deductions and the charging of interest on loans were liable at this date to fall under suspicion of usury, which was both illegal and a sin condemned by the Church. Public opinion, which was relatively unmoved by the breaking of statutes by customers trading illegally, was disturbed by evidence of usury. The motive for concealing such activities from the unsophisticated and leaving no record of them wherever possible was strong. John Chirche, a London mercer with whom Soper was associated both in the customs administration at Southampton and in business, had been convicted on charges of false chevisance and usury in 1420 and had only escaped prison by repaying £31 to the defendants.[57] One cannot expect to find a great deal of direct evidence of Soper acting as a private banker in these circumstances, although his shop by the Watergate would have been as convenient for this type of dealing as for a middle-man, and there is one Chancery case of 1447 which reveals Soper lending money on his own account. The petition states that Soper lent £40 to 'oon Thomas Northereyn clerk'. Northereyn assigned a debt of his own of £10 by a writing obligatory to William Kele in London and also ordered him to pay the said £10 when received to Soper (for the which receyt the same Thomas commanded the seide Mayster William Kele to make a payment of the seide summe of x li. to youre seide besecher). Soper sent Thomas Chamberleyn to collect the money due but Kele refused to pay without written authority from Northereyn. Chamberleyn rode to Somerset from London and obtained the necessary letter under seal, but Kele still would not pay, 'the whiche he hathe refused to do and yet doth.' Kele's answer to the petition exists but is unfortunately illegible and the outcome of the case is uncertain.[58] It is thus clear that men living as far from Southampton as Somerset would turn to Soper for temporary loans upon occasion, and hard to believe that he would not have followed the customary Italian practice of charging concealed interest in the sums to be repaid.

The evidence, therefore, for Soper's trading activities is patchy and difficult to interpret. However, one can be reasonably confident that Soper continued to trade throughout his active career: that despite his appointment as collector of the customs he both owned a ship or possibly more than one ship and imported and exported goods for many years: but that as time went on he also became involved in financial operations of various kinds, including the advancement of personal loans to others. With his unique combination of skills and experiences – those of an esteemed royal official, those of a practical merchant and those of a man familiar with Italian banking methods – he was unusually well placed for this kind of business in which, despite the law, he could be well rewarded by concealed interest payments or more honestly by the payment of commission. To say that he himself became a banker is impossible because of the paucity of evidence but the facts we do possess clearly show that Soper had taken the first steps in this direction.

Similar uncertainty does not overshadow the remainder of his official career which, pursued simultaneously with his own concerns as a merchant, extended far beyond the customs house of Southampton. Enjoying the confidence of his fellow citizens his early appointment as steward of Southampton was soon followed by election as mayor in 1416 and 1424.[59] He must also have proved himself a worthy Member of Parliament. After his election to the Commons of 1413, he was re-elected in 1414, 1419, 1420, 1421, 1425, 1429, 1430–1, 1432, 1433, 1441–2, and 1448–9.[60] So long and so continuous a Parliamentary record was very unusual at the time, most burgesses being elected only once or twice: only William Chamberleyn (usually Soper's junior colleague) approached his record and one can infer from their frequent re-election that they formed an efficient team together. Service to the Crown probably took more of Soper's time than these services to his fellow citizens. His royal appointments can be conveniently divided into two classes: first those that were permanent involving the carrying out of certain duties for as long as the king pleased; secondly those that were *ad hoc* – appointments to take musters, to make inquiries (or inquisitions as they are usually termed), to arrest shipping for various purposes. His first permanent royal appointment was that of collector of customs in the port of Southampton – an appointment which lasted for nearly thirty years and formed the backbone of his career. It seems more than likely that his other appointments followed in consideration of his satisfactory record in the Southampton customs house, together with the intimate and exact knowledge of merchants and their shipping which he was so well placed to acquire. It is also, perhaps, worthy of note that at Southampton Soper always represented the royal interest in the customs. His colleagues from time to time frequently represented the interests not of the Crown, but of noble persons who had advanced money to the king and to whom this particular source of royal revenue had been pledged as a sure means of repayment. Thus, in 1423 John Foxholes was nominated by Henry Beaufort, Bishop of Winchester who had loaned the king, in March 1423, £9,333 6s 8d: and in 1431 John Chirche and Nicholas Wyfold were nominated in turn by the feoffees of the Duchy of Lancaster who had previously loaned the king £3,333 6s 8d. Soper's duties were also extended to cover the collection of special duties voted for the defence of the realm in 1423, 1427, 1429, 1432 and 1437.

His other permanent position of importance was of course, the office of keeper and governor, or clerk of the king's ships. The duties and the organisation of the office will be discussed more fully in the second half of this Introduction but at this point we can say something of how Soper first came to be associated with the king's ships. The precipitating factor seems to have been the capture at sea of a Castilian ship – the *Santa Clara* (or *Seint Cler*), freighted by two merchants trading from Castile, Juan Martinez (John Martyns) and

Agostino Lomelino (Augustine Lomelyn, a member of a Genoese family) – by a ship belonging to Soper and others in late 1413 or early 1414.[61] The ship was brought into Southampton and Soper found that he was in trouble because her owners claimed that she was covered by the terms of a safe-conduct. There must have been room for doubt in the matter because, although Soper was ordered to return to Martinez the ship's royal Castilian standards, some armour and weapons and the ship's dog in November 1414,[62] no mention was made of the ship herself and she had probably already been condemned as a prize. Thus, by February 1414, Soper had been commissioned to take carpenters and other workmen for the making and amending of a great ship of Spain at Southampton – the *Santa Clara* as his accounts make plain – which was to be reborn as the *Holy Ghost*.[63] There seems a strong possibility that Soper may have suggested this course of action to the Crown himself – the awakening royal interest in shipping would have become known in the seaport towns and in this way, the *Santa Clara* having become a royal ship, Soper would have got himself out of a potentially embarrassing position.[64]

From this slightly dubious beginning Soper's connection with the royal ships went from strength to strength. In 1416 he was associated with Robert Berde in the building of the *Gracedieu*, the *Falcon* and the *Valentine* at Southampton.[65] By 1418, at a wage of a shilling a day, he was 'surveyor of the king's ships, carracks and balingers' and in February 1420 he took over from William Catton as clerk or keeper of the king's ships, a position he was to hold continuously until 1441.[66] Even then his connection with the office was not entirely severed and he was officially controller to his successor Richard Clyvedon although by this time the office was a virtual sinecure.[67]

His third permanent position was that of verderer of the New Forest.[68] Soper was well known in the Forest – as we have seen, he made his own home on the easternmost verges. His official duties were connected with the king's pursuit of the deer – the repair of hunting lodges for example. One might imagine that his appointment had some motive also for facilitating the supply of oak from the Forest for the king's ships, but it came too late, in 1428, when the King's ships were all sold or laid up in the Hamble, to have any bearing on this matter. It was a pleasant honour for a local man of worth. Not that Soper regarded it solely as a sinecure, for it is poignant to read that in 1445 he was forced to give up the office because his health no longer permitted him to ride about the Forest.[69]

At the same time as this heavy burden of permanent administrative work Soper was also faced with a considerable quantity of occasional jobs for the Crown. Much of this work was *quasi*-military in character and closely related to the holding of musters, the arrest of transports for reinforcements to the English forces in Normandy or for ambassadors and their suites. He had, for example, to see to the safe return to Normandy of escorts for the prisoners taken in the campaigns of 1421–2.[70] The amount of such chores varied with the fortunes of the English in Normandy and was naturally greatest at the time of Henry V's expeditions, although the period of England's rapidly declining influence in France in the 1440's found Soper almost as busy smoothing the path for official travellers to France. Soper was not the only local man of importance habitually named in the commissions and mandates now surviving on the Patent Rolls and it is impossible to be completely sure whether his name was included for ornament or use. Taking into account his record in the royal administration, it seems that he was more likely to find himself actually checking the muster rolls or arguing with the no doubt somewhat truculent captains of arrested merchant ships than for example, the sheriff of Southampton (i.e. Hampshire) or Thomas, Lord Camoys. It has also been suggested that William Soper was in charge of the arrangements for the crossing of the Channel by Margaret of Anjou before her wedding to Henry VI.[71] However, it was John Breknoke and John Everdon who presented their account at the Exchequer for the expenses of the Lady Margaret coming to England, which reached the astonishing total of £5,129 2s,[72] and Soper seems to have been involved only as a personal escort for the future Queen across the Channel. This sum seems the more extraordinary when compared with the £250 which Soper received to pay off at Southampton the greater part of the ships masters and crews concerned with bringing from France to England the widowed Queen Katherine and the body of Henry V. Moreover only £76 3s 4d was spent at other ports on this occasion.[73]

Soper also became closely involved with many inquisitions of a *quasi*-judicial nature – the most important of these being concerned with the depredations of pirates in the Channel. In modern times the definition of piracy is quite clear – robbery at sea usually involving violence and the seizure of the ship as well as the goods on board. In this period, however, the position was greatly complicated by the fact that all goods or ships of the king's enemies were considered 'fair game' unless covered by a safe-conduct. Since it was by no means always clear which nations were at any one time the king's enemies (since truces were made at times for quite short periods) and since safe-conducts were of little use if the mariners could not read, there were many opportunities for the unscrupulous to help themselves to the goods of others at sea. The position was even more complicated if the goods of hostile aliens were shipped (perhaps in the names of friendly aliens) in the vessels of friendly nations. A further problem was caused by the question of whether the robbery had taken place inside or outside territorial waters, thus affecting the jurisdiction of the royal courts.[74] The only remedy for the wronged shipowners and merchants in these circumstances was to petition the king for restitution of their property; a request which was frequently answered by the appointment of a commission of inquiry. Soper, enjoying the dual position of a man of standing in Southampton and a trusted royal official, was frequently appointed when such inquiries had to be made in Southampton and its environs. With his fellow commissioners he had to set afoot a search of the cellars and back alleys of Southampton for stolen goods: for example, those of Bretons which had been shipped in Portuguese bottoms, or those of Portuguese merchants which had been shipped in the name of other aliens under the king's protection in an endeavour to ensure their safe arrival. Some pirates were evidently men of resource: one John Cornysh master of a ballinger of Plymouth whom Soper was instructed to apprehend in 1441, met in the roads off Yarmouth three Dutch vessels laden with fish and other goods of London merchants, sheltering from fear of enemies on the sea. He enticed them to put to sea again, fell on the *Buysse of Wykupse* with his thirty-six armed men, took her and finally sailed her round to Beaulieu where she was unloaded.[75] Beaulieu, a creek remote from the bustle of Southampton Water yet providing a safe anchorage, was evidently popular for the unloading of cargoes of doubtful provenance.[76]

Usually, of course, it was the more valuable cargoes of wine and other luxury goods, particularly those carried by the carracks of Portugal and Genoa, which attracted the most attention from pirates and other ruffians. The great carracks could in general outsail the smaller ships and balingers most commonly found in northern European waters but in port it was a different story. On one occasion in 1451 the carracks reached Southampton safely, but some local malefactors set out in small boats and spoiled the lighters bringing the merchandise into the town quay.[77]

In this matter of *quasi*-judicial commissions Soper was presented with a problem – the duality of his position evident throughout his career. As a merchant, a friend of the Italians, clerk of the king's ships, a customer and a worthy alderman of Southampton, whose interests exactly did he represent, especially with the truth so hard to come by? When the royal balingers the *Ane* and the *Swan* were accused of capturing the barge *Saint George* of Brittany while she was at anchor in St Peter Port, he was surely in a somewhat invidious position.[78] Similarly in 1421, he was involved in another tangled affair. Peter James and Walter Fetplace (his friends and associates), Ralph Huskard, John John and Richard Preste (all masters of royal ships) hired the royal ship the *Holy Ghost of Spain* (at the date of the petition, which is uncertain, known as the *Little Holy Ghost* of South-ampton) to go to Portugal for merchandise. On the way there, '*seiglant sur la haute meer*', they met a carrack laden with forty pokes of Spanish wool. This they seized and abandoning their original plan, returned at once to Southampton. There the partners in the scheme gave the customers (including Soper, of course) sureties for the customs due and obtained a licence to export the wool to the Staple at Calais. Even though the wool was divided between different ships, leaving at different times the wool was seized by the king's enemies and taken into Le Crotoy. However, the accounts of the customers had been charged with the sum of £57 13s 10d for duty (the partners plaintively claim that the wool was really only worth £30) and the petitioning partners beg to be excused this sum. Soper must have felt that this expedition was a disaster, with the wool lost, he himself likely to be held accountable for the customs, and in all probability no money forthcoming for the hire of the royal ship.[79]

Such total lack of success seems to have overtaken few of his enterprises. When considering the size of the fortune he built up and the use he made of it, together with such evidence as there is of his private life, we can gradually build up a much clearer picture of William Soper as a man. Soper certainly seems to have used his wealth in what might be called the classic English manner – to build up his social position by obtaining the status that attached at the time to the ownership of land. The boy who arrived in Southampton as an appren-tice from an obscure family ended his days as William Soper of Newton Bery, *armiger* – a gentleman connected by ties of friendship and obligation not only with the leading families of Southampton burgesses but also with the local gentry of Hampshire.

His first wife, Isabel, remains an obscure figure: the only clue to her parentage or family connections being that she was related to the Chamberleyn family, and may well have been a comparatively elderly widow married for her money. She was certainly pious, being granted an indult to have a portable altar in 1420 (perhaps connected with the chapel in Soper's country house mentioned by Albizzi).[80] Isabel was also godmother to Peter James' daughter Kateryn.[81]

His second wife, Joan, was rather different. William seems to have fallen in love with her when he was middle-aged and she was a young girl – a distant cousin of his first wife, living in their house and probably acting as a companion to his wife. Young girls were often placed in the households of well-connected relations or friends with the intention of acquiring social graces or even a husband. She and Soper became lovers and eventually after Isabel's death were secretly married. Yet, as Joan was Isabel's cousin in the second and third degree the union, in canon law, was incestuous and the marriage, performed without banns or proper ceremonies, void. In 1438, however, Soper managed to obtain a dispensation to remain in the marriage and absolution from excommunication because no open scandal had been caused.[82] There seems a strong possibility that Soper's projected pilgrimage to Lombardy in 1436-7 may be connected with the need for this dispensation. At this date, Pope Eugenius IV was resident in Florence, having fled from the turmoil of Rome in 1434. With him had travelled the legal machinery of the Curia through which such dispensations were granted. Florence in the year of the consecration of the Duomo of which Soper had surely heard from his Italian friends (the Martelli family, indeed, acted as patron to Donatello) was attractive to any traveller and the presence of the Pope provided an additional and compelling motive for undertaking the journey.

Joan was a member of the Chamberleyn family who were prominent throughout the fifteenth century in Southampton. William Chamberleyn, who may have been Joan's brother and who also had a daughter called Joan married to Richard Holt,[83] was Soper's colleague as M.P. in 1419, 1420, 1429, 1430-1, 1432, 1433, 1441-2. Thomas Chamberleyn, who acted on Soper's behalf in business and who was one of his executors named in his Will, may have been another younger brother. William Chamberleyn was evidently a wealthy man, sharing with Soper the honour of being among the highest rated burgesses of Southampton at the time of the levying of the so-called Feudal Aid of 1431 – in reality a form of land tax. Soper, described as 'armiger', is stated in the returns to be seised within the town of property to the annual value of £15. Chamberleyn, described as 'gentleman' is also assessed at £15; Walter Fetplace 'mercator' and William Nicholl 'mercator' at £15 and £6 respectively. Chamberleyn is also noted as holding land in military service at Henton Daubeney.[84]

There is little doubt that the assessments to this and similar taxes, undertaken by local juries according to out of date formulae, undervalued the assets of those paying the tax: however the relative wealth of one tax payer compared with another is probably fairly accurately reflected. A wider field of comparison is provided by the subsidy roll of 14 Henry VI (1435) which refers to the whole of Hampshire: – William Chamberleyn had property worth £64 per annum and Soper £50 per annum. William Brocas, the sheriff of Hampshire, was assessed at £120 and Peter James, William Nicholl and Walter Fetplace at £10, £16 and £20 respectively.[85]

Particularly in Southampton town itself Soper seems to have bought and sold property as occasion and profit offered. In 1427 for example he sold the large property on the corner of English Street and 'Bredelane' (Broad Lane) to Peter James.[86] He also granted an underlease of part of the Watergate property to John Ingoldesby for £1 per annum in 1439, retaining only the shop for himself.[87]

The full extent of his property in the town can best be judged from a survey made in 1454 to assess the burgesses' liability for the repair of the town walls.[88] At that date, he owned in the parish of Holy Rood a house rented by Gabriel Corbet, the naturalised Italian: and two houses built by himself in the grounds of the convent of the Friars Minor. Two cottages and a house next door had also formerly been his but were now owned by Thomas White. He held on lease from the corporation the house in the Watergate tower and the shop built beside the gate: the Custom House on the west side of English Street was also leased by him – this time from Winchester College. His former town residence (*capitalis tenementum*) was rented by another Italian, Filippo Larcario. A property called after his first wife 'Dame Isabell's Vaute' now belonged to Robert Bellhouse, who also rented from Soper the two houses next door. Finally, a property in the parish of St John the Baptist was rented to the Genoese Lazzaro Cattaneo and another in St Laurence to William Pyrys. The properties in the garden of the Friars Minor are particularly interesting as they are the subject of a deed which does throw some light on Soper as a man.[89] The Warden of the Friars Minor was another William Chamberleyn (almost certainly another relation of Joan) and the deed describes the most elaborate arrangements after Soper's death for a daily mass 'at the awter in the South Isle of our Churche . . . in the which Isle the said William is disposed to be buryed' for the souls of William, his mother and father, his two wives 'and all their frondes and all christen soules' and for a yearly obit. To pay for the masses and obit, William built the two cottages in the convent garden (although the income from them was reserved for himself and his wife until after their deaths), roofed the church and also presented vestments, candlesticks, censers and a silver cross. All his life William had struck bargains of one sort and another, usually to his own advantage, and he considered it only sensible to attempt to arrange matters in the next world as prudently as he had arranged them in this.

Outside Southampton Soper decided to build up an estate for himself on the western side of Southampton Water on the edges of the New Forest. All the property that he bought was in this area. A deed relating to the manor of Sherfield English near Romsey from 1428 might seem to be an exception.[90] Nevertheless, it is clear that Soper who, according to the deed, acquired an interest in the property with Sir William Cheyne, Thomas Ringwood, John Hall, John Harryes and John Conige, was not in any sense the real occupier of the manor. This had come to Thomas Ringwood two years earlier by marriage[91] and the deed probably represents a stage in the system of feoffment and re-enfeoffment necessary if a landowner wished to change his estate i.e. create an entail or limit remainders for example. The distinction between this and the process of granting title to feoffees to uses (an early form of trusteeship) is very fine and it is not entirely clear what is intended here. In 1488 the estate was still in the possession of the Ringwood family, for in that year Charles Ringwood left it to his son John.[92]

Returning to his own estates, Soper first acquired property in Fawley and Dibden in 1426, buying the land which Joan, wife of Walter Vicary of London, had inherited from her mother, the heiress of one William Woser otherwise Boteler. It consisted of some cottages and arable land in Hythe (Hethe) lying in Cadland ('Cadelande') in the parish of Fawley and a house with a garden called 'le Wose', 16 acres of land, meadows and woods in Dibden.[93] Some time before 1438, together with Richard Holte, Joan Soper's cousin by marriage, the Sopers bought a messuage and thirty-five acres of land held from the king in chief at South Langley from Richard Gould and his wife Joan.[94] At an uncertain date, Soper also bought Newton Bery, now Bury Farm, just across the water from Southampton. It was here that he retired and passed his days in peace, able to see the great carracks come to anchor and remember the days when he had built ships greater than any: no longer William Soper of Southampton merchant but William Soper, esquire, of Newton Bery, Hampshire. One feels sure that blazoned over the door would be his coat of arms: sable, a chevron between three wings argent.[95]

It was as well for his peace of mind that he was unaware of the confusion which was to overtake his estate on his death. In a manoeuvre not uncommon at the time, his property in Eling, Dibden and Fawley had been granted in 1455 to Thomas Chamberleyn who then regranted it to William and Joan for the term of their lives.[96] Following William's death in 1459, Joan, now a wealthy widow, seems to have become closely involved with the Ludlow family connected by marriage with the Ringwoods and may even have married Richard Ludlow. He is described as 'Richard Ludlow of Bery beside Southampton', at a time when the property was still in Joan's hands in the early years of the reign of Edward IV.[97] There also exists an Inquisition Post Mortem of November 1488 in which the name of the owner of the messuage and thirty-five acres of land at South Langley is given as Johanna Ludlow who is stated to have lately enfeoffed therewith John Ludlowe and Christina his wife.[98] However, a licence for entry on the Patent Rolls dated November 1482 makes clear that the grantor of this land, on this occasion, was Joan Soper late the wife of William Soper.[99] The most likely explanation is that Richard Ludlow lived with Joan who on this occasion at least used his name.

Nevertheless it is clear that, in selling this farm, Joan had ignored the rights of her Chamberleyn cousins secured by the deed of 1455 already mentioned. Thus William Fletcher, cousin and heir of Thomas Chamberleyn, was forced to go to Chancery to establish his title against another Ludlow 'of Hill Deverell, Wiltshire':[100] and it was well into the reign of Henry VIII before the Fletchers felt really secure in their property.[101]

What, therefore, is our final impression of Soper as a man? There is no doubt of his business ability, of his adaptability, his readiness to appreciate and use to his own advantage the financial skills of the Italians. He was, perhaps, sufficiently enterprising to travel to Florence himself and once there he may have seen so much to admire in the flowering of the arts that the marble tomb he built for himself in the chapel of the Friars Minor was a remembrance of those seen in Tuscan churches. He was content with the traditional teachings of the Church, well pleased to establish an obit and other charities in his will (paid for by a charge on his estates) to demonstrate to his fellow townsmen for all time his wealth, his success and his piety. His life seems to have been almost frantically busy, but for his contemporaries perhaps the best epitome of his activities and his character is that provided by Agnes Overey. This lady, when left a widow, became involved in litigation with the Fleming family over some property in Southampton. Writing to a friend she asks him to 'speke to John a Skelton that he thanke mastre William Soper for ye goodnesse and ffrendship yt he doth unto me. And that he wel speke to my Lord of Gloucestre to comande William Soper to be good friend to me and to my children as he hat ever y be. As y shal ever be a trewe bede woman to my Lord and to hym the whyle y lyve.'[102]

Thinking of Soper's multifarious contacts and positions this is perhaps the best description of him and his activities. He was the 'good friend' – who both for the Crown and for more humble citizens could be relied upon to look after their affairs in an efficient and kindly manner. He had much to be proud of in life – a former merchant apprentice who died a landed gentleman and bearer of a coat of arms. Perhaps his only sorrow was that he left no son, no heir. His memorial to posterity was rather the great ships he had built, the like of which would not be seen again in England for many years.

THE KING'S SHIPS IN THE FIRST HALF
OF THE FIFTEENTH CENTURY

By the beginning of the fifteenth century the owning of ships directly by the Crown was not unusual. The practice had relatively long antecedents, Henry II's galley commanded by Alan Tranchemer based at Southampton being perhaps the first recorded post-Conquest royal ship. The specific obligation of the Cinque Ports to provide vessels for a fifteen-day period at the royal command in return for certain privileges was still invoked on occasion but had become less useful over the years for a variety of reasons. The arrangement, comparable to the feudal obligations of the king's tenants-in-chief to provide him with land forces, was cumbersome and limited. The ports themselves, at this date, had begun to suffer from the silting up which was finally to obliterate their commercial and naval importance, so that fewer and smaller ships were available to the crown. Moreover, the loss of Normandy in 1204, which had considerably altered the strategic situation in the Channel, had provided an early stimulus to naval development. This troubled strip of water was no longer an inconvenient barrier between the two halves of one realm but a hostile frontier to be defended and a potential invasion route.

In these circumstances, the general power of arrest in time of need over all shipping in English ports attaching to the crown, from time immemorial, proved itself a powerful and flexible weapon. The vessels and their crews were obliged to serve the crown at an agreed wage for a specified period (perhaps as long as six months) thus allowing large expeditions to be mounted. Royal ships provided leadership to these somewhat motley fleets and could also be used for the smaller tasks for which arrested shipping, with its attendant disruption of commerce and unpopularity with merchants and shipowners, was not suitable – disadvantages which also applied to the Cinque Ports vessels.

King John developed a royal fleet of galleys large enough to be divided into four squadrons, the eastern, the south-eastern, the southern and the western. Some at least were based at Southampton where, in 1212, the Sheriff was ordered to build a wall for their protection in winter. Henry III kept the fleet or a portion of it in being for some considerable period; but after 1250 there are no further references to payments for the repair or the services of the royal galleys. During the period of the fleet's existence, a powerful and efficient administration was set up to deal both with these galleys and the auxiliary arrested ships. Previously arrangements had been informal and *ad hoc*, with Exchequer clerks responsible for any payments necessary. Under John, William de Wrotham, with his assistant Reginald de Cornhille, who already had a connection with the ports through the machinery set up to collect the fifteenth on French merchants' goods authorised by the Assize of Winchester, were constantly addressed in writs as *custos galliarum* and *custos portuum*. Besides handling payments out of the Exchequer they impressed ships, workmen to repair them and crewmen to sail them. In 1208, Wrotham organised the fleet for the expedition to Normandy, working through bailiffs and deputies in the various ports on the south and east coast, and also operated a similar system in 1212 by which time he had also established the beginnings of a 'royal dockyard' at Portsmouth. F. W. Brooks in his study of the naval forces of this date, felt that it was possible to see the beginnings of a system in which keepers were appointed with responsibility for a group of havens, quite independent of the sheriffs, with duties covering the beginnings of the customs administration and with some control over shipping. Henry III made some attempt to continue with this system and even de Montfort appointed Thomas de Muleton with the resounding title of Warden of the Sea and maritime parts.

By the end of the thirteenth century the English crown was again in possession of ships of its own which are normally described as galleys. As many as eight were completed in 1295 with 120 oars apiece, built at Dunwich, Ipswich, London (2), Lyme, Newcastle, Southampton and York. In 1336 the *Philip* was built for the crown at Lynn: a further ship was fitted out at Winchelsea in 1347. Two, the *St George* and *St Edward* were repaired at Bayonne about 1350: and the inventory for the *Paul* of London exists from 1373.[103] The royal galleys were a mere handful and the main reliance for the defence of the realm at sea clearly fell upon the general merchant marine of England.

As the silting up of the south eastern ports continued reducing the potential usefulness of Cinque Ports shipping in wartime, ships arrested for the royal service were based to an increasing extent on London, Southampton and the east coast ports. It was with these forces that Edward III won the battle of Sluys in June 1340, the greatest battle fought by the English since the Conquest, fittingly commemorated by the great gold noble struck for the purpose.

Edward III's reign also saw the beginning of the form of naval administration which was to endure until 1451. From 18 Edward III (1344) a separate account under the heading of clerk of the king's ships is found; at first in the Pipe Rolls series and later on from the first year of Richard II among the enrolled foreign accounts of the Lord Treasurer's Remembrancer.

At first responsibilities cannot have been very clearly defined. William de Clewere, Mathew de Torksey and Thomas de Snetesham account separately for overlapping periods of time between 18 and 37 Edward III. Robert Crull and John de Haytfield similarly account for the last years of Edward III. Although with the accession of Richard II the accounts were removed from the Pipe Rolls the duties of the office were still shared among two clerks John de Haytfield and John Lincoln. From 4 Richard II (1380–1), however, until the last year of the reign there is a break in the series, and when it resumes with the accounts of John Chamberlain, one man has sole charge of the royal ships. He was evidently a successful administrator being confirmed in the position by Henry IV and continuing to hold it until 1405.[104]

The duties of the office were by now fairly clear. The overriding concern of the clerk was naturally the ships owned by the crown; their repair, safekeeping and victualling and the payment of their crews were his business. He might also on occasion be responsible for the payment of the monies due to the masters and crews of arrested ships. He had no responsibility at all for the operation of the ships whether royal or privately owned. To use modern terms, he was a quartermaster with responsibility for the dockyard, not an admiral.

Under Richard II in 1398–9 John Chamberleyn was responsible at first for a small group of four vessels, the *Trinity of the Tower*, the *Gracedieu*, the *Nicholas* and the *George*. Besides obtaining a mast for the *Trinity* at Blakeney in Norfolk – probably imported from the Baltic – he repaired the vessels and paid the crews for a voyage to Bordeaux for wines for the royal household and for a voyage to Ireland in furtherance of the King's war. Richard II himself evidently travelled in the *Trinity* as one 'tabula mensal with 2 trestell' was provided for his use. The total expenditure came to £369 19s 11½d.

Chamberlain's second account covers the first seven years of Henry IV's reign and reveals a considerable amount of naval activity. For the whole period he received a total of £3,945 5s 1½d; £1,048 0s 7½d was intended for shipping arrested mainly for the safe-conduct of the queen from Brittany to England in 1402. Expenditure amounted in all to £4,192 0s 4½d. Six ships are mentioned in the accounts: the *Trinity* of 300 tuns and the *Nicholas* identical with those belonging to Richard II; the *Ane de la Tour*, a newly-built ballinger only briefly in royal ownership before being granted to the Archbishop of Canterbury;[105] the *Holyghost de la Tour;* the *Katherine de la Tour* of about 200 tuns purchased for £100 from the Mayor of King's Lynn and originally Portuguese;[106] and finally the ballinger *Godesgrace* or *Gracedieu de la Tour*, which was not the ship of that name formerly owned by Richard

II which had been granted to one Antony Ritz or Rys [107] with all her equipment, but a vessel newly built at Redcliff (that is Ratcliff adjacent to Wapping and Limehouse) near London.[108] There was also a river barge for the use of the royal household. Several of these vessels were elaborately decorated and must have made a brave sight riding at anchor near the Tower. The *Gracedieu* was painted red with other colours in *le celeur* and *le sterne* with a great golden eagle standing on the bowsprit and a golden crown on *le Beek* and the fore and after-castles multicoloured. The *Trinity* was also red with four gilded images of St George, St Antony, St Katherine and St Margaret on the stern and four escutcheons, two of the king's arms with gold, and two of St George with the Garter in gold; there were again two great eagles on *le celeur*. The *Nicholas* was painted black with white ostrich feathers picked out in gold, a great escutcheon of the king's arms and of St George and an image of St Christopher in pure gold. The royal barge was painted, without with red and gold, the mast being red, and within with gilded figures of the fleur-de-lys and a leopard; and another leopard, white, with a golden collar.

This squadron of ships was based at Greenwich where there were facilities of some sort for repairs and where, following the usual practice at the time, the vessels were drawn up out of the water on *les Woses* (the mudflats) during the winter months with their running rigging removed. The propinquity of this anchorage to the Tower of London probably explains the use of the suffix 'de la Tour' which was used almost as a fifteenth century equivalent of H.M.S. One must not, however, rely too much on the orderly impression conveyed by Chamberlain's enrolled accounts. Years sometimes elapsed before work undertaken was actually paid for. John Ramsey, fishmonger, who had supplied bread to the royal ships in 1404–5 to the value of £15 15s 8d did not manage to get the Exchequer to write a Warrant for Issue until March 1410.[109] Thomas Prynce, who was responsible for the painted decorations on the royal ships already mentioned, was also not paid until February 1410;[110] while one Maude Cynke, a widow living near the Tower, was reduced to great poverty and lived in fear of being thrown into jail for debt because of the reluctance of the Crown to pay for beer supplied for the *Katharine*.[111] Nicholas Shovenbergh, who had acted for Herman Brand of Danzig when Richard II bought a Danzig Ship for £67 3s 4d, had still not been paid three years after the accession of Henry IV.[112] Such delays were common to all forms of goods and services supplied to the crown and presumably were taken into account by contemporaries as far as was possible.

John Chamberlain himself had been granted, on the 6 February 1400, an allowance of 6d per day with a supplement of 5 marks a year ostensibly for life, which was paid at fairly regular intervals at least until

1405. This was in addition to his wages of 12d per day for which he accounts on the roll. The masters of the royal vessels – Laurence Monde, master of the *Holyghost,* John Golde, master of the *Katherine,* John Brembre, master of the *Gracedieu,* or *Godesgrace,* Richard Elys, master of the *Nicholas,* John Miller, master of the *Ane* and John Mayhew, master of the *Trinity* – with their crews should have been paid as and when they acted at the royal command. A skeleton crew of shipkeepers was employed during the winter when the vessels were docked: a somewhat larger crew (about half the full complement) were employed to rig the ships at the start of the sailing season and finally the full crew was employed for the actual voyages.

Chamberlain, in fact, did receive money for specific voyages from the Exchequer: for example in 1401 he received £87 12s for a voyage to be made to northern parts; in 1405 he received £620 0s 4d as one instalment and later £194 0s 4½d as another for the journey of the queen from Brittany to England; and in 1404 he received a total of £440 7s for a voyage to Bordeaux. On these occasions, it is likely that the king's mariners were paid fairly promptly, but this was not always the case. In the spring and early summer of 1403 the *Trinity,* the *Katherine* and the *Godesgrace* went on a voyage under the command of Thomas Beaufort, the Lord Admiral. With them were arrested ships mainly from King's Lynn and Hull. In this instance the ship's masters and crews were not paid until late 1412 or early 1413.[113] The ship's masters were in a somewhat stronger position than the ordinary sailors, there being a possibility of their receiving special grants in kind or in money from the Crown, as well as the usual wages and expenses. John Mayhew, the senior of the masters of the king's ships received a substantial benefit in the form of the grant of the royal ship *Nicholas* in March 1404.[114] John Golde, master of the *Katherine* also managed to obtain a grant from the Crown – that of the 'keeping of the Tronage called the Kyngesbeme' within the town of Ipswich with all due fees, profits and commodities.[115] A further possible source of income for mariners was the value of prizes taken at sea. In May 1400 John Mayhew sold to the king for £40 a *pere adamant garnisee et apparaillez dor:* [116] (a diamond set in gold) it seems probable that Mayhew obtained this as his share of a prize. The possibility of supplementing their income in this way was no doubt frequently in the sailors' minds even if diamonds were not lighted upon every day.

Chamberlain's successor John Elmeton, who was clerk for the following four years was not active on anything like the same scale; indeed the squadron of royal ships almost disappeared at this time. His receipts from all sources only totalled £216 7s 2d for the whole period while expenditure was £299 10s 8d.[117]

The *Holyghost* was granted to John Mayhew to compensate him for an unspecified loss suffered in the royal service, after completing a voyage with John Golde as master to Denmark with the Lady Philippa, the king's daughter, on her marriage. The *Trinity de la Tour* was laid up in a dock at Redcliff. The *Godesgrace* was also docked there until she was granted in December 1409 to the Earl of Somerset. The *Katherine*, already recorded by Chamberlain as having broken her back lying on *les Woses*, was completely broken up, the timber being handed over to John Montagu of Salisbury: a mast and sailyard also lying at St Katherine's by the Tower formerly belonging to the *Godesgrace* were granted to John Stanley, Seneschal of the King's Household.

The royal fleet at the end of Elmeton's term of office consisted only of the *Trinity* and the barge for use on the river with its gay awning of red and white. It is clear that the crown was uncertain of the value of royal ships and very unwilling to spend any money on their upkeep. The new clerk, John Starling, held office for only one year and seven months from November 1409 till June 1411. His period in office reveals a continuing lack of a firm policy with regard to the royal ships and must have been depressing for the clerk. Receipts totalled only £33 6s 8d, most of which came from the sale of surplus gear, while the number of ships in royal ownership was actually increased.[118] Two ships, the *Bernard* [119] and the *Christopher* were given to the king by Robert Thorley and Richard Garner respectively: the barge *Marie de la Tour* was bought and refitted at Small Hythe and the little barge *Gabriel* was also purchased. Two large vessels also came into royal ownership, probably as prizes or by forfeiture – one called either simply the *Galley* or the *Maria* or the *Jesus Maria* and the other known only as *Le Carake*. This carrack may well be identical with the *Sancta Maria et Sancta Brigida* which, while lying at Bristol, had been seized by John Starling and John Mayhew and sailed round to London with a pressed crew.[120]

By June the clerk's expenses had reached £159 2s 7¼d of which the sum of £125 15s 11¼d was owing by the crown: there was little prospect of the clerk receiving such a sum for a considerable period particularly as the royal ships were not involved in any naval expeditions of importance to bring them to the forefront of royal attention. It must have been with a sigh of relief that Starling handed over his responsibilities to Elmying Leget, an usher of the king's chamber. Leget was probably clerk until March 1413 when Henry IV died. No accounts survive for this period perhaps because there was very little for which to account. For a brief period the accession of Henry V made little difference. A certain William Loveney held office as clerk for five months from March to 28th July 1413 and his accounts state baldly that he had received no money and equally had spent none.[121]

By letters patent of 18th July 1413, however, William Catton became clerk of the royal ships, an appointment marking a radical change in the fortunes of the royal ships. This change was not foreshadowed in the terms on which he held office, which were those customary, including the normal allowance of 12d per day for himself and his clerk. The preamble to his enrolled accounts also makes clear that his responsibilities were defined as before; to be responsible for all money spent on the royal ships, all wages of shipwrights and of mariners incurred on their behalf, the safe-keeping of the same on the waters of the Thames with due allowance for money spent on artillery and for his own wages.[122] However, the increasing tension in relations between England and France evident in the later years of the reign of Henry IV, when increasingly involved negotiations with the quarrelling magnates of France had given way to the expedition to northern France led in the summer of 1412 by the Duke of Clarence, made it more and more probable that war must come. The expansion of naval activity which took place from the beginning of Catton's tenure of the clerkship was the result of a deliberate royal policy to enlarge the fleet of royal ships and place them on a war footing.

Catton accounts for the *Cog John*, the *Thomas*, the *Petit Trinity*, the *Petit Marie*, the *Grande Marie*, the *Gabriel*, the *Peter* and the *Paul* from July 1413 and it is clear that these seven were already in royal ownership. The *Petit Marie* and the *Gabriel* were identical with those accounted for by Starling. The origin of the *Peter* and the *Paul* cannot be determined. The *Thomas* had been bought from Thomas Fauconer of London for 400 marks in the previous summer.[123] The origin of the *Grande Marie* also remains obscure; her capacity was only 126 tuns and she had but one mast – too small to be John Starling's carrack which had two masts. The *Cog John* may possibly be identical with the prize taken at sea from Prussian mariners and presented to Prince John (the Duke of Bedford) in 1407.[124]

Catton's first major task, however, was the building of the *Trinity Royal* at Greenwich. The language used in the accounts is somewhat ambiguous but it seems fairly certain that the old *Trinity de la Tour*, the royal flagship continuously from the days of Richard II which had been laid up in a dock for some two years, was dismantled and her timbers re-used in the construction of a yet more glorious successor, so that from the shards of a vessel of 300 tuns phoenix-like arose one of 540 tuns. Certainly the operation was not performed for reasons of economy as the sum spent amounted to £1,686 15s 11¼d. More likely was the shortage of suitable and properly seasoned timber near London, as supplies were sought from Eltham, Hatfield, Colchester, Croydon, Ealing, Bromley and Bexley among other places. She was certainly as gaily decorated as before as supplies of white lead, red lead, vermilion, copper, verdigris, varnish, gold, 'smarer lake', 'jude fyne', 'fleymsoker', 'Ruskynoker' and 'Tynfoil' were laid in for this purpose.

During the accounting period the *Rodcogge*, originally known as the *Flaward de Gerrant*, the *Philip*, and the *Katherine*, also joined the squadron of royal ships in June 1414, March 1414, and February 1415 respectively. These and the other vessels were maintained in a sea-worthy condition at a cost which varied from £12 8s 10½d for the *Paul*, to £120 14s 2½d for the *Thomas*. Only £8 2s 10d was spent on the *Peter* but this vessel was granted by the king to Gilbert Umfraville and John Cornewaill at their petition at the end of 1414. The *Cog John* was unfortunately lost, sinking off the Breton coast when returning with wines from Bordeaux on 7 October 1414.[125]

In the absence of any documents indicating the state of mind of the king and his councillors on naval matters at this date, the interpretation of the remainder of this first account of Catton's presents some diffi-culties. The usual practice during the reign of Henry IV had been for the ships to be commissioned in the early summer when they usually undertook voyages 'to keep the seas', although occasionally going on more domestic errands to Bordeaux for wines for the royal household, for example. Catton did not totally ignore military expeditions which remained the raison d'être of the royal ships, but he devoted a con-siderable amount of time and effort to hiring out the royal ships to merchants for trading voyages on the merchants' own account. Some went to Bordeaux or La Rochelle for wines, landing them at Bristol, Hull, London or Southampton: others went to Newcastle for coal or to Danzig for pitch, tar and timber.

To use the royal ships in this way on this scale was unprecedented; the total sum accruing to the clerk of the king's ships for freight charges for this period was over £2,000. This was a very considerable sum at this period and must have been the result of a deliberate act of policy. It is not possible to determine whether the impulse came from Catton himself, who was not as far as we know of merchant stock but a 'career' royal official, or from the king in council. However, one motive may well have been the fact that the hulls of wooden ships re-quire maintenance whether or not they are at sea; to hire them out to merchants in this fashion would produce a financial gain to the crown without a corresponding increase in dockyard expenses. The consider-able expense of maintaining a squadron of ships ready for action would thus be mitigated to a certain degree. It was, also, possible for Catton to face with equanimity the prospect of the ships, for which he was responsible, being absent from home waters because the summers of 1413 and 1414 saw little naval activity in the Channel with attention concentrated on the diplomatic exchanges between England and the quarrelling factions in France.

In 1415 attention was naturally focused on military matters, to the exclusion of trading voyages, culminating in the Agincourt expedition and the re-opening of the war with France. It should be noted that the expenses of ships, whether royal or privately owned, which took part in the Agincourt expedition do not appear in Catton's accounts. He clearly states that, on this occasion, responsibility lay with the Treasurer for War and merely notes which ships were placed under the aegis of this official and the period of time concerned.

Catton's second account, however, for the period 1416–1419 covers the period when as the French war progressed command of the Channel became vital to ensure the continued reinforcement and supply of the English armies in France. A system which had dealt satisfactorily with a squadron of between half-a-dozen and a dozen ships, with perhaps one new one building, was strained to the utmost as the royal fleet grew and naval activities of all kinds multiplied.

Total receipts accounted for by the clerk of the king's ships for this period amounted to £12,310 0s 4d.[126] The greater part of this sum, £8,809 9s 8½d came from the Exchequer as grants for various purposes, mainly repairs and wages for certain expeditions. Another large sum, also from royal funds, came from the king's chamber. A further £1,442 5s 2½d came from freight payments for merchants as previously. This practice had evidently proved itself so profitable that even during wartime certain royal ships were available for hire transporting wines, iron, corn, beans and salt fish among other merchandise. Moreover, the *Marie Breton* was hired to Roger Hemming, her master, for a year for £10 in 1415–16. There were also small sums due to the crown from the sale of prize goods taken at sea by royal vessels: for example, 5 quarters 8 bushels of beans on one voyage, 13 barrels of white herring on another, and as much as £182 5s 4d from the sale of iron, wool fells etc. on a third. Surplus supplies were also sold as were ships no longer considered suitable for the royal service. The *Rodcogge* and the *Petit Trinity* were sold in 1418: the *Agase*, a carrack wrecked on the mud flats, the *Marie Hulke*, the *Philip*, and the *Galley* in the following year.

Activities were no longer concentrated in the Thames below the Tower but had spread to other ports in the south of England particularly Southampton. No fewer than 36 ships were the responsibility of Catton and his single clerk at the highest point reached by Henry V's squadron of royal ships. Of these thirteen were prizes – the *Marie Hampton*, the *Marie Sandwich*, the *George*, the *Agase*, the *Katherine*, the *Paul*, the *Christopher*, the *Andrew*, the *Peter*, the *Christopher of Spain*, the *Marie Spaniard*, the *Marie Hulke*, and the *Holyghost of Spain*. One, the *Craccher*, was a gift to the king from John Hawley of Dartmouth, a well-known sea captain whose exploits were frequently indistinguishable from those of a pirate. Another, the ballinger *Nicholas,* had been previously in the possession of the Duke of Bedford and was transferred to the king in 1417. Three more – the *Little John,* the *James* and the *Swan* – appear as new entries in the list because of 're-grading'. It was evidently usual for the very largest of the king's vessels to have what is called a 'follower': a smaller vessel which would act in concert with it and which had no separate entry in the accounts. For some reason this practice was discontinued in certain cases and the 'follower' of the *Holyghost* appears as *James,* and that of the *Trinity Royal* as the *Swan.* The *Little John,* which may at one time have belonged to the Duke of Bedford but whose origin is otherwise obscure, may possibly have been the follower of the *Cog John* which had been lost at sea. Two ships had been bought, the *Nicholas* and the *Katherine* both in 1415.[127]

Of the newly-built ships Catton was personally responsible only for those which were built on the borders of Kent and Sussex – one the great ship *Jesus* at Winchelsea, the other the ballinger *George* at Small Hythe on the river Rother. William Soper, as has been mentioned in the first part of this introduction, was responsible for rebuilding the prize the *Saint Clare of Spain* into the new *Holyghost de la Tour,* building the new ballinger *Ane,* and repairing the *Saint Gabriel de Heybon* in Brittany, renamed the *Gabriel de la Tour.*[128] The work on the *Holyghost* and the *Gabriel* was finished in time for them to have joined the squadron of king's ships by the opening date of Catton's second account. The *Ane* took a little longer but was ready by November 1416.

These projects, however, were dwarfed by the greatest enterprise of all: the astonishing scheme to build a ship of 1,400 tuns estimated capacity – the *Gracedieu* – work on which together with her two accompanying balingers the *Valentine* and the *Falcon* had begun in 1416 in a specially built dock at Southampton.[129] The work was on such a scale that workmen had been sought for her from as far afield as Devon and Cornwall.[130] Robert Berde had charge of the works under the general supervision of Soper and it might be thought that the introduction of new men specially commissioned to build these ships with no direct responsibility to the clerk of the king's ships betokened some lack of confidence by the Crown in Catton himself. It seems more likely that these commissions were nothing more than an attempt to get things done in a situation of some urgency, when, as has been said, the whole administration of the royal ships was badly overstrained.

The practical result of this division of responsibility was that Catton retained control over events in Greenwich – the old royal dockyard area – and the Kent-Sussex borders, while Soper was in charge in Southampton. Catton had had to scour the woods of Kent, Middlesex and Essex to find enough suitable timber for building the *Trinity*

Royal. When the Crown embarked on shipbuilding enterprises on a scale never before attempted, Southampton must have seemed overwhelmingly suitable as a base. The great oak woods of the New Forest were at hand; a secure deep water anchorage lay waiting; seamen were available to man the ships and Southampton was a more convenient base for Channel operations than the Thames, taking into account the tricky passage round the coast of East Kent and up the estuary. Southampton and its environs had in fact become the usual 'home port' for many of the royal ships. In 1417, no fewer than twelve royal ships were anchored at Hamble for the winter including the *Jesus* and the *Holyghost*. Soper, himself, had taken the muster of Richard Spicer esquire and forty archers in his company ordered to guard the king's ships against the invasion and malice of his enemies.[131]

When Catton retired in 1420 rewarded for his labours by the grant of the *Gabriel de la Tour*, and the *Grand Gabriel*, a definite attempt seems to have been made to consolidate and reorganise the administration of the king's ships. Soper was appointed clerk, and, while the building of the *Gracedieu* continued at Southampton, facilities were also to be provided for the repair and refitting of the other ships in the same port. His salary was more than doubled from a shilling a day to forty pounds a year, with provision for a deputy.[132] The main anchorage of the king's great ships in the Hamble river was also to be fortified, to guard against the possibility of French raids, a familiar hazard in Southampton Water but unlikely in the waters of the Pool of London or off Greenwich or Deptford. With the benefit of hindsight it is clear that this effort by the king and his council to provide a strengthened administration for the king's ships had come too late. The dangerous situation in the Channel presented by the French alliance with Genoa had been overcome and from the very first it seems that Soper was in charge of a declining department. However, contemporaries would have taken a different view and Soper certainly set about his task, which amounted to the transfer of the royal dockyard from Greenwich to Southampton, with vigour and enthusiasm.

The total number of royal ships had declined slightly it is true. Besides the sales already noted, and the grant to Catton of the *Grand Gabriel* and the *Gabriel de la Tour*, the *Petit Marie* had sunk off Cornwall,[133] and the *Little John* was a useless wreck outside the walls of Southampton soon to be sold for £1 3s 6d. The *Christopher of Spain* and the *Marie Spaniard*, two prize vessels, had been granted to royal servants in the late summer of 1419. Soper also soon disposed of the king's half share in the *Marie Breton* and the *Margaret* which were used mainly on commercial voyages.[134] New vessels were to replace them very adequately in terms of attacking power; the new great boat for the *Trinity Royal*, the *Valentine* and the *Falcon*, the ballinger *Roos* which had been forfeited to the king in February 1420 at Bayonne and then brought to England, and most important of all the enormous *Gracedieu*; all of these were in service by the summer of 1420.

Work was pushed forward on the building of a forge and storehouse for the king's ships at Southampton, facilities which had not existed at Greenwich. Solidly built of 'holyngston' and ragstone it cost nearly £200. The 'bulwark' or tower at Hamble to defend the anchorage there, which had been started by Soper in the autumn while Catton was still clerk, was less solid being made entirely of timber, but it was garrisoned by a company of soldiers under the command of Thomas Trewarrak and at least two sentries watched day and night for a multitude of Spanish galleys which were rumoured to be hiding along the coast waiting for a chance to burn the king's great ships at their moorings. Among other repairs a major refit, almost a complete rebuilding, was also undertaken of the *Thomas* at Deptford where she had been waiting on the stocks since October 1418 having been earlier beached at Wapping. To supervise the work Soper sent his factor David Savage.

However, on a rough calculation taking into account all money received by Catton, all money received by Robert Berde, and all money received by William Soper before he was appointed Clerk of the King's ships on 3 February 1420, it is clear that the rate of royal spending shows a decline for the period 1420-2 from the peak reached in the period 1415-20. During this latter period these three men had received from the crown and other sources a total of approximately £20,000 or an average of £5,000 per annum. For the two and a half years from February 1420 till Henry V's death in August 1422 Soper received just over £5,500 in all, a sum comparable to the £5,451 which Catton had received for his first years in office from July 1413 to March 1415 for many fewer ships. These sums do not, of course, represent the total liability of the crown for naval expenditure during this period. While the clerk's accounts do include some sums provided for the wages of royal ships' crews while at sea, and also some payments to arrested shipping, the greater part of payments under these headings were handled separately sometimes by the Treasurer for War, William Kynwollmersh, and sometimes by the individual ships' captains. Nor was the royal Exchequer the only source of income of the clerk of the king's ships. Some of the money referred to above came from the sale of prizes, some from the sale of surplus stores, and some from the freight payments made by merchants mentioned earlier, a practice which was continued by Soper. Nevertheless the totals do provide a rough scale on which to measure the activity of the office of the clerk of the king's ships. At the time Soper would probably have felt that the lower level of both receipt and expenditure was quite understandable in view of the facts that no new ships were under construction, and that following the successes of previous years on land and sea the Channel was firmly in English control.

We must now consider the royal ships of this period in more detail. It is already clear that they differed greatly in size; did they also differ in rig, in the construction of the hull, and in use? Unfortunately, the technical details of naval architecture in the fifteenth century in northern Europe in general and England in particular are extremely controversial and from the nature of the evidence complete certainty on many points is very difficult. Although treatises on shipbuilding survive from the Mediterranean region, like that written by Giorgio Timbotta about 1445 preserved in the Cotton collection, there are no comparable shipwright's manuals for England and it seems unlikely that any such document was written at this time.[135] There are many inventories of ship's gear similar to that in the Phillipps manuscript, but these cannot be relied on to give a complete list of the equipment of any particular ship: they record what was actually on board on the date the count was made, not what should have been available for the proper functioning of any particular ship. With regard to rigging especially, a list of the names given to various ropes and cables does not convey a picture of how they were set up. We are not completely without any representation at all of the ships of this date, but those that do exist were not intended as technical drawings and raise as many problems as they solve.

An important group come from the seals of seaside towns and it is hard to say to what extent the ship represented has been distorted to fit into a medallion. There are also church carvings and various drawings of ships most commonly as background detail in pictures with a religious or narrative purpose.[136]

Only one piece of archaeological evidence exists. The wreck of the *Gracedieu*, struck by lightning and burnt as she lay on the mud of the Hamble River in 1439, can still be seen at extreme low water at equinoctial spring tides. An expedition in 1874 did little more than collect souvenirs and cause damage to the wreck.[137] A later investigation, in 1933, led to a partial survey of the vessel and the discovery and careful recording of certain details concerning the wreck's planking.[138] It has also been suggested that a wreck found off what is now American Wharf at Southampton in 1848 may be the *Jesus* and that even now some worthwhile information might be obtained from the fragments of the vessel which are possibly still concealed by the mud of the harbour bed. The identification is only speculative, however, and the timbers raised in 1848 have long since disappeared.[139]

In these circumstances it is plain that the whole subject of fifteenth century naval architecture in England is fraught with difficulties and that many of our conclusions must be tentative.

One fact is reliable: the size of contemporary vessels, whether those of the king or those in private ownership, was estimated in tuns i.e. the number of tuns of Bordeaux wine with which a vessel could *per estimationem* (as estimated) be laden. It is clear that this figure was arrived at by some formula and there seems no reason to doubt Major-General Prynne's suggestion that the formula used in Elizabethan days could well have been used in the fifteenth century that is 'depth of hold × keel length × main beam divided by 100=the tunnage.'[140]

Some idea of the difference between the estimated tunnage and the actual load carried by a vessel can be gained from the figures surviving from a voyage to Bordeaux for wine made by the following ships in 1414: the *Thomas* of 180 tuns had a cargo of 136 tuns; the *Petit Trinity* of 120 tuns one of 104 tuns; the *Petit Marie* of 80 tuns one of 56 tuns; the *Cog John* of 220 tuns one of 207 tuns and the *Grand Marie* of 126 tuns one of 103 tuns – a difference varying from 30% to 6% in the case of the *Cog John*.[141]

On other voyages at the same period the *Thomas* carried cargoes of 137 tuns and 141 tuns, and the *Petit Marie* as much as 67 tuns I hogshead. The *Redcog* whose nominal burden was 120 tuns made four voyages to Bordeaux for wine between 1414–16: her cargo varied from 111 tuns 1 hogshead to 123 tuns 1 pipe. The tunnage formula was clearly not completely accurate.[142]

The ships are also classified in the accounts into four classes – barges, ballingers, carracks, and *naves* i.e. ships. The term *barge* nowadays is applied to a very wide range of vessels from the powerless flat-bottomed craft towed by tugs to the sailing barges of the Thames Estuary. In the fifteenth century, it is clear that the term could also be used in several ways. The barge for the king's household, dating from the time of Henry IV, was evidently an oared river craft of a ceremonial nature very similar to those well known from sixteenth-century pictures. Two other vessels appear listed as barges, the *Marie Breton* and the *Valentine*. The king was concerned with two ships called *Marie Breton*: the one known as the barge *Marie Breton* was owned by the king and Richard Rowe in partnership and seems to have been brought into the royal fleet to transport corn and other provisions and reinforcements to Normandy.

The *Valentine*, newly built under Robert Berde's supervision, was involved in a military expedition mounted by the Earl of Devon, but otherwise undertook more peaceful voyages transporting the Ambassador of the Count of Foix to Bordeaux and carrying wool to the Low Countries. From their inventories both were single-masted vessels: the *Valentine* also was equipped with 48 oars, while the *Marie Breton* apparently had none. The barge would seem to have been a roomy but slow cargo vessel not well-fitted to a warlike role. The provision for rowing the *Valentine* may well have been an innovation of Berde's making her appear more like a ballinger – by which name she is described in one document.[143]

Ballingers indeed seem to have been one of the most successful of late medieval ship types. In many ways they represented an amalgam of the nordic tradition of the Viking long ships with the galleys of the Mediterranean. As a ship type, ballingers enjoyed a wide geographical spread and perhaps a somewhat unsavoury reputation as the vessel beloved by pirates. As J. Bernard states: *partout où un mauvais coup était perpétré il y avait bien des chances que l'on decouvrit un baleinier.*[144] Most were small and of shallow draught to enable them to enter small ports and sail as far as possible up an estuary. Of those in royal ownership none were larger than 120 tuns, while the three smallest were from 24–30 tuns. The type clearly underwent development during the period from 1400–36 and considerable differences exist between the various ships described by this term in the royal accounts. As many as fifteen vessels came into this category: of these eleven were single-masted and four were at least two-masted. Most were also equipped with oars often as many as thirty or forty: it is hard to give precise numbers as oars are obviously an easily damaged item of naval equipment and it is impossible to tell from the inventories how many were missing or were intended for spares. Of the two-masted vessels none dates earlier than 1416: two, the *George* of 120 tuns (described at one stage as being *ad modus unius gallee* – in the style of a galley)[145] and the *Ane* also of 120 tuns were built at the royal order; the first at Small Hythe, the second at Southampton, the third, the *Roose* of 30 tuns was forfeit to the king in February 1420 at Bayonne and then sailed to England. These three are clearly stated to have had a great mast and a mizzen. The fourth of this group the *Petit Jesus* is unique. Originally the follower or tender of the *Jesus*, she was refitted as a single masted ballinger in the period 1422–7. Then in 1435, she was again completely rebuilt and this time emerged as a three-masted vessel possessing a great mast, a mizzen and a 'fuk or foke' or fore mast.[146]

Although this apparent confusion might appear to destroy any justification of using the term 'ballinger' to describe a definite type of vessel, it is clear that despite their differences in appearance these vessels were operated in a very similar manner. Fortunately detailed accounts exist for the *Ane* (2-masted, 120 tuns) the *Craccher* (single-masted, 56 tuns) and the *Nicholas* (single-masted, 120 or 140 tuns) which enable one to make such a comparison. From September 1416–March 1419 the *Ane* (120 tuns) made at least fifteen voyages and the crew employed varied from 140 sailors, 1 constable and 4 pages to as little as 45 sailors, 1 constable and 4 pages.[147]

The larger crews of between 130–143 men were all employed on voyages of an essentially warlike nature described variously as: watching for enemies at sea; or sailing on the sea. The smaller crews varying from 57 to 95 were employed when the *Ane* was either being used as a transport, for example taking artillery to Caen, or food and an ambassador and his servants across the Channel; or was supporting the royal forces at the siege of a town or castle apparently accessible by water, like Falaise, Honfleur, Caen or Rouen.[148] The same pattern is provided by the crew figures for the *Craccher* of 56 tuns. Ninety-one crewmen were employed on a voyage to keep the seas and 51 when provisions were transported to Caen and Rouen.[149]

The figures for the *Nicholas* of 120 tuns approx. show much less variation: this vessel was evidently very successful as a warship and was employed on every expedition mounted in the last years of Henry V. The voyages in the extant accounts of Robert Shadde, her master, are all for keeping the seas and do not mention any cargo. The crew varies from 100 to 120, the most usual figure being 107. On one occasion the crew rose briefly to 146 men; the smallest crew is 99 men on the only occasion when a passenger is mentioned, the *Nicholas* being employed to take the king himself to Calais.[150] It is suggested that the main reason for the great variation in crew sizes was whether it was intended to use oars in a battle situation or not. All ships of this date probably used oars to manoeuvre in harbour or in similar situations when the wind was adverse. One of the distinguishing features of the ballinger was that in a sea fight when the main aim was to close with an enemy ship, grapple with her and board her, the oars would be used to control the ship in the necessarily confined circumstances when reliance on the wind alone could leave a ship helpless and at the mercy of her enemies. If a ballinger put to sea without her oarsmen she presumably did not intend to stand and fight but would run from any would-be attackers. If this is so, differing sail plans would be irrelevant to the classification of a ship as a ballinger.

Carracks form the most easily defined group in the royal fleet. All were of Mediterranean origin, from Genoa, being prizes captured by various royal ships in the actions in the Channel which will be described below. Of the total of eight, renamed when in royal hands, the *Marie Hampton*, the *Marie Sandwich*, the *Paul*, the *Peter*, the *Christopher*, the *George*, the *Andrew*, and the *Agase*, the tunnage of all but the *Agase* is known: four were of 600 tuns, one of 660 tuns, one of 500 tuns, and one of 550 tuns. There is very little information available concerning the *Agase* which was apparently wrecked off the quay at Southampton in a storm very soon after she was captured by Hugh Courtenay off Netley; most of the others, however, were two-masted with a mainmast and a mizzen. It seems likely that they may have closely resembled the ships drawn by Maso Finiguerra intended as illustrations of a universal history, originally discovered by Ruskin and published by Bernard Quaritch under the title of *A Florentine Picture Chronicle*. Finiguerra's dates are 1426–64, and one would expect that these pictures were drawn sometime in the late 1440s–1450s.[151] The more famous series of drawings in the Victoria and Albert Museum by the probably Flemish WA or W are later, probably 1460–80, and certainly the Craek in the series is a more sophisticated vessel with three masts and a fore topmast.[152] The ex-voto model in the Prins Hendrick Museum, Rotterdam, known as the Mataro model, probably dates from the first half of the fifteenth century but seems to show a much smaller vessel of around 80 tuns. However, it also is two-masted with a main and mizzen mast. The great weight of pictorial evidence and the fact that the lateen rig had been known in the Mediterranean area from the Dark Ages, make it most likely that the mizzen masts of these vessels were rigged in this manner, although there is no evidence to confirm or deny this available from the inventories of Soper and his colleagues. The main mast similarly seems to have been square-rigged.

The hulls of these vessels, following the normal Mediterranean methods, would be carvel-built, that is to say with edge to edge planking. They were steered by a stern-post rudder – a northern innovation which the Basque pirates from Bayonne are credited with introducing to the Mediterranean in the early fourteenth century. Certainly their size, and the weight of their hulls gave them a great advantage in the close-quarters sea-fighting of the day. To contemporaries they seemed supremely successful and majestic fighting vessels. Of all the incidents at sea at this period nothing so impressed itself on the minds of the chroniclers as the capture of the carracks.

The largest group of vessels in the royal fleet some twenty in number are described simply as *naves* the normal Latin word for 'ships'. However, the word is clearly used in a technical sense (the general term employed in the MSS. is 'vessellamentum') since this word is never used of vessels in the other groups already described. Despite this, one must be cautious in trying to establish common features between ships so evidently disparate as the *Gracedieu* of 1,400 tuns on the one hand and the *Margaret* of 70 tuns on the other. The class was obviously not entirely homogenous, and may in fact be divided into several sub-groups.

The most outstanding of these is undoubtedly that comprising what became known as the 'King's great ships', the *Gracedieu*, 1,400 tuns, *Trinity Royal*, 540 tuns, *Jesus*, 1,000 tuns, and the *Holyghost de la Tour*, 740 or 760 tuns. These four vessels were built or extensively re-modelled successively during the reign of Henry V, the *Trinity Royal* being completed in 1413, the *Holyghost* in 1415, the *Jesus* in 1416 and the *Gracedieu* in 1420. To a far greater extent than any other ships

available in England at this date these four were built as warships –
their suitability for use as merchant vessels was hardly considered. The
Genoese carracks were efficient fighting ships because of the lawless
conditions usual at sea at this period. The king's four great ships were
designed to be the English answer to the carracks in a sea fight. This
was the reason for their gradually increasing size: in the boarding and
ramming tactics of the period superior size was an inestimable advantage.

Their sail plan may well also have been influenced by that of a
carrack. The evidence is scanty and somewhat confused but it seems
clear that the *Trinity, Holyghost,* and *Jesus* were all two-masted with
a main and mizzen looking probably rather like the carved bench-end
from St Nicholas Chapel, King's Lynn, now in the Victoria and Albert
Museum, where again the mizzen is lateen-rigged. The *Gracedieu,*
however, was certainly three-masted with a great mast, a mizzen, and
presumably a foremast. The inventories list her as having three *velis
cum iii bonettis et le shrowde cum toto apparatu* (sails with three
bonnetts and all the necessary cordage) but also mention four masts not
including that for her boat. The fourth mast may have been a topmast
or a spar used for the flags and streamers she flew but there is unfortunately no way of reaching a definite conclusion.

The Mediterranean influence did not extend to the hulls of these
ships. These were clearly clinker built with over-lapping strakes secured
by nails clenched on their further ends.[153] In the case of the *Gracedieu,*
probably the largest clinker-built ship ever made, the technique can
be studied in detail from the portions of planking recovered from the
Hamble River in 1933. Each strake uniquely consists of three layers of
planking, two twelve inch planks overlaid on the inside with an eight
inch plank with an overlap of four inches. These were secured with
square iron nails five-eighths of an inch thick driven from inside the
ship riveted over circular roves on the outside some six to eight inches
apart. The interior timbers were secured with trenails sixteen inches
apart driven from the outside. Her estimated length on the keel was
about 125–127 feet and beam about 48–50 feet. These dimensions can
be compared with those of the ship apparently under construction for
Henry V in Bayonne in 1419 with a keel length of 112 feet. The three
other great ships came more within the accepted bounds of contemporary ship size being comparable to the carracks already mentioned and
those ships described in a letter from Cotton Vespasian C XII fol. 127.

Also yff be plessying to the kyng ther by twey new carrakes of
makyng at Batholem the on of XIII C botts ther other of XC
botts. He may haffe hem yff hyt lyke hym.[154]

Of the remaining 16 vessels grouped as 'naves' the tunnage of 13 is known varying from 70 tuns in the case of the *Margaret* owned in partnership by the king and John William to 330 tuns in the case of the *Nicholas* bought for the royal fleet in 1415. Only one and that of foreign origin the *Holyghost of Spain* of 290 tuns, a prize captured in 1419 by Hugh Courtenay and Thomas Carrew, was two-masted. The others, larger in general than the ballingers, seem to have been more the transports of the fleet, or merchantmen than specifically fighting vessels. Perhaps more than the other vessels in royal ownership they corresponded to the stereotype late medieval ship with a deep hull, very beamy, with fore and after castles, a single mast with a square sail and a stern post rudder. Of such a vessel there is a very good modern model in the National Maritime Museum. Two were certainly cog ships (the *Redcog* or *Flaward* and the *Cog John*) the most widely used sea going vessel of northern Europe particularly associated with the Hanseatic ports whose pre-eminence, secure in the fourteenth century, was now threatened by the more sophisticated vessels being developed under Mediterranean influence. From its name, the *Marie Hulke* may be an early example of a later type of north-east European vessel, the hulk, which continued in use until the mid-sixteenth century.[155]

The royal ships, therefore, do provide a large enough and varied enough sample to enable one to reach certain conclusions about English ships in the first half of the fifteenth century. R. Morton-Nance has stated that: 'the chief contribution of the fourteenth century to ship development was the introduction into the Mediterranean of the square-sailed northern rig of the Basque pirates and its imitation there by the Genoese, Venetians and Catalonians. The chief contribution of the fifteenth century was the bringing back to northern and western Europe of a cog improved into the carrack form by contact with the traditional Mediterranean or "Latin" ship.'[156] This process can almost be seen at work in the royal fleet with the building of gradually more sophisticated vessels culminating in that of the *Gracedieu*. Indeed the introduction of the two-master with a lateen mizzen, as we have shown is some fifteen years earlier than Morton-Nance's date of c.1430 and the *Gracedieu* may well have been rigged in the style of his 1450 vessel as early as 1420. With regard to the hull, however, carvel-building had not been accepted at all by Soper's shipwrights even though there were examples of it to hand in the royal carracks of Genoese origins.

No evidence is available from the accounts of the clerks of the king's ships to support the suggestion that a foremast was added to the single main mast of the northern ship before the mizzen despite the handling problems discussed by Sir Alan Moore in his *Rig in Northern Europe*.[157] It is clear that the second mast was a mizzen, and that the foremast came later, first in the *Gracedieu* and then in the rebuilt *Petit Jesus*. All the masts were stayed fore and aft with forestays and backstays and were provided with *headropes* or shrouds. The sails were reefed by the removal of bonnetts at the foot. More exact detail about the construction of the hull and the rigging must remain uncertain from the nature of the evidence.

In the same way there is little detailed evidence concerning the way in which the ships were handled and crewed, and the life of those on board. Navigational instruments supplied as part of the ship's normal equipment were a lead and line, a compass contained in a binnacle and a 'diol' or running glass. Some kind of portolan or rutter may have been used but these were the personal property of the master and would not figure in the ship's inventory. The master, who received a wage of 6d per day was in complete charge of the sailing of the vessel assisted by mariners at 3d per day and a few boys at 1½d. An extra weekly payment of 6d per week, known as a *regardum*, was also sometimes made to the sailors. A constable is sometimes mentioned particularly on the larger ships and there was also occasionally a clerk (the modern purser?) and a quartermaster although they did not receive wages any different from those of an ordinary sailor. By modern standards the vessels were almost grotesquely overcrowded. The sizes of the crews employed on various balingers have already been noted and it must be remembered that when setting out on a voyage to keep the seas a ship would also have on board men at arms and archers under separate command.

Thus on the carrack *Mary de la Tour*, for Thomas Carrew's expedition in 1417, in addition to the crew of about 100 men, 62 men at arms and 134 archers, under the command of their captains Janken Edward and Thomas Legate, were embarked; making a total of approximately 398 men on a ship of around 500 tuns.[158] On the *Petite Trinity* a much smaller vessel were 18 men at arms, 40 archers and their captains Thomas Taplegh and John Saintbarb. The food provided for these men, crammed together and expected on occasion to be at sea (though not continuously) for as long as six months, was very monotonous. On a voyage to Le Crotoy Richard Rowe provisioned the balinger *Petit Jesus* with bread, flour, beef, salt meat, five pipes of beer, 7½ pipes of wine, some salt, 6 lb of candles and 500 billets of wood (for cooking?) Other ships on the same expedition took salt fish, fresh fish, biscuit and mutton.[159]

Despite these overcrowded conditions and the disadvantages which the royal vessels of this date might seem to suffer from compared with later and more highly developed sailing ships, there is no doubt that they could give a good account of themselves both in the sea-fights of the day and on more mundane errands. During the reign of Henry V, the royal ships not only provided the nucleus for naval expeditions but were useful in maintaining communications, carrying supplies and in what is delicately called 'the king's secret business'.

As noted previously royal ships were also used for merchant voyages throughout the reign of Henry V. In the period 1413–15, for example, the *Cog John*, the *Grand Marie*, the *Petit Trinity*, the *Petit Marie*, the *Philip*, the *Katherine*, the *Grand Gabriel*, the *Redcog*, the *Nicholas*, the *Margaret* and the *Marie Breton* all made the voyage to Bordeaux for wines on various occasions, in some cases more than once. The *Petit Trinity* and the *Philip* went to Newcastle for coal; and the *Petit Trinity* made another voyage to Prussia for naval stores.[160] The *Redcog*, formerly known as the *Flaward de Gerrant* had also made the journey from Chester to Dublin with the king's lieutenant, John Stanley.[161] Turning to more warlike expeditions, in the autumn of 1414 three small balingers the *Gabriel de la Tour* (30 tuns), the *Peter* (24 tuns) and the *Paul* (24 tuns) were sent north to protect the east coast fishing fleet against the malice of the king's enemies. Provision was then made for the *Grand Marie,* the *Gabriel de la Tour,* the *Petit Trinity* and the *Philip* to leave on a voyage to Bordeaux for wine. They sailed at the end of December and were caught by a storm off the Isle of Wight which forced them to take shelter off Camber near Winchelsea. News then came that Lord Talbot was to lead an expedition in the Channel and they all returned to London, setting sail for a more warlike cause on 20 February having been joined by the *Paul* and the *Katherine* and a few arrested ships.[162]

During the summer of 1415 attention was concentrated on the great assemblage of vessels slowly gathering on the south coast for the king's invasion of France. Very little of this activity and excitement is reflected in the returns of the clerk of the king's ships, as all the naval payments whether for royal or arrested ships were handled by the treasurer for war – and Catton merely records the date his ships left to join the king and the date they returned. The *Trinity Royal*, as for many years past was the royal flagship and carried the king himself and his immediate entourage, but also included in the great fleet that set sail from Southampton that August day were the *Grand Marie*, the *Petit Trinity*, the *Petit Marie*, the *Philip*, the *Katherine*, the *Nicholas*, and the *Redcog*.

When the king returned from France, the hero of Agincourt, to entertain the Emperor Sigismund and conduct lengthy negotiations with the various French factions, he left the garrison at Harfleur in an increasingly difficult position. Although reinforcements under the command of the Earl of Dorset had arrived in January 1416 in a squadron led by the *Trinity Royal* and including the *Gabriel Harfleur* and the *George,* by the summer of the same year the town was invested both by land and sea where the French had a great advantage through their alliance with the Genoese. No fewer than eight of the great Genoese carracks had come north, and also 12 galleys under the command of Gioanni de' Grimaldi.[163] The situation, from the English point of view, had deteriorated to such an extent that the French felt sufficiently confident to attack Portland and the Isle of Wight.[164] The Duke of Bedford was put in command of the fleet raised to oppose the French and their allies and had difficulty at first in putting to sea owing to contrary winds. His total strength is given by the Italian chroniclers as about 300 ships,[165] and included the *Holyghost*, the *Petit John*, the *Trinity Royal*, the *Swan* and the *James*. The enemy was sighted at dawn on 15 August and almost immediately a furious battle began at the mouth of the Seine. It is clear that the English outnumbered their opponents, for a portion of the French forces remained in the harbour at Harfleur and played no part in the fighting, and the Genoese galleys had drawn off largely because Grimaldi had been killed in an earlier attack on English ships sailing in convoy to Bordeaux for wine. The Spanish vessels (also allies of the French) fled, as soon as they saw the size of the English fleet. The great carracks of the Genoese took the brunt of the English attack and held on all day. In the evening, however, three were taken[166] and the others fled, one of them later foundering on the sandbanks off Honfleur.[167] The English were now victorious and returned in triumph to Southampton with the three captured carracks soon to be re-named the *Marie Hampton*, the *Marie Sandwich* and the *George*.[168]

The tremendous strength of the Genoese carracks in the boarding tactics of the period were further demonstrated in an epic fight that occurred later that same summer off Calais. A Genoese carrack with a crew of 62 men was sighted and chased up the Channel by six ballingers with (according to Guistiniani) a total complement of 1,500 men under the command of the 'Duca di Vernich' (the Earl of Warwick). The battle raged, but one sailor alone, though wounded and nearly choking in his own blood, threw the boarding ladders back from the carrack's deck to the English ships below and the gallant vessel made good her escape suffering eight dead and 50 wounded.[169] The English writer of the *Gesta Henrici Quinti* also described how the carrack towered a spear's length at least above the ballingers which only drew off when their missiles were exhausted.[170]

In the summer of 1417 English naval activity reached its peak. Three squadrons were at sea at various times, one led by the Earl of Huntingdon, one by Thomas Carrew, and one by Pons, Lord Castelhon. The chroniclers were most impressed with the activities of the Earl of Huntingdon who captured four more carracks soon known as the *Paul*, the *Christopher*, the *Andrew* and the *Peter*.[171] However, the Lord Castelhon captured the ballinger *Katherine*, the *Christopher of Spain*

and the *Marie Spaniard*, and Carrew the *Holyghost of Spain* and the
Agase. Huntingdon had with him the pick of the royal ships, the
Trinity Royal, the *Holyghost*, the *Gabriel de la Tour*, the *Petit John*,
the *Nicholas* and the *Gabriel Harfleur*. The Lord Castelhon had one of
the newly captured carracks the *Marie Sandwich*, and also the *Grand
Marie* and the *Petit Trinity*.[172]

For the summer patrol in 1418 Thomas Duke of Exeter was the
admiral assisted by John Arundel. The newly-captured carracks *Peter*,
Christopher and *George* led the royal contingent with the *Craccher*, the
Ane, the *Katherine*, the *Nicholas* and the ballinger *George*. Among the
supporting arrested ships was Soper's own *Julyan of Hampton* of 140
tuns: others came from Fowey, Tiegnmouth, Plymouth and Newcastle.

In the following two summers, the patrols were led by Hugh Courtney, Earl of Devon, with John Hawley of Dartmouth and Thomas
Carrew. By this time, the Channel was firmly in English control and
the ships probably saw little action.

Courtney's expedition of 1420 is of great interest; first of all because
of the rather extraordinary happenings at its outset and also because it
seems clear that on this occasion, the fleet was led by the *Gracedieu*. It
has always been suggested that this great ship was a failure, that she
never put to sea, and that she was almost a royal *folie de grandeur*.
However, Soper definitely states in his account for 1420–2 that she
came into his charge *post viagium Comitis Devon super salva custodia
maris completum* (after completing a voyage with the Earl of Devon
concerned with the safe-keeping of the sea).[173] Also in the early spring
of 1420 the masters of the following ships received commissions to
raise crews for their vessels; the *Swan*, the *Valentine*, the *Falcon*, the
James and the *Trinity*; and at the same time John Gyrdelet, quartermaster of the *Gracedieu* received a similar commission.[174] Finally, we
still have the report to the Council made by William Moryng, Knight,
and Peter Garneys, *armiger*, who went to Southampton in May 1420 to
take the muster of the 50 men-at-arms and 1,000 archers commanded
by Hugh Earl of Devon, the Lord de Botreaux, Thomas Carrew, and
John Hawley and also to muster the ships' crews, all setting forth on an
expedition to keep the seas. According to the report everything went
wrong: the Earl of Devon refused to muster his men at all. When
they went on board the *Gracedieu*, one of the quartermasters, William
Duke of Dartmouth seized the muster roll by force from Peter Jordan
clerk of the same ship, and threatened to throw it into the sea. After
the fleet had left Southampton a group of Devon men on the same
ship under the command of William Payne mutinied and insisted on
being put ashore on the Isle of Wight. When the commissioners inter-
vened they answered them with *verbis contumeliose* (rudely) and tore

the clothes of one of their servants. The sailors on the *Jesus* also refused to be mustered. It is a relief to discover that the Lord de Botreaux and Thomas Carrew humbly obeyed and mustered their retinues while the commissioners were probably almost glad that they could not even attempt to muster John Hawley's men because of storms at sea.[175]

There also exists a letter written by Humphrey Duke of Gloucester, to Henry V when the latter was in France, describing how he had visited the *Gracedieu* as she was about to sail on the expedition led by the Earl of Devon already described. The original of this letter cannot now be traced, but it was published in facsimile in 1865 in the collection of facsimiles of national manuscripts edited by Sir Henry James by whom it was ascribed to the reign of Henry IV with the Prince of Wales (later Henry V) as the author. There is no doubt, however, of its true provenance: it is signed H.G. and besides describing activities of the Duke of Bedford and Tiptoft dating from this period and Humphrey's own marriage plans also mentions the visit of the captive King of Scots to Henry V in France which took place in 1420. It is pleasant to read how, 'your gret ship the *Grace Dieu* is ever as redy and is the fairest that ever men saugh I trowe in good faith: and this same day th' Erle of Devonshir my cosin maad his moustre in her and al others have her moustre the same tyme that shal go to the see.' This was not written of a ship that was a failure from her inception but of what seemed to contemporaries to be an outstandingly successful and daring experiment which had justified the faith shown in her by her builders. She was built as a deliberate act of policy. 'Whate hope yt was the kynges grette entente of the shippes and what in mynde he mente? It was not ellis but that he caste to be Lorde rounde aboute environ of the see' as the author of the Libelle of English Policy put it. The *Gracedieu* was the victim not of faulty shipbuilding techniques but of the rapidly changing political and strategic situation in the Channel.

Turning from the great expeditions, it is possible to gain an idea of the errands undertaken by some of the smaller of the king's ships by studying the accounts presented by certain ships' captains at the Exchequer.

Robert Shadde of the *Nicholas*, for example, was at sea in May 1417 with the *George* and the *Ane*. He then joined the Earl of Huntingdon and after the capture of the carracks went to assist at the sieges of Touques and Caen bringing special orders from the king. After cruising off the Isle of Wight he returned to Portsmouth on 23 December. He was at sea under the orders of Arundel from April to July 1418 and then crossed to Normandy to the sieges of Rouen and Honfleur, bringing provisions from England and on one occasion taking Henry himself to Calais. In 1419–20 he was again at sea with Hugh Courtney and in 1421 with William Bardolf.[176] Richard Rowe was master in turn of the *Swan* and the *Valentine*. As master of the first he was at the siege of Rouen from September 1418 till the fall of the town in January 1419. As master of the second he took the ambassadors of the king to the Count of Foix to Bordeaux in July 1422.[177]

Stephen Welles, the master of the balinger *Craccher*, must have been seldom in port between 1416–18. When not at sea looking for the king's enemies, or serving in the large expeditions he was at the sieges of Touques, Caen and Rouen bringing victuals, important passengers or artillery. Later he and his ships brought supplies to France for the siege of the castles of Falaise, and of Honfleur.[178] Ralph Huskard and the balinger *Ane* were used in a very similar way: as well as assisting in certain secret business of the king they also watched for enemies at sea and brought stones to the sieges mentioned above.[179]

The death of Henry V had the far-reaching effects on the royal ships and on the office of the clerk of the king's ships which are detailed in the Phillipps M.S. Almost immediately an order was made to sell as many of the ships as possible with the greater part of the proceeds being handed over to the late king's executors.[180] It is a curious fact that this process is far better known to historians and has been far more frequently described than the earlier days of success and expansion.[181]

The ostensible cause was the clause in Henry V's Will stating that sufficient ships – at that time the personal property of each individual king – should be sold in order to provide his executors with funds to pay his debts. However, the obligation to the royal executors amounted only to 1,000 marks (£666 13s 4d) and the total raised by the sale of the royal ships not including the assessed value of the *Grand Marie* amounted to just over £1,000.[182] It seems that the motive behind the sales was strategic and practical as much as legal. The upkeep of the fleet was expensive and the ships when sold would still be available to the crown under the general power of arrest in an emergency, the occurrence of which seemed unlikely in view of English control over both sides of the Channel. The reasoning of the council seemed impeccable particularly as the late king's four great ships the *Jesus, Holyghost, Trinity Royal* and *Gracedieu* were not to be sold, and two smaller vessels were also retained, the balinger *Gabriel Harfleur*, soon to be lost at sea,[183] and the *Petit Jesus*, the follower of the *Jesus*, refitted and re-named. Richard II and Henry IV had possessed similar small squadrons of royal ships and the council perhaps felt it was more sensible to follow precedent in this matter than attempt to maintain anything on the same scale as Henry V's fleet of 36 vessels.

Despite the order for sale, however, Soper was confirmed in his position as clerk at the same salary as before which was paid fairly regularly until 1436.[184] The details of administration were altered, perhaps following the model of the customs: a controller was appointed: that is the keeper of a counter-roll or duplicate set of accounts – as some sort of accounting safeguard. Both Soper's clerk, John Foxholes, and the controller Nicholas Banastre were at various times also his colleagues in the Southampton customs [185] and there was no suggestion that he was subordinate to the controller, whose activities were probably purely formal.

There was no sudden cessation of expenditure on the royal ships. The *Grand Marie*, before being granted to Richard Buckland in partial satisfaction of debts, was completely re-fitted at a cost of £182 9s 10d. The *Petit Jesus* was reconstructed, and £143 6s 1½d, £70 7s 5d, £83 7s 3d and £70 16s 3d were spent on the upkeep of the *Gracedieu, Holyghost, Jesus* and *Trinity Royal* respectively. The other ships before their sale were in the care of ship-keepers whose task was sometimes arduous in times of rough weather. Those on board the *Thomas,* moored at Plymouth, were granted special payments for working day and night to bail her out during a storm.

It is difficult nowadays to come to any conclusion as to whether the ships sold were disposed of at their true value or whether they were, especially the ballingers, 'indecently snapped up'.[186] The expense of keeping wooden ships in good repair was substantial and it is impossible today to have any very clear idea of the real condition of a vessel described as merely *debilis* (in poor condition). The carracks *Christopher* and *George*, the ships *Thomas* and *Holyghost of Spain* fetched good prices, £166 13s 4d, £133 6s 8d, £133 6s 8d and £200 respectively, obviously reflecting their seaworthy condition. The price fetched by the ballingers varied considerably; the *Roose* a total wreck went for £1 6s 8d: the *Nicholas* fetched £66 13s 4d: the others, the *Swan*, the *Craccher*, the *George*, the *Ane*, the *Falcon* and the *Katherine Breton* average around £30. The last sale, that of the *Roose* took place in 1425. The purchasers, among whom figure several royal mariners – Ralph Huskard, John William, Richard Rowe, John Jon – and also well-known English and alien merchants – Nicholao Iustiniani, a Venetian, John Chirche a London mercer – probably were well satisfied with their bargains but there seems to be little evidence of any real irregularity or sharp practice on the behalf of Soper or his colleagues.

Indeed the surplus from the sale of the ships amounting to approximately £334 plus the proceeds of the sale of surplus stores and the newly-built forge and storehouse of £107 2s 9d were not immediately handed to the Exchequer. Soper was given permission to retain these funds to cover himself for moneys spent on behalf of the crown for which he had not been re-imbursed from the time of the building of the *Holyghost* onwards; also included were his expenses incurred when arranging the sale of the ships when with Banastre he had ridden from

Southampton to Bristol, Plymouth, London, Winchelsea, Sandwich, Saltash and Greenwich. Even with this windfall he was still substantially out of pocket at the end of the accounting period.[187] The second half of the accounts here edited are almost melancholy reading. Each spar, each rope, the smallest piece of ironwork, whatever its condition, in the possession of the office of the king's ships at Southampton is accounted for under the name of the ship to which it had once belonged no matter how long had passed since that ship was sold, or had foundered, or had rotted away on the mud. For example, Lord Talbot's expedition had captured in the Channel four little Breton ships laden with salt, wine and bacon in early 1415.[188] They were brought into Winchelsea harbour; some of the wine was sold, the bacon and provisions were sent to the victualler of Calais and in a little while the Bretons were sent home in a specially hired small boat after payment of ransom. However, while odd pieces of equipment from their little boats – undecked and of a capacity of only 40, 34, 30 and 30 tuns respectively – were sold, the vessels themselves remained in royal hands and were included in inventories thereafter, although they must soon have been little more than wrecks. Equally the names of the *Galley*, the *Redcog*, the *Petit Trinity* and the *Philip*, among others, linger in the accounts even though they had all been sold as being in a totally unseaworthy condition before the death of Henry V. Similarly in the inventories attached to the accounts of Soper and his successor Richard Clyvedon for the years after 1427, the names of the dispersed ships live on, attached to mouldering heaps of old cordage, rotten sails, and worm-eaten boards.

During the succeeding years the attempt to keep the four great ships in a seaworthy condition was gradually abandoned. By 1432 only the *Gracedieu* was still afloat although her great mast and yard had been lowered. The others were in docks specially constructed on the mud flats, the *Trinity Royal* and the *Holyghost* at Hamble, the *Jesus* at Southampton.[189] Originally they had been docked so that repairs could be carried out but as the years went by and the money was not forthcoming from the Crown it was clear that these docks could well be their graves. Yet it is not true that they had been completely abandoned to their fate – shipkeepers were still employed and their equipment was in a rented store and a *'hovell'* specially built for the masts and sails. The *Petit Jesus* was in commission bringing the king a share of a prize in August 1430.

During the period 1432–6 even this level of activity was reduced: the *Gracedieu* was also beached in the Hamble river at Bursledon, stripped of her remaining equipment and although she was protected by a 'hegge' dug out of the mud to make a dock there was no pretence that any future repairs were contemplated. As much old equipment as possible was sold, some of the canvas sail cloth going to painters. The only centre of positive activity was the *Petit Jesus* which was completely rebuilt and re-rigged to a different design during this period: even so the clerk's total expenditure was under £150.[190] Soper finally relinquished the clerkship in April 1442.[191] In January 1439 the *Gracedieu* had been struck by lightning in the middle of the night and had burnt to the water-line.[192] The other hulks lay rotting on the mud and for his last two and a half years in office expenditure did not exceed £4 16s 4d against receipts of £6 10s 11½d.[193]

His successor Richard Clyvedon, a yeoman of the chamber previously supervisor and clerk of the New Forest to whom Soper was appointed controller [194] seems to have made quite strenuous efforts to wind up the office and dispose of the old stores and things salvaged from the hulks. A total of £61 2s 7d had been raised from this source by July 1447 and the *Jesus* had been disposed of to servants of Cardinal Henry Beaufort, Bishop of Winchester, during the previous winter.[195] By April 1452 there was evidently nothing saleable left. Old ironwork had been cut up, melted down, weighed and sold: the old timber had been brought to Southampton from Hamble, including the last salvaged fragments of the *Holyghost* lately sunk at her moorings, and all sold off.[196]

Two anchors, formerly belonging to the *Gracedieu* and the *Trinity Royal* were also handed over to be used in private shipping fighting for the king; rather against the will of Clyvedon's deputy who declared belligerently that the king could write twenty letters under the privy seal and he still would not hand over the anchors! The last account of the clerk of the king's ships disclosed a profit of £56 19s 6½d, on which practical and commercial note the crown ceased to have any naval administration until 1480.

Alfred the Great, Henry V and Henry VII have all at various times been considered the Father of the Royal Navy. It is clear that while Henry V did inherit a small group of ships and a tradition of royal leadership in naval affairs, under his own son and successor the tradition seemed to wither and die. The great flowering of naval interest in Henry's V's reign seems almost like the blooming of an exotic plant which could not long sustain itself in a hostile climate. Despite this lack of continuity, the naval achievements of the reign cannot be ignored; contemporaries, like, for example, the author of the *Libelle of English Policye*, were made forcibly aware of the importance of sea power; under the stimulation of war, technical improvements were made in the design of ships which continued to bear fruit throughout the years ahead. William Catton and William Soper were careful men, administrators and accountants, never directly involved in the hurly-burly of a battle at sea; yet their establishment of a royal dockyard was essential to any continuing military success at sea and a clear demonstration of the possibilities inherent in the operation of a royal navy.

THE METHOD USED IN EDITING AND TRANSLATING THE TEXT OF THE ACCOUNTS

Soper's account book for 1422–7 is written, like nearly all public documents of this date, in Latin. However, it is not the Latin of Cicero, nor even that of the medieval scholar. It is a serviceable, standardised, technical language used with familiarity by the clerk and consisting largely of a collection of conventional phrases which could be strung together as necessary. It is written in a highly abbreviated form using a large number of standard contractions: wherever an unfamiliar term must be used, the clerk does not search for a Latin word but writes down the usual everyday one, usually English, very occasionally something which seems nearer to French. In this translation, the aim has been to provide a text which is clearly understandable and is as close to the original as is consistent with that aim. The punctuation (very nearly non-existent in the original) has been modernised. Some repetitions of 'aforesaid' and similar words have been omitted. Proper names but not identified place names have been left in the original spelling. Words (mostly technical terms) which appear to be in contemporary English in the manuscript have been left in the original spelling and printed in italics. The meaning of most of them will be found in the glossary. All figures have been changed from Roman to Arabic numerals.

In the original, there are running headings at the top of each folio. These have all been omitted. The few marginal notes in the manuscript which seem to have been made by somebody checking the arithmetic have also been omitted. In the inventory section of the accounts some more substantial alterations have been made. The form in which the inventory is made up (goods received, additions and deletions, goods remaining) involves an enormous amount of repetition. In the text as printed, the 'goods received' section is kept, together with the alterations noted which are usually few in number. The 'goods remaining' section has been omitted, because in general it merely repeats the substance of the 'goods received' section.

Further details of the careers of many of the individuals mentioned in the accounts will be found in Appendix III – the biographical index. Only the names of the more obscure workmen about whom nothing further could be discovered have been omitted.

The Accounts and Inventory of
William Soper

THE ACCOUNTS

[F.1r.] The particulars of account of William Soper Keeper and Governor of the ships of our Lord King Henry VI as required by a writ under the Privy Seal given the second day of the month of December in the second year of the aforesaid King addressed to the Treasurer and Barons of the Exchequer, delivered with this account and enrolled with the writs addressed to the same Treasurer and Barons of the Exchequer on roll twenty of Hilary Term in the said second year. The account is made up under the oath of the said Keeper from the last day of August in the tenth year of the Lord Henry V lately King of England on which day indeed the said King died to the fifth day of March next following in the first year of our present King and also made up as directed by letters patent under the Great Seal of England given on the aforesaid fifth day of March in the said first year as similarly by virtue of letters under the Privy Seal of the said Lord King given and enrolled as above, under the supervision and testimony of Nicholas Banastre, the Controller, and under the oath of the said Keeper of the King's ships to wit including all manner of receipts in cash for the office howsoever received together with various foreign cash receipts from the sale of various ships, carracks and other vessels whatsoever belonging to the said late King, sold by virtue of a Royal Writ under the Privy Seal received by the aforesaid Keeper; and including all manner of purchases, outlays, costs and expenses made or laid out by the same for the purpose of the repair, governance and safekeeping of the same ships, carracks and other vessels belonging to the said late King up to the time of the sale of the same for the benefit of the King at various times during the accounting period by the said Keeper acting at the order of the King's Council and the said Royal Writ. Also including all manner of costs, outlays and expenses made by the same during the construction and restoration of the King's ship *Grand Marie* lately newly renovated at Southampton by order of the said late King confirmed by the Council of the present King. Moreover also concerning the repair and improvement of the four great ships belonging to the present King, called *Gracedieu, Jesus, Trinity Royal* and *Holyghost,* and of other vessels in the care of the said office with the large and small boats, equipment and other things whatsoever, together with the wages of carpenters, caulkers, and other workmen whatsoever working and labouring on the aforesaid construction, making, repair, and improvement; also concerning the payment of the wages, bonuses, emoluments, and transport fees of the masters and sailors of the same ships (if there are any of any kind) together with the payment made by the aforesaid Keeper of transport dues, freight, towage, pilotage, and boat hire for the same; moreover also concerning the wages of sailors remaining in the same ships for the governance and safe keeping of the same in the port of Southampton and elsewhere at various times; to wit concerning all receipts and expenses from the last day of August in the tenth year of King Henry V lately King of England on which day the same late King died to the last day of August in the fifth year of our present King Henry VI, that is to say for five complete years. (William Soper has already drawn up his accounts for the previous period and will draw up further accounts elsewhere for the period after this date).

[F.1v.] *Receipts from the Royal Exchequer*
Michaelmas Term, the first year.   nothing.
Easter Term, the first year.
   The same (i.e. Soper) accounts for: £112 received from the Treasurer and Chamberlains of the Exchequer on the 12th July, Easter Term, in the first year of the present King; to wit into his own hands by an assignment made that day for the office of the King's ships to provide supplies for the governance and safe keeping of various great ships of the King together with their tenders.
Easter Term, the second year.
   Also concerning: £57 2s 7d similarly received from the same Treasurer and Chamberlains at the aforesaid Receipt of the Exchequer on the 5th June, Easter Term, in the second year of the present King, to wit the money was received personally by an assignment made that day as an advance on his office for the improvement and repair of the aforesaid great ships with various other expenses and costs incurred for this same office.
   Total for this term: £169 2s 7d.
Michaelmas Term, the second year.
   Also concerning the £31 13s 7d similarly received from the aforesaid Treasurer and Chamberlains at the Receipt of the Exchequer on the 15th November, Michaelmas Term, in the second year of our aforesaid king: to wit the money was received personally by an assignment made that day for various repairs, outlays, costs and expenses incurred for the governance and safe keeping of the said great ships, and for other necessities for the office.

Michaelmas Term, the second year.

Also concerning £30 similarly received from the same Treasurer and Chamberlains at the Receipt of the Exchequer on 28th January, Michaelmas Term, in the second year of the same King: to wit the money was received by Simon atte Forde as an advance on the office for the supply and improvement of various cables and ropes by the same Simon for the governance and safe custody of the same great ships and other vessels in the care of the office aforesaid.

[F.2r.] Michaelmas Term, the second year.

Also concerning £13 8s 5d similarly received from the aforesaid Treasurer and Chamberlains at the Receipt of the Exchequer on the 2nd March in Michaelmas Term in the said second year of the King aforesaid; to wit the money was received by Simon atte Ford of Bridport as an advance on the office for cables and ropes bought from and supplied by the same Simon for the ships mentioned above.

Total for this term: £75 2s.

Michaelmas Term, the third year.

Also concerning £77 16s 8d similarly received from the same Treasurer and Chamberlains at the aforesaid Receipt of the Exchequer on 27th November in Michaelmas Term of the third year of the Lord King aforesaid; to wit the money was received personally as an advance on the office on two occasions: on the first £72 16s 8d; on the second £5.

Easter Term, the third year.

Also concerning £80 received from the same Treasurer and Chamberlains at the same Receipt on 26th June of the said third year in money given to him personally for his aforesaid office.

Also concerning £100 similarly received from the same Treasurer and Chamberlains at the aforesaid Receipt of the Exchequer on 9th July in Easter Term in the said third year of the aforesaid Lord King: to wit the money was received personally through an assignment made that day as an advance on the office.

Easter Term, the third year.

Also concerning £76 10s similarly received from the aforesaid Treasurer and Chamberlains at the aforesaid Receipt of the Exchequer on the same day in July of the said third year: to wit the money was received personally through an assignment made that day as an advance on the office of the King's ships.

Total for this term: £256 10s.

Easter Term, the fourth year.

Also concerning £46 13s 4d similarly received from the same Treasurer and Chamberlains at the said Receipt of the Exchequer on the 25th July in Easter Term in the fourth year of the said King to wit the money was received personally by an assignment made that day as an advance on the same office of the King's ships.

Total for this term £46 13s 4d.

Michaelmas Term, the fifth year.

Also concerning £40 similarly received from the aforesaid Treasurer and Chamberlains at the said Receipt of the Exchequer on the 5th December, in Michaelmas Term, in the fifth year of the said present Lord King to wit the money was received personally through an assignment made that day as an advance on the same office of the King's ships.

Michaelmas Term, the fifth year.

Also concerning £15 similarly received from the same Treasurer and Chamberlains at the said Receipt of the Exchequer on the 21st February in Michaelmas Term in the said fifth year of the same present King to wit the money was received personally through an assignment made that day as an advance on the repair and improvement of the King's ships.

Total for this term £55.

Total received from the Exchequer: £680 4s 7d.

[F.2v.] Foreign Receipts from the Sale of the King's ships covered by the period of this account: to wit:

Freight Payment.

Also concerning £20 similarly received from Neron Victor (Nerone Vetturi), a Lombard, and various other merchants as payment for the freighting of a certain Royal ship called The *Holyghost of Spain* for a voyage made between the first of April in the said first year (the day this ship first sailed to Zealand laden with various merchandise) and the 15th of June next following when it returned; to wit the money was received for the benefit of the King under the controlment aforesaid, after all expenses, costs, wages and port dues of the sailors for this voyage had been paid.

Freight Payment.

Also concerning £10 similarly received from Paul Morrell (Paolo Morelli) and various other merchants of Southampton as payment similarly for the freighting of a certain Royal barge called *Valentine* for a voyage lately made to Calais laden with wool and other merchandise to wit between the 28th of March in the said first year, the day the ship sailed on this voyage with the aforesaid destination and the 30th of June next following when it returned, to wit the money was received under the controlment aforesaid after all expenses, costs, wages and port dues of the master and sailors for this voyage had been paid.

Ballinger called *Katherine.*

Also concerning £20 similarly received from John Sterlynge of Greenwich, as the proceeds of the sale of a certain royal ballinger in bad repair called the *Katherine Breton* sold to him with various equipment and other things by the said Keeper of the King's ships on the 5th of March in the first year of the present King under the controlment aforesaid on the order and advice of the King's Great Council by virtue of the aforesaid Royal Letters.

[F.3r.] Carrack *Christopher.*

Also concerning £166 13s 4d received from John Morgan of Bristol as the proceeds of the recent sale of a certain royal carrack called *Christopher de la Tour* sold to him with various equipment and other things by the said Keeper of the King's ships on the 23rd of May in the first year of the present King, for the benefit of the King under the controlment aforesaid, by virtue of letters of the same Lord King directed to the said keeper dated as above in the preamble to this account on the advice and with the consent of the Great Council.

The Ship *Thomas.*

Also concerning £133 6s 8d similarly received from John Chirche, mercer of London, as the proceeds from the sale of a certain royal ship called *Thomas de la Tour* sold to him with various equipment and other things by John Stafford, Treasurer of England and the said Keeper, on the 5th September in the first year of the said King for the benefit of the King on the advice and by order of the Great Council mentioned above.

The *Holyghost of Spain.*

Also concerning £200 similarly received from John Radeclyff, Ralph Huskard, Henry Baron and John Wodefford of Southampton as the proceeds from the sale of a certain royal ship called *Holyghost of Spain* sold to them with various equipment and other things by the said Keeper of the King's ships on the 15th of June in the said first year of the present King, for the benefit of the King under the controlment aforesaid, by virtue of the said Royal Letters on the order and advice of the King's Great Council as quoted above.

The Ship *Grand Marie.*

Also concerning £151 11s 1d received from Richard Bukland of London as a proportion of the value (£200) of a certain royal ship called *Grand Marie de la Tour*, so valued and handed over to the same Richard with various equipment and things in satisfaction of two tallies for a total of £148 8s 11d, due to him, which were to be cancelled at the Receipt of the Exchequer, on the authority of a certain Royal Writ under the Privy Seal dated the 3rd of July in the first year of King Henry VI, addressed to the accountor, John Foxholes and Nicholas Banastre. The tallies remain with these particulars and will be answered for below by the accountor.

Ballinger *Nicholas.*

Also concerning £66 13s 4d similarly received from John More, William Straunge, Richard Rowe and others of Dartmouth as the proceeds of the sale of a certain royal ballinger called *Nicholas* sold to them with various equipment and things, by the said Keeper of the King's ships on the 11th of September in the first year, for the benefit of the King, under the controlment aforesaid, by virtue of the said Royal Letters and the order and advice of the Great Council as has already been quoted at length.

The Ship *Grand Marie.*

Also concerning £200, the value of a certain royal ship called *Grand Marie de la Tour* with her equipment of various kinds, so valued by certain worthy men of the town of Southampton before John Foxholes, William Soper and Nicholas Banastre by order of a certain writ under the Privy Seal of the King Henry VI dated the 3rd of July in the first year of his reign addressed to the said John, William, and Nicholas, which remains with these particulars. The ship was valued and delivered to Richard Bukland by virtue of the same writ.

[F.3v.] Ballinger called *Craccher.*

Also concerning £26 13s 4d similarly received from John Cole, Thomas Assheldon, and John William of Dartmouth and Kingswear as the proceeds of the sale of a certain royal ballinger called *Craccher* sold to them by the said Keeper with various things and equipment of different kinds on the last day of April in the first year for the benefit of the King under the controlment aforesaid by virtue of the said Royal Letters and by the advice and order of the Great Council as noted above.

Royal Ballinger called *Swan.*

Also concerning £18 similarly received from John William, Thomas Downynge and Nicholas Stephens of Kingwear, as the proceeds of the sale of a certain royal ballinger called *Swan* sold to them by the said Keeper with various equipment and other things on the first day of April in the said first year for the benefit of the King under the controlment aforesaid by virtue of the said Royal Letters on the advice and order as defined above.

Ballinger called *Falcon*.

Also concerning £50 similarly received from Adam Forster of London as the proceeds of the sale of a certain royal ballinger called *Falcon* sold to him by the said Keeper with various equipment and things on the first day of June in the said first year for the benefit of the King by virtue of the said Royal Letters on the same order and advice of the Great Council as quoted above.

Ballinger called *George*.

Also concerning £20 similarly received from William Bentley of Plymouth as the proceeds of the sale of a certain royal ballinger called *George*, of which Edward Hoppyer was lately master, sold to him by the said Keeper with various equipment and other things on the last day of August in the said first year for the benefit of the King under the said controlment by virtue of the said Royal Letters on the order and advice of the said Great Council of the King as quoted above.

Barge called *Valentine*.

Also concerning £80 similarly received from Jack Jon and John Emery of Southampton as the proceeds of the sale of a certain royal barge called *Valentine* sold to them by the said Keeper with various equipment and other things on the first of March in the second year of the present King for the benefit of the King under the controlment aforesaid by virtue of the said Royal Letters on the advice and order of the said Great Council of the King as is explained more clearly in the preamble.

[F.4r.] Ballinger *Ane*.

Also concerning £30 similarly received from John Slogge of Saltash as the proceeds of the sale of a certain royal ballinger called *Ane* sold to him by the said Keeper with various equipment and other things on the 27th of June in the second year of the said King for the benefit of the King under the controlment aforesaid by virtue of the said Royal Letters on the same advice and order of the Great Council of the King as noted above.

Carracks called *Paul* and *Marie Sandwich*.

Also concerning £26 similarly received from Richard Patyn, Richard Preste of Hamble, John Gladwyn and William Gladwyn of Shottes-hall[197] in the county of Southampton as the proceeds of the sale of two royal carracks, worn out and in bad condition, called *Paul* and *Marie Sandwich* sold to them without any equipment or other things by the said Keeper of the King's ships on the 10th September in the third year of the present King, for the benefit of the King, under the said controlment by virtue of the said Royal Letters and by the order and advice of the said Great Council as reported previously.

Carrack called *Peter*.

Also concerning £13 6s 8d similarly received from Robert Morynge and William Tassyer of Southampton as the proceeds of the sale of one carrack, worn out and in bad condition called *Peter* sold to them on the 23rd October in the third year of the present King by the said Keeper of the King's ships, without any equipment or other things, for the benefit of the King, under the said controlment by virtue of these said Royal Letters on the order and advice of the said Great Council as is more fully noted above.

Ship *Nicholas*.

Also concerning £5 similarly received from John Reynold, shipwright, as the proceeds of the sale of a certain royal ship, worn out and in bad condition and sunk in the *wose*, called *Nicholas* sold to him in May in the second year of the present King by the said Keeper without any equipment or other things, for the benefit of the King, under the said controlment, by virtue of the said Royal Letters on the order and advice of the Great Council as recorded above.

Ship *Katherine*.

Also concerning £5 similarly received from John Perss and others from Greenwich in the county of Kent as the proceeds of the sale of a certain royal ship, worn out and in bad condition, called *Katherine* sold to them on the 6th March in the third year of the same King without any equipment or other things, for the benefit of the King, under the controlment aforesaid by virtue of these said Royal Letters on the order and advice of the said Great Council of the King as defined previously.

Ballinger called *Roose*.

Also concerning £1 6s 8d similarly received from William Castell of Southampton as the proceeds of the sale of a certain royal ballinger called *Roose* worn out and in bad condition, which was broken up by various storms and strong winds into several parts and was afterwards sold to the same William on the 17th February in the third year of the present King by the said Keeper without any equipment, for the benefit of the King under the controlment aforesaid by virtue of these said Royal Letters on the order and advice of the Great Council of the King then forthcoming.

[F.4v.] Sale of one Anchor.

Also concerning £5 similarly received from Scortefegon, Patron of a certain Genoese carrack as the proceeds of the sale of one anchor lately belonging to this office for the royal carrack called *Peter* sold to the same Patron on the 4th April in the third year of the present king by the said Keeper of the King's ships for the benefit of the King under the controlment aforesaid.

Sale of Sawn Boards.

Also concerning £19 12s 3½d similarly received from Walter Fettepas of Southampton and various other men as the proceeds of the sale of 1125 pieces of sawn board, planed and finished called *Waynscott* (to wit each whole board so finished making two pieces) as a parcel of a certain consignment of boards among other things lately received by indenture from Robert Berd, clerk, and others; sold to them for the same sum on various occasions in June in the third year of the said King by the said Keeper, for the benefit of the King under the controlment aforesaid, to wit charging 7d for each whole board of two pieces, the total being as above.

Sale of sawn *rigold*.

Also concerning £2 1s 5¾d similarly received from the said Walter Fettepas and other men of the same town of Southampton as the proceeds of the sale of 64 pieces of sawn board, finished and planed, called *rigold*, (each whole board making two pieces so finished) as a parcel also of the consignment of finished *rigold* similarly received as above by indenture from the said Robert Berd and others to wit sold to the same Walter and his associates on various occasions in July and August in the said third year, by the said Keeper for the benefit of the King, under the controlment aforesaid, namely charging 1s 2¼d for each whole board containing two pieces, total as above.

Storehouse.

Also concerning £66 13s 4d similarly received from the Master of Godshouse[198] at Southampton as the proceeds of the sale of a certain store house and forge adjoining the said house lately newly built for the same office of the King's ships at Southampton: [199] sold to him on the third of June in the second year of the present King by the said Keeper for the benefit of the King, under the controlment aforesaid by virtue of a certain Royal Writ under the Privy Seal dated 26th May of the said second year addressed to the said Keeper and exhibited with this account.

Old Sails.

Also concerning £9 3s 4d similarly received in the following two installments, to wit as the proceeds of the sale of two old sails in bad condition lately belonging as follows: one sail in bad condition – that is one course and one *bonnett* formerly belonging to the royal carrack *Andrew* sold to John Mase of London, artist, for £4 16s 8d on the 8th August in the second year of the present King, for the benefit of the King under the controlment aforesaid; and another sail in bad condition – that is a course with a *bonnett* lately belonging to the royal carrack *Peter* sold to Richard Herman of Colchester on the 22nd November, in the third year of the same Lord King for £4 6s 8d, under the same controlment.

[F.5r.] Carrack *George*.

Also concerning £133 6s 8d similarly received from Nicholas Justinyan and his associates as the proceeds of the sale of a certain royal carrack called *George*, sold to them with various equipment and other things by the said Keeper on the 10th August in the first year of the present King, for the benefit of the King, under the controlment aforesaid, on the order and advice of the Great Council of the King and by virtue of the said Royal Letters.

Prizes taken by the Royal Ballinger called *Petit Jhesus*.

Also concerning £17 15s similarly received from the proceeds of the sale by auction of various merchandise and other stuff lately assigned to the King, under the said controlment from a certain prize captured at sea near Brittany and Spain from the enemies of the same Lord King: to wit in August in the fifth year of the said King by a certain royal ballinger called *Petit Jhesus* acting with a group of various other ships and ballingers belonging to other people, all of which were together occupied in a voyage for the safekeeping of the sea in the said fifth year.

Sale of one Anchor.

Also concerning £4 13s 4d similarly received from Jacob Spynell of Southampton as the proceeds of the sale of one anchor lately belonging to the said office of the King's ships intended for the royal carrack called *Marie Sandwich*; sold to the said Jacob by the Keeper of the King's ships on the 8th July in the fourth year of the present King, under the controlment aforesaid for the benefit of the King.

Total foreign receipts £1350 4s 4$\frac{1}{4}$d.

Overall total of receipts £2030 8s 0$\frac{3}{4}$d.

[F.6r.][200] Royal Carrack called *George*.

These expenses and costs have been incurred and expended, as described below in this account, by the said Keeper of the King's ships firstly for the repair, fitting out, and governance of various ships and carracks, and indeed the governance and repair of various other vessels of the Lord Henry V lately King of England and similarly for the safe keeping and governance of the same in the Port of Southampton and elsewhere, looking after them up to the time of their sale as is made clear below to wit:

Payments and bonus payments.

The same accounts for the rent of an outhouse on the waterfront at Sandwich for the safekeeping of the sails and bonnetts and various other equipment belonging to the royal carrack *George de la Tour,* to be stored there up to the time of the handing over of the same carrack, by an agreement concerning the outhouse made for the benefit of the King, with Thomas Haddon 3s 4d. Also for money paid as a bonus to Peter Johnson and various other men working both at moving the said sails and bonnetts with great care out of the outhouse and rigging and ordering them and other equipment again during this period and also for their extra care and work in looking after and mooring the carrack in the port there to keep her safe during a storm 20s.

Total 23s 4d.

Wages of sailors, keeping the said carrack.

Also for the wages of Peter Johnson and five other sailors his colleagues, called *shipkepers,* each earning 3d a day while living on the said royal carrack called *George* (burden estimated at 600 tuns) in the port of the town of Sandwich to take care of her after a certain voyage to Bordeaux completed on the 23rd April as appears in the preceding account of the said Keeper concerning the said voyage: to wit for this safe keeping from the 23rd April in the first year of the present King to the 10th August next following (under the supervision and with the knowledge of the said controller), on which date the said carrack was delivered, following the advice and order of the King's Council, to the care and control of Antony Hongare and his companions according to an indenture as appears more fully therein, that is to say for 109 days, counting the last day and not the first, £8 6s 6d.

[F.6v.] Wages of the master for this safe-keeping.

But William Richman master of this same royal carrack did not receive any wages (usually at the rate of 6d a day) for living on the *George* to take care of her in the port aforesaid at this time because he receives a fee of ten marks a year granted to him by the Council of the present King to be paid by the Treasurer of England, during pleasure.

Total expenses for this carrack £9 6s 10d.

Royal Ship called *Grand Marie de la Tour*.

These are the costs and expenses which have been incurred and expended by the said Keeper of the King's Ships for the complete repair at Southampton of a certain royal ship called *Grand Marie de la Tour*, undertaken at the direction and order of the said late King Henry V on the 24th July in the tenth year of his reign and followed through and completed at the direction and order of the Council of the present King. This royal ship immediately after her complete repair at Southampton was sold by the advice of the Great Council of the present King, by the said Keeper under the said controlment to Richard Bokeland of London together with her equipment by virtue of a Royal Writ directed to the same William Soper and others.

[F.7r.] To wit, firstly for 26 pieces of timber bought from William Bens to make *shores* to put round the said ship and used in this way at the time of her repair, at 1½d each, total 3s 3d.

Also for 6 great pieces of timber then needed for *bordstokkes* at 4d each, total 2s: and 9 other pieces of timber, price as above, total 3s similarly bought from Walter Cole and used for the works on this ship: total 5s.

Also for 2 great pieces (of timber) bought from Roger Bokfost to make *bemes* for the same royal ship and used in the same works, total price, 6s 8d.

Also for 100 pieces of timber for *wronges* and *stodel* at 4d each, total 33s 4d; and for 60 pieces of timber at 12d each, total 60s; and for 35 pieces of timber for *wales* and *bensenges* at 20d each total 58s 4d; and for one large piece of timber needed for a certain *kne* at 3s 4d bought from John Chamberleyn on various occasions and used for the reconstruction of this ship. Total £7 15s.

Also for two wheelbarrows similarly bought and used for the works on this ship from Nicholas Weston, total price 16d.

Also paid to Richard Burgeys, smith, of Southampton for making two *gemeletts* used in the works necessary on the said royal ship at the time of her refitting 4d.

Also paid to Thomas Smyth of Southampton for 6 *augers* used similarly on the works on this ship at the time of her refitting 2s.

Also for 4 mwt nails called *sporcanaill* bought from the said Robert Smyth for the works on this ship and used for this work at 2s 6d per mwt, total 10s.

Also for 2 iron *stapuls* weighing 28 lb bought from Richard Burgeys and used in the works on this ship at 1¼d a pound, total 2s 9d.

Also for 7 mwt 5½ cwt of iron bought from John Seldere to make *roff* and *clenchnaill boltes, spikes* and various other ironwork for the work on this ship and in fact used on this work, at 46s 8d per mwt, total £17 13s 0½d.

Also for 40 *clovebord* bought from William Tangle for the work on this said royal ship and in fact used on this work at a total cost of 13s 4d.

Also for 69 clovebord, at 14d each, total 74s 9d, and for 100 boards called *sawbord,* bought from Henry Brampton for the work on the said ship and used therein, at a total cost of £4 12s 9d.

Also for 52 sawn boards, similarly bought from Nicholas Weston for the work on and refitting of this royal ship and used on these works, at a total cost of 18s, for the benefit of the King.

Also for 100 boards called *waynscot,* bought from the said William and Nicholas for the work on and refitting of this said royal ship and used therein, at a total cost of 13s 4d.

Total £35 10s 3½d.

[F.7v.] Carriage and freight payments.

Also paid to Richard Crokker, Richard Bery, John Stoker, John Colman, John Whetnal, Richard Twyman, William Prence, Richard Boteler, William Chapelayn, John Cole, William Andrewe and John Hekeley, to wit 12 carters for the carriage of 24 cart loads of timber from nearby in the New Forest in the county of Southampton to the said town of Southampton at a charge of 10d a cart load, total 20s; and to the said carters for the carriage of 38 cartloads of timber from further off in the royal New Forest to the same place, similarly for the refitting of the same royal ship, at a charge of 12d a cart load, total 38s – joint total 58s.

Also to the same John Hekeley for the carriage of 16 cart loads of timber from the same royal New Forest to the same place for the refitting of the said royal ship at a charge of 12d a cart load, total 16s.

Also to Richard Edderes of Weston[201] for the carriage of 60 cartloads of timber from Woolston Wood[202] to the sea for the works on this royal ship at a charge of 2d a cart load total 10s.

Also to Richard Reve, carter, similarly carting timber for *knowes* then needed for the refitting of this royal ship, that is to say from Woolston to the sea charging for two cart loads of this timber 8d.

Also to John Forbour, carter, for 36 cartloads of *mosse* for *wynelynges* then made for the refitting of the said ship and used therein, at a charge of 2d a cartload, total 6s.

Also to John Hekeley, carter, for three cartloads of *heeth* then needed for *bremynge* in the refitting of this ship and used for the burning of boards called *berdynge,* at a total cost including carriage of 5s 4d.

Also to John Cheseman hired with his cart to carry *turves* required for making and finishing the head of a certain dike called a *dam* needed for the construction of the said ship, to wit for eight days at a charge of 12d a day, total 8s.

Also to Richard Carpenter similarly hired with his cart to carry these turves to make and finish this dike to wit for five days, at a daily charge as above, total 5s.

Also to John Hekeley for one cartload of heath for *bremynge* then needed to burn the boards called *berdynge,* during the work on this said ship, at a total cost including carriage of 2s 8d.

Also to William Tangle for the freight of 152 sawn boards from Havant to Southampton for the work on and refitting of this same royal ship at a charge for freight agreed with him of 5s.

Total 116s 8d.

[F.8r.] Wages of carpenters called fellers and sawyers.

Also for the wages of Thomas Stride, a carpenter called a feller, for 45 working days at a daily rate of 6d, total 22s 6d; of Ralph Stride, a carpenter – feller, for 21 working days at a daily rate of 5d; total 8s 9d; and Robert Heye, a carpenter – feller, for 18 working days, daily rate as above; total 7s 6d; to wit all working, felling timber and splitting it for the works on the said royal ship in the royal New Forest and elsewhere in the county of Southampton, that is to say between the 1st September in the said first year and 28th October next following: total 38s 9d.

Also for the wages of the said Thomas at 6d a day, of Ralph and Robert at 5d a day, working, felling and splitting timber there for the works on the said royal ship being reconstructed at Southampton, to wit between 28th October aforesaid and Christmas next following, that is to say each of them for 42 working days; total 56s.

Also for the wages of Walter Sawyer and Richard Standeley his colleague, sawyers, working there and sawing planks of timber and other things necessary for the works aforesaid to wit both of them for 16 working days during the period of this royal ship's reconstruction at a daily rate of 5d; total 13s 4d.

Also paid to Thomas Osmond working and helping a carpenter there called a sawyer to saw a certain *knowe* and other things needed for the works on this royal ship to wit for three working days during the period of this ship's reconstruction at a daily rate of 5d; total 15d.

Overall total 109s 4d.

Wages of labourers.

Also for the wages of Henry Goldmyth, John Dogman, John Barowe, William Stride, Hugh Long, Thomas Smyth, William Wilforde, John Senger and John Tirry to wit in all nine labourers working there on the making of a certain dike called a *dam* recently ordered for the reconstruction of the said ship and also on the blocking and widening of the same, to wit each of them for 18 working days, at a daily rate of 5d; total 67s 6d.

Also for the wages of John Wodgreve, Richard Adam, John Wyndesore, John Tommsr and Ralph Carpenter similarly working and digging to make [F.8v.] this dike called a *dam* and on other things there, to wit each of them for six working days, daily rate as above; total 12s 6d.

Also for money paid to various sailors for their expenses when working on the conducting and towing of the said ship from the Itchen to the port of Southampton where she was to be refitted; total 7s 8d.

Overall total £4 7s 8d.

Wages of the master-carpenter and carpenters called *berders*.

Also for the wages of John Hogkyn master-carpenter, at 8d a day, working on the renovation of this royal ship called *Grand Marie* lately refitted in the said town of Southampton, to wit for 120 working days between 24th July in the tenth year of the Lord Henry V lately King of England and 5th March in the first year of the present King; total £4.

Also for the wages of John Bysshoppe for 122 working days, John Davy for 182 working days, Phillip Weble for 115 working days, Thomas Herry and John Carpenter both of them for 156 working days, Galfrid Piers for 182 working days, Thomas Moleyn for 193 working days, John Southern for 110 working days, Henry Baker for 76 working days, Richard Dorset for 48 working days, William Danyell for 75 working days, John Nobelet, Roger Payn and Robert Baker, all of them for six days, Henry Carter for 131 days and Henry Kagent for 10 working days; to wit all carpenters called *berders* working there on the repair of this same royal ship within the same period, all at a daily rate of 6d; total £39 7s.

Also for the wages similarly of John Power, a carpenter called a *berder* working there on the repair of this same ship that is to say for 66 working days within this period, daily rate as above; total 33s.

Also for the wages of another master-carpenter called William Bachyne at 8d per day because the aforesaid John Hogkyn was ill for a certain time, working there on this repair of this same royal ship, to wit for 102 working days between 24th July in the tenth year of the Lord King Henry V and 5th March in the first year of our present King; total 68s.

Also for the wages of John Merssh for 100 working days, John Wanester for 15 working days, Peter Awmesbery for 101 working days, John Halle for 14 working days, Thomas Snoke for 22 working days and Water atte Verne for 110 working days, to wit all carpenters called *berders* similarly working there on this repair of the said royal ship within the same period, that is to say for a total of 361 days; total £9 0s 6d.

Overall total £57 8s 6d.

[F.9r.] Wages of carpenters called *clenchers*.

Also for the wages of John Smyth, Bawdewyn Burgeys, William Traharn, John Kynge, John Carter, William Melgowe, and Peryn Hogkyn, to wit seven carpenters called *clenchers* similarly working there on the repair of the said royal ship to wit each of them for 121 working days between the said 24th July in the tenth year of the late King and the said 5th March in the first year of our present King at a daily rate of 5d; total £17 12s 11d.

Also for the wages of Monet Robert, Robert Baker, William Breche, and John Downe four similar carpenters working there on the works of the same royal ship, to wit each of them for 156 working days within the same period, daily rate as above; total £13.

Also for the wages of Symon atte Welle, a carpenter called a *clencher*, for 111 working days, and Thomas Pelete, a carpenter called a *clencher*, for 151 working days, similarly working there on the repair of the said royal ship within the same period, both of them at the daily rate as above; total 109s 2d.

Also for the wages of William Haye, a carpenter called a *clencher*, for 108 working days similarly working there on the repair of the said royal ship within the same period, daily rate as above; total 45s.

Also for the similar wages of six carpenters called *clenchers*, each for 51 working days working there on the repair of the said royal ship within the same period; total £6 7s 6d.

Wages of carpenters called *holders*.

Also for the wages of William Rawlyn, Henry Stevene and Peter, carpenters called *holders*, each of them at 4d a day, working at the said town of Southampton on the repair of the said ship, to wit each of them for 156 working days between the said 24th July in the tenth year of the late King and the said 5th March in the first year of our present King; total £7 16s 0d.

Also for the wages of John Dorset, a carpenter called a *holder*, working there on the said repair of this ship, to wit for 55 working days, within the same period, at a daily rate of 3d; total 13s 9d.

Also for the wages of John Maynejon and Thomas Bolfford, both of them for 100 working days and Thomas Cheyney and Henry Corkeley, both of them for 70 working days and John Cornissh for 60 working days, to wit all carpenters called *holders* similarly working there on the repair of the said royal ship within the same period, all at a daily rate of 4d, as above; total £16 13s 4d.

Grand total £67 15s 4d.

[F.9v.] Wages of Smiths.

Also for the wages of Richard Nansake, a smith employed for 72 working days, William Smyth for 63 working days, William Deen for 107 working days, Richard Harpe for 36 working days, John Talbote for 9 working days and Richard Bayle for 6 working days, to wit all six smiths employed for the benefit of the King to make *clenchnaill, rooff* and *anned, boltes, spikes, bondes* and various other ironwork for the repair of the said royal ship between the said 24th July in the tenth year of the late King and 5th March in the first year of our present King, that is to say in all for 293 working days each at a daily rate of 5d; total £6 2s 1d.

Total expenses on this ship £182 9s 10½d.

Royal Carrack called *Christopher de la Tour.*
Purchases and other necessities.

Also for one piece of timber bought by the said Keeper after the said 5th March, from John Bollour and used there on the repair of this same royal carrack called *Christopher,* under the controlment aforesaid, price 4d.

Also for money paid to one Southampton man for himself and his horse lately sent by the Keeper of the King's ships from the same town of Southampton to Bristol on business concerning the delivery of this carrack and its equipment to various men of that town after its sale lately made for the benefit of the King, to wit receiving for his time and for his work 4s 8d.

Total 5s.

[F.10r.] Wages of Caulkers.

Also for the wages of Roger the caulker at 6d per day while on board and working on the same royal carrack called *Christopher* and her great and small boats in the port of Bristol for in turn caulking, fitting out and *ransakenges* the same, and blocking up certain splits and cracks occurring in the cabin, to wit from 13th March in the first year of the present Lord King till 23rd May next following, under the said controlment, that is to say for 71 days, counting the last day and not the first; total 35s 6d.

Wages of sailors caretaking the said royal carrack.

Also for the wages of John Twesyll and Roger Caltour and seven other sailors their companions called *shipkepers* all at 3d a day, being continually on board the said royal carrack called *Christopher* (burden estimated at 600 tuns) to look after and keep her safe in the said port of Bristol after a certain voyage from Bordeaux completed in the said month of March in the said first year as appears more fully in the previous account of the Keeper of the King's ships, to wit for this caretaking from 13th March in the first year to 23rd May next following, (on which day the said carrack was sold with her equipment to John Morgan of Bristol, on the order and advice of the King's Council, by the Keeper, for a certain sum of money accounted for in the Foreign Receipts of this account, under the supervision and oath as above) that is to say for 71 days, counting the last day and not the first; total £7 19s 9d.

Wages of the Master for this caretaking.

But William Tenderley, Master of the same royal carrack was not paid any wages at 6d per day for being similarly on board the same royal carrack called *Christopher*, to look after her and keep her safe in the port of Bristol during the same period because he received a certain fee of ten marks granted to him during pleasure by the Royal Council to be paid every year by the Treasurer of England; Total nothing.

Total expenses for this carrack £10 0s 3d.

[F.10v.] Royal Ballinger called *Roos de la Tour*.
Purchases and other necessities.

And the same similarly accounts for any purchases, outgoings, costs and payments whether wages, gifts and bonuses of sailors or other expenses; inasmuch as nothing was spent on port dues, wages for sailors or anything else necessary for the repair or safekeeping of this royal ballinger called *Roos* within the accounting period by the Keeper of the King's ships, with the exception strictly speaking of the wages of sailors called *shipkepers* acting as caretakers for the same.

Total nothing.

Wages of sailors keeping the said royal ballinger.

Also for the wages of Walter Richard, a sailor called a *shipkeper* at 3d a day while continuously on board the royal ballinger called *Roos* (burden estimated at 30 tuns) in the port of Southampton in order to look after the same, to wit from the last day of August in the tenth year of the late King, on which day the late King died, to 5th March next following under the oath of the said Keeper, that is to say for 186 days, counting the last day and not the first. Total 46s 6d.

Further wages of sailors keeping the said ballinger.

Also for the similar wages of the said Walter Richard, a sailor called a *shipkeper,* while continuously on board the said royal ballinger called *Roos* in the same port of Southampton in order to look after the same, to wit, under the supervision and with the knowledge of the Controller, from the abovesaid 5th March, in the first year, on which day the tenure of the said Controller began, to 1st April next following, on which day the said ballinger was beached on the mudflats (*Le Wose*) because of her bad repair without any *shipkeper* on board, that is to say for 27 days, counting the last day and not the first. Total 6s 9d.

Wages of the Master for this caretaking.

But John Yafford, Master of the said royal ballinger called *Roos* (usual daily rate 6d) received no wages during this period being absent from the safekeeping of the said ballinger because he was engaged on his own business at that time.

Total nothing.

Total expenses for this ballinger 53s 3d.

[F.11r.] Royal Ballinger called *Swan de la Tour.*
Purchases and other necessities for the same.

And the same accounts similarly for any purchases, outgoings, costs and payments whether wages, gifts and bonuses of sailors or other expenses; inasmuch as nothing was spent on port dues and the wages of sailors or any other payments necessary for the repair and safe-keeping of the same royal ballinger called the *Swan* within the accounting period by the said Keeper of the King's ships, except strictly speaking the wages of sailors called *shipkepers* acting as caretakers for the same.

Total nothing.

Wages of sailors keeping the said royal ballinger.

Also for the wages of John Harry, a sailor called a *shipkeper* at 3d a day while continuously on board the same royal ballinger called *Swan* (burden estimated at 20 tuns) in the said port of Southampton in order to look after the same to wit from the last day of August in the tenth year of the Lord Henry V, late King of England, who indeed died on that day, to the 5th March next following in the first year of the present King, under the oath of the said Keeper, that is to say for 186 days, including the last day and not the first.

Total 46s 6d.

Further wages of sailors keeping the said ballinger.

Also for the similar wages of John Harry, a sailor, while continuously on board the royal ballinger called *Swan* in the port of Southampton in order to look after here there, to wit, under the supervision and with the knowledge of the Controller, from the said 5th March in the first year, on which day the tenure of the said Controller began, to 1st April next following when the said ballinger, on the advice and order of the Royal Council was sold by the Keeper of the King's ships together with various equipment, to John William, Thomas Downynge and Nicholas Stephenes [F.11v.] of Kingswear for a certain sum of money which is accounted for above among the Foreign Receipts of this account, all this under the supervision of the Controller, that is to say for 27 days, counting the last day and not the first.

Total 6s 9d.

Wages of the Master for this caretaking.

But Robert Downynge, Master of the said royal ballinger *Swan* received no wages (usually at the rate of 6d a day) while on board the same ballinger in the port of Southampton during the whole period of this caretaking because he received every year from the Treasurer of England a fee of five marks granted to him by the present Royal Council during pleasure.

Total nothing.

Total expenses for this ballinger 53s 3d.

[F.12r.] Royal Ship called *Thomas de la Tour*.
Purchases and other necessities for the same.

And the same accounts similarly for any purchases, outgoings, costs and payments whether wages, gifts and bonuses or other expenses; inasmuch as nothing was spent on port dues and the wages of sailors or any other payments necessary for the repair and safekeeping of the said royal ship *Thomas* within the accounting period by the said Keeper of the King's ships except, strictly speaking, the wages of sailors called *shipkepers* acting as caretakers for the same.

Total nothing.

Wages of sailors keeping the said royal ship.

Also for the wages of Reginald Horton, and three other sailors

his colleagues, called *shipkepers,* all at 3d a day while continuously
on board the same royal ship *Thomas* (burden estimated at 180 tuns)
in the port of the town of Plymouth in order to look after the same,
particularly on account of the unusual necessity to keep watch day
and night because of the danger of the anchorage there and storms
occurring there; to wit from 4th December, in the first year of the
present King to 5th March next following, under the oath of the said
Keeper of the King's ships, that is to say for 90 working days, counting
the neutral day.

Total £6.

Further wages of sailors keeping the said ship.

Also for the similar wages of the aforesaid Reginald and three other
sailors his colleagues called *shipkepers,* while continuously on board
the same ship in the port aforesaid in order to look after the same,
to wit, under the supervision and with the knowledge of the Controller,
from the said 5th March in the first year, on which day the tenure of
the said Controller began, to 5th September next following on which
day the said royal ship was sold together with various equipment to
John Chirche, citizen and mercer of London [F.12v.] on the order
and advice of the Royal Council by the Treasurer of England and the
said Keeper for a certain sum of money which is accounted for above
among the Foreign Receipts of this account, that is to say for 185
days, counting both days.

Total £12 6s 8d.

Wages of the Master for this caretaking.

But William Cheke, Master of the aforesaid royal ship called
Thomas, received no wages at this time (usually at the rate of 6d
per day) for the caretaking of this ship in the port of Plymouth as
recited above, because he was engaged on his own business at the time
and because he was ill.

Total nothing.

Total expenses for this ship £18 6s 8d.

[F.13r.] Royal Ballinger called *George de la Tour.*
Purchases and other necessities for the same.

And the same accounts for any purchases, outgoings, costs and
expenses whether wages, gifts or bonuses or other payments; inasmuch
as nothing was spent on port dues and the wages of sailors or any
other payments whatsoever necessary for the repair and fitting out
of a certain royal ballinger called *George* within the accounting period
by the said Keeper of the King's ships except, strictly speaking, the
wages of sailors called *shippkepers* acting as caretakers for the same.

Total – nothing.

Wages of sailors keeping the said royal ballinger.

But for the wages of John Ade, a sailor called *shippkeper,* at 3d a day, while continuously on board the said ballinger called *George* (burden estimated at 120 tuns) in the port of Southampton in order to look after the same, to wit from the last day of August in the tenth year of the Lord Henry V, late King of England, on which day the King died, to the said 5th March next following in the first year of the present King under the oath of the said Keeper of the King's ships, that is to say for 186 days counting the last day and not the first.

Total 46s 6d.

Further wages of sailors keeping the said ballinger.

Also for the similar wages of the said John Ade while continuously on board the said royal ballinger called *George* in the port of Southampton in order to look after the same, to wit from the said 5th March on which day the tenure of the Controller began, to the last day of August next following, on which day the said royal ballinger was sold, together with various equipment, to William Bentle of Plymouth, on the order and advice of the present Royal Council, [F.13v.] by the said Keeper of the King's ships with the said Controller for a certain sum of money which is accounted for above among the Foreign Receipts of this account, that is to say for 178 days, counting the neutral day.

Total 44s 6d.

Wages of the Master for this caretaking.

But Edward Hoppier, Master of the said royal ballinger called *George,* received nothing either for his wages (at the rate of 6d a day) or for his fee of five marks a year (granted by letters patent of the late King, etc.) because he was not involved in the caretaking of this same ballinger for the whole period, being engaged in his own business.

Total nothing.

Total expenses for this ballinger £4 11s.

Royal ballinger called *Ane de la Tour.*
Purchases and other necessities for the same.

And the same accounts similarly for any purchases, outgoings, costs and expenses whether wages, gifts and bonuses or any other payments such as port dues and wages of sailors or any other payments whatsoever necessary for the fitting out and repair of a certain royal ballinger called *Ane*; during this accounting period nothing was spent by the said Keeper except strictly speaking the wages of the sailors called *shippkepers* acting as caretakers for the same.

Total nothing.

[F.14r.] Wages of sailors keeping the said royal ballinger.

But for the wages of Henry Davy, a sailor called a *shippkeper* at 3d a day while continuously on board the said royal ballinger *Ave* (sic) (burden estimated at 120 tuns) in the said port of Southampton in order to look after the same, to wit from the last day of August in the tenth year of the said Henry V, late King of England who died on that day, to 5th March next following in the first year of the present King under the oath of the said Keeper, that is to say for 186 days counting the last day and not the first.

Total 46s 6d.

Total before the appointment of the Controller – as above.

Further wages of the sailors keeping the said ballinger.

Also for similar wages for the said Henry Davy while continuously on board the same royal ballinger called *Ane* in the said port of Southampton in order to look after the same from the said 5th March, on which day the tenure of the Controller began to 27th June in the second year of our present King, on which day the said ballinger with various equipment was sold to John Slogge and others from Saltash in Cornwall, on the advice and order of the Royal Council, with the controlment aforesaid, for a certain sum of money which is accounted for above among the Foreign Receipts of this account, that is to say for 478 days, counting the neutral day.

Total 119s 6d.

Wages of the Master for this caretaking.

But Ralph Huskard, Master of the aforesaid royal ballinger called *Ane,* received nothing either for his wages (at the rate of 6d a day) or for his fee of five marks a year, granted by letters patent of the said late king, etc. because he was not involved in this caretaking for the whole period, being engaged at this time with his own business.

Total nothing.

Total expenses for this ballinger £8 6s.

[F.14v.] Royal Ballinger called *Craccher de la Tour.*
Purchases and other necessities for the same.

And the same accounts for any purchases, outgoings, costs and expenses whether wages, gifts and bonuses or any other payments; inasmuch as nothing was spent on port dues and the wages of sailors or any other payments whatsoever for the repair, fitting-out and safe-keeping of a certain royal ballinger called *Craccher* by the said Keeper of the King's ships within the accounting period except, strictly speaking, the wages of sailors called *shippkepers* acting as caretakers for the same.

Total nothing.

Wages of sailors keeping the said royal ballinger.

Also for the wages of John Cokeryngton, a sailor called a *shippkeper* at 3d a day while continuously on board the same royal ballinger called Craccher (burden estimated at 56 tuns) in order to look after the same in the said port of Southampton, to wit from the last day of August in the tenth year of the said Henry V, late King of England, on which day the late King died, up to 5th March next following in the first year of the present King, under the oath of the said Keeper, that is to say for 186 days counting the last day and not the first.

Total 46s 6d.

Further wages of sailors keeping the said ballinger.

Also for the similar wages of the aforesaid John Cokeryngton while continuously on board the said royal ballinger in order to look after the same similarly in the port of Southampton, to wit from the said 5th March in the first year on which day the tenure of the said Controller began, as is mentioned in the preamble to this account, to the last day of April next following when the said ballinger with various equipment was sold by the said Keeper to John Cole, John William and Thomas Asscheldon of Dartmouth and Kingswear, on the advice and order of the Royal Council, with the controlment aforesaid for a certain sum of money which is accounted for above among the Foreign Receipts of this account: that is to say for 57 days, counting the neutral day.

Total 13s 9d.

[F.15r.] Wages of the Master for this caretaking.

But Stephen Welles, Master of the said royal ballinger called *Craccher* received nothing either for his wages at 6d a day or for his fee of five marks a year granted to him by royal letters patent, being absent from this caretaking during the said period because he was occupied with his own business at the time.

Total nothing.

Total expenses for this ballinger 61s 3d.

Royal Ballinger called *Faucon de la Tour.*
Purchases and other necessities for the same.

And the same accounts for any purchases, outgoings, costs and expenses whether wages, gifts and bonuses, or any other payments; inasmuch as nothing was paid for port dues and the wages of sailors or other payments whatsoever for the repair and fitting out of a certain royal ballinger called *Faucon* by the said Keeper of the King's ships within the accounting period, except, strictly speaking, the wages of a sailor called *shippkeper* acting as caretaker for the same ship.

Total nothing.

[F.15v.] Wages of a sailor keeping the said royal ballinger.

Also for the wages of Michael Grogall, a sailor called *shippkeper* at 3d a day while continuously on board the same royal ballinger called *Faucon* (burden estimated at 80 tuns) in order to look after the same in the said port of Southampton to wit from the last day of August when the late King died to 5th March next following in the first year of the present King, that is to say for 186 days, counting the last day and not the first under the oath of the Keeper of the King's ships;

Total 46s 6d.

Further wages of a sailor keeping the said ballinger.

Also for the similar wages of the said Michael Grogall while similarly continuously on board the said royal ballinger in order to look after the same in the same port of Southampton to wit from the said 5th March in the said first year on which day the tenure of the Controller began, as is more fully mentioned in the preamble of this account to 1st June next following when the said ballinger with various equipment was sold by the order and advice of the Great Council of the King to Adam Forster, a merchant of London, by the said Keeper, for the King's benefit, under the said controlment for a certain sum of money which is accounted for above among the Foreign Receipts of this account, that is to say for 87 days counting the neutral day and not the last.

Total 21s 9d.

Wages of the Master for this caretaking.

But George Mextowe, Master of the said royal ballinger called *Faucon,* received nothing for his wages at 6d a day, being absent from this caretaking of the same ballinger in the port of Southampton for the whole of the said period because he was engaged overseas and elsewhere on his own business continuously for the whole period as above.

Total nothing.

Total expenses for this ballinger 68s 3d.

[F.16r.] Royal Carrack called *Marie Sandewych.*
Purchases and other necessities for the same.

And the same accounts similarly for any purchases, outgoings, costs and expenses whether wages, gifts and bonuses or any other payments; inasmuch as nothing was spent on port dues and wages of sailors or any other payments whatsoever for the caretaking, fitting out and repair of a certain royal carrack called *Marie Sandewych de la Tour* by the said Keeper of the King's ships within the accounting period except, strictly speaking, the wages of sailors called *shipp kepers* acting as caretakers for the same carrack.
Total nothing.

Wages of sailors keeping the said royal carrack.

But for the wages of Thomas Ivell, a sailor called *shippkeper* at 3d a day while continuously on board the same royal carrack called *Marie* (burden estimated at 550 wine tuns) in the said port of Hamble in order to look after the same to wit from the last day of August in the tenth year of the said Lord Henry V, late King of England who died on that day to 5th March next following in the first year of the present King, under the oath of the said Keeper, that is to say for 186 days, counting the last day.
Total 46s 6d.

Further wages of sailors keeping the said carrack.

Also for the similar wages of the said Thomas Yvell while continuously on board the said royal carrack in order to look after the same in the port of Hamble to wit from the said 5th March in the first year, when the tenure of the said Controller began, as is mentioned more fully in the preamble of this account, to 1st May next following when the said royal carrack because of her bad condition was beached on the *Wose* (mudflats) for the benefit of the King, that is to say for 57 days counting the last day and not the first under this controlment.
Total 14s 3d.

[F.16v.] Wages of the Master for this caretaking.

But John Merssh, Master of the said royal carrack called *Marie Sandwich* received nothing for his wages at 6d a day or for his fee of ten marks a year granted to him by royal letters patent, etc. being absent from the caretaking of the carrack for the whole of the said period because he was engaged on his own business undertaken at the same time.
Total nothing.
Total expenses for this carrack 60s 9d.

[F.17r.] Royal Ballinger called *Nicholas*.
Payments and other things.

And the same accounts similarly for any purchases, outgoings, costs and expenses whether wages, gifts or bonuses or any other payments; inasmuch as nothing was spent on port dues and wages of sailors or other payments whatsoever for the caretaking, repair, and fitting out of a certain royal ballinger called *Nicholas*, by the said Keeper of the King's ships within the accounting period except, strictly speaking, the wages of sailors called *shippkepers* acting as caretakers for the same ballinger.

Total nothing.

Wages of sailors keeping the said royal ballinger.

Also for the wages of John James and one sailor, his companion, called *shippkepers* both at 3d a day while continuously on board the same royal ballinger called *Nicholas* (burden estimated at 120 tuns) in the port of London in order to look after the same after the completion of a voyage towards the northern parts to keep the seas in the fishing season as appears more fully in the previous account of the said Keeper of the King's ships, to wit from 3rd October in the first year of the present King to 5th March next following, 102 days counting the neutral day.

Total 75s. 6d.

Further wages of sailors keeping the said ballinger.

Also for the similar wages of the aforesaid John James and one sailor his companion while continuously on board the same royal ballinger in the said Port of London in order to look after the same from the said 5th March in the first year to 4th September next following on which day the said royal ballinger with various equipment on the advice and order of the King's Great Council was sold by the said Keeper of the King's ships, for the benefit of the King, under the controlment aforesaid, to John More, William Straunge, Richard Rowe, Walter Bacheller and John Reede of Dartmouth for a certain sum of money which is accounted for above among the foreign receipts of this account, that is to say for 190 days, counting the first day and not the last.

Total £4 15s.

Wages of the Master for this caretaking.

But Robert Shadde, Master of the said royal ballinger called *Nicholas* received nothing for his wages at 6d a day nor for his fee of five marks a year granted to him by royal letters patent during pleasure, etc., being away from the ballinger and from this caretaking for the whole of the said period because he was occupied on his own business both overseas and elsewhere.

Total nothing.

Total expenses for this ballinger £8 10s 6d.

[F.17v.] Royal Barge called *Valentyn de la Tour.*
Purchases and other necessities.

And the same accounts similarly for any purchases, outgoings, costs and expenses whether wages, gifts and bonuses or any other payments; inasmuch as nothing was spent on port dues and wages of sailors or other payments whatsoever for the caretaking, repair and fitting-out of a certain royal barge called *Valentyn* by the said Keeper of the King's ships within the accounting period except, strictly speaking, the wages of sailors called *shippkepers* acting as caretakers for the same ship.

Total nothing.

Wages of sailors keeping the said royal barge.

But for the wages of Thomas Burgeys and William Morrys, sailors called *shippkepers*, both at 3d a day while continuously on board the same royal barge called *Valentyn* (burden estimated at 100 tuns) in the port of Southampton in order to look after the same, to wit from the last day of August in the tenth year of the Lord Henry V, late King of England, on which day the same King died, to 5th March next following in the first year of the present King, that is to say for 186 days, counting the last and not the first.   Total £4 13s.

Further wages of sailors keeping the said barge.

Also for the similar wages of the said Thomas and William while continuously on board the said royal barge called *Valentyn* in the said port in order to look after the same similarly, to wit from the said 5th March in the first year, the day on which the tenure of the Controller began as is more fully noted in the preface of this account, to 28th March next following, that is to say for 23 days counting the last day and not the first.   Total 11s 6d.

Total of this page 104s 6d.

[F.18r.] Wages of sailors in victuals, together with money wages and port dues of sailors for the same voyage.

Also from the said 28th March, mentioned above, the same accounts similarly because the said royal barge was hired by Paul Morell and various other merchants of Southampton for a voyage to Cales (Calais) laden with wool and various other merchandise, and was engaged on the said voyage, going and coming back, to the last day of June next following on which day the said ship was unloaded after the said voyage. Wherefore, for victualing the same ship, and for the wages and port dues of the sailors at this time nothing was spent because the said barge, for the advantage of the King, was handed over to the said merchants by the said Keeper for a certain sum of money not including any expenses incurred by the merchants themselves on this voyage, to be accounted for to the said Lord King, which is accounted for above among the foreign receipts of this account.

Total nothing.

Wages of sailors keeping the said royal barge.

Also for the wages of John Elcome, a sailor called a *shippkeper*, at 3d a day while continuously on board the same barge in the said port of Southampton in order to look after the same after the said Cales voyage was completed, from the last day of June in the said first year to 1st March next following, on which day the said barge with various equipment was sold, by the said Keeper of the King's ships, on the advice and order of the King's Council, to John Jon and John Emery of Southampton, under the controlment aforesaid, for a certain sum of money which is accounted for above among the foreign receipts of this account, that is to say for 243 days, counting the neutral day.

Total 60s 9d.

Wages of the Master for this caretaking.

But Richard Rowe, Master of the said royal barge called *Valentyn*, received nothing for his wages at 6d a day or for his fee of five marks a year granted to him by royal letters patent etc., being absent from this caretaking for the accounting period because he was engaged on his own business travelling both at home and overseas.

Total nothing.

Total expenses for this barge £8 5s 3d.

[F.18v.] Royal Ship called *Holigost of Spain*.

Purchases and other necessities for the same ship.

And the same accounts similarly for any purchases, outgoings, costs and expenses whether wages, gifts and bonuses or other payments; inasmuch as nothing was spent on port dues and wages of sailors or other payments whatsoever for the governance, repair and fitting out of a certain royal ship called *Holigost of Spain* within the accounting period except, strictly speaking, that noted below and also the wages of sailors called *shippkepers* paid to look after the same ship.

Total nothing.

Further purchases of necessaries.

Also for 8 *pulley shives* bought from John Bollour of Southampton and used for the repair and making of various *pulleys* belonging to the said ship, outside the controlment aforesaid, gross price 8d.

Also for 3 cwt nails called *pompnaill,* price per cwt 2d, 6d, and 5 cwt nails called *hacchnaill*, price per cwt 6d, 2s 6d, and for 3 cwt nails called *calfatenaill*, price per cwt 12d, 3s, bought from Robert Smyth and used on the repair of the same royal ship and her boats, total 6s.

Also for 7 boards called *waynscott* bought from William Nicholl and used in the similar repair of the said ship and her boats, price a piece 4d, 2s 4d.

Overall total 9s.

Wages of sailors keeping the said royal ship.

Also for the wages of John Jon, Master of the said royal ship called *Holigost of Spain de la Tour* (burden estimated at 290 tuns) at 6d a day and two sailors both at 3d a day while on board the said royal ship in the port of Southampton in order to look after the same after a certain voyage from Bordeaux completed in the same port of Southampton on 17th January in the first year of the present King, as is more fully recited in the preceding account of the Keeper, to wit from the said 7th January in the said year to 5th March next following, that is to say for 46 days, counting the neutral day, on the oath of the said Keeper.   Total 46s.

Overall total without controlment 55s.

[F.19r.] Further wages of sailors keeping the said ship.

Also for the wages of two sailors each at 3d a day while continuously on board the said royal ship called *Holigost* in the said port of Southampton in order to look after the same to wit, under the said controlment, from the abovesaid 5th March in the first year to 1st April next following, that is to say for 27 days counting the first day and not the last.

Total 13s 6d.

Wages of sailors including victualing expenses, with payments and port dues for the same etc.

And the same renders his account, because from the said 1st April noted above, the said royal ship was engaged on a certain voyage to Celand (Zealand) by virtue of a freight agreement made for the benefit of the King, with Neron Victor (Nerone Vetturi) and various other merchants. A certain sum of money, free of all costs and expenses, was to be answered for by them to the King and was answered for among the foreign receipts of this account. They returned to the said port of Southampton on 15th June next following and the said ship was then unladen there and, on the same day of June, the same royal ship, with various equipment and other things, was sold, by the said Keeper of the King's Ships, on the advice and order of the Great Council of the King, under the controlment aforesaid to Ralph Huskard, Henry Baron and John Wodefford of Southampton for a certain sum of money which is answered for above among the same foreign receipts of this account.

Total nothing.

Total expenses for this ship 68s 6d.

[F.19v.] Royal Ballinger called *Gabriell Harflewe.*

Purchases and other necessities.

And the same accounts similarly for any purchases, outgoings, costs and expenses whether wages, gifts and bonuses or other payments; inasmuch as nothing was spent on port dues or wages of sailors or any other payments whatsoever for the governance, repair and fitting-out of a certain royal ballinger called *Gabriell Harflewe* within the accounting period except, strictly speaking, the wages of sailors called *shippkepers* paid to look after the same ballinger.

Total nothing.

Wages of sailors keeping the said royal ship.

Also for the wages of Richard Holme, a sailor called a *shippkeper* at 3d a day while continuously on board the same royal ballinger called *Gabriell Harflewe* (burden estimated at 40 tuns) in order to look after the same to wit from the last day of August in the tenth year of the Lord King Henry V, late King of England who died on that day and 5th March next following in the first year of the present King, outside the period of controlment, that is to say for 146 days, the last day counted and not the first.

Total 46s 6d.

Further wages of sailors keeping the said ballinger.

Also for the similar wages of the said Richard Holme, while continuously on board the royal ballinger called *Gabriell* in the same port of Wynchelse (Winchelsea) in order to look after the same to wit, under the controlment aforesaid, from the said 5th March in the said first year to 8th May next following on which day the said royal ballinger because of her bad repair and dilapidation was beached on the Wose (mudflats) that is to say for 63 days, counting the neutral day.

Total 15s 9d.

Wages of the Master for the safe keeping of this ship.

But Andrew Godfrey, Master of the said royal ballinger called *Gabriell Harflewe* received nothing for his wages at 6d a day, or for his fee of 5 marks a year lately granted to him by letter patent of the Lord King etc., being absent from this safe keeping for the accounting period because he was engaged at the same time on his own business.

Total nothing.

Total for this ballinger 62s 3d.

[F.20r.] Royal Ship (in poor repair) called *Katrine de la Tour*.
Purchases and other necessities for the same.

And the same accounts similarly for any purchases, outgoings, costs and expenses or any wages of the Master and sailors or gifts and bonuses or other things whatsoever for the repair or fitting out or the safe keeping or the *rigg* or the improvement or anything else at all done for the governance of a certain ship in bad repair called the *Katrine de la Tour* within the accounting period, and nothing was spent by the said Keeper of the King's Ships, under the said controlment, except the items noted below.

Total nothing.

Payment of money for the hire of a *dook*.

Also for money paid by Robert Purfote, carpenter of London in the name of the said Keeper to William Ramessey of Depford Strande (Deptford) for the hire of, and mooring within a certain digging there called a *dook* of a royal ship called *Katrine*. This digging was recently made in a certain garden belonging to William himself for the support of the same dilapidated ship and the money was due, being in arrears, from the last day of August in the tenth year of the said Lord Henry V, lately King of England to 5 March in the first year of the present King, to wit receiving annually for this *dooke* by an agreement made with him for the greater convenience of the King 6s –

Total 3s 1d.

Further payment of money for hire of a *dok*.

Also for money paid similarly by the said Robert Purfote of London a carpenter, in the name of the said Keeper of the King's ships, to the said William Ramessey for the hire of a certain digging called a *dook* hired from him for the same royal ship called *Katrine*, at Depford Strande, to provide for the support of the said royal ship because of her dilapidation, to wit, under the said controlment, from the said 5th March in the first year of the present King to 6th March in the third year of the same Lord King that is to say for two years and one day, receiving annually for this hire of the *dook* as agreed above for the benefit of the King.

Total 12s 0¼d.
Total expenses for this ship 15s 1¼d.

[F.20v.] Royal Ship (in poor repair) called *Nicholas.*
Purchases and other necessities.

And the same accounts similarly for any purchases, outgoings, costs and expenses or any wages of the Master, sailors, or any one else, whether gifts or bonuses or any payments whatsoever for the repair, improvement and fitting-out or for the safe keeping, or any thing else necessary for the keeping of a certain dilapidated ship called *Nicholas de la Tour* within the accounting period, stating that nothing was spent by the Keeper of the King's ships himself or his deputies between the last day of August in the tenth year of the said Lord Henry V, late King of England who died on that day and 23 May in the second year of the present King on which day, under the said controlment, the said dilapidated ship without any equipment or other things, was sold by the said Keeper, for the benefit of the King, by virtue of the said letters under the Privy Seal to John Reynold, *shipwryght*, for a certain sum of money which is answered for above among the foreign receipts of this account.

Total nothing.
Total expenses for this ship nothing.

Concerning four dilapidated ships captured from Bretons.

And the same accounts similarly for any purchases, outgoings, costs and expenses or any wages of sailors or anyone else or for any gifts and bonuses to sailors or other workers or any payments whatsoever for the repair, improvement, and fitting out, also for the safe keeping or anything else for the governance of four dilapidated ships lately taken from Bretons, within the accounting period, by the Keeper himself or his deputies, in fact nothing.

Total nothing.
Total expenses for these four ships nothing.

[F.21r.] Royal Ballinger called *Katrine Britton.*
Purchases and other necessities for the same.

And the same accounts similarly for any purchases, outgoings, costs and expenses or wages, gifts and bonuses or other payments to the Master and sailors; inasmuch as nothing was spent on port dues and wages of the same or any other payments whatsoever for the governance, repair and fitting-out of the royal ballinger called *Katrine Britton* within the accounting period, except, strictly speaking, the items written below.

Total nothing.

Wages of sailors keeping the said royal ship.

Also for the wages of one sailor called a *shippkeper* at 3d a day while continuously on board the same royal ballinger called *Katrine* in the port of the town of Harflew (Harfleur) to look after the same, to wit, from the last day of August in the tenth year of the Lord Henry V, late King of England who died that day to 25th February next following in the first year of the present King when finally because of the bad repair of the same ballinger and various cracks suddenly appearing in the same, and because of the illness of the Master, the said ballinger was sold, for the advantage of the King, by the said Keeper of the King's ships, on the order and advice of the King's Great Council under the controlment aforesaid, to John Sterlynge of Greenwich for a certain sum of money which is answered for above among the foreign receipts of this account; that is to say for 177 days counting the neutral day.

Total 44s 3d.

Wages of the Master for this safe keeping.

But John Sterlinge, Master of the said royal ballinger called *Katrine* received nothing for his wages at 6d a day or for his fee of five marks a year granted to him by royal letters patent during pleasure etc. being absent from this safe keeping during the accounting period because, at that time, he was very ill.

Total nothing.

Total expenses for this ballinger 44s 3d.

[F.23r.] Royal Ship called *Gracedieu de la Tour*.

These expenses and costs, listed below in this account by the said keeper of the king's ships, have been incurred and provided at various times as much for the repair and fitting out of the great ships and other vessels of the Lord King as, similarly, for the governance and safe keeping of the same in the port of Hamble and elsewhere of which, to wit the aforesaid ship called *Gracedieu* is now under discussion.

Purchase of necessities.

Also for one pottle of oil bought, that is between the death of the Lord Henry V late King of England and 5 March next following, from Henry Chaundeler of Southampton and used in the same ship for caulking and fitting-out the same: price 8d.

Also for 10 boards called *waynscott* bought in the same place within the same period from Peter James and used in the repair of the same ship and her boats; price a piece 4d: total 3s 4d.

Also for 3 barrels of pitch similarly bought from Walter Fettypas within the said period and used in the caulking and fitting out of the same ship and her great boats, price a barrel 4s, total 12s.

Also for 8 oars similarly bought within the same period for the same Royal ship, price a piece 14d, total 9s 4d.

Also for 6 shovels similarly bought within the same period from Thomas Armorer of Southampton for the same ship and her boats for bailing out sand and water from the same on several occasions: price 12d.

Also for a certain *gymled* similarly bought within the same period for the same Royal ship, price 6d. Also for 5 cwt nails, price per cwt 6d, total 2s 6d; and 3 cwt nails, price per cwt 2d, total 6d, similarly bought within the same period from Robert Smyth and used in the repair of the same ship and her great boats, joint total 3s.

Overall total 29s 9d.

Wages of sailors keeping the said Royal ship.

Also for the wages of John Honywell *shippkeper* and overseer, for the benefit of the king, of the stocks and all equipment of the same ship at 4d a day, according to the contract made with him, and 6 sailors, his colleagues each at 3d a day, while continuously on board the same Royal ship called *Gracedieu* (burden estimated at 1400 tuns) in the port of Hamble, in order to look after the same and her great boats, to wit from the last day of August, in the tenth year of the said Lord Henry V, who died on that day, to 5th March next following in the first year of the present King, counting the last day and not the first, that is 566 days, including the wages of Robert Lawte a sailor called *shippkeper* at 3d a day who was similarly continuously on board the same Royal ship as a caretaker for 184 days within the same period.

Total £19 7s.

Total outside the period of controlment

£20 16s 10d.

[F.23v.] Also for 3 cwt nails, similarly bought from Peter Lokkyer of Southampton, that is under controlment, after 5th March in the first year, and used in the similar repair of the said ship, price per cwt 5d, total 15d.

Also for 200 lb of wax bought from John Godynowe of Southampton after 5th March and used in the greasing and *talwynge* of the same Royal ship, price a hundred 9s 4d, total 18s 8d.

Also for 600 pieces of wood called *fire wodde* similarly bought in lots from Andrew Bour within the same period and used there for the heating of pitch, tar, wax and other necessities for the repair of the aforesaid ship, price 3s.

Also for 4 cwt nails called *calfatenaill* similarly bought after the same date from Robert Smyth of Southampton and used in the repair of the said Royal ship, price per cwt 12d, total 4s.

Also for 6 cwt nails similarly bought within the same period and used on the repair of the said ship and her boats, price per cwt 4d, total 20d.

Also for 1 pottle of oil bought there at the same time and used on the caulking and fitting-out of the same ship, price 6d.

Also for a certain iron *ladyll* bought from John Sonday for the same ship, price 5d.

Also for 6 sheepskins similarly bought from Thomas Boucher for *mappoldes* and necessities then made and used in the *pitchynge*, *tarrynge* and *talwynge* and other works on the same ship, gross price 15½d.

Also for 2 hundreds of fuel bought there at the same time and used for *bremynge* during the repair of the said Royal ship, gross price 12d.

Also for 4 *watirscoupes* bought from Thomas Armorer of Southampton for the same ship and her boats, to bail out water and sand from the same ship, price each 2d, total 8d.

Overall total 32s 5½d.

Further wages of sailors keeping the said ship.

Also for the wages of the said John Honywell, a sailor called *shippkeper* and overseer for the benefit of the king as above at 4d, and 7 sailors called *shippkepers*, each at 3d a day, while continuously on board the same Royal ship in the said port of Hamble in order to look after the same and her great boats, to wit under the said controlment from the said 5th March, in the first year on which day the tenure of the controller began, as noted at length in the preamble of this account to the last day of August next following in the said first year, finishing on the same day, that is for 169 days, counting the last day and not the first.

Total £18 12s 9d.

[F.24r.] Wages of a Carpenter.

Also for the wages of Henry Baker, a carpenter, at 5d a day while on board the same Royal ship called *Gracedieu* in the said port working there on the repair of the same ship and various faults, necessary items and cracks in the same and also on board the Royal ship called *Holigost* and her boats and similarly while in attendance there, for the benefit of the King, during the period of safe keeping under the controlment aforesaid, to wit from 23 April, in the said first year to 1 September next following that is to say for 130 days, counting the neutral day.

Total 54s 2d.

Wages of a Caulker.

Also for the wages of a caulker called John Sonday at 4d a day by agreement made with him for the benefit of the King while similarly on board the same Royal ship in the same port, working on caulking and *ransakying* of the same ship, and also the ship *Holigost* and her great boats and while in attendance there for the benefit of the King during the above-mentioned safe keeping to wit under the said controlment from 13 March in the said first year to 1 September next following that is to say for 171 days, counting the neutral day.

Total 57s.

Further wages of the sailors keeping the said ship.

Also for the wages of the said John Honywell, a sailor called a *shippkeper* and overseer for the benefit of the King, as above, at 4d a day and 7 sailors his colleagues, each at 3d a day while continuously on board the same Royal ship in the said port in order to look after the same and her great boats to wit, under the controlment aforesaid from the said 1 September in the second year of the present King, beginning the same day to the last day of August next following, in the said second year finishing on that day, that is to say for 365 days, counting both days, payment being made on four occasions during this period.

Total £38 5d.

Further wages of a carpenter.

Also for the wages of Henry Baker, a carpenter at 5d a day by agreement made with him for the benefit of the King similarly while on board the said ship working continuously on the repair, renewal and blocking up of various faults and cracks and other things needing mending or making for the same ship, her boats, and various other Royal vessels or while in attendance for the safe-keeping mentioned above to wit for 182 working days within the same period under the said controlment in the said second year of the present King.

Total 75s 10d.

[F.24v.] Further wages of a caulker.

Also for the wages of the said John Sonday, a caulker, at 3d a day by agreement made with him for the greater benefit of the King, while working and caulking in the said ship and her great boats and also in various other Royal ships and vessels on the repair and fitting out of the same and similarly while in attendance for the safe keeping mentioned above in the said port in the said second year to wit under the said controlment within the said period for 181 working days.

Total 60s 4d.

Further wages of sailors keeping the said ship.

Also for the wages of Peter Bottesowe a master mariner and over-seer, for the benefit of the King as mentioned above and 7 sailors his colleagues called *shippekepers*, of whom the said overseer received 4d a day and each of the others 3d a day while continuously on board the same Royal ship called *Gracedieu* in the said port of Hamble for the similar safe-keeping of the same with her great and small boats to wit, under the controlment aforesaid from 1 September in the third year of the present King, beginning the same day, to 1 September next follow-ing in the fourth year of this King beginning the same day, that is to say for 365 days counting the first day and not the last.

Total £38 5d.

Further wages of a carpenter.

Also for the wages of the said Henry Baker, a carpenter at 5d a day by agreement made with him for the greater benefit of the King simil-arly while working in this Royal ship and her great boats and various other vessels of the said office on the renewal and repair and *ransakynge* of the same and while in attendance for this safe keeping mentioned above to wit under the controlment aforesaid for 362 days in the said third year being paid on four occasions.

Total £7 10s 10d.

Further wages of a caulker.

Also for the said wages of John Sonday, a caulker, at 4d a day for the benefit of the King retained as above, while working and caulking in this Royal ship, her great boats and in other vessels of the said office on the fitting out and caulking of the same and while similarly in attendance in the said port for the safe-keeping of the same, to wit under the said controlment for 361 days in the said third year that is to say paid on four occasions in the same period.

Total £6 4d.

Further purchase of necessities.

Also for 3 cwt nails bought in the said third year from Richard Marke of Southampton and used in the repair of the same ship and her boats.

Price 15d.

Also for a certain consignment of ox leather bought from Roger Boneiour and used in the repair of the pumps (*dez pompes*) of the said ships

Price 14d.

Also for a certain consignment of fuel bought from Richard Reve and used in the caulking and fitting out of the said Royal ship.

Price 12d.

Also for one pottle of oil bought from Henry Mantell and used in the fitting out and caulking of the same ship.

Price 5d.

Also for 3 sheepskins bought from William Boucher then made into *mappoldes* and used in the caulking and fitting out of the same ship.

Price 9d.

Total 4s 7d.

Total expenses for this ship £143 6s 1½d.

[F.25r.] Royal ship called *Holigost de la Tour*
Purchase of necessities.

Also for 12 boards called *waynscott* bought from William Nicholl between the foresaid death of the Lord Henry V and the said 5 March in the first year of the present King for a certain Royal ship called *Holigost* and used in the repair of the same ship and her boats, price a piece 3½d, total 3s 6d.

Also for 6 lbs of candles bought within the same period from Robert Chaundeler and used on occasions on the *ransakynge* and repair of the same ship under the *(les) carlynges* in the same, price a lb. 1½d.

Total 9d.

Also for 6 cwt nails called *pompnaill,* price per cwt 2d, total 12d, and 2 cwt nails, price 3d per cwt, total 6d, bought from Peter Lokkyer of Southampton within the same period and used in the repair of the same ship and her boats, total 18d.

Also for 5 cwt nails, price per cwt 6d, total 2s 6d and 7 cwt nails price per cwt 10d, total 6s 3d [sic] and 4 cwt nails price per cwt 5d, total 20d bought in parcels within the same period from Robert Smyth of Southampton and used similarly in the making and repair of the same ship and her boats.

Total 10s 5d.

Also for 4 pieces of timber bought within the same period for the same ship and used in this repair of the same Royal ship, price 2s.

Also for 1 piece of timber similarly bought from John Tournour within the same period and used on the repair of the same ship, price 12d.

Total 19s 2d.

Wages of sailors keeping the said Royal ship.

Also for the wages of Thomas Chewrell, a sailor called a *shippkeper* and three sailors his colleagues each at 3d a day while continuously on board the same ship called *Holigost*, burden estimated at 760 wine tuns, in the said port of Hamble in order to look after the same with her great boats to wit from the last day of August in the tenth year of the Lord Henry V lately King of England who died that day to 5 March next following in the first year of the present King, that is to say for 186 days, counting the last day and not the first.

Total £9 6s.

[F.25v.] Also for the similar wages of Thomas Arclowe, a sailor called *shippkeper* while continuously on board the same Royal ship called *Holigost* in the said port of Hamble for this safe-keeping of the same ship and her boats to wit for 32 days within the same period.

Total 8s.

Total expenses outside controlment

£10 13s 2d.

Purchases of necessities.

Also for a certain consignment of ox leather bought under the said controlment after 5 March as mentioned above from John Cordwaner of Southampton and used on the repair of the *pompes* in the same ship together with 3 cwt nails bought at the same time from Peter Lokkyer and used on this repair, gross price 2s 4d.

Also for money paid to various Hamble men for bread and ale, meat and candles bought from the same within the same period for the benefit of the King to save wages and used for men, women and other labourers working overtime to save the same ship because of various leaks and stoppings up made in the same.

Total 10s.

Also for 158 quarters of wax bought after 5 March from John Godynowe and used in the fitting out and *talwyng* and various other necessities in the same, price 16s 2d.

Also for 4 sheepskins bought from the said John within the same period for *mapoldes* made for and used in the repair of the said ship.

price, 10d.

Also for 1 thousand of fuel bought within the same period and used for caulking and heating pitch and tar and other necessities for the mending and fitting-out of the said ship and various other Royal vessels and for drying and heating the said ship at the time of her fitting out and stopping up, total 5s.

Also for a certain piece of ironwork called a *flappe* bought from Peter Lokkier within the same period and used in the repair of the (*del*) *pompe* of the said ship, price 4d.

Also for 2 dozen candles bought from John Chaundeler of Tychefeld (Titchfield) within the same period and used in this ship and in other Royal ships and vessels in *serchynge* for various faults and *lekynges* occurring in the same at various times and also for blocking up and mending the same under *les hacches* because of the lack of daylight, price a dozen 18d, total 3s.

Also for 4 *pompe boxes* bought within the same period from John

Bollour of Southampton and used on occasions in the repair of the *pompes* in the same Royal ship

gross price 12d.

Overall total. 38s 8d.

[F.26r.] Further wages of sailors keeping the said ship.

Also for the wages of the said Thomas Arclowe, a sailor called a *shippkeper* and 4 sailors, his colleagues, each at 3d a day while continuously on board the same royal ship in the said port of Hamble for the similar safe-keeping of the same ship and her great boats to wit from the said 5 March in the said first year when the tenure of the said controller in the office of King's ships first began as is more fully recorded in the title of this account, to the last day of August next following, the first year finishing on that day, that is to say, counting the last day and not the first for 179 days.

Total £9 3s 9d.

Bonus payments to sailors and others.

Also for the money paid as bonuses, for the benefit of the King to William Osmond and various sailors and other men working overtime in the said ship at baling out water and sand from the said ship until the *lekkynges* and *rent* were mended, as mentioned above and also at *morynge* and looking after the same both inside and out and various other works performed at the same time for the safety of the said ship, together with 8d given to the same workers in ale so that they would work better, to wit receiving for their bonus payments 12s 8d.

Also for money similarly paid as a bonus for the greater use to the King of Davy Owen, *dyver*, for swimming and *dyvinge* in the water under the bottom of the same ship and working there to block up and mend underwater these *rent* and cracks and on the *serchynge* and *ransakyng* of the same cracks and *rent* in the same period for the safety of the said ship receiving by agreement made with him for this bonus, 6s 8d.

Total 19s 4d.

Further wages of sailors.

Also for the wages of the said Thomas Arclowe and four sailors his colleagues called *shippkepers* each at 3d a day while continuously on board the same Royal ship in the said port in order to look after the same and her great boats to wit from 1 September in the second year of the present King beginning that day to the last day of August in the third year of our said present Lord King finishing that day under the said controlment, that is to say for two whole years consisting of 730 days counting both days, being paid on 8 occasions in the same period.

Total £45 12 6d.

[F.26v.] Wages of the master for this safe-keeping.

But Jurden Brownynge, master of the said Royal ship called *Holigost*, received nothing for his wages at 6d a day while similarly on board the said Royal ship in the said port for the safe-keeping of the same during the said period nor for his fee of ten marks a year, granted to him by Royal letters patent because the said master for the whole of the said period was engaged on his own business overseas and elsewhere.

total nothing.

Total expenses for this ship £70 7s 5d.

Royal Ship called *Jhesus de la Tour*.
Purchases of necessities.

Also for 4 great boards called *pruc deles* (Prussian deal from the Baltic) bought from William Nicholl of Southampton, to wit between the death of Henry V late King of England and 5 March in the said first year for the Royal ship called *Jhesus* and used to repair the same, price a piece 14d, total 4s 8d.

Also for 8 boards called *waynscot* similarly bought from the said William within the same period and used in the repair of the said ship and her boats, price a piece 3½d, total 2s 4d.

Also for 6 cwt nails, price per cwt 6d, total 3s and 2 cwt nails price per cwt 10d, total 20d bought from Robert Smyth of Southampton within the said period and used in the similar repair of the same ship and her boats, total 4s 8d.

Also for the money paid to Richard Smyth to mend an anchor belonging to the ship within the said period, 5s 2d.

Also for 1 hundred of fuel bought from John Toller and used to heat pitch, tar, *rosen* and wax for the caulking and fitting out of the same Royal ship. Price 6d.

Overall Total 17s 4d.

[F.27r.] Wages of Sailors keeping the said Royal ship.

Also for the wages of Bartholomew Scledale and three sailors his colleagues called *shippkepers* each at 3d a day while continuously on board the same Royal ship called *Jhesus* burden estimated at 1000 tuns, in the said port of Hamble in order to look after the same and her great boats to wit, from the last day of August in the 10th year of the said late King who died that day to 5 March next following in the first year of the present King, that is to say for 186 days counting the last day and not the first, outside controlment.

Total £9 6s.

Further wages of a sailor keeping the said ship.

Also for the similar wages of Paston Renward a sailor called *shippkeper* while on board the same Royal ship called *Jhesus* for this safe-keeping of the ship and her boats in the same port of Hamble to wit for 120 days within the said period.

Total 30s.

Wages of a caulker.

Also for the wages of John Eliote, a caulker at 4d a day for the benefit of the King, by agreement made with him while working and caulking in the same Royal ship and her great and small boats and also on *ransakynge* and *serchynge* and repairing various other vessels of the same office and while in attendance in the said port for this safe-keeping and supervision of the same to wit for 86 days within the same period outside controlment. Total 28s 8d.

Total expenses outside controlment £13 2s.

[F. 27v.] Purchases of necessities.

Also for 4 *flappes* of iron bought from Peter Lokkyer of Southampton under the controlment aforesaid after the said 5 March in the first year and used to mend the *watirpompes* of the same Royal ship.

gross price 16d.

Also for 2 cwt nails called *pompnayll* bought from the said Peter within the said period and used in the similar repair of the said pompes price per cwt 2d, total 4d.

Also for 4 cwt nails called *hachnayll* within the same period bought from Robert Smyth and used there for the repair of the said ship and her great boats, price per cwt 5d, total 20d.

Also for 3 hundreds and a half of wax bought after the said 5 March from John Godynowe to mix and heat with tar and *rosen* to repair and fit out the same ship, her great boats and various other vessels of the said King and used in this work price 18s.

Also for a certain parcel of fuel called *billet* bought after the said 5 March and used in heating wax and tar and for various other things necessary for the repair of the same ship and her boats price 2s 6d.

Also for 100 lb wax bought from Nicholas Swadelynge and used in the repair and fitting out of the same ship and in the heating of the same with pitch and tar price 9s 4d.

Also for 4 cwt nails called *pompnaill* bought on another occasion from John Compton and used in the repair of the *pompes* and other necessities of the same ship price 8d.

Also for 3 cwt nails called *pompnaill* bought on another occasion from Peter Lokkyer within the same period and used in the repair of *watir-dales* and *pompes* in the same Royal ship price per cwt 2d.

total 6d.

Also for 3 sheepskins bought from Thomas Boucher within the same period for *mappoldes* used in the repair and fitting out of the same ship, price a piece 3d,   total 9d.

Also for a certain parcel of ox leather bought after the said 5 March and used in the mending and fitting out of the *pompe* of the same Royal ship called *Jhesus*   price 4½d.

Also for 3 sheepskins bought on another occasion after 5 March in the said first year for *mappoldes* used in the repair and fitting out of the said ship,   Gross price 4½d.

Also for 1 hundred of fuel bought from John Osmonde and used in the heating of pitch, tar and wax for the repair and fitting out of the same ship and her great boats,   Price 6d.

Also for 2 lb candles bought from William Boucher and used in the *ransakynge* and repair of this ship,   Price 3d.

Also for 2 cwt nails called *pompenaill* bought from Peter Lokkyer and used in the repair *dez pompes* in the same, price 4d. Also for 1 cwt nails called *hacch naill* similarly bought from the said Peter and used in the repair of the said Royal ship,   price 6d.

                                                          Total 37s 8d.

[F.28r.] Further wages of sailors keeping the said ship.

Also for the wages of Bartholomew Scledale and 4 sailors his colleagues called *shipkepers* each at 3d a day while continuously on board the same royal ship in the said port of Hamble in order to look after the same ship and her boats to wit under the said controlment from the said 5 March in the said first year when the tenure of the said controller in the office of the king's ships first began, as noted more fully in the title of this account, to wit to the last day of August next following in the first year finishing on the same day, that is to say for 175 days, counting the last day and not the first.

                                                          Total £9 3s 9d.

Wages of a caulker.

Also for the wages of the said John Eliot, a caulker, at 4d a day for the benefit of the King by agreement made with him while working and caulking in the same ship and in her great and small boats and also while caulking, *ransakynge* and *serchynge* various other vessels of the same office and while in attendance in the said port for the said safe-keeping of the same ship and her boats, to wit, during the said period under the said controlment.

                                                          Total 59s 8d.

Further wages of sailors keeping the said ship.

Also for the wages of the said Bartholomew Scledale and 4 sailors his companions called *shippkepers* each at 3d a day while continuously on board the said royal ship called *Jhesus* in the same port of Hamble to look after the same ship and her boats, to wit, under the said controlment from 1 September in the second year of the present King, beginning on that day and the last day of August next following in the said second year finishing on that day, that is to say for 365 days, counting both days, under this controlment.

Total £22 16s 3d.

Further wages of a caulker.

Also for the wages of the said John Eliote, a caulker, at 4d a day by agreement made with him while similarly working and caulking in the same ship and her boats and while overseeing the repairs and *ransakynge* of other vessels of the said office and while in attendance in the said port for the said safe-keeping mentioned above in the said second year, to wit for 181 working days under the said controlment within the said period.

Total 60s 4d.

[F.28v.] Further wages of sailors keeping the said ship.

Also for the wages of the said Robert Cole and 4 other sailors his colleagues called *shippekepers* each at 3d a day while similarly on board the same royal ship in the said port of Hamble in order to look after the same to wit from 1 September in the third year of the said King, beginning on the same day to the last day of August next following in the said third year finishing on that day, to wit for 365 days counting both days, being paid on four occasions under the said controlment.

Total £22 16s 3d.

Further wages of a caulker.

Also for the wages of the said John Eliot, a caulker, at 4d a day for the benefit of the King by agreement made with him while working and caulking on this ship, in the other great ships of the King and their great boats and while in attendance for this safe-keeping mentioned above, to wit under the said controlment in the said third year for 334 days within the same period of this safe-keeping, to wit being paid on five occasions.

Total 111s 4d.

Total expenses for this ship £83 7s. 3d.

Royal ship called *Trinite Riall*.
Purchases of necessities.

Also for 7 pieces of timber bought from John Prest, between the death of the said late King and abovesaid 5 March in the said first year, for the repair of the royal ship called *Trinite Riall* and her boats and used in the repair of the same ships and boats: gross price 16d.

Also for 6 large boards called *del* bought from William Nicholl within the same period and used in the repair of the same ship and her boats, price a piece 15d. total 7s 6d.

Also for 4 cwt nails, price per cwt 6d, total 2s and 3 cwt nails price per cwt 8d, total 3s 4d bought on occasion within the said period from Robert Smyth and used in the repair of the said ships and her boats.

total 7s 10d.
Overall total 16s 8d.

[F.29r.] Wages of sailors keeping the said royal ship.

Also for the wages of Richard French a sailor called a *shippkeper* and 4 sailors his colleagues each at 3d a day while continuously on board the same royal ship called *Trinite Riall* burden estimated at 540 tuns in the said port of Hamble in order to look after the same and her great and small boats, to wit from the last day of August in the tenth year of the Lord Henry V, late King of England who died that day to 5 March next following in the first year of the present King, that is to say for 186 days, counting the last day and not the first.

Total £11 12s 6d.
Total expenses without controlment £12 9s 2d.

Further purchases of necessities.

Also for a certain iron *flappe* for *le pompe* bought from Peter Lokkyer of Southampton under the said controlment, to wit after the abovesaid 5 March as mentioned before and used in the repair of the *pompe* of the said royal ship,   price 4d.

Also for 1 cwt 3 qua of wax similarly bought at the same period from Thomas Boucher of Southampton and used there in the fitting out, *talwynge* and caulking of the same ship and her great boats,

Gross price 16s 2d.

Also for 500 pieces of wood called fuel bought after the said 5 March in the first year from Robert Poynell and used for *bremynge* while caulking and fitting out this ship and her great boats   price 2s 6d.

Also for 2 cwt nails called *pompnaill* price 4d, and 2 cwt nails price per cwt 3d, total 6d bought at the same time from the said Peter Lokkyer and used in the repair of the same ship   total 10d.

Also for 5 *pompeboxes* bought from John Bollour within the same period and used in the repair of the *pompes* in the same ship,

gross price 14d.

Also for 5 cwt nails called *calfatenaill* price per cwt 12d, total 5s, and for 5 cwt nails price per cwt 10d, total 4s 2d, bought in various lots from Robert Smyth after 5 March, and used in the repair of the said ship and her great boats.

Overall total 9s 2d.

Also for a certain parcel of fuel bought from Richard French in the same period and used for *bremynge* at the time of the fitting-out and repair of the same ship: price 9d.

Total 30s 10d.

[F.29v.] Further wages of sailors keeping the said royal ship.

Also for the wages of the said Richard French, a sailor called a *shippkeper* and 4 other sailors his colleagues each at 3d a day while continuously on board the said royal ship in the said port of Hamble in order to look after the same and her great and small boats to wit, under the controlment aforesaid from 5 March in the said first year when the tenure of the said controller in the office of the King's ships first began as noted more fully in the title of this account, to wit to the last day of August next following in the said first year finishing that day, that is to say for 170 days, counting the last day and not the first.

£11 3s 9d.

Further wages of sailors keeping the said ship.

Also for the similar wages of the said Richard French and 4 sailors his colleagues called *shippkepers* while on board the same ship in the said port to look after the same and her great and small boats, to wit, under the said controlment from 1 September in the second year of the said Lord King, beginning that day to the last day of August next following in the said second year finishing that day, that is to say for 365 days, counting both days, in four instalments.

Total £22 16s 3d.

Further wages of sailors keeping the said ship.

Also for the similar wages of the said Richard and 4 sailors called *shippkepers* while continuously on board the said royal ship in the port of Hamble in order to look after the same together with her great and small boats, to wit, under the said controlment from 1 September in the third year beginning that day to the last day of August next following in the said third year finishing that day, that is to say for 369 days, counting both days to wit paid in four instalments.

Total £22 16s 3d.

Wages of the master for this safe-keeping.

But William Yalton, master of the same royal ship received nothing for his wages at 6d a day or for his fee of 10 marks a year granted to him by royal letters patent, as mentioned in the previous account of the said keeper, during the whole period of safe-keeping, because he was engaged during the whole period on his own affairs both at home and abroad.

Total nothing.

Total expenses for this ship £70 16s. 3d.

[F.30r.] Various other payments.

Purchases of paper and other necessities for the same office.

Also for parchment, wide paper, bound and unbound and wax, ink and various other necessities for the same office of the said keeper of the King's ships, needed by the keeper himself, or his deputies on various occasions both here and elsewhere, bought and supplied within the same accounting period together with the expenses of binding this book.

Total 13s 4d

Wages of one purveyor.

Also for the wages of a purveyor for the said office of the King's ships, at 6d a day while engaged in working and travelling on horseback on various purchases and purveyances of timber, boards, pitch, tar and various other supplies for the building of the royal ship called *Graun Marie* lately rebuilt and also for other ships and vessels belonging to the said office and while arranging the carriage, freight and shipping of supplies for the said office, and while in attendance and working on the supervision of all the ships and vessels of the office and their equipmen and supplies because the ships' masters were not on duty during the accounting period, to wit for his wages from the last day of Augus in the tenth year of the said late King to 5 March next following, tha is to say for 186 days, counting the last day and not the first.

Total £4 13s

Also from 5 March, to wit under the said controlment to the las day of August in the third year of the said Lord King finishing that da for his similar wages, whether working or in attendance in the sam office for the same tasks, to wit for 908 days, counting the neutral day

Total £22 14s

Overall total £22 14s [sic

Total for this page £23 7s 4d.

[F.30v.] [203] Expenses of William Soper, keeper of the King's ships, an of the controller of the said office incurred in the sale of the roy ships, to wit:

Also for the costs and expenses of the keeper himself, for himself an for his four horses and for the costs and expenses of the said Nichol

Banastre the controller of the said office for himself and for his three
horses while travelling to promote the sale of various royal ships and
other vessels and their supplies and equipment, as appears itemised
below: to wit riding from Southampton to Bristol and elsewhere for
the sale of the royal carrack *Christofre* and its equipment to John
Morgan of the same town in May in the first year of King Henry VI,
that is to say, travelling there, staying there and returning home for a
total of 16 days on several occasions, each receiving 2s a day, while
negotiating the sale and collecting the money.   64s.

Also for the similar costs and expenses of the same keeper and controller of the same office, to wit, riding with their own horses from
Southampton to Plymouth and elsewhere to promote the sale of the
royal ship *Thomas* and two royal ballingers called *George* and
Katherine Britton together with their equipment to wit, the ship
Thomas with her equipment to John Chirche of London in September
in the said first year: the said ballinger *Katherine Britton* with her
equipment to John Sterlynge and others in March in the said first year:
and the said ballinger called *George* with her equipment to William
Bentley between August and September in the said first year, that is to
say travelling there, staying there and returning home for a total of 19
days on various occasions each receiving as above while negotiating the
said sales and collecting the money.   Total 76s.

Also for the similar costs and expenses of the said keeper and controller of the said office, to wit riding with their own horses from
Southampton to London and Winchelsea to promote the sale of two
royal ships called *Holigost of Spain* and ship *Graunt Marie* and a royal
ballinger called *Faucon* with their equipment, to wit the said ship
Holigost to John Radeclyff and others in June in the said first year: the
ballinger called *Faucon* with its equipment to Adam Forster in June in
the said first year: and the said ship *Graunt Marie* with its equipment
to Richard Buckland in August in the said first year that is to say for a
total of 14 days on various occasions including travelling there, staying
there and returning home each receiving as above while negotiating
the sale and collecting the money   Total 56s

Also for the similar costs and expenses of the said keeper and controller of the same office to wit riding with their own horses from
Southampton to Dartmouth and Falmouth to promote the sale of three
royal ballingers called *Craccher*, *Nicholas* and the ballinger *Swan* with
their equipment; to wit the said ballinger called *Craccher* with her
equipment to John Cole and others in April in the said first year; and
the ballinger called *Swan* with her equipment to John William and
others in the said month of April in the said first year; and the ballinger called *Nicholas* with her equipment to John More and others in
September in the said first year, that is to say including travelling there,

staying there and returning home for a total of 11 days on various occasions both receiving as above while negotiating the sale and collecting the money.   Total 44s.

Also for the similar costs and expenses of the said keeper and controller of the same office, to wit riding with their own horses from Southampton to Sandwich and Winchelsea to promote the sale of the royal carrack called *George* with its equipment and also various stores belonging to the said office sold to Nicholas Justinian and others between July and August in the said first year, that is to say including travelling there, staying there and returning home for a total of 13 days on various occasions, each receiving as above, while negotiating the sale and collecting the money.   Total 52s.

Also for the similar costs and expenses of the same keeper and controller of the said office, to wit riding with their own horses from Southampton to Saltash and elsewhere in Cornwall to promote the sale of the ballinger called *Ane* with her equipment to John Slogg in June in the second year of the said King Henry VI, to wit including travelling there, staying there and returning home for a total of 9 days on various occasions, each receiving as above while negotiating the sale and collecting the money.   Total 36s.

Also for the similar costs and expenses of the said keeper and controller of the said office, to wit riding with their own horses from Southampton to London and Greenwich to promote the sale of two ships called *Nicholas* and *Katerine* without their equipment, to wit the said ship called *Nicholas* without equipment to John Reynold in May in the said second year and the said ship called *Katerine* without equipment to John Piers and others in March in the third year of King Henry VI, that is to say including travelling there, staying there and returning home for a total of 12 days on various occasions, each receiving as above, while negotiating the sale and collecting the money.   Total 48s.

Also for the similar costs and expenses of the said keeper and controller of this office to wit, riding with their own horses to the town of Hamble, and the town of Shotteshalle and elsewhere in Hampshire and also to the town of Poole and elsewhere to promote the sale of two royal ballingers, one called *Valentine* with her equipment and one called *Rose* (sic i.e. *Roose*) without equipment and also three carracks in bad repair, the *Paul* and the *Marie Sandwich,* and the carrack called *Peter* without their equipment; to wit the said ballinger called *Valentine* with her equipment to John Jon and others in March in the second year of King Henry VI; and the said ballinger called *Rose* without equipment to William Castell in February in the third year of the said King Henry VI; and two carracks called the *Paul* and the *Marie Sandwich* without equipment to John Gladwyne and others in September in the third year of the said King Henry VI; and the carrack called *Peter* without equipment to William Morynge and others in October in the said third year, that is to say including travelling there, staying there and returning home for a total of 7 days on various occasions, each receiving as above, while negotiating the sale and collecting the money and making inquiries for men to repair these vessels, Total 28s. All this authorised by a writ under the privy seal dated 26 June in the eighth year of the said present king addressed to the Treasurer and Barons of the Exchequer and enrolled among the memoranda of the eighth year among writs addressed to the Barons in Trinity Term on the third roll from the King's Remembrancer.

Overall total of days, 101.

[F.31r.] Gross purchases for the office of the King's Ships.

Also for 2 loads of pitch, each load containing 12 small barrels bought at various times between the death of the said late King and 5 March next following from Robert Burton for the same office of the King's ships: price a barrel 3s 4d.

Total £4.

Also for 40 large oars bought within the same period from John Derkey of London for the use of the same office of the King's ships: price each 16d. Total 53s 4d.

Also for 24 tools called *shovelles* similarly bought for the same office of the King's ships within the stated period from John Bollour of Southampton for moving ballast on various occasions when *lekkynges* and *ransakynges* suddenly happened on various vessels of the said office and also used for various other works price each 2d.

Total 4s.

Total without controlment £6 17s 4d.

Further purchases.

Also for 20 *pompe boxes* bought from John Bollour under the said controlment to wit after the aforesaid 5 March in the said first year for the same office of the King's ships, gross price, by the account drawn up with him on 3 April in the same first year, 6s 8d.

Also for 8 cwt nails called large *pompe naill* similarly bought from John Compton of Southampton within the same period for the office of the King's ships, price per cwt 4d, by an account drawn up with him on 7 May in the said first year, total 2s 8d.

Also for 6 large barrels of tar bought from John Jonson after the said date for the office of the King's ships, price a barrel by an account drawn up with him on the same day in May 6s 8d. Total 40s.

Also for a certain large brazen cauldron called *bras potte* bought

from Thomas Brasyer of Winchester to heat pitch and tar and wax and various other necessities for the fitting out and repair of the great ships and vessels in the ownership of the said office, weighing 97 lb, price a lb. 3d, by agreement made with him on 13 July in the said first year,
total 24s 3d.

Also for 4 large cables of white (i.e. untarred) Bridport yarn and 16 ropes called *hauncers* bought within the same period from Simon atte Ford of the same town, each cable weighing 1 mwt 2 cwt – total 4 mwt 8 cwt and each *hauncer* weighing 1½ cwt 12 lb – total 2 mwt 5½ cwt 24 lb (sic) overall total 7 mwt 3½ cwt 24 lb at a price of 13s 4d per cwt, by agreement made with him on the last day of February in the second year of the present King–   Total £49 2s 9½d.

Also for 9 ropes called *hauncers* of the same yarn bought from the said Simon atte Ford for the said office of the King's ships, each *hauncer* weighing 1 cwt 1 qua 20 lb – total 1 mwt 2 cwt 3 qua 12 lb and 9 small ropes of the same yarn similarly bought for the same office weighing altogether 8 cwt 9 lb. Overall total 2 mwt 3 qua 21 lb, price per cwt as above by agreement made on the same date
[F.31v.] – Total £13 9s 2d.

Also for 60½ stones of *ocom fyn* (fine oakum) bought after the said 5 March from Robert Norffork and Katerine Douchwoman of London for the same office of the King's ships price a stone 4d by agreement made with them on 10 June in the said second year of the King,
Total 20s 2d.

Also for 12 ells of canvas bought from Richard Goslyn for making *sarplers* in which this oakum was transported so that it would be better looked after and these 12 ells of canvas were afterwards used for the repair of the sail of the great boat of the royal ship called *Jhesus*, price an ell 5½d.   Total 5s 6d.

Also for money paid similarly for the carriage of the same *ocom* to the Thames and for boat-hire for the same to a certain ship in the Pool (of London)   total 10d.

Also for 12 large barrels of tar bought from George Huske for the same office of the King's ships, gross price, for the greater benefit of the King by agreement made with him on 22 June in the said second year   £4.

Also for money paid to Robert Freng a sailor for freight dues for these 60½ stones of *ocom*, to wit from London to Southampton for this office of the King's ships receiving for the freight dues by agreement made with him for the benefit of the king   3s 4d.

Also for 8 large barrels of tar bought from Thomas Freland on various occasions for the same office of the King's ships, price a barrel 6s 4d by agreement made with him in June in the said second year,
total 50s 8d.

Also for 5 cwt nails called *calfatenaill* bought from Peter Lokkyer for the same office of the King's ships, price per cwt 12d by agreement made with him on 16 July in the second year,   Total 5s.

Also for 4 cwt nails similarly bought from the said Peter for the same office of the King's ships, price per cwt 4d, by agreement made with him at the same time in the second year   Total 16d.

Also for 5 large ropes and 6 *hausers* of white yarn bought for the same office of the King's ships, from John Froy total weight 6 mwt 3 cwt 1 qua 11 lb, price per cwt 13s 4d by agreement made with him on 7 October in the said third year of the Lord Henry VI. Total £42 4s 7d.

Also for 5½ cwt 8 lb of *rosen* bought from Auncell Spyser for the same office of the King's ships price per cwt 5s by agreement made with him in January in the said third year,   Total 27s 10¼d.

Also for 13 large barrels of tar bought from William Nicoll for the same office of the King's ships, price a barrel 6s 8d by agreement made with him on 12 March in the said third year.   Total £4 6s 8d.

Also for 2 loads of tar consisting of 24 large barrels bought from John Jon for the office of the said King's ships gross price, by agreement made with him for the benefit of the King on 3 May in the said third year,   £7

Also for 6½ cwt 4 lb. of *rosen* bought from John Wodland of Southampton for the same office of the King's ships gross price, for the benefit of the King by agreement made with him on 22 May in the said third year, [F.32r.]   26s.

Also for money paid to John Brasyer of Southampton for mending a certain large bronze pot belonging to the said office of the King's ships for heating pitch, tar, wax and other necessities in the same office receiving by agreement made with him   14d.

Also for 4 sheep skins bought from Thomas Boucher for making *mappoldes* used in the repair and caulking of various great royal ships,   price 12d.

Also for 300 pieces of fuel bought from Robert Ellys for the same office of the King's ships and used in the repair and fitting-out of various royal ships and boats in the third year,   price 18d.

Overall Total £131 11s 2d.

Total for gross purchases £138 8s 6d.

Release of money to the executors of the will of King Henry V.[204]

Also for money released to Robert Babethrop and John Wodouse, the executors of the will of King Henry V, lately King of England, by indenture drawn up on 20 May in the second year of the present King, still in the possession of the said Robert and John and the Keeper of the King's ships concerning the payment of 1,000 marks, the proceeds of the sale of royal ships and other property of the office, lately assigned to the executors on the advice and order of the King's Great Council in order to pay various debts of the late king: that is £160 from the sale of the royal carrack *Christopher*, £80 from the sale of the royal barge *Valentine*, £26 13s 14d from the sale of the royal ballinger *Craccher* and £133 6s 8d from the sale of the ship *Thomas,* all this money being in the hands of John Stafford, Treasurer of England; and £148 8s 11d, a portion of the proceeds of the sale of the royal ship *Graunt Marie,* the money coming from the redemption of two tallies lately issued at the Receipt of the Exchequer for certain victualls and stores bought or provided for the Household and Wardrobe of the late King by Richard Buckland:

total due under this indenture
£548 8s 11d.

[F.32v.] Also for the money similarly released on another occasion without an indenture to the said Robert and John as part of this payment of 1,000 marks, as mentioned above, to wit the proceeds of the sale of a certain storehouse and forge adjoining the same lately newly built for the same office at Southampton, sold by authority of a royal writ under the privy seal dated at Westminster 26 May in the said second year addressed to the said keeper and exhibited with this account (also taking into account the evidence of certain tallies relating to this release drawn on the said Receipt of the Exchequer for the said keeper of the king's ships).

Total £66 13s 4d.

Also for the money similarly released on another occasion without an indenture as part of this payment of 1,000 marks, as defined above, to the same Robert and John, executors of the will aforesaid, to wit a portion of the proceeds of the sale of a certain royal ship called *Holigost of Spain de la Tour,* the release of the money being recorded by a tally lately also drawn on the Receipt of the Exchequer for the said keeper.

Total £51 6s 8d.

By authority of the said royal writ under the privy seal.[205]
Also for the money paid to Richard Bokeland for certain victuals and stores for the Household and Wardrobe of the Lord King Henry V, father of the present King, purchased and provided by the said Richard for royal use from his own money, total £148 8s 11d, included in a writ under the privy seal of King Henry VI, dated 3 July in the first year ordering jointly and severally John Foxholes, clerk, William Soper and Nicholas Banastre to sell certain great ships and other vessels be-

longing to the King and to account to the King for the receipts, noted above in item 8 under foreign receipts.

Total £148 8s 11d.

[F.33r.] These are the various outgoings costs and expenses including the wages of carpenters called *berders*, *clenchers* and *holders* and the wages of sawyers, caulkers, and other craftsmen and workmen whatsover incurred by the said keeper of the king's ships under the controlment aforesaid for the same office of the King's ships and for the repair of a certain royal ballinger called *Petit Jhesus*, also including various other gross purchases similarly bought and provided on various occasions by the said keeper for the same office between 1st September in the fourth year beginning on the same day and the last day of August in the fifth year of the said King, finishing on the same day, to wit:

Also for 1 dozen *pomp boxes* bought from John Boollour of Southampton and all used in the repair of *les pompes* in these great royal ships called *Gracedewe*, *Jhesus*, *Trinite Riall* and *Holigost* and in their great boats during the accounting period, price 3s 4d.

Also for 14 *pomp boxes* similarly bought from the said John, and used to repair the said *pompes* in the same 4 royal ships and their great boats called *folowers*, total price   3s 9d.

Also for the money paid to Peter Lokkyer of Southampton for all his work on various ironwork and other necessities made to repair the said *pompes* during the same accounting period,   6s 6d.

Also for 6 cwt nails called *pompnaill* bought on another occasion from Robert Smyth and used to mend these *pompes*, price per cwt 2d,   total 12d.

Also for a parcel of ox leather similarly bought from John Boveioure and used in the repair of these *pompes* of the said 4 royal ships, price 9d.

Also for 80 small pieces of timber bought from the Abbot of Titchfield [206] to make *piles* and *stakes* used in the repair of the *stakynge* and *pilynge* in the port of Hamble, for the greater security of the said 4 great royal ships, gross price 20d.

Also for the money paid to John Harry for the carriage of this timber, to wit from the park at Titchfield to the said port of Hamble gross receipts for this carriage for the benefit of the King, 2s.

Also for 4 pieces of timber bought similarly from the said Abbot of Titchfield to make *trenails* used in the repair of the said 4 royal ships and their great and small boats during the same accounting period, price 16d.

Also for the wages of Richard Rilleford a carpenter working there on the felling and trimming of this timber intended for making *trenails* during the same accounting period, [F.33v.] receiving 6d a day, total 5s.

Also for 1 cwt nails, price 7½d, 7 cwt nails price per cwt 1d, total 7d, and 4 cwt nails called *scepnaill* price per cwt 5d total 20d, bought from Richard Burgeys and Robert Kenne of Southampton and used in the making and repair of these 4 great royal ships with their boats at the same period, total 2s 10½d.

Also for 1 load of tar, consisting of 12 large barrels, bought from John Wyote of Southampton and used in the fitting out and repair of the said 4 royal ships with their great and small boats gross price 70s.

Also for 11 barrels of pitch bought from the said John and used similarly in the *calkynge* and fitting out of the said 4 ships and in the repair of their great boats by agreement made with him on 8 May in the fourth year of the said King, gross price 36s 8d.

Also for 1,000 lb of *rosyn* bought from John Etheriche of Southampton and used there in the *rosenynge* and fitting out of these 4 great royal ships with their great and small boats, price a hundred 3s 4d by agreement made with him on 18 May in the said fourth year, total 33s 4d.

Also for 1,000 lb of *rosyn* similarly bought from Richard Rakyll and used in the repair of the said 4 ships and their great and small boats, price a hundred as above by agreement made with him on 13 June in the said fourth year, total 33s 4d.

Also for money paid to Richard Marcus, a smith for mending and making various items of ironwork belonging to the same royal ships, receiving, by agreement made with him for the greater benefit of the King, 2s.

Also for money paid to the same Richard for various items of ironwork made by himself for the same ships and used in the repair of the said 4 royal ships, price 13d.

Also for a certain piece of ironwork called a *pomp yerde* similarly bought from the same Richard and used in the repair of the *pomp* of the said royal ship called *Jhesus,* price 8d.

Also for 20 stones of *ocom* bought from Isabella Roger of Southampton and used in the caulking and fitting out of the said 4 ships and their great boats, price a stone 4d, total 6s 8d.

Also for 8 sheepskins bought from William Boucher of Hamble to make *mappoldes* used for *picchynge, tarrynge* and *rosenynge* the same royal ships, and their great and small boats, price each 3d. total 2s.

Also for 1 gallon of oil bought in two parcels and used in the caulking of the said 4 ships and their great and small boats, price 10d.

Also for a quantity of fuel bought in separate lots from John Davy and used when *bremynge* to heat [F.34r.] pitch, tar, wax and *rosyn* and for various other necessary tasks when repairing the said 4 great royal ships and their great and small boats, price 2s.

Also for 1 cwt nails, price 5d, 2½ cwt nails called *calfatenaill,* price per cwt 10d, total 2s 1d, 2 cwt nails, price per cwt 6d, total 12d, and 3 cwt nails, price per cwt 8d, total 2s, bought on various occasions from Richard Burgeys and Richard Markes and used in the repair of the said 4 royal ships and their great and small boats, total 6s 6d.

Also for money paid to John Brownynge for transporting timber with his horses and carts for the repair of the *stakynge* and *pil* at the port of Hamble for the safe keeping and greater security of the same royal ships moored at Hamble, to wit receiving for 17 carts, by agreement made with him for the greater benefit of the King, a gross payment of 2s.

Also for the wages of Andrew Caller, John Kene, Richard Kene, and John Gerard, 4 labourers working on the repair of this *pilynge* and *stakynge* at the port of Hamble, for the greater security and safekeeping of the same royal ships and also for various other work carried out there for 55 working days during the accounting period, each receiving 4d a day, total 18s 4d.

Also for 1 cwt nails bought from William Smyth of Hamble and used for the repair of this *pilynge* and *stakynge,* price 6d.

Also for 2 cwt nails, price per cwt 5d, total 10d, and for 1 cwt nails, price 4d, similarly bought from Richard Burgeys of Southampton, and used in the repair of this *pilynge* and also in the repair of the said 4 ships and their boats, total 14d.

Also for 1 lb of candles bought and used in the ransaking and *serchynge* of various faults in the royal ship *Gracedewe* needing repair on various occasions, price 1½d.

Also for a certain parcel of ox leather similarly bought from Nicholas Deen and used in the repair of the *pomp* of the same ship called *Gracedew,* price 8d.

Also for 1 piece of timber bought and used in the repair of the same royal ship called *Gracedieu,* price 2½d.

Also for 3 cwt nails bought on various occasions from Richard Markes and used in the repair of the said 4 royal ships and their great and small boats, price per cwt 5d, total 15d.

Also for 300 pieces of fire wood bought from John Osmond and used for heating pitch, tar and *rosyn* needed to repair the *Gracedieu* and the other great royal ships, price 18d.

Also for 6 sheepskins, price 18d and 1 jar of oil price 5d, similarly bought and used in the caulking and [F.34v.] fitting out of the same great royal ships and their boats, total 23d.

Also for 2 lb of candles bought and used on occasions for the repair, *ransakynge* and *serchynge* of the same great royal ships,   price 3d.

Also for 3 pots of *lute* price 4½d, and 13 pieces of timber for making *pomp stavys* price including carriage 18d, used in the repair and caulking of the said royal ships and for the mending of their *pompes*, total 22d.

Also for 200 pieces of fire wood bought on another occasion from the said John Osmond, price 12d, and for 4 sheepskins for making *mappoldes* inclusive price 12d, and for 2 pots of *lute* for *picchynge* and *rosenynge* price 3d, and for 1 jar of oil with 2 lb of candles, price 8d bought and used in the repair of the royal ship *Trinite Riall* and other great royal ships and their great and small boats,

total price 2s 10d.

Also for 7 large cables of white Normandy yarn weighing together 7 mwt 1½ cwt 21 lb and 17 ropes of various sorts called hausers of the same yarn weighing 2 mwt 2 cwt 1 qua 7 lb, joint total 9 mwt 4 cwt, price per mwt 115s, per cwt 11s 6d, bought from John Rove of Cane (Caen) in Normandy by an agreement made with him on 21 March in the said fifth year, also including 7s 8d paid to various labourers and sailors for the stowing and carriage of the same to the storehouse in Southampton, during the same period,   total £54 8s 8d.

Overall total £67 3s 10d

Royal ship called *Gracedieu.*
Wages of sailors keeping the said royal ship.

Also for the wages of Richard Bowden a sailor and 7 other sailors called *shipkepers* each at 3d a day while on board the said royal ship called *Gracedieu* in the port of Hamble in order to look after same and also her great and small boats to wit under the said controlment from 1st September in the fourth year of the said King, beginning on that day and the last day of August next following in the said fourth year ending that day, that is to say for 365 days, counting both days,

total £36 10s.

7s 6d must be deducted for the wages of one sailor who was absent from this safekeeping of the same ship for 30 days within the above period because of a certain illness and bodily weakness.

Overall total £36 2s 6d.

Wages of a carpenter.

Also for the wages of Henry Baker, a carpenter at 5d a day, by agreement made with him for the greater benefit of the King, while similarly working on board this royal ship and her great and small boats and also other royal ships to carry out repairs and other works and while in attendance for this safekeeping already mentioned, to wit under the said controlment for 315 days within the accounting period.

total £6 11s 3d.

[F.35r.] Wages of a caulker.

Also for the wages of John Sonday, a caulker at 4d a day, by agreement made with him for the benefit of the King whilst similarly on board the same royal ship called *Gracedieu*, to caulk the same and her great and small boats, and other ships of the said office and while in attendance in the said port for this safekeeping, to wit under the said controlment for 365 days in the said fourth year.

total £6 20d.

Further wages of sailors keeping the said royal ship.

Also for the wages of the said Richard Bawden, on another occasion, and 7 other sailors called *shipkepers,* each at 3d a day while similarly on board the said ship called *Gracedieu* in the said port of Hamble in order to look after the same and while continuously in attendance for the safe-keeping of her great and small boats to wit under the said controlment from 1st September in the fifth year, beginning that day to the last day of August next following in the said fifth year finishing that day, that is to say for 365 days counting both days.

total £36 10s.

Further wages of a carpenter.

Also for the wages of Olyver Carpenter at 5d a day by agreement made with him for the greater benefit of the King while on board and working on this royal ship and her great and small boats and in other ships of the said office and their great boats and while in attendance for their safe keeping, to wit under the said controlment for 365 days in the fifth year of the said King, total £7 12s 1d.

11s 5d must be deducted for 27 days' wages of the same carpenter because he was away from this job for this period because he was busy on his own affairs for so many days.

overall total £7 10d.

Further wages of a caulker.

Also for the wages of the said John Sonday, caulker, at 4d a day, by agreement made with him for the greater benefit of the King while similarly working on and caulking the said royal ship and other great ships and boats of the said office and also while in attendance in the said port for the safe keeping of the same, to wit under the said controlment for 365 days in the fifth year.

total £6 20d.

Wages of the master for the safe keeping of the said ship.

But William Payn, master of the same royal ship was paid nothing during the whole period by the said keeper for his wages, at 6d a day or for his fee of 20 marks a year lately granted to him by royal letters patent, as appears more fully in the preceding account of the said Keeper.

Total nothing.

Total expenses for this ship £98 7s 11d.

[F.35v.] Royal ship called *Trinite Riall*.
Wages of sailors keeping the said Royal ship:

Also for the wages of Richard French and 4 other sailors, his companions, each at 3d a day while on board the same royal ship called *Trinite Riall* in the said port of Hamble in order to look after the same and her great and small boats to wit under the said controlment from 1st September in the fourth year beginning the same day, to the last day of August next following in the said fourth year, finishing the same day, that is to say for 365 days, counting both days, total £22 16s 3d.

15s must be deducted for the wages of two sailors who were absent at various times, during this period, from this safe-keeping – to wit both of them for 30 days because they were busy during this period of absence on their own affairs.

Final total £22 15d.

Further wages of sailors keeping the said ship.

Also for the similar wages of the said Richard French and 4 other sailors his companions each at 3d a day, while on board the same Royal ship called *Trinite Riall* in the said port of Hamble for the similar safe-keeping of the same and also her great and small boats to wit under the said controlment from the said 1st September in the fifth year beginning that same day to the last day of August next following in the said fifth year finishing that day, that is to say for 365 days, counting both days.

total £22 16s 3d.

The wages of the master for this safe-keeping.

But William Yalton, master of the same royal ship called *Trinite Riall,* was paid nothing by the said Keeper either for his wages of 6d a day or for his fee of 10 marks a year lately granted to him during pleasure by Royal letters patent as was more fully recorded in the preceding account of the said keeper.

total nothing.

Total expenses for this ship £44 17s 6d.

[F.36r.] Royal ship called *Jhesus de la Tour*.
Wages of sailors keeping the said royal ship.

Also for the wages of Robert Coole, a sailor called *shipkeper* and 3

other sailors his companions, each at 3d a day while on board the same
royal ship called *Jhesus* in the said port of Hamble in order to look
after the same and her great and small boats to wit under the said
controlment from 1st September in the said fourth year beginning that
day to the last day of August next following in the said fourth year,
finishing that day, that is to say for 365 days, counting both days.

Total £18 5s.

Wages of a caulker.
 Also for the wages of John Eliote, a caulker, at 4d a day, by agreement made with him for the benefit of the king while similarly working and caulking on the same royal ship and her great and small boats
and also while *ransakynge* and *serchynge* and mending various faults
in the same and while in attendance in the same port for this safe-
keeping of the same to wit under the said controlment, for 344 days
within the stated period.

Total 114s 8d.

Further wages of sailors keeping the said ship.
 Also for the wages of the said Robert Coole, a sailor called a *shipkeper* and three other sailors his companions, each at 3d a day while
similarly on board the same royal ship called *Jhesus* in the said port of
Hamble in order to look after the same and also her great and small
boats, to wit under the said controlment from 1st September in the
fifth year beginning that day to the last day of August next following
in the said fifth year finishing that day, to wit for 365 days counting
both days.

Total £18 5d.

Further wages of a caulker.
 Also for the wages of the said John Eliot, caulker, at 4d a day by a
further agreement made with him for the benefit of the king while
working and caulking in the same royal ship, and her great and small
boats, and also while *ransakynge* and *serchynge* and mending various
faults in the same and other royal ships and while similarly in attendance in the said port for this safe-keeping as above, to wit under the
said controlment for 365 days in the fifth year.

Total £6 20d.

[F.36v.] Wages of the master for the safe-keeping of the said ship.
 But John Williams master of the same royal ship received nothing
for his wages due at 6d a day while on board the same royal ship in
the said port of Hamble in order to look after the same during this
accounting period because the said master received as a gift and grant

from the said king by letters patent twenty marks sterling for life as is more plainly set out in the same letters patent.

Total nothing.

Total expenses for this ship £48 6s 4d.

Royal Ship called *Holigost de la Tour*

These are the expenses and various costs incurred by the said keeper of the King's ship for the wages of various workmen working continuously very often by night and by day to bale out water and sand from the said royal ship because of her worn out condition and poor repair and because of certain leaks and splits which suddenly appeared because of the wildness of the wind and storms, and to strike and lower the masts and other rigging and *takelyng* of the same ship and also to construct a certain digging called a *dooke,* newly made so that the said royal ship could be dragged into place in the same *dooke* to be repaired, to wit between 10 April in the said fourth year and 21 June next following, to wit:

Purchases of timber and other necessities for the same.

For 100 small pieces of timber for *shores* then needed bought from the Abbot of Titchfield and used on occasion for the *shorynge* and repair of the said royal ship called *Holigost* after she had been placed in the *dooke* for her repair, gross price for the benefit of the king aforesaid 6s 8d.

Also for 10 pieces of timber similarly bought from the said Abbot of Titchfield for *undir-stokkes* then made and used on the same works for the said royal ship. Gross price for the benefit of the king   6s 8d.

Also for two [F.37r.] pieces of timber bought from Richard Osmond and used for *undir-strokkes* then needed to put underneath the same royal ship in the *dooke* and for her repair, gross price for the benefit of the king   12s.

Also for money paid to the said Richard Osmond, carter, transporting with his cart and horses all this timber, from Titchfield and elsewhere to this same newly-made *dooke* near Southampton, that is receiving for this carriage a gross payment of 5s by agreement made with him for the benefit of the king.   Total 19s. 4d.

Wages of sailors keeping the said royal ship.

Also for the wages of the said Jurden Brownynge a sailor called *shipkeper* and 4 other sailors his companions, each at 3d a day while on board the same royal ship called *Holigost* in the said port of Hamble in order to look after the same and her great and small boats to wit under the said controlment from 1st September in the fourth year of the said King, beginning the same day to 21 June next following, that is to say for 293 days counting the first day and not the last.

Total £18 6s 3d.

Wages of labourers.

Also for the wages of 4 sailor-labourers, that is Richard Bewes, John Garnyssey, Gerald Pon and Philip Payn working and digging to clear and haul out water and sand from the said ship because of her bad repair and certain splits and cracks, which suddenly appeared through various storms and the wildness of the wind, in the said port of Hamble and also working on the making of a *dook* lately ordered for the repair of this ship, moreover also on the *strikynge* and lowering of the masts and other rigging and unloading the stores of the same ship, to wit all under the said controlment, for 34 working days, each at 4d a day, in May and June in the said fourth year.   Total 45s. 4d.

Also for the similar wages of William Osmond, a labourer and 80 other labourers his companions working on digging and making this same *dook* for the said ship to wit between them for a total of 654 working days in the said months in the fourth year, each receiving a daily wage as above,   total £10 18s.

Also for the similar wages of 16 labourers working on the construction of the same digging called a *dooke* being made for the same royal ship, to wit between them for 65 working days under the said controlment in the months of June and July in the said fourth year, each receiving a daily wage as above,   total 21s. 8d.

Overall total £14 5s.

Also for the wages of the said Jurdan Brownynge, a sailor called *shippkeper* at 3d a day while on board the same royal ship after she was lifted on *les stokkes* in the said *dook* to be repaired, supervising the safe keeping of the ship and various equipment of the same and also clearing and hauling out water and sand from the same, very often by night and by day to salvage the same, to wit from the said 21 June in the fourth year of the said King to the last day of August in the fifth year of the same King, finishing that day, that is to say for 436 days counting the last day and not the first.

Total 109s.

[F.37v.] These are the various expenses on food incurred by the said Keeper of the King's ships for the greater benefit of the King in order to save on the wages of various master craftsmen and 80 sailors while they were working for two days within the stated period in the fourth year, on lowering and removing the masts and various other equipment from the said royal ship and also on sailing, towing, guiding and hauling this worn out ship onto *les stokkes* in the same *dook* at the said time, to wit:

Also for 1½ pipes of *sider* bought by the said Keeper of the King's ships from Richard Kempe of Hamble, and used during the works mentioned above. Gross price 8s.

Also for 4 dozen loaves bought from Robert Baker of Southampton and used on the works of this royal ship, price 12d a dozen, total 4s.

Also for various quantities of fish bought from various Southampton men and used similarly in these works, to wit guiding and sailing this royal ship onto *les stokkes* and dismantling the masts and other equipment from this royal ship as mentioned before, within the same period, total 4s 9d.

Also for 6 lb candles bought from William Here and used in ransacking and *serchynge* various splits and cracks that must be repaired in the same and also, at night time, in hauling out and clearing water and sand from the same royal ship within the same period so that she might be repaired, price per pound 1½d. Total 9d.

Overall total 17s 6d.

Total expenses for this royal ship £39 17s 1d.

Total expenses for the four preceding ships £231 8s 9d.

Royal ballinger called *Petit Jhesus de la Tour*

Purchase of timber and boards for the same.

Also for 4 pieces of timber bought from the Abbot of Titchfield and used in the repair of the same royal ballinger called *Jhesus* otherwise called the *Graunt Folower* of the same ship. gross price 3s 4d.

Also for 60 pieces of timber similarly bought from the said Abbot of Titchfield used in the similar repair of the same ballinger gross price, for the benefit of the King, 5s.

Also for 2 pieces of timber bought from Richard Osmond for *walees* then made for and used in the repair of this same ballinger, price 16d.

Also for a certain piece [F.38r.] of timber bought from Richard Screveyner for a certain *bitbeme* then needed for the same ballinger and used in her repair. Price 4d.

Also for 1 piece of timber similarly bought from John Austeyn for a certain *stempne pece* then made and used for the repair of the same ballinger, price 11d.

Also for 50 boards called *waynscott* bought from William Nicholl of Southampton and used in the repair of the same ballinger, price 16s 8d.

Also for 100 boards called *waynscott* similarly bought from John Emory and used in the work on this same ballinger, price 40s.

Also for 22 sawn boards similarly bought from William Osmond and used in the repair and *celynge* of the same ballinger, price 3s 5d.

Also for 15 boards called *waynscott* bought from the said William

Nicholl and used in the repair of the same ballinger, gross price for the benefit of the king 6s 3d.

Also for 21 sawn boards bought from the said John Carpenter and used in the repair of the said royal ballinger, gross price 5s 3d.

Also for 2 large boards from Prussia called *deles* bought from the said William Nicholl and used in the repair of the same ballinger, gross price 3s.

Also for 1 large piece of timber bought from the said John Carpenter and used in the repair of the said royal ballinger, price 20d.

Also for 6 pieces of timber bought on another occasion from the Abbot of Titchfield and used on the repair of the same ballinger, gross price 2s.

Total £4 9s 10d.

Smith's work with nails and other pieces of ironwork.

Also for money paid to Richard Marcus, smith, for 3 cwt 18 lb of iron made into *rooff naill, boltes, spikes* and various other items of ironwork, bought for and used for the works on and repair of the same royal ballinger, at a price per cwt worked (including the iron) of 14s with additions at 1½d per lb. Total 44s 3d.

Also for money paid to Richard Burgeys, smith of Southampton for working 1 cwt 24 lb of iron into *clenchnaill* and various other items of ironwork bought from him and used on the same repair of the same royal ballinger at a price per cwt so worked up including the iron of 16s 4d, extra pounds at 1¾d. Total 19s 10d.

Also for money paid to the said Richard Marcus for his work on *sharpynge* old nails coming previously from the same ballinger and used in the repair of the said royal ballinger 6d.

Also for 2½ cwt nails bought from the said Richard, and used in the repair of the same royal ballinger, price per cwt 6d, total 15d.

Also for 5 cwt nails called *calfatenaill* bought from the said Richard Burgeys and used on the [F.38v.] repair of the same royal ballinger, price per cwt 8d, total 35s 4d.

Also for 1 mwt nails called *sporkatenaill* bought from the said Richard Burgeys and used in the repair of the same ballinger, gross price for the benefit of the king 3s 4d.

Also for various items of ironwork bought from the said Richard Burgeys and used on the repair *del rothir* (of the rudder) of the same ballinger, gross price by agreement made with him, 3s 4d.

Also for 2 cwt nails called *calfatenaill* bought from the said Richard and used in working on and repairing the *calfatynge* of the same ballinger, price per cwt 8d, total 16d.

Also for 4 cwt nails called *hacchnaill* similarly bought from the said

Richard Burgeys and used in the work on and repair of the *hacches* of the same ballinger, price per cwt 6d, total 2s.

Also for money paid to Richard Marcus for 57 lb of iron worked into *boltes, cheynes* and various other items of ironwork bought from Richard himself and used on the repair of the same ballinger, price per lb 1½d, total 7s 1½d.

Also for 1 cwt nails price 8d, and for 2 cwt nails, price per cwt 6d, total 12d, similarly bought from the said Richard Burgeys and used on the repair of the same royal ballinger, total 20d.

Overall total £3 7s 11d.

Purchase of necessities for the same royal ballinger.

Also for 3 large barrels of pitch bought from William Nicholl of Southampton and used in the *picchynge*, fitting out and repair of the same royal ballinger called *Petit Jhesus*, price a barrel 6s 8d.

Total 20s.

Also for 4 pieces of canvas called *Olonnes* [207] bought from William Payn of Southampton and used in making a certain sail and 1 *bonnett* newly ordered for the same royal ballinger, gross price for the benefit of the king   £4 6s 8d.

Also for 9 ells of *fyn* canvas similarly bought from the said William and used in the work on the same sail for the same royal ballinger, price 4s 6d.

Also for 3 small ropes called hawsers bought from the said William Nicholl and used for *bolt ropes* and other necessities in the making of the said sail and also for 3 *copul hedropes* weighing in all 2 cwt 26 lb, price per cwt 13s 4d, total 29s 8½d.

Also for 2 *pulleys*, price 12d and for 3 *pulleys* price 18d and for 11 *pulleys* price 22d and for a certain *pomp boxe* price 3d bought from John Bollour of Southampton and used and put in position during the repair and fitting out of the same royal ballinger, total 4s 7d.

Also for a certain brazen cauldron called *pich ketyll* similarly bought from Peter James of Southampton for the same royal ballinger, price 6s 8d.

Also for 36 oars bought from the said John Bollour to be used in the same royal ballinger, gross price for the greater benefit of the King, 60s.

Also for 1 cwt 3 lb of wax similarly bought from Adam Boucher of Southampton and used in *talwynge* and fitting out of the same royal ballinger price [F.39r.] 8s.

Also for 52 lb of *rosyn* similarly bought from Walter Fettepase of Southampton and used in the *rosenynge* and fitting out of the same royal ballinger, gross price 2s 1d.

Also for 1 axe similarly bought for the same royal ballinger, price 7d.

Also for 1 pair of *garnett* similarly bought from the said Richard

Marcus and used in the making of *bredecotes* in the same royal ballinger, price 4d.

Also for 2 *watir scopes* bought and used for throwing water and sand out of the said royal ballinger, price 4d.

Also for 17 ells of canvas bought from William Nicholl and used to make and mend the sail and *bonnetts* of the same ballinger, price an ell 6d, total 8s 6d.

Also for 2 lanterns bought for the same royal ballinger, price 12d.

Also for a certain parcel of fuel similarly bought for *bremynge* then thought necessary and used in *rosenynge, picchynge* and *talwynge* the said ballinger, price 12d.

Also for 100 needles called *sailneld* bought from William Harry and used in the making of the said sail and bonnetts of the same ballinger, price 6d.

Also for a certain *saillboxe* similarly bought for the same ballinger because of the great care taken with her, price 8d.

Also for 1 *dioll* similarly bought for the same royal ballinger, price 8d.

Also for 5 *skayn* of thread similarly bought from Walter Fettepase and used in the making of the same sail and bonnetts, gross price for the benefit of the King, 2s 1½d.

Also for 6 small cords called *lyn* similarly bought from the said William Nicholl and used in the making of the said sail and bonnetts, gross price 6s 9d.

Also for 2 lbs of *fillace* bought from Peter Jamys and used in the making of the said sail and bonnetts, price 8d.

Also for 4 pieces of *stroppes* bought and used in the similar making of the same sail and bonnetts, price 8d.

Also for 2 small ropes called hawsers of black twine bought from the said William Nicholl for *stetying* then made for the same royal ballinger weighing 73 lb, gross price for the benefit of the King, 8s 3d.

Also for 2 virges of cloth called *saye* bought and used for making a certain *fane-cloth* for the same royal ballinger, price 6d.

Total £12 14s 9¼d.

Wages of carpenters.

Also for the wages of Thomas Came, a master carpenter called *shipwright* working on the said ballinger called *Petit Jhesus* which was to be repaired at Southampton, that is to say in all for 37 working days to wit between 10 April in the fifth year of the said King and 22 June next following, receiving 8d a day, total 24s 8d.

Also for the wages of 5 carpenters, *berders,* to wit William Piers for 15 working days, [F.39v.] Thomas Meleyn for 6 working days, Henry

Kegwyn for 22 working days, Richard Rylford for 19 working days and Robert Gower for 22 working days, that is to say in all between them for 85 working days within the same period, working on the same repairs for the ballinger, each receiving 6d a day, total 42s 6d.

Also for the wages of 3 carpenters called *clenchers,* to wit Roger Payn, William Danyell and Maurice Robert, each for 17½ working days between the said 10 April in the said fourth year and 22 June next following, each of them receiving 5d a day, similarly working on the repair of the same royal ballinger, total 21s 10½d.

Also for the wages of Thomas Pyllet, a carpenter called a *clencher* for 8 working days similarly receiving 5d a day, total 3s 4d. and for the wages of 4 carpenters called *holders*, to wit John Moynet for 10 working days, receiving 4d a day, total 3s 4d, Henry Stephen, John Collyn both for 19 working days, daily rate as above, total 12s 8d, and John Philippe for 16 working days, daily rate as above, total 5s 4d. All employed on the works for the same royal ballinger between 10 April in the said fourth year and the said 22 June next following, overall total 24s 8d.

Also for the wages of 4 carpenters called *berders*, to wit John Stephen, William Trouche both for 12 working days, at 6d a day, Total 12s. Richard Weste for 10½ working days, daily rate as above, total 5s 3d, and John Bisshope for 8 working days, daily rate as above, total 4s, to wit all employed on the works for the same ballinger within the stated period, overall total 21s 3d.

Also for the wages for 4 more carpenters called *clenchers*, to wit David Swayn for 12 working days, at 5d a day, total 5s. John Rede and William Monford, both for 11½ working days, daily rate as above, total 9s 7d, and Nicholas Stacy for 4½ working days, daily rate as above, total 22d, to wit all employed on the works for the said ballinger within the stated period, overall total 16s 5½d.

Also for the wages of 4 carpenters called *holders* on another occasion, to wit Thomas Went for 6 working days, at 4d a day, total 2s; John Rede and Thomas Blerake both for 12 working days, daily rate as above, total 8s; Henry Stephen for 9½ working days, daily rate as above, total 3s 2d, to wit all employed similarly on the works of the said royal ballinger, that is to say between the said 10 April in the said fourth year and 22 June next following under the controlment aforesaid, overall total 13s 2d.

Also for the wages of three carpenters called *berders*, to wit Richard Rilfford for 5½ working days at 6d a day, total 2s 9d and Thomas Melayn and William Barre both for 7 working days, at 6d a day, total 7s and John Hede and David [F.40r.] Swayn, *clenchers* both for 5½ working days, at 5d a day, total 4s 7d, and Robert Mildewe for 6 working days, at 4d a day, total 2s, to wit all employed on the works of

the same royal ballinger during the stated period under the controlment of the said controller, overall total 16s 4d,

Final total £9 0s 9d.

Wages of sawyers.

Also for the wages of 4 sawyers, to wit Henry Ducheman and
Thomas Fleynghatte both for 3½ working days, at 6d a day, total 3s 6d,
and John Spenser and Robert Wynboll working on another occasion
both for 4 working days, both on the same daily rate as above, total
4s, to wit all employed on sawing timber, planks, and boards for the
same works for the same royal ballinger within the stated period of
her repair as mentioned above.

Overall total 7s 6d.

Wages of the master and mariners for *riggynge* the same.

Also for the wages of John Robyn, the master of the same royal
ballinger called *Petit Jhesus* at 6d a day, and 7 sailors each at 3d a day
while on board working on the *riggynge* of the same ballinger in the
port of Southampton after the said ballinger had been launched from
le dooke after her repair, and on her victualling and fitting out because
of a voyage to be made on the advice and order of the Great Council
to the sea coast of Spayn and Brittany and elsewhere to keep the seas;
also they were working in the same to raise the mast and secure the
shroude to wit from the said 22 June in the said fifth year to 2 July
next following, that is to say for 10 days, counting the last day and not
the first, total 22s 6d.

Deductions must be made from the above sum for the advantage and
benefit of the King for the purchase and provision of victuals during
the period of this *rigg*, bought by the bursar of the same ballinger for
the same master and mariners on several occasions, to wit, bread, ale,
butter, beef, mutton and salt and fresh fish and various other foodstuffs,
total 8s 2½d.

Final total 14s 3½d.

[F.40v.] Wages of the master and mariners including victuals during the
keeping of the seas.

Also for the wages of the said master and 31 mariners, each at 3d a
day, lately retained to set forth in the said royal ballinger on a similar
voyage during the war of the said King to be made towards the said
coasts of Spayn, Brittany and elsewhere to keep the seas, as mentioned
above. To wit under this controlment from the said 2 July in the said
fifth year, on which day they first sailed from Southampton to 3
October next following, on which day they returned to the said port

and the said master and mariners were then paid off for this voyage, to wit the outward voyage, return voyage and any delay totalled 93 days, counting the last day and not the first, total £37 3s.

Deductions must then be made for the advantage and benefit of the King, for the provision and purchase of victuals for the said war voyage made by the bursar of the same ballinger during the stated period on various occasions for the same master and mariners to wit, bread, ale, butter, beef, mutton and salt and fresh fish and various other food-stuffs, total £15 12s 4½d.

Final total £21 11s 7d.

Total expenses for this royal ballinger £51 6s 10¾d.

Also for money paid to Richard Bokeland of London in partial pay-ment of £148 8s 11d recorded on 2 tallies drawn on the Receipt of the Exchequer of King Henry V, dated 29 July in the tenth year of the same late King, levied on John Butler and John Norton, lately collec-tors of the subsidy on wools in the port of London, and owed to the said Richard to pay for various victuals and stores bought for the household of the said late King, to wit one of the said tallies for £110 9s 9d was returned to the Receipt of the Exchequer to be can-celled with this account by direction of the said royal writ under the Privy Seal dated 3 July in the first year, mentioned above under foreign receipts.

£110 9s 9d.

Total £110 9s 9d.

[F.41r.]

Also for money owed to the said William Soper, the accountant, for cables, ropes and other necessities used in the making and repair of various royal ships belonging to the said office, together with the wages and emoluments of sailors from the time of William Catton lately Keeper of the royal ships by an account made with him on 22 January in the eighth year of King Henry V, lately King of England, recorded in a list of debts presented with these particulars (as also recorded in William Catton's account for the period from 21 March in the fourth year of the said late King to 7 February in the seventh year of the same late King, enrolled on the third roll of foreign accounts of King Henry VI) where he was owed £127 5s 6d of the total sum of £230 15s 10d owed to sundry creditors; the debt is also recorded in the account of William Catton enrolled on the third roll of the King's Remembrancer, by direction of a royal writ under the Privy Seal dated 26th June in the eighth year of the said present King directed to the Treasurer and Barons of the Exchequer and enrolled among the memoranda of the eighth year among the writs directed to the Barons during Trinity Term.

£127 5s 7d.

Also [208] for money owed to the same William Soper, the accountant, from the balance due on his account of the third year of King Henry V lately King of England, for the building of a certain royal ship called the *Holigost of Southampton*, at Southampton, and the repair of a certain ship called *Gabriell* on the order of the said late King, as is recorded in the account of the said William Soper, the accountant, for the said third year for this building and repair in his account on the fifth roll (i.e. account roll E) of King Henry VI: Total £73 13s 9¼d included on the said royal writ mentioned in the preceding particulars.

Total £73 13s 9¼d.

Also[209] for money paid to the said Nicholas Banastre, the controller of the said office as a reward for his work for the same office and also for arranging the sale of various royal ships, carracks and other vessels at a daily rate of 6d to wit from 5 March in the first year of the said King Henry VI to the last day of August in the fifth year of the same Lord King, finishing on that day, that is to say for 4 years and 179 days within the period of this account.

Total £40 19s 6d.

Overall total of expenses and allowances £1,413 13s 9d.
Of this, £616 14s 1¾d is owing.[210]

THE INVENTORY

35. Bulk purchases made during the period of this account.
36. Royal ship called *Gracedewe*.
37. Ship called *Holigoste*.
38. Ship called *Jhesus*.
39. Ship called *Trinite Riall*.
40. Items in store for this office.
41. Royal ballinger called *Petit Jhesus*.

[F.42r.] The particulars of account of William Soper, keeper and governor of the ships of the said lord King Henry VI drawn up by authority of the said writ under the privy seal dated 2 December, as mentioned before, and also the said letters patent under the Great Seal of England dated 5 March in the first year of the said Lord King and also the privy seal letters of the king dated and enrolled as noted above in the preamble of this account; concerning all manner of equipment, stores and other things whatsoever in the storehouse in London, or Southampton, or elsewhere in hand from previous accounts of the said keeper, belonging to the said office; moreover also concerning all manner of ships, barges, ballingers and boats and other vessels whatsoever in the possession of the office, together with their equipment and also concerning various ships, carracks, barges and ballingers and other vessels whatsoever lately sold together with their equipment by the order and advice of the King's Great Council, within the accounting period for the benefit of the King by the said keeper under the said controlment; or hired out for a certain time; or captured and robbed at sea, or as a gift, sold, provided or given by the King to any person.

And also concerning various equipment and stores and other necessities whatsoever bought or provided by the said keeper or his deputy for the said office during the said period and similarly concerning all manner of equipment and stores used, broken or damaged or provided or lost at sea in storms and sunk intended for the safe-keeping, fitting-out or defence of the same ships and vessels, between the last day of August in the tenth year of the Lord Henry V lately King of England who died on that day and the last day of August in the fifth year of the present King finishing on that day.

1.[212] Various goods and equipment received, in the storehouse in hand from previous accounts of the said keeper: that is to say:

Iron *gaddes* for *le topp* from the royal ship *Trinitee Riall*	15
A large anchor called Marie from the same ship *Trinite Riall*	1
Guns in bad condition, without chambers, from *le storehouse* in London	2

[F.42v.] 2. Various foreign goods received in store in London in hand from previous accounts of the said keeper: that is to say:

Pieces of cork lately received from Richard Buckland without
an indenture to make *boyes* for the office of the king's ships.   40
Small *coffres* of *quarells* for the royal carracks, from the store
at Southampton   41

The various items listed below from the foreign goods were used, broken or damaged in various ships, carracks and other royal vessels on various occasions in the maintenance, safe-keeping and defence of the same between the last day of August in the tenth year of the Lord Henry V, lately king of England who died that day and the last day of August in the fifth year of the present king, finishing on that day. That is to say:

[F.43r.] Items used:

Pieces of cork lately received from Richard Buckland without an
indenture to make *boyes* for the same office of the king's ships   29
These were delivered to make 4 *boyes* for the safe-keeping and
fitting out of the royal ships noted below: 2 for the ship
Graunt Marie: 2 for the royal ship called *Jhesus*, (see under
these ships).[213]
Small *coffres* of *quarrells* for the royal carracks from the
store at Southampton   2
These were delivered, shot off or damaged to provide for the safe
keeping and defence of the royal ships noted below:
in a certain royal barge called *Valentyn* and in the royal ship
called *Holigost of Spain* and various other vessels belonging
to the same office while sailing to Flanders and Calais during
the accounting period.

3. Various goods and equipment received from bulk purchases, in hand from earlier accounts of the same keeper: that is to say:

Ironwork called *cabilhokes* for making cables and ropes
for the office of the king's ships   6 no weight given
Large iron chains containing 80 links ordered to chain off
the port of Hamble 2 weighing together 9 mwt 6 cwt 1 qua 20 lb.[214]
Large oars, coming from a purchase lately made from Richard
Buckland intended for various ballingers, each 24ft. long   102
(50 for royal ballinger called *George*, 49 for royal ballinger
called *Ane*. 3 for ballinger called *Gabriell Harflewe de la Tour*).
Cable from bulk purchases   1: weighing 1 mwt 2 cwt 3 qua. 26 lb.
Oars   1
Towe for caulking the royal ships and carracks   6 cwt 1 qua. 22 lb.

[F.43v.] Various goods and equipment listed below from these bulk purchases in hand from earlier accounts, were used, broken or damaged in various ships and other royal vessels on various occasions for their safe-keeping between the said last day of August in the tenth year of the said late king who died that day and the last day of August in the fifth year of the present King, finishing on that day: that is to say:

Items used.

Ironwork called *cabilhokes* for making cables and ropes for the same office of the king's ships   1 no weight given.

Large oars from a certain purchase lately made from Richard Buckland for various ballingers, each 24 ft. long   10

(that is, in the royal ballinger called *George*, 4, royal ballinger called *Ane*, 3, royal ballinger called *Gabriell Harflewe*, 3.)

Cable from bulk purchases in earlier years.

                                1 weighing 1 mwt 2 cwt 3 qua 26 lb.

Oars   1 delivered and used for the benefit of the king in the safe keeping and repair of the great ship of the said Lord King called *Gracedieu de la Tour*, on various occasions during the accounting period.

Towe for caulking the ships and carracks of the Lord King   6 cwt 1 qua 22 lb

Delivered and used, for the benefit of the King, for the fitting out and caulking of the royal ship called *Graunt Marie* while she was being rebuilt and also for the repair of the royal ships called *Jhesus*, and *Faucon* and *Valentyn* on various occasions, during the accounting period.

[F.44r.] 4. Equipment of the ship called *La Galley*.

Various goods and equipment received, formerly belonging to the ship called *La Galley* and in hand from earlier accounts; that is to say:

Iron *grapnell*   1

Oars in bad repair in the storehouse for the royal *Galley*   4

[F.44v.] 5. Royal carrack called *George*.

Royal carrack called *George de la Tour* received, with various equipment and goods in hand from earlier accounts, that is to say:

Topp   1
Mast   1
Bowspret   1
Parrel for the mast   1
Pairs of *hedropes*   2
Pendantz for *les pollances*   2
Sail   1

(that is 1 body with 1 *bonnett*, for the same carrack).

Anchors for the same	4
Mesan maste	1
sailyard for the same *mesan*	1
Small sail called *mesan*	1
Bytakyll	1
Cannons	3 with 6 chambers
Peyntynge hokes for the anchor	2
Small boat called *cooke*	1
Iron chains for *le shrowde*	2 (no weight given)
Hawsers of black yarn from Lynn[215] to be used for *pollancre* ropes	3 (weighing 7 cwt 1 qua)
Hawser for *upties* of white yarn from Lynn for the same carrack	2 (weighing 8 cwt 1 qua)
Hawsers of the same yarn to be used for a *forstey*	1 (weighing 5 cwt 7 lb)
Hawsers for *upties* for *le mesane*	1 (weighing 1 cwt 14 lb)
Hawsers for *hedropes* for the same *mesan*	1 (weighing ½ cwt 21 lb)
Bonnett newly made from a mended sail of the said royal carrack	1 (containing 450 ells of canvas from Vitré)
Pulleys for the same carrack	15
Large *pulleys*	1
Cable for *boyropes*	1 (weighing 3 cwt 3 qua 4 lb)
Hawser for *bowlyn*	1 (weighing 4½ cwt 14 lb)
Hawser for *haliers*	1 (weighing 1 cwt 10 lb)
[F.45r.] Great boat called *bark*	1
Great anchor for the same carrack	1
Scalynge ladders with 6 iron *hokes* for the same	2
Outside receipts: that is to say:	
Anchor coming from the royal carrack called *Marie Hampton*	1
Purchases in hand from earlier accounts, that is to say:	
Hawsers of white yarn from Holland for *handropes* and *botropes* (weighing 2½ cwt 10 lb)	2
Large cables in bad repair	2
Hawser for using for *boiropes* (inclusive weight for these 2 items 2 mwt 7 cwt 3 qua 14 lb)	1
Bedewe	1
Watirscopes	3
Brass pots for the same carrack	2
Large cables of white yarn from Bridport (weighing 1 mwt 8½ cwt 7 lb)	2
Small rope of the same yarn to be used for *cranelynes* (weighing ½ cwt 21 lb)	1

Hawser of the same yarn to be used for *yardropes* and *hoke ropes*   1
(weighing 3 qua 12 lb)

Hawsers of Dutch yarn for *lyfftyng* and *stetynges* for the same carrack   3
(weighing together 5 cwt 7 lb)

Large cable of *fyn* white yarn from Bordeaux   1
(weighing 1 mwt 4 cwt)

Hawser to be used for *shetes*   1
(weighing 15 cwt 3 qua 15 lb)

Hawser to be made into *hedropes* for *le mesan*   1
(weighing 1 cwt 1 qua)

Oars for the same carrack	14
New *pulleys* for the same carrack	6
Lanterns for the same carrack	4
A certain *pompe* for the same	1
Axe for the same	1
A certain *nawger* for the same	1
Large oars for the same	8
[F.45v.] Shovels, another lot, for the same	6
A certain *sondyngled*	1
A certain piece of ironwork called a *dregge*	1

Foreign receipts, part of the parcel of 170 pieces of cork from the store house for making *boyes* for the safe keeping of this carrack, that is to say:

Boyes for the same carrack   2

Foreign receipts lately coming from the royal ship *Nicholas* for the safe-keeping of this carrack, that is to say:

Cable of Dutch yarn	1 (weighing 7½ cwt 3 lb)
Brass pot	1
Cable from store of Lynn yarn	1
Hausers of the same yarn	3

Foreign receipts during the accounting period coming from the carrack *Peter* for the safe-keeping of this carrack, that is to say:

Hawser for a *forstey*	1 (weighing 8½ cwt)
Hawser for *hedropes*	1 (weighing 2 cwt 3 qua 6 lb)
Hawser in bad condition for a *truss*	1 (weighing 1 cwt 3 qua 21 lb)
Rope for *takkes*	1 (weighing 1 cwt)

In the said royal carrack called *George*, the goods and equipment listed below were used up or broken or damaged in the maintenance, fitting out and safe-keeping of the same, on various occasions between the last day of August in the tenth year of the said late king who died that day and 12 August in the first year of the present king, that is to say:

Items used.

Pair of *hedropes*	1
Pendants for *les pollances*	1
Peyntynghokes for the anchor	1

Hawser of black yarn from Lynn to be used for
pollancre ropes   1 (weighing 2 cwt 14 lb)
Hawser for *hedropes* for the same *mesan*
       1 (weighing ½ cwt 21 lb)

[F.46r.] *Pulleys* for the same carrack   2
Cable for *boiropes*   1 (weighing 3 cwt 3 qua 4 lb)

Purchases from previous years, that is to say:

Hawser of white Dutch yarn for *handropes* and
botropes   1 (weighing 1 cwt 1 qua 4 lb)
Large cable in bad condition   1 (weighing 1 mwt 1 cwt 3 qua 10 lb)
Watirscoupes   1
Hawser of Dutch yarn for *lyfftynges* and *stetyng* for the
same carrack   1 (weighing 1½ cwt 5 lb)

Oars for the same carrack	4
Lantern for the same carrack	1
Large oars for the same carrack	2
Shovels, another parcel, for the same	2

Foreign receipts during the accounting period lately coming from the
carrack called *Peter* for the safe-keeping of this carrack, that is to say:

Hawser in bad condition for a *truss*   1 weighing 1 cwt 3 qua 21 lb)
Rope called *takkes*   1 (weighing 1 cwt)

The said keeper of the king's ships is not responsible for the said
royal carrack called *George* and her various equipment and goods
from 11 August in the third year of the present king because the said
keeper with the agreement and on the order of the King's Great Council
handed over the said carrack and her equipment under the said
controlment, on the said 10 August in the first year of the present
king, to Antony Hongaris, Prancato Justinian and Nicholas Justinian
for them to control for a period laid down in a certain indenture and
then when they should have restored the said carrack and her equipment to the service of the king on the above said 11 August in the
third year of this king they themselves paid a certain sum of money
to the king for this carrack and her equipment for which the said
keeper of the king's ships accounts above among the foreign receipts
of this account.

[F.47v.] 6. Royal ballinger called *George de la Tour*.
Receipt of the royal ballinger called *George* with various equipment
and goods, in hand from previous accounts during the tenure of the
said keeper of the king's ships, that is to say:

Anchors for the same ballinger   3
Ropes called hawsers of white yarn for making
five pair of *hedropes* with one *forestey,*
4 *bacsteyes* and 2 upties   5 weighing all together 1 mwt 2 cwt
                                  3 qua. 13 lb)
Ropes called hawsers of the same yarn for making
yardropes, and *priall ropes*   2 (weighing together 1 cwt 3 qua 5 lb)
Sailyerd   1
Bowspret   1
Pulleys   8
Leads called *sondyngledes*   2
Sail in bad condition called *mesan*   1
                                  (containing 72 ells of canvas of Vitré)

Pulleys   5
Topp castell   1
Small boat   1
Mast parraill   1
Hawser for *pollancr ropes*   1 (weighing 1 cwt 1 qua 16 lb)
Small rope called *sondynglyn*   1 (no weight)
Cables for the same ballinger   2 (weighing together 1 mwt 2 cwt 7 lb)
Bonnett for the same.   1 (containing 80 ells of canvas)
Truss parraill for the same   1
Sondynglyn   1 (no weight gíven)
Purchases from previous years, that is to say:
Cables of Dutch yarn   2 (weighing 7 cwt 1 qua 18 lb)
Hawsers for *shetes* and *boyropes*
                                  2 (weighing 3 cwt 3 qua 21 lb)
Hawsers for *stetyng* and *bowlyn*
                                  2 (weighing 2½ cwt 14 lb)
Bonnett for the sail of the same ballinger
                                  1 (containing 98 ells of canvas)
Oars for the same ballinger   17
A certain *pompe f*or the same ballinger   1
Foreign receipts lately coming from the ship called *Petit Trinity* for
the safekeeping of this ballinger, that is to say:
Hawsers for *warpropes*   2 (weighing 7 cwt 14 lb)
Sail   1 (that is 1 body of the sail with 2 *bonnetts*)

[F.48r.] The following goods and equipment were used up, broken or
damaged in the said royal ballinger called *George* in her maintenance
and safe-keeping on various occasions between the last day of August
in the tenth year of the said Lord Henry V lately king of England who
died that day and the last day of August in the first year of the present
king finishing on that day, that is to say:

Items used.
Ropes called hawsers of white yarn to be used for 5 pairs *hedropes*
with 1 *forestey* 4 *bacstyes* and 2 *upties*
                            2 (weighing together 3 cwt 1 qua 3 lb)
Rope called hawser of the same yarn to be used for *yerdropes*
and *priallropes*   1 (weighing 3 qua 2 lb)
Pulleys   2
Small rope called *sondynglyn* 1 (no weight given)
Cable for the same ballinger   1 (weighing 6 cwt 3 lb)
Purchases from previous years, that is to say:
Hawser for *shetes* and *boyropes*
                            1 (weighing 1½ cwt 14 lb)
Hawser for making *stetynges* and *bowlynes*.
                            1 (weighing 1 cwt 12 lb)
Oars for the same ballinger   4
Foreign receipts coming from the royal ship called *Petit Trinite* for the
safe keeping of the same ballinger, that is to say:
Hawser for *warpropes*   1 (weighing 3½ cwt 10 lb)
Bonnett for the same ballinger 1 (containing 80 ells of canvas)
Trussell parraill for the same
ballinger   1
Sondynglyn   1 (no weight given)
The said keeper of the king's ships is not responsible for the said
royal ballinger called *George* with her various equipment and goods
after the above last day of August in the first year of the present king,
finishing on that day. On that day the same ballinger and her goods
was sold, by the said keeper of the ships, for the benefit of the king
under the said controlment, to William Bentley of Plymouth for a
certain sum of money, as ordered by the King's Great Council and by
royal letters under the Privy Seal noted more fully in the preamble of
this account. The keeper accounts for the money assigned to the royal
service above among the foreign receipts of this account.

[F.49r.] 7. Equipment of the royal ship called *Philippe*.
Receipt of various goods and equipment formerly belonging to the
royal ship called *Philippe* in hand from earlier accounts, that is to say:
Pairs of *hedropes*, in bad condition, for the same   3
Anchor   1 (that is on the ship called *Nicholas*)
Axe   1
[F.49v.] Various goods and equipment which formerly belonged to
the said ship called *Philippe* were handed over to and used in various
ships and other royal vessels on various occasions for the benefit of
the king, for the maintenance and safe-keeping of the same between
the said last day of August in the tenth year of the said late king who

died that day and the last day of August in the fifth year, finishing that day, that is to say:

Items used or handed over:

Pair of *hedropes* in bad repair for the same office   1

(Handed over by the said keeper of the king's ships for the benefit of the said king for the maintenance and safe keeping of the royal barge called *Valentyn* within the accounting period),

Axe   1

(Handed over by the said keeper of the king's ships for the benefit of the king for the maintenance and safe keeping of a certain ship called *Trinite Riall* within the accounting period)

[F.50r.] 8. Royal ship called *Thomas de la Tour*

Receipt of the royal ship called *Thomas* with various equipment and goods in hand from previous accounts during the tenure of the said keeper, that is to say:

Mast in bad condition	1
Parrel for the mast	1
Anchor	1
Iron guns	4 that is each with 3 chambers
Old *basnetts*	15 with 11 *ventaills*
Close brestes in poor condition	4
Vambraces in poor condition	2
Rer braces in poor condition	5
Hauberks	4
Hammers	3
Dartes	3 dozen
Bows	4
Sheaves of arrows	6
Pollaxes	4
Shields in poor condition	2
Anchor	1
Sail	1 that is 1 body with 2 bonetts
Pulleys for *le shrowde*	3
Cable of Dutch yarn	1 (weighing 8½ cwt 1 qua)
Hedropes in bad condition	6
Hawser of white yarn for *upties*	1 (weighing 4 cwt 3 qua 8 lb)
Cable of white yarn	1 (weighing 6½ cwt 24 lb)
Hawser of the same yarn for making *bowlynes*	
	1 (weighing 1 cwt 1 qua 22 lb)
Hawser of the same yarn for making *truss*	
	1 (weighing 1½ cwt 17 lb)
Pulleys	2

Foreign receipts lately coming from the ship called *Phelippe* for the safe-keeping of this ship, that is to say:

Takkes	2
Stetynges	2
Yerderopes	1 (weighing 3 qua)

[F.50v.] Foreign receipts, that is to say:

Lanterns lately belonging to the office of the king's ships	6

Foreign receipts lately coming from the royal ship called *Katerine* for the safe-keeping of this ship, that is to say:

Anchors	2
Sondyng led	2
Brass cannon	2
Axes	2
Touches of iron for the cannon	3
Grapnell	1 with an iron chain for the same

Foreign receipts lately coming from the ship called *Nicholas* for the safe-keeping of this ship, that is to say:

Hawser of black yarn for making *upties*	
	1 (weighing 5 cwt 2 qua 14 lb)
Hawser for a *forstey*	1 (weighing 6 cwt 1 qua)

Foreign receipts lately coming from the royal ship called *Rodcogge* for the safe-keeping of this ship, that is to say:

Anchors	2
Sondyngledes	1
Cannon in bad condition	1
Iron chains for the *hedropes*	2
Anchor for the boat	1

Purchases from previous years, that is to say:

Large mast for the same ship	1
A certain spar called a *sailyerd*	1
small boat called *cook*	1
Brass pot	1
Brass measure	1
Brass bell to mark the watches of the sailors in the same	1
Iron candlesticks	4
Large *bedewe*	1
Axe	1
Large *compasses*	1
Large shovels	9
Pulleys	12
[F.51r.] A certain *firepan*	1
Large pulleys	2
Tin measure for the same ship	1

Large *fan*	1
Bonnett newly made	1 containing 133 ells of canvas
A certain hawser of Bordeaux yarn for using for *wareshetes*	
for the same	1 (weighing 3 cwt 3 qua 21 lb)
Cables of the same Dutch yarn	2 (weighing 1 mwt 3 cwt 16 lb)
Oars for the same	5
A certain *pompe* for the same ship	1
Hawsers of black Bridporte yarn for *stetynges* and *truss*	
	2 (weighing 1½ cwt 2 lb.)
A certain rope called *bast*	1 (no weight given)

Foreign receipts lately coming from the artillery stores in the Tower for the safe-keeping of this ship in the accounting period, that is to say:

Pollaxes	3
Bows	4
Sheaves of arrows	5

The following goods and equipment were used up, broken or damaged in the said royal ship called *Thomas* in her maintenance and safe-keeping on various occasions, that is to say between 4 December in the first year of the present king and 5 December next following in the second year of the same king, that is to say:

Items used:

Mast in bad condition   1, (sold for the benefit of the king by the said keeper of the king's ships because of the bad condition of the mast 28 July in the second year of the present king for a certain sum of money for which he accounts above among the foreign receipts of this account).

Dartes	1 dozen
Bows	2
Sheaves of arrows	1
Shields in bad condition	2
Cable of Dutch yarn	1 (weighing 8½ cwt 1 qua.)
[F.51v.] *Hedropes* in bad condition	1
Hawser of white yarn for *upties*	1 (weighing 4 cwt 4 qua 8 lb)
Hawser of the same yarn for *truss*	1 (weighing 1½ cwt 17 lb.)

Foreign receipts, that is to say:

Lanterns lately belonging to the office of the king's ships	2

Foreign receipts lately coming from the ship called *Katerine* for the safe-keeping of this ship, that is to say:

Axe	1
Touches of iron for cannon	1

Purchases from previous years, that is to say:

Iron candlestick	1
Large *bedewe*	1
Large shovels	5

Pulleys	2
Large *fan*	1
Oars for the same ship	1

The said keeper of the king's ships has no responsibility for the said royal ship called *Thomas* with her goods and equipment from the abovesaid 5 September in the second year because on that date the said ship with her goods and equipment was sold to John Chirche merchant and citizen of London by order and advice of the King's Great Council and by royal letters under the Privy Seal, as more fully noted above. The ship was sold under the said controlment, for the benefit of the king for a certain sum of money assigned to the king's service for which he accounts above among the foreign receipts of this account.

[F.53r.] 9. Royal Ballinger called *Nicholas*.

Receipt of the royal ballinger called *Nicholas* with her goods and equipment in hand from earlier accounts during the tenure of the keeper, that is to say:

Capstan	1
Bedewe	1
Bonnett	1 containing 102 ells of canvas
Large mast	1
Sailyerd	1
Bowspret	1
Topp Castell	1
Sondynglede	1
Large hawsers for *hedropes*	3 weighing together 6 cwt 5 lb
Large hawser for *bacsteyes*	1 weighing 2 cwt 13 lb
Hawser for *warpropes*	1 weighing 1 cwt 1 qua
Small hawser for *cranelyn*	1 weighing 19 lb
Bonnetts	2 containing 182 ells of canvas
Ropes called *takkes*	2 weighing 1 cwt 1 qua
Cables of black yarn	2 weighing 1 mwt 2 cwt
Warpropes	1 weighing 1 cwt 1 qua
Pulleys for the same ballinger	3
Cable	1 no weight given
Hawser for a *forstey*	1 weighing 3 cwt 1 qua 24 lb
Hawser for *bowlyn* and *boyrope*	2 weighing together 3 cwt 1 qua 2 lb
Hawser for *upties*	1 weighing 3 cwt 2 lb

Purchases from previous years, that is to say:

Hawsers of white Dutch yarn for *pollancr ropes, yerdropes* and *stetynges*	5 weighing 3 cwt 3 qua

Cables of the same yarn 2

weighing together 8 cwt 3 qua 21 lb

Cable of white Holland yarn 1 weighing 6 cwt 2 lb

A body sail newly made for the same royal ballinger

1

containing 2 *bolts* of canvas from Oleronnes

New oars for the same ballinger 20

Hawsers of white Dutch yarn for making *stetynges* and *bowlyn*

3 weighing together 2½ cwt

[F.53v.] Cable of *fyn* white yarn from Caux[216] for the same ballinger

1 weighing 6 cwt 4 lb

Small *lyn* called *sondynglyn* 1 no weight given

Rolles of *teldes* for the same ballinger 3

Brass pot for the same ballinger 1

A certain *pompe* for the same ballinger 1

Oars for the same ballinger 4

Foreign receipts lately coming from the ship called *Katerine* for the safe-keeping of this ballinger, that is to say:

Gittons in bad condition with various embroidered patterns

1 that is with *hostric* feathers[217]

1 that is with Saint George[218]

Standardes, various embroidered

Hamour 1

The following goods and equipment were used up, broken or damaged in the said ballinger called *Nicholas* on her maintenance and safe-keeping on various occasions that is between 4 October in the first year of the present king and 11 September next following in the second year of the same king, that is to say:

Items used:

Bedewe 1

Sondyngled 1

Large hawser for *hedropes* 1 weighing 1 cwt 3 qua 7 lb

Hawser for *warpropes* 1 weighing 1 cwt 1 qua

Small hawser for *cranlyn* 1 weighing 19 lb

Cables in bad condition of black yarn.

2 weighing 1 mwt 2 cwt

Cable 1 no weight given

Hawsers for *bowlynes* and *boyropes* for the same.

1 weighing 1½ cwt 14 lb

[F.54r.] Purchases from previous years, that is to say:

Hawsers of black Dutch yarn for *pollancr ropes yerdropes* and

stetynges 2 weighing 1½ cwt

New oars for the same ballinger 4

Hawser of white Dutch yarn for making *stetynges* and *bowlynes*
for the same   1 weighing 1 cwt 14 lb
Roll of *teldes* for the same ballinger   1
Oars for the same ballinger   2

The said keeper of the king's ships is not responsible for the said
ballinger after 11 September in the second year of the present king
because on the day in September the said royal ballinger with her
goods and equipment was sold to John More, William Straunge and
various other men from Dartmouth by order and advice of the King's
great council and by royal letters under the Privy Seal, as noted in
the preamble of this account. The ship was sold for the benefit of the
king, under the said controlment for a certain sum of money assigned
to the king's service for which he accounts above among the foreign
receipts of this account.

[F.55r.] 10. Royal ship in bad condition called *Katerine*.
Receipt of the worn out ship called *Katerine* with various goods and
equipment in hand from previous accounts. That is to say:

Mast, worn out	1
Sailyerd, worn out	1
Sondynglede	1
Somerhuche, in bad condition	1
Bedewe, in bad condition	1
Lanterns, worn out	2
Iron cannon	1

The various items following from among the equipment and goods
which formerly belonged to the said ship called *Katerine* were handed
over, used up or damaged in various ships and other vessels of the
Lord King to provide for their maintenance and safe-keeping between
the last day of August in the tenth year of the said late king who died
that day and the end of this account, that is to say:

Items used:
Sondynglede   1
Bedewe in bad condition   1
Lanterns in bad condition   2 handed over for the benefit of
the king by the said keeper of the king's ships for the maintenance
and safe-keeping of the royal ship called *Trinite Riall* on various
occasions within the accounting period for which he accounts below.

The said keeper is not responsible for the said dilapidated and worn
out ship called *Katerine de la Tour* lately in a certain *dook* at Deptford
Strande after 6 March in the third year of the present king because
the said ship in bad condition was sold on that day by the said order
and advice of the King's Great Council by royal letters under the Privy

Seal to John Pers and others of Greenwich. The ship was sold by the said keeper of the king's ships, under the said controlment, for the benefit of the king for a certain sum of money assigned to the king's service for which he accounts above among the foreign receipts of this account.

[F.55v.] 1. Ship in bad condition called *Nicholas*

Receipt of the worn out royal ship called *Nicholas* with the various goods and equipment following, in hand from previous accounts, that is to say:

Sailyerd in bad condition	1
Topp	1
Awger in bad condition	1
Large Anchors	3
Boyes for the anchors in bad condition	
	1
Lantern in bad condition	1
Sondyngled	1
Sail for a boat	1
Iron *grapnell*	1

The following goods and equipment which formerly belonged to the ship in poor condition called *Nicholas* were handed over, and used in various ships and other vessels of the same office on various occasions to provide for their maintenance and safe-keeping between the last day of August in the tenth year of the said late king who died that day and the end of this account, that is to say:

Items used:	
Sailyerd in bad condition	1
Awger in bad condition	1
Boyes for the anchors in bad condition	

1 handed over for the benefit of the king by the said keeper of the king's ships for the maintenance and safe-keeping of a certain royal ship called *Holigost* on various occasions during the period of this account, for which he accounts below.

Lantern in bad condition	1
Sondyngled	1

Handed over by the said keeper of the king's ships for the greater benefit of the king for the maintenance and safe-keeping of the royal ship called *Jhesus* on various occasions within the period of this account, for which he accounts below.

The said keeper of the king's ships is not responsible for the said ship in bad condition called *Nicholas* after 4 May in the second year of the present king because on the same day in August (sic) the said royal ship in bad repair was sold by the order and advice of the King's Great Council and also by the said royal letters under the Privy Seal, more fully noted in the preamble to this account, to John Reynoll of Lymostes near Redcliff.[219] The ship was sold by the said keeper, for the benefit of the king under the said controlment for a certain sum of money assigned to the king's service for which he accounts above among the foreign receipts of this account.

[F.56v.] 12. Equipment of the royal ship called *Rodcogge de la Tour*.

Receipt of various goods and equipment lately belonging to the royal ship called *Rodcogge* in hand from previous accounts, that is to say:

Pollancr ropes in bad condition	2
Mekhoke in bad condition	1
Mast in bad condition	1
Topp castell in bad condition	1
Shovels in bad condition	2
Anchor	1
Bonnett for a sail	1

The following goods and equipment from the items which lately belonged to the said royal ship called *Rodcogge* were used or damaged in various ships and other vessels of the said office of the king's ships on various occasions to provide for their maintenance and safe-keeping between the said last day of August in the tenth year of the said late king who died on that day and the end of this account, that is to say:

Items handed over and used.

Pollancr ropes in bad condition	2
Mekhoke in bad condition	1
Shovels in bad condition	2

Handed over by the said keeper of the king's ships for the benefit of the king for the maintenance and safe-keeping of the royal ship called *Jhesus* and her great boats on various occasions within the period of this account for which he accounts below.

[F.57r.] 13. Royal ballinger called *Craccher*.

Receipt of the royal ballinger called *Craccher* with the various goods and equipment following, in hand from previous accounts during the tenure of the said keeper of the king's ships, that is to say:

Topp	1
Mast	1
Sailyerd	1
Bowspret	1
Anchors	2
Bedewe	1

Brass pot   1
Sondyngled   1
Large oars for the same ballinger   17
Small boat called *cok*   1
Large oars   3
Sail in bad condition ordered
    previously that is 1 body-sail
    with 2 bonnetts.   1
Large hawser for a *forestey*   1 weighing 3 cwt 7 lb
Hawsers for *hedropes*   2 weighing together 1½ cwt 21 lb
Hawser of black yarn for *bowlynes* and *shetes*
                                           1 weighing 1½ cwt

Purchases from previous years, that is to say:
  Hawsers of white Dutch yarn for making *stetynges, truss*, and
    boyrope for the same   5 weighing 5 cwt 3 qua 4 lb
  Cables of black Dutch yarn   2 weighing 7 cwt 1 qua 2 lb
  Cable of white yarn   1
  Hawser for an *uptie*   1
                                       weighing together 5 cwt 3 qua 26 lb
  Oars for the same   9
  Pulleys for the same   5
  Lanterns   2
  Large oars   10
  Ironwork called a *mekhoke*   1
Foreign receipts lately coming from the ship called *Rodcogge* for the
safe-keeping of this ballinger, that is to say:
  Hawsers for making *stetyng* and *truss*
                                       2 weighing 1½ cwt 24 lb

[F.57v.] The following goods and equipment were used up, damaged,
or broken in the said royal ballinger called *Craccher* on various occa-
sions to provide for the maintenance and safe-keeping of the same
between the last day of August in the tenth year of the said king
Henry V lately king of England who died that day and the last day of
April next following in the first year of the present king, that is to say:
  Items used:
  Bedewe   1
  Large oars for the same ballinger   5
  Large oars   1
Purchases from previous years, that is to say:
  Hawser of white Dutch yarn for making *stetyng, truss* and
    boyropes for the same   1 weighing 1 cwt 7 lb
  Cable of Dutch black yarn   1 weighing 3½ cwt 8 lb
  Oars for the same   3

| *Pulleys* | 1 |
| Large oars | 2 |

Foreign receipts lately coming from the ship called *Rodcogge* for the safe-keeping of this ballinger, that is to say:

| Hawser for *stetyng* and *truss* | 1 weighing 3 qua 10 lb |

The said keeper of the king's ships is not responsible for the said royal ballinger called *Craccher* with her goods and equipment after the last day of April in the said first year because on that day in April the said ballinger with her goods and apparatus was sold by the advice and order of the King's Great Council and by royal letters under the Privy Seal, as noted more fully in the preamble of this account, to John Cole, Thomas Assheldon and John William of Dartmouth and Kingswear. The ship was sold by the said keeper, for the benefit of the king under the said controlment for a certain sum of money assigned to the royal service, for which he accounts above among the foreign receipts of this account.

[F.58v.] 14. Equipment of the Ship called *Petit Trinity*

Receipt of various goods and equipment lately belonging to the royal ship called *Petit Trinity* in hand from earlier accounts, that is to say:

Topp in bad condition	1
Bowspret in bad condition	1
Parrel for the mast	1
Forstey	1
Anchors	2
Pallett	3
Jakkes	2
Pavys	4

The following goods and equipment which formerly belonged to the royal ship called *Petit Trinite* were handed over, used or damaged in various ships and other vessels of the said office, on various occasions to provide for their maintenance and safe-keeping between the last day of August in the tenth year of Henry V, late king of England who died that day and the end of this account, that is to say:

Items handed over and used:

| *Bowspret* in bad condition | 1 |
| *Forestey* | 1 |

Handed over for the benefit of the king by the said keeper of the king's ships for the repair and safe keeping of the royal ship called *Gracedieu* and her great boats, on various occasions during the accounting period for which he accounts below.

| *Palett* | 3 |

Jakkes   2

Pavys   4   Similarly handed over by
the said keeper of the king's ships for the benefit of the king on
various occasions within the accounting period for the safe-keeping of
the royal barge called *Valentyn*.

[F.59r.] 15. Royal Ship called *Graunt Marie*
Receipt of the royal ship called *Graunt Marie* with various goods and
equipment in hand from previous accounts, that is to say:

Sailyerd	1	
Bowspret	1	
Pair of *hedropes*	1	
Pairs of *bacsteyes*	2	
Parrell for the mast	1	
Anchors	3	(one broken)
Grapnell	1	
Anchor for the boat	1	
Sondyngledes	2	
Scaltrowes	3	
Berlinges	11	
Hamour	1	
Iron *gaddes* for the *topp*	25	
Boat for the same ship	1	
Cannons	3	with 9 chambers
Dartes	2	dozen
Bows	16	
Sheaves of arrows	2	
Pavis	18	
Bedewe	1	
Bonnett for the sail	1	
Sail, newly made	1	

that is 1 body sail with 1 bonnett containing 800 ells canvas

Brass pot	1	
Mekhoke	1	
Anchor	1	
Cable of white yarn	1	weighing 6 cwt 3 qua 7 lb
Mast for the same ship	1	
Berlynges	2	
Shovels	8	
Bonnett	1	containing in all 80 ells canvas
Iron *trevett*	1	
Hawser for wyndyng rope	1	
Ropes called *takkes*	2	weighing together 3½ cwt 2 lb
Hawser for *priall ropes*	1	weighing 3 qua 21 lb

Mast for the boat	1
Pulleys	2
Braspott	1
Oars	3
Hawser of black yarn to be used for *hedropes*	2 weighing together 3 cwt 1 qua
Hawser of black yarn for making *bowlynes*	1 weighing 1½ cwt 19 lb
Hawser of black yarn for making *truss*	1 weighing 3 qua 11 lb
Hawser for *upties*	1 weighing 4½ cwt 24 lb
Hawser for a *forstey*	1 weighing 2 cwt 3 qua 19 lb
Hawser for *haliers*	1 weighing ½ cwt
Lantern for the same ship	1

Purchases from previous years, that is to say:

Cable of black Dutch yarn	1 weighing 5½ cwt 14 lb
Hawsers of the same yarn for using for *pollancr ropes*	2 weighing 3½ cwt 7 lb

[F.60r.] Oars for the same ship   13

Foreign receipts lately coming from the ship called *Rodcogge* for the safe-keeping of this ship that is to say:

Hawsers for *stetynges* and *truss*	2 weighing 1½ cwt 24 lb
Hawsers for boyropes	1 weighing 2 cwt 1 qua 22 lb
Pulleys	2

Foreign receipts lately coming from the parcel of 29 pieces of *cork* from the London store house for making *boyes* for the safe-keeping of this ship; that is to say:

Boyes for the same ship	2

The various goods and equipment following were used, broken or damaged in the said royal ship called *Graunt Marie* when she was being refitted and rebuilt and during her *launchynge* and the raising of her mast and other works and to provide for her maintenance and safe-keeping on various occasions between the said last day of August in the said tenth year of Henry V lately king of England who died that day and 1 August next following in the first year of the present king, that is to say:

Items used:

Pair of *bacsteyes*	1
Broken anchor	1 handed over and broken up to

make the large ironwork of the *rothir* of the same ship and to make *bolt* nails and other pieces of ironwork and to mend the iron chains for the *hedropes* of the same ship during her rebuilding.

Sondyngledes	1
Berlinges	1
Pavis	1
Bedew	1
Bonnett for the sail	1 Handed over and used (because

of its poor, worn out condition) for caulking the ship and covering various cabins and *cotes* and making *persandes* and various other necessities during her rebuilding.

Cable of white yarn	1 weighing 6 cwt 3 qua 7 lb
Shovels	8
[F.60v.] Hawser for *wyndyngrope*	1 weighing 2 cwt 14 lb
Pulleys	2
Oars	3
Hawser of black yarn for making *bowlynes*	
	1 weighing 1½ cwt 19 lb

Purchases from previous years, that is to say
    Hawser of the same yarn for *pollancr* ropes

                                 1 weighing 1 cwt 3 qua 2 lb

    Oars for the same ship   2

Foreign receipts lately coming from the ship called *Rodcogge* for the safe-keeping of this ship, that is to say:
    Hawser for *boyropes*   1 weighing 2 cwt 1 qua 21 lb

The said keeper of the king's ships is not responsible for the said royal ship called *Graunt Marie* with her goods and equipment after 8 August in the said first year of the present king because on that day the said ship with her goods and equipment was handed over to Richard Bukland of London in satisfaction of two tallies totalling £148 8s 11d by authority of a royal writ under the privy seal dated 3 July in the first year of Henry VI directed to the accountant, John Foxholes and Nicholas Banastre, delivered with this account.

[F.61v.] 16. Royal Ballinger called *Katerine Britton.*
Receipt of the royal ballinger called *Katerine Britton* with the following goods and equipment in hand from previous accounts, that is to say:

Toppe	1
Sailyerd in bad condition	1
Bowspret	1
Pair of *hedropes* in bad condition	1
Forestey	1
Bacsteyes	1
Parrel for the mast	1
Bonetts for the sail	2

Anchors	2
Ironwork called *tricehokes*	2
[F.62r.] *Mekhoke*	1
Compas	1
Sondyngled	1
Axe for the same ballinger	1
Bedew	1
Brass pot	1
Hawser for *shetes* and *truss*	1 weighing 1 cwt 3 lb
Roll *teldes* in bad condition	1
Hawser of the same Dutch yarn for an *uptie*	
	1 weighing 6 cwt 12 lb
Hamour for the same ballinger	1

Foreign receipts lately coming from the ship called *Petit Trinite* for the safe keeping of this ship, that is to say:

Pairs of *hedropes*	2
Pairs of *bacsteyes*	1
Pavis	3

Purchases from earlier years, that is to say:

Wyndyng rope	1 no weight given
Morynge hawser	1 no weight given
Wyndyngpolley	1
Mast for the same ballinger	1
Anchor for the same ballinger	1
Body sail lined	1 that is with
	1 bonnett for the same
Boat for the same ballinger	1
Oars	6
Cables of back yarn	2 weighing together 7½ cwt 14 lb
Hawser for *stetynges, hedropes* and *yerdropes*	
	3
	weighing together 1 cwt 1 qua 17 lb
Rope called *bowlynes,* somewhat used,	
	1 no weight given

[F.62v.] The various goods and apparatus following were used, broken, or damaged in the said royal ballinger called *Katerine Britton* on various occasions to provide for the maintenance and safe-keeping of the same between the last day of August in the tenth year of the said Henry V lately king of England who died that day and 6 May next following in the first year of the present king, that is to say:

Items used:	
Copul hedrop in bad condition	1
Ironwork called *tricehokes*	1

Compas	1
Axe for the same ballinger	1
Roll teldes in bad condition	1

Purchases from previous years, that is to say:

Morynge hawser	1 no weight given
Oars	2
Hawser for *stetynges hedropes* and *yerdropes*	
	1 weighing 1 qua 14 lb

The said keeper is not responsible for the said royal ballinger called *Katerine Britton* with various goods and equipment on board the same after 6 March in the first year because on the same 6 March the same royal ballinger with her equipment and goods was sold by the order and advice of the King's Great Council and by the said royal letters noted more fully above to John Sterlynge of Greenwich. The ballinger was sold by the said keeper for the benefit of the king under the said controlment for a certain sum of money assigned to the royal service for which he accounts above among the foreign receipts of this account.

[F.63v.] 17. Royal Ballinger called *Swan*

Receipt of the royal ballinger called *Swan* with the various goods and equipment following, in hand from previous accounts that is to say:

Mast	1
Hedropes	1
Sailyerd	1
Anchors	2
Parrel for the mast	1
Pulleys for the *shrowde*	2
Sondyngledes	1
Pulleys for the same ballinger	2
Small boat called *cok*	1
Hawser for *hedropes*	1 weighing 3 qua 14 lb
Pulleys for the same ballinger	3
Axe for the same ballinger	1
Ironwork called *hammer*	1
Body-sail	1 that is to say with 1 bonnett containing 4 *bolt* of Olleron of which each *bolt* contains 32 ells of canvas: total 128 ells

Foreign receipts lately coming from the royal ballinger called *Petit John* for the safe-keeping of this ballinger, that is to say:

Anchor	1

Purchases from previous years, that is to say:

Iron chains for the same	4 weighing 24 lb
Hawser for making *bacsteyes*	1 weighing 1 cwt 9 lb
Cable for the same ballinger	1 weighing 3½ cwt 18 lb
Hawser for *yerdropes* and *takkes* for the same	
	1 weighing 1 cwt 1 qua 7 lb
Oars for the same ballinger	6
Lanterns	2
Anchor for the same ballinger	1
Hawsers of white Bridport yarn for *foresteyes, wynd-y-ng hauncer*	
and *boyropes* for the same	2 weighing 2 cwt 3 qua 5 lb
[F.64r.] Cable for the same ballinger	1 weighing 2 cwt 1 qua
A certain *sondynglyn*	1
Small rope called *cranelyn*	1
Large oars for the same ballinger	15
Mast for the same ballinger	1
Hawsers for *hedropes* and *takkes*	2 weighing 2 cwt 1 qua 3 lb

The various goods and equipment following were used, damaged or broken in the said royal ballinger called *Swan* on various occasions to provide for the maintenance and safe-keeping of the same between the said last day of August in the tenth year of the said late king, who died that day and 1 April next following in the first year of the present king, that is to say:

Items used:

Pulleys for *le shrowde*	1
Sondyngledes	1
Axe for the same ballinger	1

Purchases from previous years, this is to say:

Haunsers for *hedropes* and *takkes* for the same	
	1 weighing ½ cwt 24 lb
Oars for the same ballinger	3
Lantern	1
Hawser of white Bridport yarn for *forsteyes, wyndynghauncer* and	
boyrope for the same	1 weighing 1 cwt 1 qua 3 lb
A certain *sondynglyn*	1
Large oars for the same ballinger	2

[F.64v.] The said keeper of the king's ships is not responsible for the said ballinger called *Swan* with her goods and equipment after the said 1 April mentioned above because on that day the said ballinger with her equipment and other goods was sold to Thomas Downyng, John William and Nicholas Sthevenes by the order and advice of the said great council of the king and by the said royal letters under the Privy

Seal. The ballinger was sold by the said keeper, under the said control-ment for the benefit of the king for a certain sum of money assigned to the royal service for which he accounts above among the foreign receipts of this account.

[F.65r.] 18. Royal Ballinger called *Ane de la Tour*.

Receipt of the royal ballinger called *Ane* with the following goods and equipment in hand from earlier accounts, that is to say:

Toppe	1
Mast	1
Sailyerd	1
Bowspret	1
Pulleys	5
Anchors	3
Boat for the same	1
Bedewe	1
Grapnell	1
Boyes for the anchor	1
Bitakyll	1
Brass *shives* to be used for a certain *gire*	
	2
Hawser for making *shet*	1 weighing 1 cwt 1 qua 7 lb
Cables for the same ballinger	2 weighing together 1 mwt 1 cwt
[F.65v.] Ironwork called *hamour*	1
Axe for the same ballinger	1
Hawser for *hedropes*	1 weighing 2 cwt
Hawser for *bacsteyes*	1 weighing 2½ cwt
Hawser for *bowlyn*	1 weighing 1 cwt 14 lb
Ironwork called *mekhoke*	1

Foreign receipts lately coming from the ship called *Petit Trinite* for the safe-keeping of this ballinger, that is to say:

Rope called hawser for *upties*	1 weighing 2 cwt 1 qua
Small rope called cranelyn	1 weighing 22 lb
Bowlyn pulley	1

Foreign receipts lately coming from the ship called *Rodcogge* for the safe-keeping of this ballinger, that is to say:

Pairs of *hedropes*	5
Forstey	1
Bonnetts for the sail	2

Foreign receipts lately coming from the ship called *Graunt Gabriell* for the safe-keeping of this ballinger, that is to say:

Roll teldes	1
Sondyngled	1

Purchases from previous years, that is to say:

Small mast to be used for *le mesan* of this ballinger

                  1

Small *sailyerd* to be used for the same *mesan*

                  1

Poleys for the same ballinger   4

Hawsers of the same yarn of various kinds for making *shetes, takkes, upties, hedropes, bacsteyes, forstey, trusses* and *stetyng*

                  3 weighing 3 cwt 1 qua 2 lb

Large cable of black Dutch yarn   2 weighing 6½ cwt

Hawsers for *stetynges, trusses* and *yerdropes* for the same royal ballinger   3 weighing 4½ cwt 18 lb

Body-sail lined   1

                  that is containing 3 *bolt* of Olleron

[F.66r.] A certain *mastparraill*   1

Oars for the same ballinger   11

Lanterns for the same   2

Pulleys for the same   3

The following goods and equipment were used, broken, damaged or worn out in the said royal ballinger called *Ane* on various occasions to provide for her maintenance and safe-keeping between the said last day of August in the tenth year of the said Henry V lately king of England who died that day and 27 June in the second year of the present king, that is to say:

Items used:

Pulleys   1

Boyes for the anchor   1

Hawser for making *shetes*   1 weighing 1 cwt 1 qua 7 lb

Cable for the same ballinger   1 weighing 5 cwt 1 qua

Hawser for *hedropes*   1 weighing 2 cwt

Hawser for *bowlyn*   1 weighing 1 cwt 4 lb

Foreign receipts lately coming from the ship called *Petit Trinite* for the safe-keeping of this ballinger, that is to say:

Small rope called *cranelyn*   1 weighing 22 lb

Bowlyn pulley   1

Foreign receipts lately coming from the ship called *Graunt Gabriell* for the safe-keeping of this ballinger, that is to say:

Roll teldes   1

Sondyngled   1

Purchases from earlier years, that is to say:

Pulleys for the same ballinger   2

Hawser of the same yarn of various kinds for making *shet, takkes, upties, hedropes, bacsteyes, forsteyes, truss* and *stetyng*

	1 weighing 1 cwt 20 lb
Large cable of black Dutch yarn	1 weighing 3 cwt 1 qua 14 lbs.
Oars for the same ballinger	4
Lantern for the same	1

The said keeper of the king's ships is not responsible for the said royal ballinger called *Ane* with her goods and equipment after 27 June mentioned above because on that day the said ballinger was sold, by order and advice of the King's Great Council and by royal letters under the Privy Seal, noted more fully in the preamble of this account, to John Slogge and various other men from Saltash in Cornwall. The ballinger was sold, by the said keeper of the king's ships, under the said controlment, for the benefit of the king, for £30 sterling assigned to the royal service for which he accounts above among the foreign receipts of this account.

[F.67v.] 19. Dilapidated carrack called *Poule de la Tour*.

Receipt of the royal carrack in bad condition called *Poule* with the various goods and equipment following in hand from previous accounts, that is to say:

Topp in bad condition	1
Bowspret in bad condition	1
Pairs of *hedropes*	2
Anchors	2
Hawser for *handropes*	1
Cannon in bad condition	1
Pulleys	8
Oars in bad condition	3

Purchases from previous years, that is to say:

Ironwork called *bedewe*	1
Iron *hamour*	1
Pollancr	7

The various goods and equipment following of the said carrack were handed over, used, damaged or worn out in various ships and other vessels of the said office, on various occasions to provide for the maintenance and safe-keeping of the same, between the last day of August in the tenth year of Henry V late king of England, who died that day and the end of this account, that is to say:

Items used and handed over	
Bowspret in bad condition	1
Pairs of *hedropes*	2
Hawser for *handropes*	1
Pulleys	8

Handed over for the benefit of the king by the said keeper of the king's ships for the fitting out and safe-keeping of the king's great ship called *Gracedieu* on various occasions within the accounting period for which he accounts below.

Oars in bad condition	3
Purchases from previous years, that is to say:	
Ironwork called *bedewe*	1
Pollances	7

Handed over by the said keeper, similarly, for the use and benefit of the king, on various occasions for the safe-keeping and fitting out of the royal carrack called *Cristofre* within the accounting period for which he accounts below.

The said keeper of the king's ships has no further responsibility for the said dilapidated royal carrack called *Poule de la Tour* after 10 September in the third year of the present king because on that day of September the said carrack, in bad condition without any goods or equipment was sold to Richard Patyn, Richard Prestes of Hamble, John Gladwyn and William Gladwyn of Shotteshall in Hampshire together with another carrack in bad condition called *Marie Sandwich* by the advice and order of the king's Great Council and by royal letters under the Privy Seal. The carrack was sold by the said keeper for the benefit of the king, under the said controlment for a certain sum of money assigned to the royal service for which he accounts above among the foreign receipts of this account.

20. Royal Carrack called *Cristofre de la Tour*

Receipt of the royal carrack *Cristofre* with the various goods and equipment following in hand from previous accounts, that is to say:

Topp	1
Sailyerd	1
Bowspret	1
Pair of *hedropes*	1
Pollance ropes	4
Bonnett for a sail	1
Sailyerd for *le mesan*	1
Anchors for the same	2
Cannons	2 with 3 chambers
Hawser for *pendantz*	1 weighing 4 cwt 1 qua 7 lb
[F.68v.] Hawser for *priall ropes*	1 weighing 4 cwt
Hawser for *yerdropes*	2 weighing together 6 cwt
Hawser for *pollancr ropes*	1 weighing 1½ cwt
Anchor for the same carrack	1

Ironwork called *peyntynghoke*   1
Axe for the same carrack   1
Large cable   1 with a large hawser for *upties*
     measuring 80 fathoms, weighing together 2 mwt 1 qua 7 lb
Boyes for the same carrack   1
Large brass pot   1
Foreign receipts lately coming for the royal carrack called *Marie Hampton* for the safe-keeping of this carrack, that is to say:
   Anchors for the same carrack   2
Foreign receipts lately coming from the royal ship called *Nicholas* for the safe-keeping of this carrack, that is to say:
   Cable for the same ship   1 weighing 1 mwt 3 cwt 3 qua 4 lb
   Hawser for *stetyng*   1 weighing 3 qua 20 lb
   Hawser for *hedropes*   1 weighing 2 cwt 1 qua
   Rope called *takkes*   1 weighing ½ cwt 23 lb
   Cable in bad condition for the same ship
     9½ cwt 7 lb
Foreign receipts lately coming from the carrack called *Andrewe* for the safe-keeping of this carrack, that is to say:
   Upties for the same *mezan*   2
   Yerdropes   2
   Mekhoke   1
   Anchors   2
Purchases from previous years that is to say:
Iron *bedewes*   1
Iron *hamour*   1
Watirscoupes   3
Large oars in bad condition   24
A certain iron anchor for *la barke* of the same carrack
   1
A large piece of ironwork called *firepann*
   1
[F.69r.] A certain iron *hamour*   1
A body-sail for the same carrack   1 containing 800 ells of canvas
Mast to be used for a certain *contremaste*
   1
Pulleys for the same carrack   3
Oars for the same carrack   8
Large pulleys   3
Pulleys for the same, another lot   8
Large oars   6
Boyes newly made   3
Shovels for the same   2
Rope called *baste*   1

Cable of white Dutch yarn for making *boyropes*

    1 weighing 2½ cwt

Hawser in bad repair of white Bordeaux yarn for making
strike ropes   1 weighing 2 cwt

Large cable of the same Bordeaux yarn for the same carrack

    1 weighing 1 mwt 2½ cwt 1 qua

Cable of *fyn* white Bordeaux yarn   1 weighing 1 mwt 7 lb

Small rope of white yarn for using for *cranelyn*

    1 no weight given.

Foreign receipts lately coming from the royal carrack *Poule* for the safe-keeping of this carrack during the accounting period, that is to say:

Oars in bad repair	5
Ironwork called *bedewe*	1
Pollances	7

[F.69v.] The following goods and equipment were used, damaged, broken or worn out in the said royal carrack called *Cristofre* on various occasions to provide for the safe-keeping and maintenance of the same and her great boats between the last day of August in the tenth year of Henry V late king of England who died that day and 23 May in the first year of the present king, on which day the carrack was sold as is noted more fully below, that is to say:

Items used:

Pair *hedropes*	1
Pollancr ropes	2
Hawser for *pendants*	1 weighing 4 cwt 1 qua 7 lb
Hawser for *yerdropes*	1 weighing 3 cwt
Axe for the same carrack	1
Boyes for the same carrack	1

Foreign receipts lately coming from the royal ship *Nicholas* for the safe-keeping of this ship, that is to say:

Cable for the same ship	1
	weighing 1 mwt 3 cwt 3 qua 4 lb
Rope called *takkes*	1 weighing ½ cwt 23 lb

Foreign receipts lately coming from the royal carrack called *Andrew* for the safe-keeping of this carrack, that is to say:

Upties for the same *mesan*	2
Yerdropes	2

Purchases from previous years, that is to say:

Iron *hamour*	1
Watirscoupes	3
Large oars in bad repair	15
Pulleys for the same carrack	3

Oars for the same	3
Large oars	2
Boyes newly made	1
Shovels for the same	3
Rope called *baste*	1
Cable of *fyn* white Bordeaux yarn	1 weighing 1 mwt 7 lb

Foreign receipts lately coming from the royal carrack called *Poule* for the safe-keeping of this carrack, that is to say:

Oars in bad condition	3
Pollances	2

[F.70r.] The said keeper of the king's ships is not responsible for the said royal carrack called *Cristofre* with her various goods and equipment after the abovesaid 23 May because on that day the same carrack with her goods and equipment was sold to John Morgan of Bristol by the advice and order of the King's Great Council and by royal letters under the Privy Seal. The carrack was sold under the said controlment, by the said keeper for the benefit of the king for a certain sum of money assigned to the king's service for which he accounts above among the foreign receipts of this account.

[F.71r.] 21.   Royal Carrack in bad condition called *Andrew de la Tour*.

Receipt of the royal carrack in bad condition sunk in *le wose* (the mud) called *Andrew* with the following goods and equipment in hand from previous accounts, that is to say:

Topp in bad condition	1
Mast, dilapidated	1
Bowspret in bad condition	1
Pairs of *hedropes*	3
Forestey in bad condition	1
Pollantz ropes	2 pairs
Sail, dilapidated	1,
	that is 1 body with 1 bonnett for the same
Bowlyn	1
Iron cannon in bad condition	2
Anchors	3
Bitakyll in bad condition	1
Pulleys in bad condition	11
Oars for the boat in bad condition	4
Lantern for the same carrack	1

The various goods and apparatus below which formerly belonged to the said carrack beached and in bad condition were handed over and used in various ships and other vessels of the said office to provide for their maintenance and safe-keeping on various occasions between the last day of August in the tenth year of Henry V late king of England, who died that day and the end of this account, that is to say:

Items used and handed over:

Topp in bad condition	1
Pairs of *hedropes*	3
Forestey in bad condition	1
Pollantz ropes	2 pair

Handed over by the said keeper of the king's ships for the benefit of the king on various occasions for the safe-keeping of the royal ship called *Holigost* within this accounting period for which he accounts below.

Bowlyn	1
Anchors	2
Pulleys in bad condition	8
Oars for the boat in bad condition	4
Lantern	1

Handed over by the said keeper of the king's ships for the benefit of the king for the safe-keeping of the ship called *Holigost of Spain* during the said accounting period for which he accounts below.

Sail, dilapidated   1,

that is 1 body with 1 bonnett for the same

This sail with bonnett was sold for the benefit of the said king to John Mase of London, painter on 8 August in the second year of the present king for a certain sum of money for which the keeper accounts above among the foreign receipts of this account.

[F.72r.] 22. Royal carrack called *Peter de la Tour*

Receipt of the dilapidated carrack called *Peter* with the various goods and equipment following in hand from previous accounts that is to say:

Topp in bad condition	1
Mast in bad condition	1
Bowspret	1
Pair of *hedropes*	1
Pollantz in bad condition	1
Sail in bad condition	1, that is 1 body with 1 bonnett
Anchors	3
Parrel for the mast	1
Cannons in bad condition	3 with 4 chambers
Bitakyll in bad condition	1
Pulleys	5
Hawser for a *forstey*	1 weighing 8½ cwt
Hawser for a *hedrop*	1 weighing 2 cwt 3 qua 6 lb

Hawser in bad condition for *truss*	1 weighing 1 cwt 3 qua 21 lb
Rope for *takkes*	1 weighing 1 cwt
Cable in bad condition	1 weighing 1 mwt 3 cwt
Peyntynghoke	1
Oars in bad condition	2
Oars in bad condition	3

Purchases from previous years, that is to say:

Prussian rope called *baste,* another lot for the same carrack	1 no weight given
Bedewe for the same	1

[F.72v.] The following goods and equipment which formerly belonged to the said carrack called *Peter* were handed over and used in the said royal carrack and in various ships and other vessels of the said office to provide for the maintenance and safe-keeping of the same on various occasions between 21 December in the ninth year of the said Henry V late king of England on which day the said carrack because of her dilapidation was put into a certain *dook* at Southampton and the end of this account, that is to say:

Items used and handed over:

Pair of *hedropes*	1
Pollantz ropes in bad condition	1 pair
Pulleys	5

Handed over by the said keeper of the king's ships for the benefit of the king for the safe-keeping of the ship called *Trinite Riall* within this accounting period for which he accounts below.

Hawser for *forstey*	1 weighing 8½ cwt
Hawser for *hedropes*	1 weighing 2 cwt 3 qua 6 lb
Hawser in bad condition for *truss*	1 weighing 1 cwt 3 qua 21 lb
Rope for *takkes*	1 weighing 1 cwt

Handed over by the said keeper of the king's ships for the benefit of the same king on various occasions for the safe-keeping of the royal carrack called *George* within this accounting period for which he accounts below.

Cable in bad condition	1 weighing 1 mwt 3 cwt
Oars in bad condition	2
Oars in bad condition	3

Purchases from previous years, that is to say:

Large Prussian rope called *baste* in another lot for the same carrack	1 no weight given
Bedewe for the same	1

Used during this accounting period for the safe-keeping of this same carrack for the benefit of the king on various occasions:

Anchor	1

Sold to Scorcefegon, Patron of a Genoese carrack by the advice and order of the King's Great Council and by the said royal letters, by the said keeper of the king's ships, for the benefit of the king on 4 April in the third year of the present king for a certain sum of money for which he accounts above among the foreign receipts of this account.

Sail, in bad condition   1,

                           that is 1 body with 1 bonnett for the same
This sail in bad condition with 1 bonnett was sold to Richard Herman of Colchester on 22 November in the third year of the present king, for the benefit of the king, for a certain sum of money for which the keeper accounts above among the foreign receipts of this account.

[F.73r.] The said keeper is not responsible for the said dilapidated carrack called *Peter*, lately in *dook* in Southampton for her protection, after 23 October in the third year of the present king because on that day the said carrack in bad condition was sold to Robert Morynge and William Tassyer of Southampton by the order and advice of the King's Great Council and by the said royal letters under the Privy Seal. The carrack was sold by the said keeper of the king's ships, under the said controlment for the benefit of the king for a certain sum of money for which he accounts above among the foreign receipts of this account.

23.   Equipment of the royal carrack called *Marie Hampton*.

Receipt of the carrack in bad repair, lost at sea called *Marie Hampton* with the various equipment and goods in hand from previous accounts, that is to say:

Mast parrel in bad condition   1
Purchases from earlier years, that is to say:

Ironwork called *bedewe*   1
Oars in bad condition for the same   2

[F.73v.] 24. Royal Carrack in bad condition called *Marie Sandwich*.

Receipts of the carrack in bad condition called *Marie Sandwich* with various goods and equipment in hand from previous accounts, that is to say:

Forstey in bad condition	1
Sail in bad condition	1, that is 1 body
Anchors	2
Pulleys in bad condition	9
Rope called *takkes* of same yarn	1 weighing 1½ cwt
Bonnetts newly made	2

                         containing together 450 ells of canvas from Vitré

Boyes in bad condition for the anchor	1
Sondyngled	1
Oars in bad condition for the same carrack	3
Watirscoupes in bad condition	1

[F.74r.] The following from these goods and equipment were used, broken, damaged or worn out in the said royal carrack and in various other ships and vessels of the same office or were handed over by the said keeper for the benefit of the king to provide for the safe-keeping and maintenance of the same, on various occasions between 6 November in the ninth year of the said Henry V late king of England on which day the said carrack was beached on *le wose* because of her dilapidation and the last day of August in the fifth year of the present king, finishing on that day, that is to say:

Forstey in bad condition	1
Sail in bad condition	1, that is 1 body
Pulleys in bad condition	9

Handed over by the said keeper for the benefit of the said king for the caulking and fitting out of the four great royal ships and for the repair of other vessels of the said office and used in the safe-keeping of the same on various occasions within the accounting period.

Rope called *takkes* of the same yarn	1 weighing 1½ cwt
Boyes in bad condition to use for the anchor	
	1

used for *morynge* the same carrack called *Marie Sandwich* at times during the accounting period.

Oars in bad condition for the same carrack	3
Watirscoupes in bad condition	1

Handed over by the said keeper of the office for the benefit of the king for the fitting out and safe-keeping of the royal ballinger called *Facon* within the accounting period for which he accounts below.

Anchor   1, that is sold under the said controlment for the benefit of the king to Jacob Spynell of Southampton on 8 July in the fourth year of the said king for a certain sum of money for which the keeper accounts above among the foreign receipts of this account.

The said keeper is not responsible for the said carrack called *Marie Sandwich de la Tour* in bad condition and beached on *le wose* at Hamble for her own greater safety after 10 September in the third year of the present king because on that day the said carrack with another royal carrack in bad condition called *Poule* was sold to Richard Patyn, Richard Preste of Hamble, John Gladwyn and

William Gladwyn of Shottesshall in Hampshire by the order and advice of the King's Great Council and by the said royal letters under the Privy Seal.

The carrack was sold by the said keeper under the said controlment for the benefit of the king for a certain sum of money assigned to the royal service for which he accounts above among the foreign receipts of this account as already mentioned in the entry for the carrack called *Poule*.

[F.74v.] 25. Equipment of the ship called *Marie Hulke*.
Receipt of various goods and equipment formerly belonging to the ship called *Marie Hulke* in hand from previous accounts, that is to say:

Parrel for the mast in bad condition
                                          1
Pulleys in bad condition   1
Anchors   2

[F.75r.] 26. Royal Ship called *Holigost of Spain*.
Receipt of the royal ship called *Holigost of Spain* with the following goods and equipment in hand from previous accounts, that is to say:

Topp	1
Mast	1
Bowspret	1
Pairs of *hedropes* in bad condition	3
Bacsteyes	1 pair
Forstey in bad condition	1
Bowlyn	1
Bonnett for a sail	1
Anchors	3
Iron cannon	2 with 6 chambers
Boat in bad condition	1
Sondynglyn	1 no weight given
Cranlyn	1 no weight given
Axe in bad condition	1
Hawser in bad condition of Bordeaux yarn for a *boterope*	1 weighing 2½ cwt

Purchases from previous years, that is to say:

Ironwork called a *peyntynghoke*	1 weighing 33 lb
Iron *hamour*	1
Cables in bad condition of black Dutch yarn	3 weighing 1 mwt 8 cwt 22 lb
Hawser of the same yarn for *truss* and *boyropes*	1 weighing 2½ cwt

Rope called *cranlyn*	3 qua 23 lb
Hawser of *fyn* white yarn for *bacsteyes*	
	1 weighing 1½ cwt 21 lb
Bonnett newly made	1 containing 144 ells of canvas
Oars for the same ship	10

[F.75v.] *Skettfates*	1
Watrescoupes in bad condition	2
A certain *mesan yerd*	1
Lanterns in bad condition	2
A *bedewe*	1
Lanterns	2
Brass pot	1
Lined sail	1

that is 1 body sail with 2 bonnets containing 15 bolt of Olleron

Oars for the same ship	19
Dioll	1
Oars for the same	6
Shovels for the same	2
Cable of white Dutch yarn for making *shetes*	
	1 weighing 3 cwt 3 qua 14 lb
Cable of white Dutch yarn	2
	weighing 1 mwt 7 cwt 3 qua 4 lb

Foreign receipts lately coming from the ship called *Katerine* for the safe-keeping of this ship, that is to say:

Cable in bad condition of white yarn	
	1 weighing 8 cwt 1 qua
Hawser of white yarn for *upties*	1 weighing 5 cwt 1 qua 18 lb

Foreign receipts lately coming from the royal ship called *Nicholas* for the safe-keeping of this ship, that is to say:

Mast parrel	1
Pairs of *hedropes*	5
Bacsteyes	2

Foreign receipts lately coming from the carrack called *Marie Sandwhich* for the safe-keeping of this ship, that is to say:

Pulleys	8
Sesynge grapnell	1

that is with one iron chain of 16 links weighing 3 cwt 1 qua 6 lb

Foreign receipts lately coming from the royal ship called *Grand Gabriell* for the safe-keeping of this ship, that is to say:

Pairs of *hedropes*	5
Anchor	1
[F.76r.] *Mekhoke*	1
Bedewe	1

Foreign receipts during this accounting period coming from the carrack called *Andrewe* for the safe-keeping of this ship, that is to say:

Bowlyn	1
Anchors	2
Pulleys in bad condition	8
Oars for the boat, in bad condition	4
Lantern	1

The following goods and equipment were used, damaged, broken, and worn out in the said royal ship called *Holigost of Spain* on various occasions to provide for the maintenance and safe-keeping of the same and her great boats between the said last day of August in the tenth year of Henry V late king of England who died that day and 15 June next following in the first year of the present king, that is to say:

Items used:

Pairs of *hedropes* in bad condition	3
Forstey in bad condition	1
Bowlyn	1
Sondynglyn	1 no weight given
Cranlyn	1 no weight given
Axe in bad condition	1

Hawser in bad condition of Bordeaux yarn for a *botrope*
1 weighing 2½ cwt

Purchases from previous years, that is to say:
Cables in bad condition of black Dutch yarn
2
weighing together 1 mwt 2 cwt 8 lb

Hawser of the same yarn for *truss* and *boyropes*
1 weighing 2½ cwt

[F.76v.] Oars for the same ship	7
Watirscoupes in bad condition	2
Lanterns in bad condition	2
Oars for the same ship	9
Shovels for the same	2

Cable of white Dutch yarn for making *shetes*
1 weighing 3 cwt 3 qua 14 lb

Foreign receipts lately coming from the ship called *Katerine* for the safe-keeping of this ship, that is to say:
Cable in bad condition of white yarn
1 weighing 8 cwt 1 qua

Hawser of white yarn for *upties*   1 weighing 5 cwt 1 qua 18 lb

Foreign receipts during this accounting period coming from the carrack called *Andrew* for the safe-keeping of this ship, that is to say:

Bowlynes   1
Pulleys in bad condition   3
Oars for the boat, in bad condition 2

The said keeper is not responsible for the said royal ship called *Holigost of Spain* with her various goods and equipment after 15 June in the said first year because on that day the said ship with her goods and equipment was sold to Ralph Huskard and various others of Southampton by order and advice of the King's Great Council and by the said royal letters under the Privy Seal. The said ship was sold by the said keeper, for the benefit of the king under the said controlment for a certain sum of money assigned to the royal service for which he accounts above among the foreign receipts of this account.

[F.77v.] 27. Royal Barge called *Valentyn*

Receipt of the royal barge called *Valentyn* with the various equipment following in hand from previous accounts, that is to say:

Cokbote   1
Sondyngledes   1
Hamour   1
Oars   15
Mast   1
Bowspret   1
Cables   2 weighing 7½ cwt 3 lb
Anchors   3
Sailyerd   1
Sail   1 with 3 bonnetts and *la shroude* and all equipment.

Purchases from previous years, that is to say:

[F.78r.] Cable of black Dutch yarn   1 weighing 6 cwt 3 qua 14 lb
Hawser of the same yarn for *stetynges*
                         1 weighing 1 cwt 3 qua 18 lb
Small rope called *cranlyn* for the same
                         1 weighing ½ cwt 14 lb
Hawsers of white yarn for making *shet, takkes, warpropes,*
truss, yerdropes and *priall ropes*   5 weighing 3½ cwt 10 lb
Oars for the same   2
Oars for the same   9
Brass pot   1

Foreign receipts lately coming from the royal ship called *Marie Hulke* for the safe-keeping of this ship, that is to say:

Forstey   1
Pulleys   2
Lanterns for the same   1

Foreign receipts lately coming from the ship called *Rodcogge* for the safe-keeping of this ship, that is to say:

Hawser for *bacsteyes*	1 weighing 3 qua 21 lb
Large cable	1 weighing 6 cwt 1 qua 14 lb
Hawser for *boyropes*	1 weighing 2 cwt 1 qua 21 lb

Foreign receipts lately coming from the ship called *Nicholas* for the safe-keeping of this barge, that is to say:

| Oars for the same | 7 |

Foreign receipts of artillery coming from store and from the equipment of the ship called *Petit Trinite* for the safe-keeping of this ship, that is to say:

Jakkes in store, lately coming from the ship called *Petit Trinite*   2

Foreign receipts from the ship called *Philippe* during this accounting period, for the safe-keeping of this ship, that is to say:

Pair of *hedropes* in bad condition   1

Foreign receipts lately coming, during this accounting period, from the said ship called *Petit Trinite* for the safe-keeping of this ship, that is to say:

Palett	3
Jakkes	2
Pavis	4

[F.78v.] The following goods and equipment were used, damaged, broken or worn out on the said royal barge called *Valentyn* on various occasions to provide for the maintenance and safe keeping of the same between the said last day of August in the tenth year of Henry V lately king of England who died that day and 1 March in the second year of the present king, that is to say:

Items used:

Oars	7
Cables	2 weighing 7½ cwt 3 lb
Small rope for *crane lynes*	1 weighing ½ cwt 14 lb
Hawsers of white yarn for *shet, takkes, warp ropes, truss yerdropes* and *priall ropes* for the same	2 weighing 1½ cwt 4 lb
Oars for the same	3

Foreign receipts lately coming from the ship called *Nicholas* for the safe-keeping of this ship, that is to say:

| Oars | 7 |

Foreign receipts of artillery coming from store and the equipment of the ship called *Petit Trinite* for the safe-keeping of this ship, that is to say:

Jakkes in store coming from the ship called *Petit Trinite*   2 written off within this accounting period because of their dilapidation, the result of rot caused by the spray of sea water during various voyages at sea.

Foreign receipts lately coming from the ship called *Philippe* during this accounting period, that is to say:

Pair of *hedropes* in bad condition   1

[F.79r.] The said keeper is not responsible for the said royal barge called *Valentyn* with various equipment and goods after 1 March mentioned above because on that day the said barge with her equipment was sold to John Jon and John Emery of Southampton by order and advice of the King's Great Council and by the said royal letters under the Privy Seal. The barge was sold by the said keeper, for the benefit of the king, under the said controlment for a certain sum of money assigned to the royal service for which he accounts above among the foreign receipts of this account.

[F.79v.] 28. Royal ballinger called *Facon de la Tour*

Receipt of the royal ballinger called *Facon* with the various goods and equipment following in hand from previous accounts, that is to say:

Sondyngledes	1
Oars	21
Mast	1
Bowspret	1
Cables	2 weighing 4 cwt 1 qua 14 lb
Boat called *Cokbot*	1
Anchors	2
Sailyerd	1
Sail	1

with 3 bonnetts and *le shrowde* and all equipment

Purchases from previous years, that is to say:

Ironwork called *bedew*	1
Large *watirscoupes*	1
Oars	2
Skett fate	1
Dioll	1
Shovels	3
Cable of white yarn	1 weighing 4½ cwt

[F.80r.] Hawser of the same yarn for making *cranlynes*

	1 no weight given
Small rope called *sondynglyn*	1 no weight given
Shovels	2

Foreign receipts lately coming from the royal ballinger called *Petit John* for the safe-keeping of this ballinger, that is to say:

Hawser for a *forstey*	1 weighing ½ cwt

Hawser for making *shetes* and *bowlynes*

	1 weighing ½ cwt 18 lb
A *bowlyn pulley*	1
A *trice pulley*	1

Foreign receipts lately coming from the ship called *Rodcogge* for the safe-keeping of this ballinger, that is to say:

Axe	1
Shovels in bad condition	2

Foreign receipts during this accounting period coming from the carrack called *Marie Sandwich* for the safe-keeping of this ballinger, that is to say:

Oars in bad condition for the same carrack (sic)	3
Watirscoupes in bad condition	1

The following goods and equipment were used, broken, damaged or worn out in the said royal ballinger called *Facon* to provide for the maintenance and self-keeping of the same on various occasions between the said last day of August in the tenth year of Henry V lately king of England who died that day and 1 June next following, that is to say:

Items used:

Oars	5
Cable	1 weighing 2 cwt 14 lb

Purchases from previous years, that is to say:

Large *watirscoupes*	1
Oars	2
Shovels	3

[F.80v.] Hawser of the same for making *cranlyn*
1 no weight given

Foreign receipts lately coming from the royal ballinger called *Petit Jon* for the safe-keeping of this ballinger, that is to say:

Hawser for a *forstey*	1 weighing ½ cwt
A certain *trice pulley*	1

Foreign receipts lately coming from the ship called *Rodcogge* for the safe-keeping of this ballinger, that is to say:

Axe	1
Shovels in bad condition	2

Foreign receipts during this accounting period coming from the carrack *Marie Sandwich* for the safe-keeping of this ballinger, that is to say:

Oars in bad condition for the same carrack	3
Watirscoupes in bad condition	1

The said keeper of the king's ships is not responsible for the said ballinger called *Facon* with various goods and equipment after the said 1 June mentioned above, because on that day the said ballinger with her equipment was sold to Adam Forster of London by the order and advice of the King's Great Council and by the said royal letters under the Privy Seal as mentioned more fully in the preamble of this account. The ballinger was sold by the said keeper, under the said controlment, for the benefit of the king for a certain sum of money assigned to the royal service for which he accounts above among the foreign receipts of this account.

[F.81r.] 29. Royal Ballinger called *Roos de la Tour*

Receipt of the royal ballinger *Roos* with the following goods and equipment in hand from previous accounts, that is to say:

Topp	1
Mast	1
Sailyerd	1
Bowspret	1
Mast parrel	1
Hedropes	2 pairs
Bacsteyes	1
Forstey	1
Sail	1,
	that is 1 body sail with 2 bonnetts
Anchors	2
[F.81v.] *Pulleys*	4
Pulleys	2
Stetyng	2
Mekhoke	1
Mesan Maste	1
Sailyerd for *le mesan*	1
Hedropes for *le mesan*	3
Isynge ropes for *le mesan*	2
Mesan saill	1
Cannon	1 with 2 chambers
Bedewe	1
Boat called *cook*	1
Cable of black yarn from Zealand[220]	
	1 weighing 3 cwt 1 qua 2 lb
Hawser for *hedropes*	1 weighing 1 cwt 7 lb.
Cable of Dutch yarn	1 weighing 3 cwt 1 qua 21 lb
Hawser of the same yarn for *shet* and *takkes*	
	1 weighing 1½ cwt 27 lb
Large oars for the same	10
Lantern	1
Anchor	1
Small brass pot	1
A *sondyngled*	1
Sondynglyn	1 no weight
Hawser of the same Dutch yarn for *yerdropes*	
	1 weighing ½ cwt 7 lb

Rope of white yarn for *priall ropes* 1 weighing ½ cwt 4 lb
Large oars   17
A *skett fate*   1
Lanterns   2
Axe   1
Hamour   1
Shovels   2

[F.82r.] The following goods and equipment were used, damaged, broken and worn out in the said ballinger called *Roos* to provide for the maintenance and safe-keeping of the same on various occasions between the last day of August in the tenth year of Henry V late king of England who died that day and 1 April next following in the first year of the present king on which day the said royal ballinger was beached in a *dook* on *le wose* because of her dilapidation, that is to say:

Items used:
Pair of *hedropes*   1 pair
Forstey   1
Pulleys   2
Stetynges   1
Mekhoke   1
Hedropes for *le mesan*   1
Large oars for the same   6
Lantern   1
Sondynglyn   1 no weight given
Large oars   2
A *skett fate*   1
Shovels   2

The said keeper is not responsible for the said ballinger called *Roose* in bad condition (which had been recently beached on *le woose* because of her dilapidation and then broken up into pieces by storms and the violence of the wind) after 17 February in the third year of the present king because on that date in February the said ballinger in bad condition, broken up into pieces was sold to William Castell of Hampshire by the said order and advice of the king's great council and by the said royal letters. The ballinger was sold by the said keeper for the benefit of the king under the said controlment for a certain sum of money assigned to the royal service for which he accounts above among the foreign receipts of this account.

[F.83r.] 30. Four ships in bad condition captured from Brétons
Receipt of 4 ships in bad condition captured from Brétons with the following goods in hand from previous accounts during the tenure of the said keeper, that is to say:

Craier in bad condition without *hacches*	1, burthen 40 wine tuns
Craier in bad condition without *hacches*	1, burthen 34 wine tuns
Craier in bad condition without *hacches*	1, burthen 30 wine tuns
Craier in bad condition without *hacches*	1, burthen 30 wine tuns
Roders for the same	3

[F.83v.] 31. Royal ballinger called *Gabriell Harflew*

Receipt of the royal ballinger called *Gabriell Harflew* with the various equipment and goods following in hand from previous accounts, that is to say:

Mast	1
Pairs of *hedropes*	5
Bacsteyes	1
Forstey	1
Yerdropes	2
Anchors	2
Sail for the same	1, that is 1 body with 1 bonnett
Bedewe	1
Kettill	1
Dyoll	1
Oars in bad condition	4
Rope for *braill ropes*	1 no weight given
Hawser for *shetes*	1 weighing ½ cwt 14 lb
Hawser for *trusses*	1 weighing 3 qua 2 lb
Hawser for *upties*	1 weighing 1 cwt 1 qua
Sondyngledes	1
Hawser of black yarn for *pollancr ropes*	
	1 weighing 1 cwt

Purchases from previous years, that is to say:

Cables of Dutch yarn	2 weighing 6½ cwt 14 lb
Hawser of the same Dutch yarn for a *wyndyng-hauncer*	
	1 weighing 1½ cwt 14 lb
Small rope called *cranlyn* for the same	
	1 weighing ½ cwt 12 lb
Cable for the same ballinger	1
Hawser for *bowlynes* and *haliers* of black yarn	
	1 weighing together 4 cwt 19 lb

[F.84r.] Oars for the same ballinger 18

Lanterns	2
Sailyerd	1
A *bowspret*	1
A *pomp*	1
Boat for the same ballinger	1

Bonnett for the sail of the said ballinger

1

A *rothir* for the same ballinger   1

Foreign receipts lately coming from four dilapidated ships captured from Bretons for the safe-keeping of this ballinger that is to say:

Pulleys for the windlass   1

Mast parrel   1

Foreign receipts lately coming from the ship called *Katerine* for the safe-keeping of this ballinger that is to say:

Topp   1

The following goods and equipment were used, damaged, broken and worn out in the said royal ballinger called *Gabriell Harflew* to provide for the maintenance and safe-keeping of the same on various occasions between the said last day of August in the tenth year of the lord Henry V late king of England who died that day and the last day of the same month of August in the fifth year of the present lord king finishing on that day, that is to say:

Items used:

Pair of *hedropes*   1

Bacsteyes   1

Yerdropes   2

Kettyl   1

Oars in bad condition   4

Rope for *braill rope*   1 no weight given

Rope for *shetes*   1 weighing 64 lb

[F.84v.] Purchases from earlier years, that is to say:

Cable of Dutch yarn   1 weighing 3 cwt 1 qua 11 lb

Oars for the same ballinger   6

Lantern   1

[F.85v.] 32. Various artillery stores for the same office.

Receipt of various artillery stores, lately provided from the Tower for the same office in hand from earlier accounts.

Pollaxes   3 that is on board the royal ship called *Thomas*

Bows   3 on board the same *Thomas*

Sheaves of arrows   5 on board the same royal ship *Thomas*

Jakkes, in store lately coming from the ship called *Petit Trinite*

2

The various items below from these artillery stores were delivered to and used in various royal ships for their safe keeping and also sold for the benefit of the same king when these ships were sold on various occasions between the said last day of August in the tenth year of the lord Henry V late king of England who died that day and the last day

of the same month of August in the fifth year of the present king, that
is to say:

Deliveries and items used.

Pollaxes, that is on board the ship called *Thomas*	3
Sheaves of arrows, that is on board the same ship *Thomas*	5
Bows, that is on board the same	4

These items were sold and delivered by the said keeper of the king's
ships by order of the King's Great Council, at the time of the sale and
delivery of the royal ship *Thomas* with her equipment to John Chirche
mercer of London during this accounting period as noted above.

Jakkes in store lately belonging to the ship called *Petit Trinite*   2

These were delivered for the benefit of the said king by the said
keeper for the maintenance and safe-keeping of the royal barge called
Valentyn within the accounting period as noted above.

[F.86r.] 33. Gross purchases in hand from previous accounts.

Receipt of the various goods and equipment following in hand from
previous accounts being gross purchases for the said office, that is to
say:

Cables   3

Hawsers   5, that is of
Bridport, Lynn and Dutch yarn weighing together
                        3 mwt 9½ cwt 13 lb.

Iron *gaddes* for defence and for throwing in war-time from the
toppes of various royal ships and vessels
                        46
                        weighing together 3 cwt 1 qua 5 lb

Nails for the same royal office   1 mwt 2 cwt 27 lb
Ocom for the same office   1 mwt 3 cwt 3 qua 11 lb
Pitch for the same office   11 barrels
Large masts for the same office   2
Large oars for the same office   32
Ironwork called *cabilhokes* and *wynches* for making
    cables and ropes for the same office
                        10
Ells of canvas for the same office 35 ells 1 qua
Lanterns for the office of the king's ships
                        7
A brass pot for heating pitch, tar and other necessities
    for the same office of the king's ships
                        1
Large *pavis* for the same office   15
Pompe boxes   2
Large *deles* for the same office   2

Shovels for the same office   2
Pieces of *wynwes* for the same office
                                       2
Large boards called *rigoll*   7
Coffrs of wood ordered for keeping bows and arrows
                                       12

[F.86v.] 33. Items used from these gross purchases
Ropes and cables
  Cables   4
  Hawsers   5, that is of Bridport, Lynn and
                                       Dutch yarn weighing together
                                       3 mwt 9½ cwt 13 lb
  These were handed over and used, damaged, broken and worn out in
the maintenance and safe-keeping of the following various great ships
and vessels of the office of the king's ships on various occasions within
the accounting period, that is, in the ship called *Gracedew*
  Cables   2
  Hawsers   2 that is of Bridport, Lynn and
                                       Dutch yarn weighing
                                       1 mwt 6 cwt 1 qua 4 lb
  ship called *Jesus*
  Cables   2
  Hawser   1 that is of the above yarn weigh-
                                       ing 2 mwt 14 lb
  ship called *Holigost*
  Hawsers of this yarn from
  Bridport, Lynn and Holland   2 weighing 3 cwt 23 lb

[F.87r.] Iron *Gaddes*
  The said iron *gaddes* for defence and for throwing in wartime out of
the *toppes* of various royal ships and vessels
                                       46
                                       weighing together 3 cwt 1 qua 5 lb
  The following were delivered, used, damaged and thrown on various
occasions for the benefit of the king in various ships and other vessels
of the said office to provide for their defence and safe-keeping while
making various voyages at sea within the accounting period, that is:
  On the ship called *Holigost of Spain* on a voyage to Zealand
                                       7
  royal barge called *Valentyn* on a voyage to Cales
                                       4 weighing together ½ cwt 19 lb
[F.87v.] Nails
  The said nails for the same office of the king's ships
                                       1 mwt 2 cwt 27 lb nails

The following were handed over and used on the repair and fitting out of the various ships and other royal vessels below, and also in the building of the ship called *Graunt Marie* lately refitted at Southampton within the accounting period:

In the barge called *Valentyn* on various occasions during her repair and fitting out,	4 cwt nails
ship called *Graunt Marie* during her refitting	5 cwt nails
ship called *Trinite Riall* on various occasions while being repaired	2 cwt nails
great boat of the royal ship called *Jhesus*	1 cwt 27 lb nails

Ocom

Ocom for the same office of the king's ships 1 mwt 3 cwt 3 qua 11 lb

This was handed over and used in the repair, caulking, and fitting out of the various ships and other royal vessels below and also in the building of the said royal ship called *Graunt Marie* lately ordered during this accounting period, that is, in:

ship *Holigost of Spain*	1 cwt 14 lb
royal barge called *Valentyn de la Tour*	½ cwt 11 lb
ballinger called *Nicholas*	1 cwt 3 qua
royal ship called *Gracedewe de la Tour*	1 cwt 3 qua 17 lb
ship called *Graunt Marie* during her rebuilding	4 cwt 21 lb
ship called *Jhesus*	½ cwt 9 lb
ballinger called *Ane*	½ cwt 18 lb
ship called *Trinite Riall*	1 cwt 14 lb
ship called *Holygost* with her boats	1 cwt 19 lb
ship called *Thomas*	1 cwt 3 qua

[F.88r.] Pitch

Pitch for the same office of the king's ships   11 barrels

These were handed over and used for the repitching, *ransakynge* and repair of various faults suddenly occurring in the various royal ships below and also for the caulking of the same on various occasions during the accounting period, that is:

in the royal barge called *Valentyn de la Tour*	2 barrels
ship called *Trinite Riall de la Tour*	3 barrels
royal ballinger called *Ane*	1 barrel
ship *Jhesus* with her great boats	3 barrels
royal ship called *Holigost* with her boats	2 barrels

Masts

Great masts for the said office.[221]

[F.88v.] Oars.

Great oars for the said office 32.

These were handed over and used in the fitting out and safe-keeping of the various ships and other vessels of the office below on various occasions within the accounting period, that is:

In the ship called *Gracedew* and her boats	7 oars
royal ballinger called *Roos*	3 oars
ballinger called *Faucon*	4 oars
Royal ship called *Jhesus* with her boats	6 oars
ship *Holigost* with her boats	4 oars
ship called *Thomas*	2 oars
ballinger called *Georg*	4 oars
royal ballinger called *Ane*	2 oars

Canvas

Ells of canvas for the same office	33 ells 1 qua

These were handed over and used on various occasions for the repair of various sails and bonnetts and for the making and mending of various other necessities in the said office during the accounting period, that is:

In the ballinger called *Nicholas de la Tour*	5 ells
royal ship called *Holigost of Spain*	7 ells
royal barge called *Valentyn*	4 ells
ship *Trinite Riall de la Tour*	11 ells
ship *Graunt Marie de la Tour*	6 ells

[F.89r.] Lanterns

Lanterns for the same office of the king's ships	7

These were handed over and used for the maintenance, safe-keeping and fitting out of the following royal ships and vessells and also on various occasions for the surveying of certain cracks and *lekkynges* suddenly occurring in the same within the accounting period, that is:

In the carrack *Christofre*	1 lantern
royal ship called *Thomas*	2 lanterns
royal ship called *Holigost*	3 lanterns
royal barge called *Valentyn*	1 lantern

Pompe boxes

Pompe boxes for the same office	2

These were handed over and used in the repair of the (*dez*) *pompes* in the royal ship called *Trinite Riall* so that water could be pumped out of this ships on various occasions within the accounting period.

[F.89v.] *Deles*

Large *deles* for the same office of the king's ships	2

These were handed over and used for the benefit of the king for the fitting out and repair of the royal ship called *Holigost de la Tour* involving the mending of the *calfatynges* of the same ship within the accounting period.

Shovels

Shovels for the same office of the king's ships   2

These were handed over and used for the shifting of ballast and sand within various ships and other royal vessells for the maintenance of the same and also for the removal of ballast in order to mend various *rentynges* and other faults in the same within the accounting period.

Wynwes

Pieces of *wynwes* for the same office   2

These were handed over and used to bind and repair the sails and bonnetts of the royal ship called *Holigost of Spain* and the royal barge called *Valentyn* on various occasions within the accounting period.

Rigold

Large boards called *rigold* for the same office   7

These were handed over and used for the benefit of the king to make various cabins and various other necessities needed for the works on the royal ship called *Graunt Marie* at the time of her refitting during this accounting period.

[F.90v.] 34. Foreign receipts in hand from previous years.

Receipt of various goods and stores in hand from the foreign receipts of previous years for the office of the king's ships, that is:

Large *bylwes* lately coming from the royal ship called *Gracedewe* used for making nails and various other ironwork for the said office in the smithy[222] of the same office.   2

Iron *tongges* of various kinds lately similarly coming from the same royal ship called *Gracedewe* for the making of nails and other ironwork for the same office in the same smithy 8 pairs with 1 iron *firestaff*.

Iron apparatus for hanging up anchors while making or repairing the same similarly coming from the same ship called *Gracedieu* to be used in the said smithy.   1

Cables of various kinds recently ordered of black and white Dutch yarn coming from a certain recent purchase and provision of yarn for the same office.   3

Ropes called hawsers of various kinds similarly newly ordered of the same black and white Dutch yarn from the same recent purchase and provision for the said office.   2 weighing together 4 mwt 1½ cwt 1 6lb

Oaks from the royal New Forest in Hampshire received by indentures under a royal writ from John Hull and others as above, felled and sawn.   29

[F.91r.] Strings for bows for the same office, as above among the gross purchases,

2½ gross, that is 360 strings.

Bows for the same office of the King's ships lately received by the said indenture from John Acclan, yeoman of the late King, for the maintenance of the office of the king's ships.   50

Sheaves of arrows similarly received from the said John Acclan by indenture for the office of the king's ships.   114

Waynscott boards, sawn and shaped, and planed recently received by indenture under a royal writ from Robert Berd, clerk,[223] for the same office of the king's ships.   1125 pieces (counting 120 to the 100)

Boards called *rigold* sawn, shaped and planed received from the said Robert by indenture for the office of the king's ships.   64 pieces.

[F.91v.] 34. Items used from these foreign receipts from previous years. Ropes and cables

Cables of various kinds recently ordered of black and white Dutch yarn coming from a recent purchase and provision of yarn for the same office.   3

Ropes called *hauncers* of various kinds similarly newly ordered of the same black and white Dutch yarn coming from this recent purchase for the said office.   2   weighing together 4 mwt 1½ cwt 16 lb

Of which the following were handed over, used, damaged, broken and worn out in the maintenance and safe keeping of the various ships and other vessels of the office of the king's ships noted below, on various occasions during the accounting period, that is:

In the royal ship called *Trinitee Ryall*	1 cable
Royal barge called *Valentyn*	1 cable
Ship called *Holygost* for *boiropes*	2 hawsers
	weighing in all 1 mwt 9½ cwt 16 lb

[F.92r.] Oaks

Oaks from the royal New Forest in Hampshire received by indenture under a royal writ from John Hull and others, as above, for the office of the king's ships, sawn and felled.   29

These were handed over and used in the repair of the *stakynge* and *pilynge* at Hamble and the repair of various ships and vessels of the office and also the rebuilding of the ship called *Graunt Marie* lately undertaken at Southampton, on various occasions within the accounting period, that is:

In the royal ship called *Jhesus* with her great boats	5 oaks
barge called *Valentyn*	2 oaks
royal ship called *Gracedieu de la Tour* with her great boats	6 oaks
royal ship called *Graunt Marie* for her rebuilding	11 oaks

royal ship called *Trinite Riall* with her boats   3 oaks
port of Hamble for repair of the *pilynge* and *stakynge*   2 oaks

[F.92v.] *Waynscott*

Waynscott boards, sawn, shaped and planed recently received by indenture under royal writ from Robert Berd, clerk for the same office of the king's ships.   1125 pieces (120 to the 100)

These were sold, under the said controlment for the benefit of the king by the said keeper of the king's ships by order of the said royal letters under the Privy Seal to Walter Fettepas and various other men of Southampton on various occasions in the third year of the present king, receiving for each whole board (that is with two pieces sawn and shaped) 7d, total £19 12s 3½d for which he accounts above among the foreign receipts of this account.

Rigold

Board called *rigold,* sawn, shaped and planed similarly received from the said Robert by indenture for the office of the king's ships   64 pieces

These were sold similarly under the said controlment for the benefit of the king by the said keeper of the king's ships by order of the said royal letters under the Privy Seal to the said Walter Fettepas and other men on various occasions in July and August in the said third year, receiving for each whole board (that is with two pieces sawn and shaped) 14½d, total 40s 5¾d for which he accounts above among the foreign receipts of this account.

[F.93v.] 35. Gross purchases during the accounting period for the same office.
Purchases.

Wooden *pompe boxes* for the said office of the king's ships   20
Nails called *pompnaill* for the office of the king's ships   8 cwt
Large barrels of tar for the same office   6
Large barrels of tar for the same office   12
        (total 18 barrels)
A certain large *brasse pott* used in the caulking and fitting
   out of ships in the same office   1
Lastes of pitch, each *last* comprising 12 small barrels
       2 comprising 24 barrels
Large oars for the same office of the king's ships
     40
Shovelles for the said office   24
Large cable of white yarn from Bridport for the same office
     4
     each cable weighing 1 mwt 2 cwt, total 4 mwt 8 cwt

Ropes called *hauncers* of the same Bridport yarn
16
each weighing 1½ cwt 12 lb, total 2 mwt 5½ cwt 24 lb

[F.94r.] Small ropes of the same Bridport yarn for the same office
9 weighing together 8 cwt 9 lb

Stones of *ocom* for the office of the king's ships
40½

Large barrels of tar for the same office
12²²⁴

Large barrels of tar for the same office
8

Large barrels of tar for the same office
13

Lasts of tar for the same office   2 lasts comprising 24 barrels
Overall total of tar 45 barrels

Nails called *calfatnaill* for the office
5 cwt

Nails for the office of the king's ships
4 cwt

Total 9 cwt nails.

Large cables for the office of the king's ships
5

Hawsers of white yarn for the office of the king's ships
6
weighing together 6 mwt 3 cwt 1 qua

Rosen for the same office   5½ cwt 8 lb
Roosen for the same office   6½ cwt 4 lb

Total 1 mwt 2 cwt 12 lb.

Large cables of white yarn from Normandy for the office of the king's ships
7 weighing 7 mwt 1½ cwt 21 lb

Ropes of various kinds called hawsers from the same Norman yarn
17
weighing 2 mwt 2 cwt 1 qua 7 lb

[F.94v.] 35. Items used from these gross purchases for the same office

Pompe boxes

The said 20 wooden *pompe boxes* for the office of the king's ships.
These were handed over and used in the repair of the *watrepompes* in the following various ships and other vessels of the said office to pump out water from the same for their maintenance and safe-keeping on various occasions within the accounting period, that is:

In the royal ship called *Jhesus*	4 *boxes*
royal ship called *Trinite Riall de la Tour*	3 *boxes*
royal ship called *Gracedieu de la Tour*	5 *boxes*

royal ballinger called *Georg*	2 *boxes*
royal barge called *Valentyn*	2 *boxes*
royal ship called *Holigost de la Tour*	4 *boxes*

Nails.

The said 8 cwt nails called *pompe naill* for teh office of the king's ships.

These were handed over and used in the repair and fitting out of the following various royal ships and other vessels and in the making and repair of various masts and necessities for the same on various occasions within the accounting period, that is:

In the royal ship called *Gracedieu de la Tour*	2 cwt 25 lb nails
royal ship called *Holigost de la Tour*	3 cwt nails
royal ballinger called *Ane* and the ballinger called *Roos*	1 cwt nails
great masts of the ship *Jhesus* and the royal ship called *Trinitee Riall*	1 cwt 75 lb nails

[F.95r.] Barrels of tar.

The said 6 large barrels of tar for the office of the King's ships.

The said 12 large barrels of tar for the same office   Total 18 barrels.

These were handed over and used in the preparation and *tarrynge* of various ropes and cables and other necessities in the following various royal ships and vessels and also to repair same on various occasions within the accounting period, that is:

In the royal ship called *Gracedieu de la Tour* with her great boats	4 barrels
royal ship called *Holigost de la Tour*	3 barrels
royal ship called *Jhesus de la Tour* with her boats and masts	5 barrels
royal ship called *Trinitee Riall* with her boats	3 barrels

Lasts of pitch.

The said *lasts* of pitch, each *last* comprising 12 small barrels; 2 *lasts* comprising 24 barrels.

These were handed over and used in the caulking and *ransakynge* of the following various royal ships and other vessels and also in the building and fitting out of the royal ship called *Graunt Marie* and various other necessaries in the said office on various occasions during this accounting period, that is:

In the royal ship called *Graunt Marie de la Tour*	6 barrels
royal ship called *Gracedieu* with her great boats	5 barrels
ballinger *Craccher*	1 barrel
ballinger called *Georg*	1 barrel
ship called *Jhesus de la Tour*	3 barrels

royal ship called *Trinitee Riall*	2 barrels
royal ship called *Holigost de la Tour*	2 barrels

[F.95v.] Oars.

The said 40 large oars for the office of the king's ships.

These were handed over and used for the maintenance and safe-keeping of the following various ships and other vessels of the same office on various occasions within this accounting period, that is:

In the royal ballinger called *Georg*	3 oars
ship called *Graunt Marie* when she was being built for her *launchynge* and maintenance.	9 oars
ship called *Thomas*	4 oars
ballinger called *Nicholas* for *sterynge sculles*	2 oars
ballinger called *Facon*	5 oars
ship called *Trinitee Riall de la Tour*	6 oars
ship called *Holigost of Spain de la Tour*	2 oars
ballinger called *Ane*	1 oar
ship called *Holigost*	3 oars

Shovels

The said 24 *shovelles* for the said office of the king's ships.

These were handed over and used on various occasions for shifting ballast and sand inside and outside the various ships and other royal vessels following when taking on ballast and for moving ballast here and there in the same when *ransakynge* various faults suddenly occurring in the same within this accounting period, that is:

In the ship called *Graunt Marie* at the time of her building	7
royal ship called *Gracedieu de la Tour*	3
royal ballinger called *Ane*	2
royal ballinger called *Roos*	2
royal ship called *Trinite Riall de la Tour*	5
royal ship called *Holigost de la Tour*	5

[F.96r.] *Roosen*

The said 5½ cwt 8 lb of *roosen* for the same office of the king's ships
The said 6½ cwt 4lb *rosen* for the same office.

(total 1 mwt 2 cwt 12 lb)

These were handed over and used in the repair and *ransakynge* of the various royal ships and other vessels of the office following and for the caulking and *rosenynge* of the same on various occasions during this accounting period, that is:

In the barge called *Valentyn de la Tour*	1 cwt 2 lb *rosen*
royal ship called *Jhesus* with her boats	3½ cwt *rosen*
royal ship called *Gracedieu* with her great boats	4 cwt 1 qua *rosen*

royal ship called *Holigost de la Tour* with her
    great boats   2 cwt 6 lb *rosen*
royal ship called *Trinite Riall* with her great boats   1 cwt 1 qua 4 lb

Nails
    The said nails called *calfatnaill* for the same office of the King's
ships.   5 cwt
    The said nails for the same office.   4 cwt
                                        Total 9 cwt

These were handed over and used in the repair of the following various royal ships and also in the repair of (*del*) *bulwerke* on various occasions within this accounting period, that is:
    In the wooden tower called *bulwerke*   3½ cwt nails
    royal ship called *Trinitee Riall*   2 cwt 1 qua nails
    royal ship called *Holigoste*   3 cwt 1 qua nails

[F.96v.] Cables and ropes
    The said large cables of white Bridport yarn for the same office of the king's ships   4 of which each cable weighs
                                         1 mwt 2 cwt
                                  Total 4 mwt 8 cwt
The said 16 ropes called hawsers with 18 other ropes called hawsers, being in two parcels, both of the same white Bridport yarn for the same office
    34, that is weights as above under three headings, 4 mwt 6½ cwt 17 lb
                  Overall total 9 mwt 4½ cwt 17 lb
These were handed over and used, damaged, broken and worn out in the maintenance, fitting out and safe keeping of the following various royal ships and other vessels and in the binding, fitting out and assembly of various great masts and other necessities for the same ships on various occasions within this accounting period, that is:
[F.97r.] In the ship *Trinite Riall*
    Hawsers and ropes for the binding and assembly of the great mast and *saill yerds* and various other necessities of the same royal ships and her boats   3
    Hawsers for *boyropes* for the safe keeping and maintenance of the anchors and cables of the same royal ship   2
    Total 5 hawsers weighing 4½ cwt 3 lb
Ship *Gracedieu*
    Great cables for *le rood* for the safe keeping and maintenance of the said royal ship.   2
    Hawsers for *boiropes* for this maintenance and keeping of the anchors and cables and boats of the said ship   4
    Hawsers and small ropes for the binding and repair of the great mast and various other necessities   3

Hawsers for *bote ropes* for the keeping and maintenance of the great
boats of the same royal ship   2
Total 2 cables 9 hawsers weighing 3 mwt 7 cwt 2 lb
Ship *Jhesus*
Large cables for *le rood* and *morynge* for the safe keeping and
maintenance of the same royal ship   1
Hawsers for *boiropes* for the maintenance and keeping of the
anchors and cables of this ship   3
Hawsers for *hedropes* for the maintenance and fitting out of the
same royal ship   1
Hawsers for *bote ropes* for the maintenance and *morynge* of boats   2
Hawsers and ropes for the rigging and binding of the great mast and
kele ropes and various other necessities for the same royal ship   2
Total 1 cable 7 hawsers
weighing 2 mwt 6 cwt 3 qua 6 lb
[F.97v.] Ship *Holigost*
Large cables of the said yarn for *morynge* for the maintenance and
safe keeping of the said ship   1
Hawsers for *bote ropes* and *morynge* the great boats and various
other necessities in the same   2
Hawsers for *bacsteyes* used for the maintenance and fitting out of
the same royal ship   1
Hawsers for *boiropes* for the safe keeping of the anchors and cables
and other necessities in the same ship   2
Hawser for *wyndynghauncer* and various other necessities made for
the maintenance of the same   1
Total 1 cable 6 hawsers weighing 1 mwt 8½ cwt 11 lb
Barge *Valentyn*
Hawsers for *forsteyes* and various other necessities for the keeping
and maintenance of the same royal barge   1
Hawsers and other ropes for *stetyng* and *boyropes* and other necessi-
ties for the keeping and fitting out of the said barge   2
Total 3 hawsers weighing 3 cwt 1 qua 14 lb
Total of cables, as above,   4
Total of hawsers and other ropes used,   31
weighing in all 9 mwt 1 qua 8 lb

Barrels of Tar
The said 8 barrels of tar, 13 barrels of tar and 2 lasts comprising 24
large barrels all for the same office of the King's ships, total 45 barrels
Of which the following were handed over and used in the preparation and *tarrynge* of various ropes and cables and in the *tarrynge* de
shrowdes in the various ships following and in the preparation, repair

and *tarryng* of the same on various occasions within the accounting period, that is:

In the ship *Trinite Riall* with her boats	7 barrels
royal barge called *Valentyn*	3 barrels
royal ship called *Gracedew*	12 barrels
ship *Holigost* with her boats	8 barrels
ship *Jhesus* with her boats	11 barrels

Ocom

The said stones of *ocom* for the office of the king's ships 60½ stones.

These were handed over and used in the repair and *ransakynge* of the following various royal ships and other vessells of the same office and also in the caulking and fitting out of the same on various occasions within this accounting period, that is:

In the royal barge called *Valentyn*	6 stone
ship called *Jhesus* with her boats	11½ stone
ship *Gracedieu* with her boats	14 stone
ship *Holigost* with her boats	10½ stone
ship *Trinite Riall* with her boats	7 stone

[F.98v.] 36. Royal ship called *Gracedieu*

Receipt of the royal ship called *Gracedieu* with the various goods and equipment following, in hand from previous accounts, that is:

Receipts

Great mast	1
Boats for the same	2
Cokbotes	1
Sondyngledes	3
Hamours	6
Oars	17
Shovels and mattocks	7
Augers	6 of which 2 long
Masts	3 of which 1 for a boat
Bowspret	1
Large hawsers	4
Cables	5 weighing 5 mwt 5½ cwt 3 lb
Polleys	61
Pompes	2
Pots	3
Saws	2
Anchors	13 of which 2 for a boat
Guns	3 with 3 chambers
Mesan	1
Boyes of *Cork*	2

Wooden *boys* called *dobbles*	2
Wooden *lath*	1
Wayshell	1
Pikoys	2
Clenchhamours	2
Iron *crowes*	2
Iron socket for the *pompstaff*	1
Iron hame	1

[F.99r.] Iron *gaddes* for throwing in the *topp*

102

Iron rams	2
Iron shovels	1

Brazen *sives* and *cross braces* made out of 1000 lb of copper and 200 lb. of *belbrass* and 900 lb. of *potbras* and *panbras* and the remains of 8 brazen *shives*

51

Sailyerdes	2
Sails	3 with 3 bonnetts and the *shrowde* and all equipment.

Purchases from previous years, that is:

Large cable for the same	1 weighing 2 mwt 4 cwt 3 qua
Bellows for the same ship for firing the cannon	
	2

Foreign receipts for earlier years lately coming from the carrack called *Petir* for the maintenance of this ship, that is:

Anchors	2
Grapnell	1

Foreign receipts from earlier years lately coming from the carrack called *Andrew* for the maintenance of this ship, that is:

Pairs of *hedropes*	2
Bacsteyes	2
Pollantz ropes	2
Upties	1

Foreign receipts from earlier years lately coming from the ship called *Nicholas* for the maintenance of this ship, that is:

Anchor	1
Hamour	1
Small anchor for a boat	1
Bedew	1

Stores from the Great Wardrobe that is coming lately from the same ship called *Nicholas*

Stremer of St Nicholas variously embroidered[225]

1

Gittons in bad condition variously embroidered
                                       1, that is of St Edward [226]
Cables coming from store of white yarn from Lynn
                                       2
Hawsers of the same yarn   3
[F.99v.] Purchases during this accounting period, that is:
Oars   8
Shovels   6
A certain *gymlete*   1
A certain iron *ladell*   1
Watir scopes   4
Foreign receipts lately coming from the ship called *Petit Trinite* for
the maintenance of this ship within this accounting period, that is:
Bowspret in bad condition   1
Forstey   1
Foreign receipts lately coming from the carrack called *Poule* for the
maintenance of this ship and her great boats within this accounting
period, that is:
Bowspret in bad condition   1
Pairs of *hedropes*   2
Hawser for *handropes*   1
Pulleys   8
The following equipment and goods were used, damaged, broken and
worn out in the said royal ship called *Gracedieu* and in her boats in
order to provide for the maintenance and safe-keeping of the same be-
tween the last day of August in the tenth year of the lord Henry V
late king of England who died that day and 1 September in the sixth
year of the present king, beginning on that day, that is:
Items used:
Hamours   1
Oars   4
Shovels and mattocks   2
Large hawser   1
Pulleys   2
Brass pot   1
Cork boyes   1
[F.100r.] *Waysshell*   1
Iron rams   1
Iron shovels   1
Foreign receipts from previous years lately coming from the carrack
called *Andrew* for the maintenance of this ship, that is:
Pairs of *hedropes*   2
Bacsteyes   2
Pollantz ropes   2

Upties   1

Foreign receipts lately coming from the carrack called *Poule* for the maintenance of this ship, that is:

Bowspret in bad condition   1

This was delivered and used, after it had become dilapidated to make various *dobles* and *spornewaters* and various other necessities needed for the fitting out and maintenance of the same royal ship on various occasions during this accounting period.

Pulleys   3

[F.101v.] 37. Royal ship called *Holigost de la Tour*.

Receipt of the royal ship called *Holigost de la Tour* with the following various goods and equipment in hand from previous accounts, that is:

Topp	1
Mast	1
Pairs of *hedropes*	3
Sailyerd	1
Bowspret	1
Pollancr ropes	2
Anchors for the same ship	8 – of which one is called Tynktawe and formerly belonged to the ship called *Trinite Riall*.
Large sail	1, that is one body sail with 4 bonnetts.
Trice hokes	2
Hamours	1
Pulleys	11
Kettyll	1
Cannon	6 that is with 12 chambers for the same ship
Cros bowes	5
Iron *grapnell*	1 that is with an iron chain containing 12 links
Sperr Shaftes	26
Iron *gaddes* for the (*le*) *topp*	57
Basnetts in bad condition	24
Bows	6
Sheaves of arrows	58
Ventailles in bad condition	6
Great boat	1
Mast for the same boat	1
[F.102r.] *Botes* anchor	1
Oars for the boat	3

Small boat called *cok*   1
Supplies from the Great Wardrobe that is
A sign of *worsted* embroidered with *hostric* (ostrich) plumes comprising a cover for three bonnetts of the sail of the same royal ship
                                            1

A *stremer* in bad condition embroidered wtih the Holy Spirit for the same ship[227]   1

Gittons diversely embroidered	2, that is
1 with the Royal Arms [228] and	
1 with St Edward.	
Standardes diversely embroidered	2, that is
1 with the Holy Spirit	
1 with an *anteloppe.*[229]	
Copper pot called *kettyll*	1
Ropes called *takkes*	2 weighing 2 cwt
Hawser for warprope	1 weighing 2 cwt
Cable of white yarn for *shet*	1 weighing 4½ cwt 6 lb
Ironwork called *pompyerd*	1 weighing 63 lb
Cable of Bridport yarn	80 fathoms long
	1 weighing 1 mwt 2 cwt
Hawser for a *forstey*	1 weighing 5 cwt 1 qua
Hawsers for *hedropes*	3 weighing 7 cwt 1 qua 14 lb
Hawsers for *bacsteyes*	2 weighing 4 cwt 3 qua 14 lb
Hawser for *bowlyn*	1 weighing 2 cwt 10 lb
Small oars for a boat	3
Mekhoke for a sail	1
Small cable for *boiropes*	1 weighing 4½ cwt 4 lb

Purchases from previous years, that is:
Lanterns in bad condition for the same ship
                                            2
[F.102v.] Large cables in bad condition of white yarn
                                            3
Small cable of the same yarn for making *warschetes*
                                            1
Large hawsers in bad condition of the same yarn for making *warpropes*   2

Total weight of the above	5 mwt 5 cwt 1 qua 5 lb

Purchases from previous years already debited
Ironwork called a *flaill* for the (*le*) *wyndlasse* of the said ship used to raise the sails more quickly in the same way as a carrack for the benefit of the king   1 weighing 6½ cwt 14 lb
Cable of the same yarn   1 weighing 1 mwt 1 cwt 7 lb
Hawsers of the same yarn needed for *upties* and *handropes*

	2 weighing 6½ cwt 10 lb
Small rope called *sondynglyn*	1 no weight given
Oars for the same ship	22
Watirscopes	2
Lanterns for the same ship	2
Ironwork called *hamour*	1
Ironwork called *bedew*	1
Small *lyn* called *sondynglyn*	2

Cable of Dutch black yarn for the same royal ship

	1 weighing 2 mwt 3 cwt
Small ropes called *cranelyn*	2 weighing ½ cwt 22 lb

Foreign receipts from previous years part of the parcel of 170 pieces of cork in store for making *boyes* for the upkeep of this ship that is:

Boyes for the same ship	2

Foreign receipts from previous years coming from the ship called *Nicholas* for the maintenance of this ship, that is:

Truss pulleys	2
Braill pulleys	2
Axe	1
Hawser for a *wyndyngrope*	1 weighing 2½ cwt.

Foreign receipts from previous years coming from Lynn yarn in store for the maintenance of this ship, that is:

Cables of the same yarn	2
Hawsers of the same yarn	3

Anchor coming from store lately belonging to the (*le*) *Trinite de Ryall* (sic)   1 called Tynktawe.

Cables coming from Lynn yarn in store

	2
Hawsers of the same yarn	3

[F.103r.] Foreign receipts from previous years lately coming from the ship called *Trinite Riall* for the maintenance of this ship, that is:

Large anchor called Tynktawe	1

Purchases during this accounting period, nothing.

Foreign receipts lately coming during this accounting period from the equipment of the ship called *Nicholas* for the maintenance of this ship, that is:

Sailyerd in bad condition	1
Awger in bad condition	1
Boyes for anchors, in bad condition	
	1

Foreign receipts lately coming during the accounting period from the carrack called *Andrew* for the maintenance of this ship, that is:

Topp in bad condition	1
Pairs of *hedropes*	3

Forstey in bad condition	1
Pollantz ropes	2 pair

The various goods and equipment following were used, broken, damaged, and worn out in the said royal ship called *Holigost* and in the maintenance of her great boats in order to provide for the maintenance and safe-keeping of the same between the last day of August in the tenth year of the said Lord Henry V late king of England who died that day and 1 September in the sixth year of the present king, beginning on that day, that is:

Items used:

Topp	1
Pair of *hedropes*	1
Pulleys	2
Oars for a boat	2
Hawser for *warpropes*	1 weighing 2 cwt
Cables of white yarn for making *shetes*	
	1 weighing 4½ cwt 6 lb
Cable of Bridport yarn 80 fathoms long	
	1 weighing 1 mwt 2 cwt
[F.103v.] Small oars for a boat	1
Small cable for *boyropes*	1 weighing 4½ cwt 4 lb
Oars for the same ship	2
Watirscoupes	2

Foreign receipts from previous years coming from the ship called *Nicholas* for the maintenance of this ship, that is:

Trice pulleys	2

Foreign receipts from previous years coming from Lynn yarn in store for the maintenance of this ship, that is:

Cable of the same yarn	1
Hawser of the same yarn	1

Purchases during this accounting period, nothing.

Foreign receipts lately coming during this accounting period from the same ship *Nicholas* for the maintenance of this ship, that is:

Sailyerd in bad condition	1

This was delivered and used for the benefit of the king, after it had worn out for the making of *dobles* and *spornewatrs* and other necessities for the maintenance and repair of this same ship on various occasions during this accounting period.

[F.105r.] 38. Royal ship called *Jhesus de la Tour*

Receipts of the royal ship called *Jhesus de la Tour* with the following goods and equipment in hand from previous accounts, that is:

Great anchors for the same ship	2 no weight given

Great anchor newly made for the same ship

1 weighing 1 mwt 5½ cwt

Anchor newly made for the same   1 weighing 2 mwt 2 cwt 24 lb
Anchor newly made for the same   1 weighing 1 mwt 8 cwt 1 qua 6 lb
Anchor newly made for the same   1 weighing 1 mwt 4½ cwt
Anchor newly made for the same   1 weighing 1 mwt 4 cwt 3 qua
    Total 8 mwt 5 cwt 1 qua 2 lb

[F.105v.] *Sailyerd*   1
  Brass pot   1
  Mast   1
  Sail   1

that is one bonnet somewhat used for the great boat, called *folwer*, of the same ship.

Whole equipment for the same mast

1

Lined sail   1

with 4 lined bonnetts for the same ship comprising 1823 ells of canvas from Vitry.

Ropes called hawsers of white yarn for making *hedropes*

5 weighing 1 mwt 9 cwt 1 qua 4 lb

Large hawser of the same yarn for a *forstey*

1 weighing 7 cwt 4 lb

Hawsers for *warpropes*   2 weighing 6 cwt 1 qua 7 lb
Hawser for *stetyng*   1 weighing 2½ cwt 2 lb
Hawsers for *bowlynes*   2 weighing 4 cwt 3 qua 19 lb
Small boat called *bark*   1

Ropes called hawsers of white yarn for *bacsteyes*

2 weighing 5 cwt

Axe for the same ship   1

Purchases from previous years, that is:

A certain large piece of ironwork called a *flaill* for raising the sails of this ship more easily   1 weighing 3 cwt 18 lb
Iron chains with four iron bolts   3 weighing 1½ cwt

Hawsers of Dutch yarn for *handropes*

5 weighing 5 cwt 21 lb

Hawsers of the same yarn for making *truss* and *boyropes*

2 weighing 7 cwt 21 lb

Hawsers of the same yarn for making *upties*

2 weighing 1 mwt 1 cwt 14 lb

[F.106r.] Ropes called hawsers needed for *hedropes, warpropes* and *bacsteyes*   7 weighing 9 cwt 3 qua 20 lb

Ropes called hawsers of white Dutch yarn needed for *braill ropes* and *pollancre ropes, bote ropes* and *trisynge ropes*

6 weighing 7 cwt 7 lb

Hawser of the same yarn for making *boyropes*
                              1 weighing 1 cwt 14 lb
Hawser of black Dutch yarn for *haliers, yerdropes* and *shetes*
                              3 weighing 7½ cwt 4 lb
Large cables of the same yarn   3
                              weighing 2 mwt 1 cwt 3 qua 14 lb
Small ropes called *cranelyn*   2 weighing 1 qua 22 lb
Ironwork called *hamour*   1
Lanterns   2
Oars for the same ship   30
Pulleys for the same ship   7
Small shovels for moving ballast for the same royal ship
                                10
A mast called a *mesan mast*   1
Mekhoke for the same ship   1
Beddewes for the same ship   2
A *fane* for the same ship   1 comprising 33 virges of *say*
Brass *pulleys* for the same ship 4
Small *lyn* called *sondynglyn* 1
Foreign receipts from previous years part of the parcel of 170 pieces
of cork in store for making *boyes* for the upkeep of this royal ship,
that is:
Boyes for the same ship   3
Foreign receipts from previous years lately coming from the carrack
called *Poule* for the maintenance of this ship, that is:
Canon in bad condition   2 with 1 chamber
Gondell   1
Pulleys   5
Oars in bad condition   4
Watirbaill   1
Sondynglyn   1
Cable of black Dutch yarn   1 weighing 1 mwt 4 cwt 4 lb
[F.106v.] Foreign receipts from previous years lately coming from the
royal ship called *Katerine* for the maintenance of this ship, that is:
Cable for *boyropes*   1 weighing 1½ cwt 2 lb
Cable for the same ship   1 weighing 8 cwt 21 lb
New *pulleys*   3
Oars for the same ship   4
Foreign receipts from previous years lately part of the Lynn yarn in
store for the maintenance of this ship, that is:
Cable   1
Hawsers of the same yarn   5
Purchases, that is nothing.
Foreign receipts during this accounting period lately part of the

parcel of 29 pieces of cork for making *boyes* for the upkeep of this ship, that is:

Boyes for the same ship	2

Foreign receipts during this accounting period lately coming from the equipment of the ship called *Rodcogge* for the maintenance of this ship, that is:

Pollancr ropes in bad condition	2
Mekhoke in bad condition	1
Shovels in bad condition	2

Foreign receipts during this accounting period lately coming from the equipment of the ship called *Nicholas* for the maintenance of this ship, that is:

Lantern in bad condition	1
Sondynglede	1

The following various goods and equipment were used, broken, damaged and worn out in the said royal ship called *Jhesus* and in her great and small boats in order to provide for the maintenance and safe-keeping of the same, that is on various occasions between the last day of August in the tenth year of the said late king who died that day and 1 September in the sixth year of the present king, beginning on that day, that is:

Items used:

Rope called hawser of white yarn for making *hedropes*	
	1 weighing 3 cwt 12 lb
Hawser for *warpropes*	1 weighing 3 cwt 7 lb
Hawser of Dutch yarn for *handropes* for the same	
	1 weighing 1 cwt 14 lb

Rope called hawser of white Dutch yarn needed for *braill ropes, pollancr ropes, bote ropes* and *trisynge* ropes

	1 weighing 1 cwt 3 lb
[F.107r.] Hawser of the same yarn for making *boyropes*	
	1 weighing 1 cwt 14 lb
Large cable of the same yarn	1 weighing 7 cwt 1 qua 10 lb
Oars for the same ship	3
Small shovels for moving ballast in the same royal ship	
	3
Beddewes for the same ship	1

Foreign receipts from previous years lately coming from the carrack *Poule* for the maintenance of this ship, that is:

Pulleys	2
Oars in bad condition	2
Sondynglyn	1

Foreign receipts from previous years part of the Lynn yarn in store for the maintenance of this ship, that is:

Cables	1
Hawsers of the same yarn	2
Purchases, that is nothing	

Foreign receipts during this accounting period lately coming from the equipment of the ship *Rodcogge* for the maintenance of this ship, that is:

Pollancr ropes in bad condition	1
Shovels in bad condition	2
Mekhoke in bad condition	1

[F.108v.] 39. Royal ship called *Trinitee Riall*

Receipt of the royal ship called *Trinitee Riall* with the following various goods and equipment in hand from previous years, that is:

Large hawsers for *forsteyes*	2
Ropes for *bacsteyes*	1
Pairs of *hedropes* of white yarn	4
	weighing 2 mwt 7 cwt 10 lb
Sondyngledes	4
Lined sail	1 that is 1 body with 3 bonnetts for the same royal ship
Pulleys for the (*le*) *shrowde*	9
Large *pulleys*	3
Susternes	2
Brass *pulleys* for *les gires*	2
Brass *pulleys* for hoisting the mast	2
Brass *shyves* for *peynt ancor*	2
Bowspret	1
Mast parrels	2
Topp for the same ship	1
Iron chains for the (*le*) *shrowde*	34
Iron chains to *peynt* the (*les*) *ancors* of the same royal ship	
	2 that is with 2 iron *hokes* for the same
Brass *shives* to be used for the same	
	2
Anchor	1
Mekhokes	2
Firepan	1
Bitakyll covered with lead	1
Boyes for the anchor	2
Large anchor the gift of Sir John Blount to the said late king	
	1

Gilded crown of copper for the (*le*) *toppe*
1

Spyndell of iron for the same crown
1

Wooden leopard painted [230]   1
[F.109r.] Gilded crown of copper for the same leopard
1

Gilded *septr* of copper for the (*le*) *capstan* of the same ship
1 that is worked as three flowers *delic* [231]

Stores from the great Wardrobe, that is:
A sign for the sail of the said ship embroidered with the Royal Arms in *worsted* cloth   1
A cover of *worsted* enough for three bonnetts of the same sail
1

Stremers variously embroidered   1 that is of St Mary [232]
Gittons variously embroidered   3 that is:
   of the Holy Trinitee   1 [233]
   of St Edward   1
   of *hostric* feathers   1
Standards in bad condition, variously embroidered
2, that is:
   of St Mary   1
   of *hostric* feathers   1
Various equipment from store acquired at sea and elsewhere, that is:
   Lyfftynges   1
   Iron *trevett*   1
   Sheerhoke   1
   Boyes   2
   Crosse bowes   8
   Quarell for the same   177 (a hundred being 5 x 20)
   Iron cannon   5, that is coming from Nicholas Merbury by way of Stephen Thomas, with 8 chambers
Lances coming from the same Nicholas by way of the said Stephen
18
   Gaddes of iron for the (*le*) *topp*   81
   Ironwork called *tricehokes*   2
   Ironwork called *bedewes*   1
   Ironwork called *grapnell*   1
[F.109v.] Large hawser for *upties*   1 weighing 6½ cwt 6 lb
   Hawsers for *hedropes*   2 weighing 4 cwt 10 lb
Large cable of white Lynn yarn 80 fathoms long

	1 weighing 1 mwt 2 cwt 3 qua
Ropes called *takkes*	2 weighing 3 cwt 3 qua
Brass pot called *pich kettil*	1
Mekhoke	2
Cable of Bridport yarn	1 weighing 1 mwt 1 cwt 1 qua
Small mast for a boat	1

Purchases that is from previous years

Sailyerd for the same great boat	1
Iron chains for the same boat	6
Cables of black Dutch yarn	2
	weighing 1 mwt 8 cwt 3 qua 20 lb

Hawsers of the same yarn for *truss, stetynges* and *yerdropes*

                                            6
                              weighing together 2 mwt 1 cwt 12 lb

Cable for the same yarn	1 weighing 8 cwt 3 qua 15 lb
Large shovels	3
Small ropes called *cranelynes*	2 weighing ½ cwt 14 lb
Bedewes for the same ship	2
Oars for the same ship	23
Lanterns	3
A *sailyerd* for the same	1 comprising 2 spars

Hawsers of white Dutch yarn for *priall ropes*

                                            2
                              weighing together 2 cwt 1 qua 14 lb

Large hawsers of the same yarn needed for *boyropes*

                              1 weighing 3½ cwt 21 lb

| Small ropes called sondynglyn | 2 |

Foreign receipts from previous years from the store house lately coming from the ship called *Katerine* which formerly belonged to a certain old royal *Hulke,* that is:

Anchor formerly in the old *Hulke* recently on board the ship called *Katerine*	1

[F.110r.] Foreign receipts from previous years lately coming from the ship called *Rodcogge* for the maintenance of this ship, that is:

Brass pot	1
Iron *hamour*	1
Cable for the same ship	1 weighing 8 cwt 4 lb

Foreign receipts from previous years coming from Lynn yarn in store for the maintenance of this ship, that is:

| Hawsers of the same yarn | 3 |

Purchases, that is – nothing.

Foreign receipts during this accounting period coming from the equipment of the ship called *Philippe* for the maintenance of this ship, that is:

Axe   1

Foreign receipts during this accounting period lately coming from the carrack called *Peter* for the maintenance of this ship, that is:

Pair of *hedropes*   1
Pollantz ropes in bad condition   1 pair
Pulleys   5

Foreign receipts during this accounting period lately coming from the ship called *Katerine* for the maintenance of this ship, that is:

Sondyngled   1
Beddewe in bad condition   1
Lanterns in bad condition   2

The following various goods and equipment were used, damaged, broken and worn out in the said royal ship called *Trinite Riall* and in the great and small boats of the same in order to provide for the maintenance and safe-keeping of the same, that is between the last day of August in the tenth year of the Lord Henry V late king of England who died that day and 1 September in the sixth year of the present king beginning on that day, that is:

Items used:

Pair of *hedropes* of white yarn   1 weighing 2 cwt 6 lb.
Sondyngledes   1
Pulleys for the (*le*) *shrowde*   2
Mekhokes   1
Boyes for anchor   1
Ironwork called *bedewes*   1

[F.110v.] Large cable of white Lynn yarn 80 fathoms long
                                                        1 weighing 1 mwt 2 cwt 3 qua
Cable of black Dutch yarn   1 weighing 9 cwt 1 qua 8 lb
Hawser of the same yarn for *truss, stetynes* and *yerde ropes* for the same royal ship   1 weighing 1 cwt 4 lb
Large shovels   3
Bedewes for the same ship   1
Oars for the same ship   4
Large hawser of the same yarn needed for *boyropes*
                                                        1 weighing 3½ cwt 21 lb

Foreign receipts from earlier years coming from Lynn yarn in store for the maintenance of this ship, that is:

Hawsers of the same yarn   3

Foreign receipts during this accounting period lately coming from the equipment of the ship called *Philippe* for the maintenance of this ship, that is:

Axe   1

[F.112v.] 40. Receipt of various goods and stocks in bad condition in store.

Receipt of various goods and stocks in bad condition found to be in store for the same office of the king's ships, that is:

Old *pulleys* in store for the same office of the king's ships
168

Cables in bad condition in store for the same office
20

Old hawsers in store for the same office of the king's ships
18

Old lanterns in store for the said office of the king's ships
8

A parcel of brass in store for making and mending *pulley shives* in the same office of the king's ships
24 lb

Iron chains in bad condition in store lately coming from various ships and carracks in bad condition, or worn out or sunk
56

A great brass pot similarly in store, used for the fitting out and caulking of the great ships and other vessells in the said office
1

Old brass cooking pots in store for the same office of the king's ships 8
of which one is iron.

A worn out body sail lately coming from the old ship called *Hulke*
1

A sail in bad condition in store 1

[F.113v.] 41. Royal ballinger called *Petit Jhesus*

Receipt of the royal ballinger called *Petit Jhesus* otherwise called the (*la*) *Graunt Folower* of the royal ship called *Jhesus* with the following various goods and equipment, that is:

Receipts recently provided for in the same royal office, and as a favour debited without a valuation within this accounting period, that is:

Mast	1
Topp	1
Sailyerd	1
Bowsprett	1
Pairs of *hedropes*	2
Bacsteyes	2
Anchors for the same	2
Cables in bad condition	3
Forstey	1

Yerdropes	2
Pollancr ropes	2
Beddewe	1
Shetes	2
Boyes for the anchor	1
Upties	2
Axe	1

Purchases during this period, that is:

Sail	1 that is 1 body with 1 bonnett
Pairs of *hedropes*	2 weighing 3 qua 6 lb
Pulleys	2
Pulleys	3
Pulleys	11

A brass cooking pot called a *pitch ketyll*

	1
Oars for the same ballinger	36
Axe for the same ballinger	1
Watirscoupes	2
Lanterns for the same ballinger	2
A *saill boxe*	1
Dioll for the same ballinger	1

Small ropes called hawsers of black yarn needed for *stetynges*

	2 weighing ½ cwt 23 lb
A *fane cloth*	1

[F.114r.] The following various goods and equipment were used, broken, damaged and worn out in the said ballinger called *Petit Jhesus* in order to provide for the maintenance and safe-keeping of the same, that is during the period of the construction of the said royal ballinger and also after the building of the same, that is in all between 10 April in the fifth year of the present king and 1 September next following in the sixth year of the said king, beginning on that day, that is:

Items used:

Cable	1
Yerdropes	1
Shetes	1
Axe	1
Pulleys	1
Pulleys	2
Oars for the same ballinger	3
Watirscoupes	1

[F.115r.] Receipt of tallies.

The same accountant accounts for two tallies levied at the Receipt of the Exchequer in the tenth year of King Henry V on the collectors of the subsidy on wools in the port of the City of London for £148 8s 11d received from Richard Bukland of London by virtue of the said royal writ under the Privy Seal dated 3 July in the first year of King Henry VI, mentioned above in the foreign receipts of this account.

Total of tallies 2

Delivery of tallies.

The same accounts that these tallies have been delivered to the Receipt of the Exchequer to be cancelled in the term and year as contained in the memoranda rolls at the same Receipt by virtue of the said writ.

Appendices

EXPENDITURE ON SHIP REPAIRS, c.1417 (FRAGMENTARY ACCOUNT)

Further wages of carpenters

. . . next following that is each for 31 working days by agreement made with them on 28 August in the said ninth year, total £13 3s 6d.

Also for the wages of John Burley, William Atteley, John Gostard, John Gerrard, William Hechys, Richard Reynoll, John Tentgrowe and Robert Leker that is 8 carpenters – clenchers each for 29½ working days engaged on the same works at 5d a day, total £4 18s 4d and Nicholas Kebell, David Fraunces, William Boche, Robert Straunge, Wilfrid Monyng, Richard Romeney and John Bell, that is 7 carpenters each for 26 working days engaged on the same works, daily rate as above, total 60s 8d, all engaged within this accounting period by agreement made with them on the same day in August in the said ninth year, combined total £7 19s

Overall total £32 11s 2d

Total expenses for *pilynge and stakynge*

These are the payments for freight, boat-hire and carriage and various bonuses, gifts and other payments to sailors,[235] made by the said keeper of the king's ships through the said office on various occasions for the benefit of the said late King, for working and for travelling on business for the said office during this accounting period, as appears below, that is:

Payments for freight and porterage and other payments.

Also for money paid to 12 labourers called *portours* for transporting 4 mwt 5 cwt 3 qua 23 lb *rosen* recently bought from Sansote de la Suse, a Portuguese (together with various other supplies belonging to the said office of the king's ships) from a certain place in Southampton called the *Weyhuse*[236] to *le Storehuse* of the same office for a gross payment by agreement made with them for greater convenience of the king of 3s 4d.

Also for money paid on another occasion during this accounting period to William Tonge and various other labourers his colleagues called *portours* for transporting a certain parcel of cables and ropes, acquired for the same office, weighing 9 mwt 2½ cwt 25 lb and other necessities from the house of William Lenn in London to *Sevenokeskey*[237] including the hire of boats to take the same to a certain ship in *le Poole*:[238] total 5s.

Also for money paid to Robert Bristowe and his various colleagues called *portours* for the transport of 43 stones of *ocom* severally from various houses at a distance in London to the river Thames including the hire of boats to take the said *ocom* to a certain *craier*[239] of Fowey called *Katerine* moored in *le Pole* [Pool] and also 120 large oars for the same office: total 8s 8d.

Also for money paid to William [Dorse of folio] Kyff master carpenter and 7 carpenters working on the preparation and ordering of 6 large masts to be transported to Southampton on *tow* bearing in mind that they should not be damaged by this towing and using for this purpose 12 pieces of wood, the necessary nails and requisite ironwork, receiving in all by agreement made with him for the greater benefit of the king 26s 8d.

Also for money paid to William Wymonde master of a *craier* called *Katerine of Fowy* and Nicholas Topewall master of another ship called *Christofre of Fowy* for the freight of 9 mwt 2½ cwt 25 lb of ropes, 120 large oars, 43 stones of *ocom*, and 967 stones of Lynn yarn for making ropes received for the royal stores by authority of an indenture of William Catton and 23 lanterns, together with the towing of the said 6 large masts from London to Southampton receiving in all by agreement made with them 3 April in the eighth year of the said king   £9 6s 8d.

And to Robert Welyng and 21 labourers his colleagues working on unloading the said stores on-board the two ships from Fowey and carrying the same to a certain building called the *storehouse* in Southampton and unloading the said 6 masts and carrying them on shore receiving as a bonus for the greater benefit of the king by agreement made with them 11 May in the same year – 20s.

Also for money paid to William Shusshe for the freight of 2 mwt 8 cwt 33 lb of *fyn towe* and a parcel of tar and other necessities for the same office of the king's ships recently bought from Galtret Bardy in Flanders, that is carrying the same from Middelburgh [240] to Southampton receiving for this freight by agreement made 8 June in the said eighth year £4 6s 8d.

Also to John Hasyll of Hamble for the rent of a house there for the safe keeping of various stores and necessities belonging to the said office from the royal store that is from 4 February in the seventh year of the said king to 23 March in the ninth year of the same lord king – total 10s.[241]

Also for money paid to Walter Tonton master of a *barge* from Barnstable for the freight of 23 cables and 32 hawsers weighing 17 mwt 1½ cwt 20 lb bought from Richard Bukland and William Lenn of London and of five large ropes called *bastes* and 159 stone of *towe* recently bought from Cecilia Asshton, Isabella Roger and Agnes Bron for the same office, that is receiving for the carriage of the same from London to Southampton, by agreement made with him 17 September in the eighth year of the said king, £4.

Also for money paid to William Kempe master of a *craier* of Bridport called *Katerine* for the freight of 47 small ropes and 8 *cranelyn* with 144 *skayn* of yarn lately bought from William Mounford at Bridport for the same office, that is receiving for the carriage of the same [new folio] to Southampton by agreement made with him 7 November in the said year, 13s 4d.

Also for money paid to William Swayn master ropemaker for his work in making 6 great cables and 17 large hawsers of various kinds of black and white Lynn yarn, recently ordered at Southampton for the same office, using 744 stones of yarn received by an indenture of William Catton from the royal stores purchased in Lynn, weighing all together 11 mwt ½ cwt, at an agreed price per cwt made up, of 12d, for the benefit of the king, the account being made up on 20 August in the said year, total 110s 6d.

Also for money paid to David Roche master of a ship called *Marie Welfare* of Dartmouth for the freight of 10 large masts for the same office, part of a purchase of 22 masts recently made from John Renwell and for 2 *sailyerd* from the royal store and 2 great *bastes* 6 cables, 9 hawsers and 2 dozen *scoupes* recently bought for the same office from Thomas Estfeld, mercer, that is receiving for the carriage of the same in the same ship from London to Southampton, by agreement made with him in the same month of April in the said year, £12 6s 8d.

Also for money paid to 18 sailors working on the loading and stowing of the said masts for 3 working days as a bonus paid to them for the greater benefit of the king: 20s.

Also for money paid to William Miller, carpenter and 8 carpenters, his colleagues, working on the *shorynge* and stowing of the said 8 masts so that they should not be damaged but kept safely and for the protection of the ship, using for this work 23 pieces of timber, and ironwork and other necessities, receiving by agreement for the greater benefit of the king, 24s.

And to John Serle for the carriage of 4 great *bechys* for the same office of the king's ships, that is from the royal New Forest in Hampshire to the town of Southampton to wit 4 cart-loads, at a rate per cart-load of 12d by agreement made with him 3rd April in the ninth year of the said king: total 4s.

And to John Kolte, carter, 9s William Sprenge, 20d, Richard Storke 7s 4d, Thomas Paye 4s, Sandro Knoll 11s 3d, John Helier and John Bron 14s 5d between them, Simon Sleyhonde 7s 6ds. John Person 5s John Roger 15s 2d, Thomas Pembrigge 3s 4d, Roger Storme and John Holl 11s 4d between them, all for carting 107 large pieces of timber for the same office that is, from the said royal New Forest to Southampton between 1 April in the said ninth year and 12 August next following, by agreement made with the same 18 August in the said year.

Total £4 10s
Overall total £47 5s 6d.[242]

[Dorse of Folio]

Gross Wages of Carpenters and other workmen for the same office of the King's ships.

Gross wages of carpenters and other workmen.

Also for the wages of Thomas Stride, carpenter for 15 working days, daily rate 6d, total 6s 6d. Robert Peccard and William Piers both at 6d a day, for 6 days, total 6s: John Joffr and John Wynard both for 6 working days at 5d a day, total 5s: Ralph Stride for 5 working days, daily rate as above, total 2s 1d; and John Stride for 6 working days at 4d a day, total 2s: working on the felling and trimming of timber in the said royal New Forest and also working on the repair of various royal ships and carracks in August in the eighth year of this king, total 22s 7d (sic)

Also for the wages of Richard Brigge, smith, and Richard Crope both for 38 working days at a daily rate of 6d, total 38s; Edward Clerk and John Dokeman both for 56 working days, at a daily rate of 5d, total 46s 8d: and John Burnham, smith, for 11 working days daily rate as above, total 4s 8d: working in a royal *forge* at Southampton making *clenchnaill, roeffs, spikes, bolt, bondes* and various other ironwork for the same office out of royal iron in store in the custody of the said keeper received from various prize vessels captured at sea, working there in July, August and September in the said year, total £4 7s 3d.

Also for the wages of John Sonday, caulker, for 117 working days, at a daily rate of 6d total 53s 6d: Andrew Garner, caulker for 111 working days, daily rate as above total 55s 6d: and John Eliote, caulker, for 55 working days, daily rate as above, total 27s 6d; working on caulking the various carracks and great ships of the King both inside and outside on their bottoms, that is between 1 April in the ninth year of this king and 20 September next following by agreement made with them 27 September, overall total £7 18s.

Also for the wages of John Belford, caulker, for 90 working days, at a daily rate of 6d working on caulking the same great ships and carracks of the King, between 22 April in the ninth year of the said King and 1 November next following by agreement made with him on 13 of the same month in the said year, total 45s. Also for the wages of William Savage, master carpenter, called *carrek carpenter* at a daily-rate of 8d continuously working on the great royal ships, carracks and ballingers because of his own skill in the work, because of the repairs for the said ships and carracks and because [New Folio] [243] . . . of the repair of various faults suddenly occurring in the same that is for 99 working days within the said period, total 60s.

Also for the wages of John Bysshoppe, carpenter called *berder* for 115 working days, daily rate 6d, total 57s 6d: Thomas Melon for 63 working days, daily rate as above, total 31s 6d: Richard Dorsete and David Yevan both for 115 working days, daily rate 5d total £4 15s 10d: and John Colyn for 71 working days, daily rate 4d, total 23s 8d working on the repair of the said ships and carracks when needed suddenly under the supervision of the said master carpenter from 13 July in the ninth year of the said king to 1 January next following by agreement made with the same 4 January in the above year, total £10 8s 6d.

Overall total £28 4s 10d.

[Dorse of Folio] Royal ship called *Jhesus de la Tour*

Purchase of timber and boards.

Also for 18 pieces of timber bought and used for the repair of various cabins of the said ship called *Jhesus,* price a piece 3d, total 3s 6d.

Also for 34 sawn boards bought from Richard Bron, carpenter, of Southampton used for the repair of the same ship, price each 4d, total 11s 4d.

Also for 100 boards called *waynscott* (long 100 that is 120) bought from William Fetepase [244] of Southampton and used for making and repairing cabins in the same and various other necessities, total price 40s.

Also for 8 *plankes* called *dels* bought from Richard Davi of London and used in the repair of *calfatynge* of the said ship, price each 14d, total 9s. 4d.

Also for 120 boards called *waynscott* (long 100 that is 120) similarly bought on another occasion from the said William for making a *somercastell* newly ordered to protect . . .[245] and used on various other necessities, price a hundred 41s, total 46s 8d.

Also for 27 pieces of timber bought from Robert Hoore and used for making the said *somercastell* and other necessities, price each 6d, total 13s. 6d.

Also for 9 pieces of timber bought from the said Robert and used in the repair of the said ship, price each 4d, total 3s.

Also for 12 pieces of timber bought for making *knowes* and used to repair the said royal ship, price each 6d, total 6s.

Also for 28 pieces of timber bought from William Water of Southampton for making *bailles* and other necessities and used in the works on this ship price each 4d, total 9s.

Also for 130 boards called *waynscott* bought from Peter James of Southampton and used for making the masts of the said ship and various other necessities price each 4d, total 36s 8d.

Also for 3 pieces of timber bought from the said William and used in the making and repair of the said masts, gross price 3s 6d.

Also for 1 large piece of timber similarly bought and used when making the masts for *lerynges* price 10s.

Also for 42 pieces of timber bought from the said Robert Hoor and used in the renovation of the masts and other necessities in the said ship, price each 2d, total 7s.

Also for 35 boards called waynscott . . .

[New folio]

Purchases of nails and other ironwork. Also for 6 cwt nails bought from Robert Smyth of Southampton and used in the repair of the said ship, price per cwt 6d, total 3s.

Also for various ironwork called *clench* and *annede, bolt* and *spikes* weighing altogether 1 cwt 4 lb bought from the said Robert and used in the same repairs, price per lb 1¼d, total 12s 1d.

Also for various ironwork called *bondes* and various *spikes* bought from the said Robert and used to make the said masts, weight 1 qua 18 lb, price per lb as above, total 3s 9d.

Also for 5 cwt nails called *calfatenaill* price per cwt 12d, total 5s and 4 cwt nails called *spikes* price per cwt 12d, total 4s, and 4 cwt large nails price per cwt 16d, total 5s 4d, 6 cwt large nails price per cwt 2s, total 12s, and 9 cwt nails price per cwt 12d, total 9s, bought from John Lokier of Southampton on various occasions and used in the repair of the said ship and its masts, overall total 35s 4d.

Also for 1 mwt nails called *bordnaill* price per cwt 6d, total 5s and 4 cwt nails price per cwt 2d, total 8d, and 6 cwt nails price per cwt 9d, total 4s 6d and 8 cwt nails price per cwt 6d, total 4s bought on various occasions from Robert Smyth of Southampton and used in the repair of the said ship and her boats during this accounting period, total 14s 2d.

Also for various large nails called *lernails* and various *spikes* bought from the said Robert and used for the renovation of the large mast weighing 2 cwt 3 qua 16 lb, price per lb 1¼d, total 33s 9d.

Also for 9 large *bolt* bought from the said Robert for the repair of the same ship weighing ½ cwt 12 lb, price per lb 1¼d, per cwt 12s 8d, total 7s 1d.

Also for 2 mwt 2 cwt nails, price per cwt 3d, total 5s 6d and for 1 cwt 1 qua large nails called *lernail* and various *spikes* weighing 2 cwt 1 qua 20 lb price per lb 1¼d, total 28s 4d, bought from the said Robert and used for the making and renovation of the said large mast, overall total 33s 10d.

Also for a large piece of ironwork called *le flaille* bought from the said Robert and placed and fastened on *le* (the) *wyndlas* of the said ship, to raise the sail of the said ship more easily in the style of a carrack, weighing 3 cwt 28 lb, price per lb 1½d, total 45s 6d.

Also for various pieecs of ironwork called *siropes* and *wegges* bought from the said *Robert* and used for making the same *wyndlas* and *le flaill* weighing 1 qua 27 lb price per lb 1½d, total 6s 10½d.

Also for 3 iron chains with 4 iron *bolt* bought from the said Robert for the same ship weighing 1½ cwt price per lb 1½d, total 21s.

Also for 10 large *bolt* with 10 *forlokes* and various nails called *spikes* bought from Peter Lokier of Southampton and used in the repair of the said ship, weighing 1 cwt 1 qua 6 lb price per lb, 1¼d, total 18s 3d.

Also for 4 iron bolt bought on another occasion from the same Peter and used to stabilize and set up the mast of the same ship weighing 1 qua 12 lb price per lb 1¼d . . .

[Dorse of Folio] . . . with 13 iron *bolts* and 2 cwt large *spikes* bought on another occasion from the said Robert and used in the making of the said mast, recently renovated, weighing 8 cwt 3 qua 27 lb price per cwt 13s 4d, total 119s 9½d

overall total £17 19s 7d.

Purchases of cable and ropes.

Also for 5 hawsers of Dutch yarn bought from William Lynne of London needed for *handropes* for the same royal ship, weighing 5 cwt 21lb price per cwt 8s, total 41s 6d.

Also for 3 hawsers of the same yarn similarly bought from the same William for making *trusses* and *boiropes* for the said ship, weighing 1 mwt 1 qua 24 lb, price per cwt as above, total £4 3s 8¼d.

Also for 2 hawsers of the same yarn for making *upties* bought from the said William for the same royal ship, weighing 1 mwt 1 cwt 14 lb, price per cwt as above, total £4 9s.

Also for 10 ropes called hawsers bought from Richard Bukland needed for *hedropes warpropes* and *bacsteys* weighing all together 1 mwt 5 cwt 1 qua 27 lb price per cwt 8s, total £6 3s 10½d.

Also for 11 ropes called hawsers of white Dutch yarn needed for *braill ropes, pollancre ropes* and *bote ropes* and *tryssyngropes* bought from John Mascall of London weighing 1 mwt 1 cwt 18 lb price per cwt 10s, total 111s 7d.

Also for 1 hawser of the same yarn bought from the said John for making *boiropes* for the same ship weighing 1 cwt 14 lb price per cwt as above, total 11s 3d.

Also for 5 hawsers of black Dutch yarn bought from William Lynne for making *haliers, yerdropes* and *shetes* for the said royal ship, weighing 1 mwt 1 cwt 14 lb, price per cwt 8s, total £4 9s.

Also for 3 large cables of the same yarn bought from the said William for the same royal ship, weighing 2 mwt 1 cwt 3 qua 14 lb price per cwt 8s, total £8 15s.

Also for 4 small ropes called *cranelynes* bought for the same royal ship weighing 3 qua 12 lb price per lb 1½d, total 12s.

Also for a certain rope called a large *sondynglyn* bought from Auncell Spicer of Southampton gross price with no given weight 8s 8d.

Also for 2 ropes for making *haspynglynes* similarly bought from the said Auncell on another occasion and used to repair the sails of the said ship weighing 1 cwt 4 lb price per cwt 14s, total 14s 6d.

Also for 10 ropes . . .[246]

APPENDIX II[247]
EXPENDITURE ON REPAIRS TO SHIPS TAKING PART IN THE DUKE OF BEDFORD'S EXPEDITION OF 1416 (FRAGMENTARY ACCOUNT)

[F.116r.]
. . . parcel of fuel needed for *bremynge* price 8d, bought from him and used in the repair of the said ballinger by agreement made with him 17 May in the said fourth year, total 9s 8d.

Also to Robert Smyth, 3s for 4 iron chains weighing 24 lb, price per lb 1½d bought from the same and fixed in the same royal ballinger, by agreement made with him the same day in May in the above year.

Also to John Ternour 2s 11d for 3 *skayn* of yarn, price each 5d, total 15d and for 10 *shyves* for mending various pulleys, price each 2d, total 20d, bought and used in the repair of the said ballinger, by agreement made with him 24 May in the second year.

Also to John Wryght 16s 8d for 5 long pieces of timber needed for *revesynges* and *walys*, gross price 6s 8d, and for 37 pieces of timber for making *laskes* and *wellynges* and various other necessities, gross price for the greater benefit of the king 10s, bought and used for the repair and building of the said ballinger by agreement made with him the same day in May in the second year.

Also for the wages of 11 carpenters that is, John Stephen and John Elys both for 18 working days, daily rate 6d – total 18s; Nicholas Stasy and William Piers both for 12 working days, daily rate as above total 12s; John Clerke and William Cornissh both for 18 working days, daily rate 5d total 15s, and Richard Burgeys for 4 working days, daily rate 5d, total 20d; and Thomas Blerake and John Hudy, holders, both for 12 working days, daily rate 4d, total 8s; Richard Langley for 6 working days, daily rate as above total 2s and Bawdewyn Burgeys for 5 working days, daily rate 4d, total 20d; that is all working on the repair and making of *portleux* and on the repair of other necessities in the same between 27 May in the said year and 16 June next following by agreement made with the same on the same day of June in the said year.

[F.116v.] These are the expenses and costs incurred by the said William Soper by order and advice of the said king for the fitting out and repair of the royal ship called *Holigost de la Tour* preparing for the voyage on the high seas of the said Duke of Bedford in the said fourth year which resulted in the capture of various carracks as mentioned above, that is:

Also to John Emory a total of 35s 8d for 1 small barrel of tar, price 4s, and for 5 *herches* of *tre* pitch, price each 4s, total 20s; and for 1 cwt 1 qua, of *fyn ocom*, gross price 11s; and for 1 pottle of oil price 8d, bought from him on various occasions and used in the repair of the royal ship called *Holigost* by agreement made with him 6 May in the fourth year of this king.

Also to Roger Sterne of Netley,[248] for 91 pieces of timber bought from him and used in the repair of the said royal ship and in the making of a certain *somercastell* in the same at a gross price for the greater benefit of the said king of 20s; together with 6s 4d paid to John Ber, John Piers, Thomas Solffe, John White and John Spenser, carters for carrying in their carts this timber from Windesser (Winsor)[249] to Southampton in April in the said fourth year by agreement made with them 8 May in the said year: total 26s 4d.

Also to John Andrew of Totton,[250] 6s for 2 dozen of (*de*) *herdel*, price per dozen 3s, bought from him and used in the making of the said *somercastell* by agreement made with him the same day in May in the above year.

Also to Richard Groundy, 15s 7d for 2 clay pots for transporting pitch, wax and tar price 4d and for 1 sheepskin for making *mappoldes* price 3d and for 3 dozen great *hardell*, price per dozen 5s. total 15s, bought from him and used in the repair and fitting out of the same ship by agreement made with him the same day in May in the above year.

Also to Robert Smyth, 15s 7½d for 45 lb of iron worked into *spikes* and other ironwork, price per lb 1½d, total 5s 7½d and for 5 cwt of large nails called *spikes* price per cwt 20d, total 10s, bought from him and used in the repair and building of the same royal ship, by agreement made with him the same day in May in the above year.

Also to William Nicholl for 53 ells of canvas called of Vitry, price 6d per ell . . .

[F.117r.] . . . of the same ship by agreement made with him 13 May in the above year, total 26s 6d.

Also to John Braisier of Southampton 26s 6d for 6 brass shyves weighing 1 qua 25 lb price per lb 5d, bought from him and placed on board and used in making various *pulleys* of the same ship by agreement made with him the same day in May in the above year.

Also to the Abbot of the House of Netley[251] 5s 4d, for 6 large pieces of timber bought from him and used similarly in the repair of the said ship and in the making of the same *somercastell*, gross price by agreement made with him the same day in May in the above year, with 3s 4d paid to Roger Kytsell and John Kytssell carters, carrying with their carts these 6 pieces of timber from there to Southampton, total 8s 8d

Also to Simon atte Meer 4s, for 48 pieces of timber called *aldrs* bought from him and used in the making of the same *somercastell* and other necessities for the same ship gross price by agreement made 22 May in the above year, with 2s paid to John Hekkele carrying with his cart this timber to Southampton, total 6s.

Also to Richard Burgeys 10s 11d for 4 cwt nails, price per cwt 8d total 2s 8d and for 4½ cwt large nails called *spikes* price per cwt 20d total 7s 6d and for 2 cwt nails price per cwt 6d, total 12d bought from him and used in the repair and making of the said ship and her *somercastell* by agreement made with him the same day in May in the fourth year.

Also to Peter James 43s for 6 large barrels of tar, price per barrel 5s 6d total 27s 6d and for 4 barrels of pitch price per barrel 3s 8d, total 14s 8d and 2 *skayn* of yarn for mending the sails price 10d bought from him and used in the repair of the said ship and in *tarrynge* various cables and ropes of the same ship by agreement made with him the same day in May in the above year.

Also to Robert Smyth 9s 1½d for 4 cwt nails, price per cwt 8d, total 2s 8d and for 2 cwt nails, price per cwt 5d, total 10d, and for 7½ cwt nails, price per cwt 7d, total 4s 4½d and for 10 lb of iron worked in *spikes* price per lb 1½d; total 15d, bought from him and used in making this *somercastell* and in the repair of the same ship, by agreement made with him 30 May in the fourth year.

Also to William Nicholl 47s for 47 lb of powder called *gounpoudir*, bought from him and used on various occasions when firing various cannon within the said ship for the defense and safe-keeping of the same while on this voyage of the Duke of Bedford when various carracks were captured and later on various other voyages, price per lb 12d, by agreement made with him the same day in May in the above year.

Also to the same [F.117v.] William Nicholl 40s, for 4 cwt of *rosen* price per cwt 4s, total 16s and for 4 lb of (*de*) *filas* price per lb 6d, total 2s and for a certain *baste* (no weight) for the same ship gross price 22s, bought from him and used in the repair and maintenance of the same ship by agreement made with him the same day in May in the above year.

Also to Thomas Armorer 28s 4d, for a certain bast (no weight given) bought from him for the same royal ship and used in the same for her maintenance and for *morynge* the same, gross price by agreement made with him the same day in May in the fourth year.

Also to Robert Smyth 13s 7½d for 1 cwt and 5 lb iron worked in *lernail, spikes, bolt* and various other ironwork, bought from him and used in the repair and building of this ship by agreement made with him 3 June in the said fourth year, price per cwt 13s.

Also to the same Thomas, 7s 4d for 1 small hawser of Dutch yarn weighing ½ cwt, price per cwt 13s 4d, total 6s 8d and for 2 *skayn* of yarn price each 4d, total 8d, bought from him and used in the binding of the (*de*) *sailyerd* and other necessities in the same ship by agreement made with him the same day in June in the above year.

Also to Peter Lockyer 6s 3½d for 4 cwt nails price per cwt 5d, total 20d, and for 2 cwt nails price per cwt 12d, total 2s and for 4½ cwt nails price per cwt 7d, total 2s 7½d bought from him and used in the repair of the same ship by agreement made with him the same day in June in the above year.

Also to William Mounford of Bridport, £111 4s 2d for 10 large cables and 2 small cables for *wareshetes,* 2 hawsers for *upties,* 1 *wyndynge hauncer* and 4 large hawsers for *warpropes* of white yarn, bought from him for this royal ship called *Holigost* and for the royal ship called *Trinite Riall* for the same voyage of the Duke of Bedford and used in the same ships for their maintenance, total weight 16 mwt 6 cwt 3 qua 7 lb, price per cwt 13s 4d according to the practice of the Treasurer of England by agreement made with him 24 May in the said fourth year of the said king.

Also to John Plompton, 6s 8d for 4 great lanterns bought from him for the same royal ship called *Holigost* and used in the same for her maintenance, price each 20d, by agreement made with him the same day in May in the above year.

Also for the money paid to William Russhe, David Gamyll, William Wase, John Redy, Henry White, and Richard Haye, that is 6 carters carrying in their carts these cables and hawsers amounting to 16 mwt 6 cwt 3 qua 7 lb and various other necessities from Bridport to Southampton for the same ships called *Holigost* and *Trinite Riall*, that is 27s each for 1 cartload by agreement made for the benefit of the king with the same 7 June in the same year, total £8 2s, with 18d paid to various labourers for loading the same at Bridport, overall total £8 3s 6d.

[F.118r.] Also for the wages of 9 carpenters, that is: Robert Skous, John Reve, John Belfford each for 9 working days, daily rate 6d total 16s 6d; Nicholas Bevys, and Richard West both for 10½ working days, daily rate 6d, total 10s 6d; John Halle for 4 working days, daily rate as above, total 2s; and John Smyth and William Heyches both for 8 working days, daily rate 5d, total 6s 8d; and Henry Stokkes for 3½ working days, daily rate 4d, total 14d; all working on the repair of the said royal ship and making this sort of *somercastell* in the same, that is between 1 June in the said fourth year and 19 of the same month next following, by agreement made with the same the same day in June in the said year.

Also for the wages of 4 caulkers, that is: John Pount for 7½ working days, daily rate 6d, total 3s 9d; Peter Boneface and John Dygo both for 9 working days, daily rate as above, total 9s; and Andrew Portingall for 8 working days, daily rate as above, total 4s; all working on the caulking of the said ship and on *ransakynge* the same between 4 June in the said year and 17 of the same month next following by agreement made with the same 11 July in the said year.

[F.118v.] These are the payments and expenses incurred by the said William Soper by order and advice of the said lord king in the making of two *somerhuches* newly ordered, that is one for the royal ship called *Holigost* and another for the royal ship called *Trinite Riall* needed for the voyage of the Lord Duke of Bedford on the high seas made in the said fourth year when various carracks were captured as mentioned above:

Also to John Choude of Southampton 15s for 45 wide boards called *waynscott* bought from him and used in the building of two *somerhuches* of war newly ordered for the defense of the same royal ships called *Holigost* and *Trinite Riall* for the voyage of the Duke of Bedford when various carracks were captured, price 4d each by agreement made with him 1 June in the said fourth year.

Also to John Emory 13s 4d for 40 wide boards called *waynscott* bought from him and similarly used in the making of the *somerhuches* for the same royal ships, price each as above, by agreement made with him the same day in June in the above year.

Also to William Peyntour of Southampton 3s 4d for 19 pieces of timber bought from him and used in the making of the said *somerhuches* for the same ships gross price by agreement made with him the same day in June in the above year.

Also to John Emory 4s for 4 Prussian *planc* called *del* bought from him and used in the making and fitting out of these 2 *somerhuches* for the said ships, price each 12d, by agreement made with him 9 June in the said year.

Also to John Sawier 12d for sawing 17 boards called *waynscott* for making these *somerhuches* used there, being paid for his work by agreement made the same day in June.

Also to John Nottebem, 6s 3d for 6 cwt nails, price per cwt 7d, total 3s 6d and for 5 cwt nails price per cwt 5d, total 2s 1d and for 2 cwt nails price per cwt 4d, total 8d, bought from him and used in making these 2 *somerhuches* for the said ships by agreement made with him the same day in June in the said year.

Also to Robert Smyth of Southampton, 2s 4d for 12 small iron fastenings called *bondes* gross price 2s and for 1 cwt nails to be used for the same royal ships with these iron fastenings price 4d, bought from him and used in the making of these 2 *somerhuches* by agreement made with him 16 June in the said year.

Also for the wages of John Hoggekyn, master carpenter for 17 working days, daily rate 8d, total 11s 4d; and John Nicholl, John Froster, and John Hillarie, each for 16 working days, daily rate 6d, total 24s; John Bron and Philip Denston [F.119r.] both for 7½ working days, daily rate 5d total 6s 3d; and Roger Austeyn for 10½ working days, daily rate 4d, 3s 6d; that is all working on making these 2 *somerhuches* for the same royal ships called *Holigost* and *Trinite Riall* ordered by advice of the said king, that is between 1 June in the said fourth year and 23 of the same month next following, by agreement made with the same on the same day in the above year of the said king: overall total 45s 1d.

These are the payments and expenses incurred by the said William Soper by order and advice of the said king for the fitting out and repair of a certain Royal ballinger called *Jamys* for the voyage of the said Duke of Bedford on the high seas in the said fourth year when various carracks were captured as mentioned above, that is:

Also to Adam Boucher of Southampton 11s 8d for 10 dozen lb of wax bought from him and used in the fitting out and *talwynge* of the royal ballinger called *Jamys*, price per dozen 14d, by agreement made with him 16 April in the fourth year of this king.

Also to Thomas Armorer 2s 6d for ½ cwt *rosen* bought from him and used in the repair of the said ballinger, price per cwt 5s by agreement made with him the same day in April in the fourth year.

Also to Auncell Spycer 19s 7d for 23 ells of canvas, price per ell 5d, total 9s 7d and for 1 *roll* of (*de*) teldes for the same ballinger price 10s bought from him and used in the repair and fitting out of the said ballinger by agreement made with him 22 April in the said fourth year.

Also to John Compton 15d for 2 *skayn* of yarn, price each 4d, total 8d, and for a parcel of fuel for *bremynge* undertaken at the time of *talwynge* and *rosenyng*, price 7d, bought from him and used in this repair and fitting out of the same royal ballinger and her sail by agreement made with him the same day in April in the said year.

Also to Thomas Armorer 11s 1½d for 1 rope called a hawser bought from him and used in the binding of the mast of the same ballinger, weighing ¾ cwt 5 lb, price per cwt 14s, by agreement made with him 6 May in the said fourth year.

Also for money paid to John Hekkes for mending the *rothir* and *helm* of the same royal ballinger within the same period, 6d.

Also to John Ternour 6d for 2 *pulleys* bought from him and used in the same ballinger for the maintenance of the same, gross price by agreement made with him the same day in April in the above year.

[F.119v.] These are the payments and expenses incurred by the said William Soper by order and advice of the said king in the repair and fitting out of a certain royal ballinger called *Petit John* similarly for this voyage of the Lord Duke of Bedford on the high seas in the fourth year when various carracks were captured from enemies from Genoa as mentioned above, that is:

Also to Walter Fettepas, 10s 6d for 21 ells of canvas called of Vitry bought from him and used in the repair of various bonetts of the sail of the royal ballinger called *Petit John*, price per ell 6d by agreement made with him 28 April in the fourth year of this king.

Also to William Nicholl 13s 4d for 40 wide boards called *waynscott*, price each 4d, and for 1 small barrel of tar price 4s and for 1 *herche* of *tre* pitch price 4s bought from him and used in the repair of the same ballinger, by agreement made with him 3 May in the said year, overall total 21s 4d.

Also to the same William 28s 4d for 1 hawser of white yarn needed for *morynge*, bought from him and used for the maintenance of the same, weighing 2 cwt 14 lb, price per cwt 13s 4d, by agreement made with him the same day in May in the above year.

Also to Richard Burgeys of Southampton 12d for 4 cwt nails, price per cwt 3d, and money paid to the same for mending one anchor belonging to the same ballinger, 8d, bought from him and ordered and used in the fitting out and repair of the same ballinger by agreement made with him 11 May in the above regnal year, total 20d.

Also to Robert Smyth 3s for 24 lb of iron worked into *spikes* and iron *bolt*, bought from him and used in the repair of this ballinger, price per lb 1½d by agreement made with him the same day in May in the above year.

Also money paid for 1 *sarr* of *moss* used in the repair of this ballinger, price 2d.

Also to the same Robert Smyth 7d for a certain iron fastening bought from him and used in mending the *helme* of the same royal ballinger.

Also to William Rede 6d for 1 piece of timber bought from him and used in making a certain *helme* for the same royal ballinger.

Also to Peter Lockyer 10s 3d (sic) for 1 mwt 2 cwt nails, price per cwt 8d, total 8s and 4 cwt nails price per cwt 6d, total 3s and 1 cwt nails price 4d bought from him and used in the repair of the same royal ballinger by agreement made with him 22 May in the said fourth year.

Also to John Braibroke 2s 8d for 5 stones of *ocom*, price per stone 4d, total 20d and for 3 sheepskins with wool needed for *mappoldes* gross price 8d, and for a certain parcel of fuel for [F.120r.] *bremynge* then being undertaken price 4d bought from him and used in the repair and fitting out of the same royal ballinger by agreement made with him the same day in May in the above year.

Also to Thomas atte Welle, *boucher*, 9s 4d for 9 dozen and 4 lb of wax bought from him and similarly used in *talwynge* and fitting out the said royal ballinger price per dozen 12d, by agreement made with him 3 June in the said fourth year.

These are the payments and expenses recently incurred by the said William Soper by advice and order of the lord king, specially commissioned to build a certain royal ballinger called *Ane*, to be constructed by the direct instruction of the king at Southampton, that is the work first beginning after 18 June in the fourth year of the said king up to 22 October next following when the said ballinger was launched, from a digging called a *dook* where she was built, onto the water to *flote* after her making, that is as below:

For 1 large piece of timber 68 feet long bought from William Parke and used for a certain *botomshyde* then needed to build this royal ballinger called *Ane* price by agreement made with him 22 June in the said fourth year of the king, 9s.

Also to John Emory 4s 8d for 1 piece of timber for making a *skegge* price 2s and for 1 piece of timber for making a *sternpost* price 20d and for 1 piece of timber needed for an *aftirkegge* price 12d, bought from him and used in the making of this ballinger by agreement made with him the same day in the above year.

Also to William Parke 6s 8d for 3 pieces of timber bought from him for making *stempne peces* used in the making of the said [F.120v.] ballinger, gross price by agreement made with him the same day in June in the above year.

Also to the same William 3s 2d for 1 piece of timber bought from him and used in the making of this ballinger price including carriage of the same from Alynton[252] to Southampton by agreement made with him 24 June in the above year.

Also to John Strady of Langley,[253] 15s for 67 pieces of timber bought from him and used in *shorynge* and making of the same ballinger gross price by agreement made with him the same day in June in the said fourth year.

Also for money paid to John Emory, a total of 4s 6d, for 6 pieces of timber bought from him and used for the (*le*) *transyngtymbre* and other necessities in the making of this ballinger, gross price by agreement made with him the same day in June in the above year.

Also to John Whetnall 16s for 24 pieces of timber bought from him for making *tilatelegges* used in the works for the said ballinger, price each 8d by agreement made with him the same day in June in the said year.

Also to John Emory 16s for 4 dozen pieces of timber called *legges* bought from him, price per dozen 4s and used in the building of this royal ballinger by agreement made with him 29 June in the fourth year of the said king.

Also to William Overey of Southampton 14s 4d, for a certain large piece called *wyndas* for the same ballinger price 13s 4d and another piece of timber price 12d bought from him and used in the building of this ballinger by agreement made with him the same day in June in the above year.

Also to William Sewer 39s 4d for 60 wide boards called *englyshbord* bought from him and used in the making of the said ballinger gross price 37s. 4d with 2s paid for the carriage of the same from Hamble to Southampton by agreement made with him 5 July in the above year.

Also to George Huskey 33s 4d for 60 wide boards called *englyshbord* 16 ft long bought from him and used in the building of the said ballinger gross price including the carriage of the same from the same place by agreement made with him the same day in July in the above year.

Also to William Warner of Poole £7 12d for 300 boards called *englyshbord* bought from him and used in the same works for the said ballinger, price per 100 40s, total £6 together with 21s paid to Richard Dey master mariner for the freight of the said 300 boards from the town of Poole to Southampton by agreement made with them 8 July in the above year.

Also to William Chyke 70s for 175 boards called wide *waynscott* bought from him and used similarly in the making of the same ballinger price 40s per hundred by agreement made with him the same day in July in the above year.

Also to William Nicholl of Southampton £13 for 650 boards called wide *waynscott* bought from him and used in the building of the said ballinger [F.121r.] at this period, price per 100 40s by agreement made with him the same day in July in the above year.

Also to John Shoude of Winchester 77s for 196 large boards called *englyshbord* bought from him and used in the works for this said ballinger price per 100 40s by agreement made with him 12 August in the said fourth year.

Also to John Emory 12s for 4 dozen sawn boards bought from him and similarly used in the building of the same ballinger price per dozen 3s by agreement made with him 22 August in the said fourth year.

Also to William Richman 16s 8d for 10 large *plankes* called *Prus del* bought from him and used in the building of the same ballinger price each 20d by agreement made with him the same day in August, in the said fourth year.

Also to John Emory 26s 8d for 16 large *plankes* called *Pruc del* bought from him and used in the building of the said ballinger price each 20d by agreement made with him 27 August in the above year.

Also to William Nicholl of Southampton 20s for 50 boards called wide *waynscott* bought from him and similarly used in the works for this ballinger price per 100 40s by agreement made with him the same day in August in the said fourth year.

Also to the said John Emory 9s for 3 dozen sawn boards bought from him and used in the building of this ballinger price per dozen 3s by agreement made with him 13 September in the said fourth year.

Also to the said William Nicholl 6s for 18 large boards called *waynscott* bought from him and used in the building of the said ballinger, price each 4d by agreement made with him 3 October in the said year.

Also to Richard Burgeys of Southampton £9 16s 10d for various pieces of ironwork called *clench* and *rooffe* bought from him and used in the making of the said royal ballinger called *Ane*, weighing in all 1 mwt 4 cwt and 6 lb price per cwt so worked 14s together with another piece of ironwork also worked for the benefit of the king by agreement made with him 23 June in the said fourth year.

Also to John Kent of Southampton £4 19s 10½d for 7 cwt 15 lb of iron worked into various pieces of ironwork called *clenchnaill* and *rooffe* bought from him and used in the same work price per cwt as above by agreement made with him 28 June in the said year.

Also to Robert Smyth of Southampton £4 7s 6d for 6 cwt, 1 qua of iron worked into ironwork called *clenchnaill* and *annede* bought from him and used in the making of the said ballinger price per cwt as above by agreement made with him the same day in June in the said year [F.121v.]

Also to Peter Lockyer 67s 4½d for 4 cwt 3 qua 7 lb of iron worked into *clenchnaill* and *annend* bought from him and used in the same works price per cwt 14s by agreement made with him 26 July in the said fourth year.

Also to Thomas Smyth of Southampton 13s 4d for 1 mwt nails called *calfatenaill* bought from him and used in the building of the same ballinger price per cwt 16d by agreement made with him 7 August in the said fourth year.

Also to the same Peter Lockyer 18d for ½ cwt nails called *spurcatenaill* price 6d and for 1 cwt nails called *spykes* price 12d bought from him and used in the works for this ballinger by agreement made with him the same day in August in the above year.

Also to John Compton 8s for 8 cwt nails price per cwt 8d, total 5s 4d and for 8 cwt nails, price per cwt 4d, total 2s 8d, bought from him and used in the building of this ballinger by agreement made with him 3 September in the said fourth year.

Also for money paid to the said Richard Burgeys of Southampton for 5 cwt 1 qua 10 lb of iron worked into *spykes, bolts, forlokes, clench* and *anned* bought from him and used in the building of the said ballinger, price per cwt 14s, by agreement made with him the same day in September in the above year, total 74s 9d.

Also to Robert Smyth, 15s 6d for 1 cwt 12 lb of iron worked similarly in large *boltes* and *forlockes* bought from him and used in the building of the said ballinger price per cwt as above, by agreement made with him 14 September in the above year.

Also to Richard Burgeys 3s 4d for 2 cwt nails called large *spykes* bought from him and used there in the making of the same ballinger, price per cwt 20d by agreement made with him the same day in September in the above year.

Also to William Sprynge of Salisbury 16s 8d for 2 mwt nails called *calfatenaill* bought from him and used in the works for this ballinger price per mwt 8s 4d by agreement made with him 21 September in the above year.

Also to the same William Sprynge 4s 4d for 1 mwt 3 cwt nails called *spurcatenaill* bought from him and used in the building of this ballinger price per cwt 4d by agreement made with him 27 September in the above year.

Also for money paid to the said Peter Lockyer for 1 mwt 2 cwt nails called *spurcatenaill* bought from him and used in the said building of this ballinger, price per cwt 4d by agreement made with him the same day in September in the above year, total 4s.

Also to the same Richard Burgeys for $\frac{1}{2}$ cwt 3 lb of iron worked into *bolt, spyke* and *clenchnaill*, price per lb 1$\frac{1}{2}$d total 7s 4$\frac{1}{2}$d and on another occasion for $\frac{1}{2}$ cwt 4 lb of iron worked into *spyke* and *forlockes* and iron *bond* price per lb as above total 7s 6d, bought from him and used in the works for this ballinger by agreement made with him the same day in September in the above year, overall total 14s 10$\frac{1}{2}$d.

[F.122r.] Also for money paid to Robert Smyth for 1 mwt nails called *calfatenaill* bought from him and used in the said building of this same ballinger and one boat for the same, price per cwt 16d by agreement made with him 5 October in the said fourth year total 13s 4d.

Also to John Compton for 1 mwt nails price per cwt 4d, total 3s 4d and 3 cwt nails price per cwt 6d, total 18d and 5 cwt nails price per cwt 5d, total 2s 1d, bought from him and used in the making of the same ballinger and her boat by agreement made with him 7 October in the above year, overall total 6s 11d.

Also for money paid to the said Richard Burgeys for a certain piece of ironwork called a *bedewe* and ironwork called a *mekhoke* bought from him and used there, gross price 12d by agreement with him the same day in October in the above year.

Also to Robert Smyth 18d for 3 cwt nails price per cwt 6d bought from him and used in the making of the same ballinger by agreement made with him 17 October in the above year.

Overall total £31 10s 6$\frac{1}{2}$d.

Purchases of necessities.

Also to John Emory of Southampton 30s for 9 small barrels of tar bought from him and used in the building of the said ballinger, price per barrel 3s 4d by agreement made with him 21 June in the said fourth year.

Also to Thomas Alfay of Southampton 45s for 10 barrels of pitch bought from him, price per barrel 4s 6d, and used in the said works for the said ballinger by agreement made with him the said day in June in the above year.

Also to Roger Kydde of Southampton 27s for 6 barrels of pitch, price per barrel 4s 6d, and similarly used in the building of the same Royal ballinger by agreement made with him 12 July in the fourth year.

Also to the same Roger 13s 6d for 3 barrels of pitch, price per barrel as above, bought from him and used in the said making of the same ballinger by agreement made with him the same day in July in the above year.

Also to John Hardegrovener of Southampton 5s 10d for 5 dozens and 10 lb of wax price per dozen 12d bought from him and used in the making of the same ballinger by agreement made with him the same day in July in the above year 5s 10d.

Also to John Dorand of Southampton for 200 lb of wax, price per hundred 8s bought from him with 4 sheepskins for making *mappoldes* price 4d each, total 16d, and used in the making of the said ballinger by agreement made with him 8 August in the above year, overall total 17s 4d.

Also to John Reynwell, citizen of London for 1 cwt 1 qua 2 lb of *fyn ocom*, price per cwt 8s, total 10s 1½d. [F.122v.] and to Richard Jon of Guernsey for 1½ cwt 23 lb of *ocom*, price per cwt 7s 4d, total 12s 5½d, bought from them and used in the making of the said ballinger, together with 20d paid for the freight of this *ocom* bought from the said John Reynwell as above from London to Southampton by agreement made with them the same day in the above year. Overall total 24s 3d.

Also to John Emory 4s 9d for 4 lagen and 3 quarts of oil bought from him and used in the oiling of the (*les*) *brewes bord* at the time of *berdyng* the same ballinger price per lagen 12d by agreement made with him 18 August in the said fourth year.

Also to John Portessey and John Bawdewyn 7s 8d for 46 *sarr* of *moss* price per *sarr* 2d, bought from them and used in *wynelynge* for the *berdynge* of the said ballinger, by agreement made with them the same day in August in the above year.

Also for the money paid to John Hekely for 1 cartload of fuel bought from him for *bremynge* and used for heating pitch, tar and wax for the making of this ballinger, by agreement made with him the same day in August in the above year, total 2s.

Also to the said John Reynwell for 294 ells of canvas called of Vitry price per 100 ells 66s 8d, total £9 11s 5d and to John Emory for 42 ells of canvas called of Vitry price per ell 6½d, total 22s 9d, bought from them and used to make a sail comprising 1 body-sail with 3 bonnetts for the same ballinger, including 5s paid to John Prest for the freight of the canvas bought from John Reynwell from London to Southampton, by agreement made with them 23 August in the said year, overall total £10 19s 2d.

Also to Thomas Armorer of Southampton 5s for 10 *skayn* of yarn, price each 6d, and to the same Thomas for[254] needles called *sailneldes* 14d, gross price, bought from him and used in the making of the said sail for the same ballinger by agreement made with him the same day in August in the above year, total 6s 2d.

Also to John Compton of Southampton for 11 lb of *filas*, price per lb 6d, total 5s 6d and to the same John for 8 pieces *wynkes*, price each 5d total 3s 4d and to the same for 17 lb of *merlynglyn* price per lb 4d total 5s 8d, bought from him and used in the making of the same sail for the same ballinger by agreement made with him the same day in August in the above year, overall total 14s 6d.

Also to William Nicholl of Southampton for a certain large mast bought from him and used in the works and for the maintenance of the same, price £10 by agreement made with him 9 September in the said fourth year.

Also for money paid to the same William for a certain *sailyerd* for the same ballinger price 20s and to the same William for a certain *bowspret* for the same ballinger price 10s bought from him and used in the same ballinger for [F.123r.] the works and for the maintenance of the same by agreement made with him 21 September in the above year, joint total 30s.

Also to Robert Flores of Southampton a total of 12s 4d for a certain small mast to be used in the same for a *mesan mast* price 10s, and to the same Robert for a certain small *sailyerd* to be used for the same *mesan* price 2s 4d bought from him and used for the works and for the maintenance of the same by agreement made with him the same day in September in the above year.

Also to John Tournour of London for 13 pulleys bought from him and used in the same royal ballinger for the works and for the maintenance of the same price each 6d, by agreement made with him the same day in September in the above year, 6s 6d.

Also to the same William Nicholl 5s 6d for 1 large barrel of tar bought from him and used there in the making of this same royal ballinger price by agreement made with him the same day in September in the above year.

Also to Thomas Armorer for 4 lb of *merlynglyn* bought from him and used in making the sail, per lb 4d, total 16d.

Overall total £33 12s 11d.

Purchases of cables and other ropes.

Also to William Mounford 9s 4d for small *lyn* called *clasplyn*, *kelyn*, and *vletlynes* bought from him and used in the making and rigging of the said sail, gross price for the greater convenience of the king, by agreement made with him 23 September in the above year.

Also for money paid to the said William for 2 cables of white yarn bought from him and used in the same for the control of the same at the time of *launchynge* and *morynge* the same weighing 8 cwt 1 qua price per cwt 13s 4d by agreement made with him the same day in September in the above year, total 110s.

Also to the same William £16 5s 11¼d for 15 hawsers of the same yarn of various kinds, bought from him for making *shetes, tackes, upties, hedropes, bacsteyes, forsteys, trusses* and *stetyng* for the same royal ballinger and used for the maintenance of the same, weighing all together 2 mwt, 4 cwt, 1 qua and 22 lb price per cwt as above by agreement made with him the same day in September in the above year.

Also to Thomas Armorer for 1 rope called *bast* for making a certain *kylerope* used in the making of the same ballinger, gross price 12d.

Also to William Nichol 2s 8d for 2 small *lyn* bought from him and used in making the said sail gross price, no weight given, by agreement made with him the same day in September in the above year, Overall total £20 8s 11¼d.

[F.123v.] Wages of Carpenters.

Also for the wages of John Hoggekyn master carpenter for 12 working days, daily rate 8d, total 8s, John Bysshoppe and Philip Webbe both for the same time, daily rate 6d, total 12s, John Stephen, John Elys, Adam Pekke, William Boll and Richard Michell, that is 5 *berders*, each for 6 working days, daily rate as above, total 15s: Richard Wilde and Henry Kagent both for 12 working days; daily rate 5d total 10s, and William Monford, Nicholas Stacy, Thomas Melon, John Verton that is 4 carpenter *clenchers* each for 6 working days daily rate 5d, total 10s, and John Meldewe, and William Reede, William Danyell and Thomas Blerake, that is 4 carpenter *holders*, each for 6 working days, daily rate 4d, total 8s, all working at

Southampton on building the same ballinger called *Ane*, that is between 18 June in the fourth year of the said king, and 8 July next following, by agreement made with them 10 July in the above year, total 63s.

Also for the wages of the said John Hoggekyn, master carpenter on another occasion for 17 working days, daily rate as above, total 11s 4d, and John Stephen, William Booll, John Bysshoppe, Philip Webbe, John Elys, Adam Peek, Richard Michell that is 7 carpenter *berders,* each for the same period, daily rate 6d, total 59s 6d, and Stephen Hed and Peter Gonsales carpenter *berders* both for 15 working days, daily rate as above, total 15s, and Henry Kagent Richard Wilde and William Mounford, that is 3 *clenchers* each for 16½ working days, daily rate 5d, total 20s 5½d, and Nicholas Stacey and Thomas Melon, *clenchers* each for 15 working days as above, total 12s, John Verton for 17 working days, daily rate as above, total 7s 1d, and John Arrowes for 11½ working days, daily rate as above, total 4s 9½d, and John Noblete for 5 working days, daily rate as above, total 2s 1d, and John Rede, Thomas Went, William Meer, and William Dainell 4 carpenter *holders* each for 17 working days, daily rate 4d, total 22s 8d, and Thomas Blerake and Simon atte Well both for 14½ working days, daily rate as above, 9s 8d and Robert Harrier for 9 working days, daily rate as above, total 3s; all working there on the making of the said royal ballinger, that is between 8 July in the said fourth year and the last day of July next following by agreement made with them the same day in the said year, overall total £8 8s 3d.

Also for the wages of the said master carpenter on another occasion for 10 working days, daily rate as above, total 6s 8d. And for 10 carpenter *berders* in all, that is John Elys for 7 working days, daily rate 6d, total 3s 6d, Adam Peke, John Stephen, William Beale, and John Bysshoppe . . .[255]

APPENDIX III
SELECT BIOGRAPHIES

This index does not include the name of every person mentioned in the Accounts. Many of them were artisans and small traders who did not possess sufficient property or importance to come to the attention of the royal or civic administration and thus be mentioned in their records. Only those persons, therefore, about whom it has been possible to discover some additional information are included in this index.

Much of the information on which these biographies are based comes from the published calendars of royal records – the calendars of Patent Rolls, of Close Rolls, of Fine Rolls and of French Rolls. Details concerning activities in Southampton will be found in the History of Southampton by J. S. Davies and in the documents published by the Southampton Record Society and in the Southampton Record Series. Other information comes from the Phillipps MS itself. These sources have not been indicated in the notes, which latter have been confined to the more unusual printed sources which might prove hard to locate, and to sources which are still in MS.

ARMORER, Thomas
Thomas Armorer was a Southampton merchant probably somewhat older than Soper. He was steward of the town from 1400–1 and 1402–3 a position analogous to that of treasurer involving control of Southampton's finances. He was then elected one of the two bailiffs of the town holding the position continuously with the exception of the years 1405 and 1408 from 1404–1414. There is a possibility that he found the confidence shown in him by his fellow citizens something of a burden because he obtained in 1412 Letters Patent discharging him from holding any municipal office for life. However, he was sent to Parliament as Southampton's senior member in May 1413 when Soper was his colleague and in January 1414 to Leicester when Thomas Marleburgh was the junior member. He continued to witness deeds as an alderman until January 1428 presumably dying at about this time.

AYLWARD, Robert
Robert Aylward was one of the most substantial merchants of Southampton in the first half of the fifteenth century. He was probably somewhat younger than Soper and traded on an extensive scale particularly with the Italians resident in and visiting Southampton. Aylward also devoted a considerable amount of time to civic duties. He was first steward in 1430, bailiff in 1433, and mayor no fewer than five times in 1436, 1441, 1442, 1449 and 1453. He owned a certain amount of property in the town, four houses in the parish of St Michael Archangel, including one on the south corner of the chancel of St Michael's church, one near the walls, and one, his own

residence, a large double tenement called the Forge.[256] He also had an interest in lands in Hampshire, Cornwall and Surrey which formerly belonged to William Nicholl.[257] His prominence naturally led to a certain involvement in government business, investigating possible cases of piracy and raising parliamentary grants.

BABETHROP or BABTHORPE, Sir Robert

Robert Babthorpe was a king's knight who was closely connected with the finance of the royal household, first as controller (under Henry V) and then as steward (under Henry VI). It has been suggested that his replacement in the latter post by the Earl of Suffolk in 1433 was connected with the superseding of Gloucester's influence in the Council by that of Bedford on the latter's return to England.[258]

He also performed services for the Crown in the Midlands, particularly Warwickshire and Leicestershire, and was in charge of the works at the castle of 'Kyllyng-worth'. His appointment as an executor of Henry V's will was no sinecure; the executors also had to face the problems of Henry IV's estate whose debts had not been paid by 1423 when an attempt was made to settle the problem of the two late kings' indebtedness simultaneously. In 1432, however, Babthorpe was still acting as executor at this date to deal with the legacies still due to Henry V's servants. He was naturally rewarded for his services to the royal household, being granted several wardships, the manor and advowson of 'Sanecomp' in Hertfordshire and an estate at Brakenholm in Yorkshire.

BANASTRE, Nicholas

Banastre was not a Southampton man but a citizen and mercer of the City of London. His first connection with Soper and Southampton was in the customs service when he was appointed controller in 1415. Thereafter he was involved in various jobs usually with Soper as his colleague taking musters, arresting shipping, investigating possible instances of piracy. On the accession of Henry VI he was first commissioned with Soper to sell the royal ships and then appointed Soper's controller in the administration of the royal ships. Banastre evidently settled down in Hampshire: by 1431 he had an estate at Idesworth in the Hundred of Portsdown worth at least £30 per annum and also had property in the town of Southampton.[259] The Hampshire property may well have come to him on his marriage to Isabel (whose family is unknown) who had been widowed twice before. Later in 1432–3 he is described as being 'of Rouen' having either established trading connections with the first city of Normandy or being concerned with royal business during the pacification and conquest of Normandy.

BELFORD, John

A ship's carpenter who was employed as a caulker and also on the making of summercastles for the *Holy Ghost*.

BERD, Robert

Robert Berd was a Southampton shipwright who was directly in charge of the building of the king's great ship the *Gracedieu* under the general supervision of Soper. The importance of the job can be gauged by the wages he received – seventy-three pounds in all at the rate of a shilling a day. He continued in the royal service as a clerk of the works after the *Gracedieu* was finished being in charge of making 'trepogetes', guns, ladders and other ordnance for the war in 1421. In 1422 he was further commissioned to arrest any carpenters, sawyers, smiths, carters and other workmen who had deserted from the king's service in France and lodge them in the nearest gaol.

BLERAKE, Thomas
A ship's carpenter, a 'holder' employed on the *Petit Jesus* and the *Ane.*

BLOUNT, Sir John
John Blount probably came from Kingston Blount near Aston Rowant in the Chilterns. He followed a military career for most of his active life. His earliest appointment was as steward and Master Forester of the forest of Rutland. He was then, in 1407, the commander of the fortress at Sangatte one of the outlying defences of Calais. By 1410 he was deputy Admiral and also Constable of Newcastle-under-Lyme and Tutbury. By 1413, he was in Aquitaine where he was in command at Soubise when the town was attacked by the Armagnacs. If he was taken prisoner when the town fell he cannot have been in confinement for long, for by the following year he was negotiating on behalf of the Crown for truces with Castile and Leon and Brittany. After the Agincourt campaign, he escorted some knightly prisoners to Conway Castle and then returned to France with the Earl of Dorset to lead a company in the defence of Harfleur. He was with the Earl on the near disastrous foray in March 1416 which cost the English dearly in supplies and men though the soldiers fought their way successfully back to Harfleur with great bravery. Perhaps it was for his courage on this occasion that he became a knight of the Garter at about this time. Indeed, his courage must have been his outstanding attribute. In 1418, at the seige of Rouen he challenged to single combat the Captain of the Porte Canchoise. He was unhorsed and killed and his body taken back into the town to be released only on the payment of 400 nobles.[260]

BOLLOUR, John
A supplier of ship's stores from Southampton who seems to have made a speciality of pump boxes although he also supplied pulley-sheaves, shovels and timber.

BOUCHER, Thomas
A Southampton butcher who supplied Soper with sheepskins, wax (tallow) and also meat for the men who worked on the laying up of the *Gracedieu.*

BROWNYNGE, Jurdan or Jordan
Jurdan Brownynge was the master of the *Holygost.* He seems to have been a Southampton man as he appears as a witness to a deed enrolled in the Black Book of Southampton. In common with the other sailors permanently employed as masters of the royal ships he was granted a pension of ten marks a year, in 1417. This was paid at yearly intervals for five years from 1418–22.[261] Brownynge did not lose all contact with the royal service on the death of Henry V. In 1431, together with other royal ships masters, he received a special payment for the king's journey to France and back.[262] More importantly, however, he supervised the complete rebuilding of the *Petit Jesus* at Bursledon in 1436.

BUCKLAND or BUKLAND, Richard

Richard Buckland was a London merchant a member of the Fishmongers Company who, not unlike Soper, also made a career in the service of the crown. He was first appointed a collector of the subsidy of tunnage and poundage in the Port of London but at the time of the Agincourt campaign became involved in the transport of the king's army to France, among other duties purchasing the *St Nicholas de Guerande* from some Bretons. A loan of 700 marks to the Crown made by himself and another merchant at this time was to be repaid from the tunnage and poundage collected in London. The service of his own two ships at the seige of Harfleur was rewarded by the grant of an inn called the Peacock in that town. From 1419 his main concern in the royal service was the administration of Calais. He was first victualler and later also treasurer of Calais, until his death which occurred between November 1436 and April 1437. His wife Joan finally settled his accounts as treasurer in 1439. She was evidently a resourceful lady who also carried on his private trading ventures after his death. Buckland during his lifetime also performed other tasks for his royal master, taking musters, hearing appeals in Admiralty cases, inquiring into the lands and services due to the king. He was not, however, like many of his contemporaries averse to trying to cheat the Crown despite his respected position in society. In 1417, prize goods taken from a Genoese carrack by his mariners were brought into Plymouth and an attempt was made to evade giving the Crown its due share of the cargo of fruit, spices and wine worth in all 278 marks. He does not seem to have been granted land by the Crown although he was appointed Captain of the king's castle of Balyngham in Picardy. His personal business activities were evidently as a merchant and shipowner. Apart from the two ships already mentioned he had a half share in the *Antony of London* of 280 tuns burden, and of course the *Grand Marie* obtained from Soper. He may have been concerned in the Baltic trade as he did on occasion supply naval stores to Soper.

BURGEYS, Richard

Richard Burgeys was a Southampton smith who supplied a considerable amount of ironwork for the royal ships. While principally concerned with the supply of nails, spikes, clenchnails and similar small goods he also made an anchor for the *Little John*, and a bedewe and mekhoke for the *Ane*.

BYSSHOPPE, John

A carpenter of this name was employed as a 'berder' on the *Grand Marie* and on the *Ane*. He may possibly be identical with the John Bishop who supplied a small quantity of tar and of timber when the *Petit Jesus* was rebuilt in 1435.[263]

CARPENTER, John

He was employed on the repairs of the *Grand Marie* and also supplied wood for the remodelling of the *Petit Jesus*. When this balinger was further rebuilt in 1435 a man of the same name also supplied a small quantity of timber.

CATTON, William

William Catton, a royal yeoman and servitor was in the service of Henry V when Prince of Wales. On Henry's accession to the throne, Catton was first bailiff of Winchelsea alone and later of both Rye and Winchelsea. His most important appointment, however, was as keeper of the king's ships, a position which he held from July 1413 until he handed over to William Soper in February 1420. This period covers Henry's invasion of France, and Catton was therefore responsible for building, converting and maintaining the greatly increased number of royal vessels which was necessary for these campaigns. He was paid only a shilling a day for this work in contrast to Soper's £40 a year and the only additional grants he received were those of the *Saint Marieknyght*, a ship forfeit to the king with all her gear at Newcastle for attempting to leave secretly with uncustomed wool and also of two ex-royal ships the balinger *Gabriel* and the ship *Grand Gabriel*. After relinquishing his post as keeper of the king's ships Catton continued in the royal service, holding musters, and as collector of customs at Chichester from July 1421. He died some time before 1431 leaving a son, Robert who became bailiff of Dover.

CHAMBERLEYN, John
This man was the clerk of the works of Henry V at Portsmouth.[264] It seems possible that he may have been a member of the Southampton family to which Soper was connected by his second wife Joan.

CHEKE, William
William Cheke joined the group of royal ship masters as a master of the ship *Marie* (probably the *Grand Marie*). He received a fee of 100 shillings per annum as master of this vessel but in 1419 was described as the master of the carrack *Paul* and by 1422 was in charge of the *Thomas*. He was also in command of the *Falcon* for at least one voyage in 1420 when his creditors maliciously took advantage of his absence from the country on a voyage to Zealand for naval stores to have him declared an outlaw for debt.

COLYN, John
A carpenter in fairly regular employment usually as a 'clencher'.

CHURCHE or CHIRCHE, John
John Churche, a citizen of London and member of the Mercers' Company to which he transferred after being master of the mystery of Linwevers, was a merchant of considerable talent and acumen.[265] The basis of his fortune seems to have been the export of cloth to Spain.[266] This cloth was most probably obtained from the Ipswich area of Suffolk, perhaps his own home county. He imported in return miscellaneous goods including iron, steel, nails, carpets and oil.[267] By at least 1432 he had his own factor resident in Seville:[268] he also had connections with Portugal sending his ship the *Margaret of Clarence* to Lisbon in 1437 and in 1438 was himself factor of the King of Portugal in England, being commissioned to obtain 60 sacks of Cotswold wool for dispatch to Florence where it was to be sold to provide funds for the purchase of cloth of gold and silver for the use of the King himself. He also seems to have undertaken at least one trading voyage to the north, to Iceland. Apart from the *Thomas*, which Churche bought from Soper, and the *Margaret of Clarence* already mentioned, he also owned the *Trinity* and the *Isabell* probably named after his wife. In 1434–5 Churche bought rigging and sails from Soper which had been intended for the King's great ships probably for the fitting out of his own vessels. The scale on which Churche traded can be judged from two letters of marque granted to him in 1438 and 1439. In the former Churche was

empowered to seize goods to the value of £2,000 from the King's enemies and in the latter the large sum of £5,332 13s 4d is mentioned as the value of the cargo of the *Margarete de Clarence* on one voyage alone. In common with most merchants of standing Churche was also drawn into the royal service. He was commissioned to find workmen for the defence of Calais and arrest ships for royal expeditionary forces. In 1430 he became a colleague of Soper in the customs administration at Southampton being appointed particularly to look after the interests of Henry Archbishop of Canterbury and the other feoffees of the Duchy of Lancaster, (who had lent large sums to the Crown), a position he held until 1438. In 1441 he was victualler of Calais and evidently used his own vessels the *Trinity* and the *Isabell* to such effect in the royal service that they were granted freedom from arrest for royal use for three years.

The no doubt considerable fortune which he acquired was invested in land: property in the City of London, and manors in Devon, Somerset and Dorset, Kent and Huntingdon.

COMPTON, John
A Southampton dealer in nautical stores who supplied Soper with nails and also with sail thread.

DANIELL, William
A carpenter working either as a 'holder' or a 'clencher' who was employed on the *Grand Marie*, the *Petit Jesus* and the *Ane*.

DOWNYNGE, Robert
Downynge was only temporarily employed as master of the *Swan* as he does not appear among the royal shipmasters granted fees, nor was he in command of any other royal ship.

EMORY or EMERY, John
John Emory was a merchant of Southampton and possibly the son of John Emory who was one of Southampton's M.P.s in 1385. He was bailiff of the town on three occasions in 1428, 1430 and 1431. He was elected mayor in 1433. He may also have been mayor in 1441 or 1442. The list of mayors in J. Sylvester Davies, *History of Southampton* shows Robert Aylward as mayor for these dates. However, a view of hosts of Foreign Merchants in the Public Record Office for Michaelmas 19 Henry VI to Michaelmas 20 Henry PI describes Emory as mayor.[269] As a merchant Emory seems to have traded extensively with Spain. He was host to a group of Spanish merchants, Peter Kyrmewe, Martyn Ochoa, Torald Gonsalve, Martyn Pagao and Ivan Iarr.[270] Martyn Ochoa acted as Emory's agent in Spain on at least one occasion, sending over wine; an arrangement which worked perfectly well until, as Emory complained, Thomas White who 'had at all tymys grete hate, malice and envie to your said suppliant' caused the goods to be arrested.[271] Emory may well also have had an interest in the Baltic trade, as the goods he supplied to Soper were mainly from this part of the world. His purchase of the *Valentine* was obviously in line with these trading activities and the probable intention was that Jack Jon (a royal ship master), should be master of the vessel.

ESTFELD, Thomas
He is described as a citizen of London and a mercer in the MS. No mercer of this name has been traced in the London records or the

Wardens' Accounts of the Mercers' Company although a man of this name is mentioned in a patent of 1432 commissioned with others to arrest one John Brown of Aldershot. It is possible that he is a lesser known relative of William Estfeld who was a very prominent mercer at this date or that the clerk made a mistake in the Christian name and that William Estfeld himself is intended here. William Estfeld came originally from Tickhill in Yorkshire. He was apprenticed to Robert Trees in 1402, as a youth, and obviously diligent and successful was one of the masters of the mystery in 1418 with Thomas Falconer, Everard Flete and John Estmond.[272] He was sheriff of the City in 1422, Mayor in 1429 and 1437 and M.P. in 1431, 1439 and 1441.[273] In 1439 he was also knighted. He had experience of the royal service being collector of tunnage and poundage in the City in 1425. He died about 1445 and was buried at St Mary Aldermanbury leaving as his memorial a legacy to build a conduit to bring the water of Paddington Spring from Tyburn to Charing Cross and the City.

FETPLACE, Walter

Although he appears in the Phillips MS only as a supplier of small quantities of naval stores to Soper, Fetplace was one of the most prominent and successful of all the merchants of Southampton in the first half of the fifteenth century and an intimate associate of Soper. His family had originally come from North Denchworth in Berkshire.[274] It is not known when Fetplace came to Southampton but by 1412 he was steward of the town. He married a Southampton girl, Alice, the daughter of John Cosyn and had one daughter, Isabel, who married Thomas Ringwood. He died in 1449 leaving the bulk of his property to Laura Ringwood, daughter of Thomas and wife of John Ludlow with the reversion to her brother also Thomas; it seems likely that these two were his grandchildren.[275] Another Walter, his apprentice, also received a substantial legacy and was probably the son of his brother John. The fact that Soper was Fetplace's executor demonstrates the close relationship between the two men. The chancery case already mentioned in the Introduction shows Soper and Fetplace using the same factor in Bilbao and almost trading as partners; they also obtained joint licences to trade with Spain in 1428–9 and 1429–30. A considerable portion of Fetplace's trade indeed was with Spain. The surviving views of hosts reveal that he imported both wine and iron from Spain, while on the '*Mortrice*' of Spain in 1433 he imported at least 10 tuns of iron; the further 16 tuns recorded in the name of an otherwise unknown Nicholas Fetplace may also have been intended for his business.[276] He was also heavily involved in trade with Italy, particularly Genoa, the patrons of whose carracks were prepared to allow English merchants to ship their own goods in these vessels.

His eminence as a merchant[277] led to an equal prominence in local government in Southampton; having been junior bailiff in 1414, Fetplace was mayor in 1419, 1426, 1432, 1439, 1443, and 1444. Deeds in the Black Book and the Southampton archives make it clear that his signature as witness was frequently in demand. His wealth as shown by the Feudal Aid of 1431 when he was described as 'mercator' and assessed at £15, and the subsidy of 1435 when he was assessed at £20 was not markedly greater than that of other Southampton merchants assessed at the same time. However, the sheriff on one occasion was in trouble for stating that his nephew, the younger Walter Fetplace had no property instead of being worth £100.[278] He owned a certain amount of property in Southampton itself – 2 messuages and 40 acres of land called Bernardeffeld in the suburbs, and another acre and a half formerly belonging to John Flemyng;[279] his own house on the west side of English Street and other town property;[280] and also the manor of Estmyll and three messuages and land in Fordingbridge.[281] This was a substantial holding of 100 acres of plough, 100 acres of pasture, 20 acres of meadow and 40 acres of wood which finally came into the Ringwood family under the terms of his will. He was not attracted to the public service and apart from one or two inquiries into suspected cases of piracy he seems to have escaped the chores which the government was only too apt to load on to men of his standing. He was a man of business, who liked to arrange his life in an orderly manner, and who, despite his family background, was never described as other than a merchant.

FFLORES, Robert

Robert Fflores or Florys was probably a Guernsey man who had migrated to Southampton, a town which had close links with the Channel Islands. He was twice bailiff of the town in 1426–8 and 1435–6. His concern in this position was the collection of the town customs at the Watergate, or water-bailiff. Quite fortuitously his accounts for his first period of office are the earliest to survive of the Southampton Port Books. Robert was married to Elena, or Ellen, but probably had no surviving children as his property (two tenements in Southampton) was left to his kinsman, Thomas Florice of Guernsey. He also made the usual bequests to local churches and the Cathedral Church of Winchester. His obit, arrangements for which were also made in his Will, was celebrated until the suppression of the chantries by Edward VI.

atte FORDE, Simon

A small dealer providing cordage for the royal ships.

FOXHOLES, John

John Foxholes was, like Nicholas Banastre, a colleague of Soper's in the customs administration of Southampton. He was appointed first of all in 1417 and is usually described as 'clerk', that is in minor orders in the Church. In 1422, one of the many occasions on which his commission was renewed he was specifically appointed to look after the interests of Cardinal Beaufort, Bishop of Winchester, who had been granted a proportion of the customs revenue of Southampton as a means of repaying part of his large loans to the Crown. His appointment was not renewed after November 1426.

GODFREY, Andrew

Andrew Godfrey was first master of the balinger *Ane* and then of the *Gabriel*. In common with the other royal ships' masters he was granted a pension; in his case of 66s 8d per annum. This was paid from 1417 to 1420.[282] He was also involved as master of the *Ane* in the incident, in the harbour of St Peter Port, which resulted in Soper being required to arrest certain royal ships' masters.

GODYNOWE, John

A Southampton tradesman who provided sheepskins and wax for the royal ships.

HEKELY, John
A Southampton carter who transported goods intended for the royal ships on several occasions. He was probably related to William Hekely a carter who appears frequently in the Southampton Brokage Books for the reign of Henry VI.

HOGGEKYN, John
John Hoggekyn was the master shipwright employed on the building and repair of the King's ships continuously from the time of the laying down of the *Gracedieu* until the repair of the *Grande Marie*. He came into the royal service as a fully trained and highly skilled man and evidently wore himself out in the service of the Crown. In July 1416 he began to assemble materials for the *Gracedieu* and in June 1421 he was granted a daily pension of 4d because in labouring long about the king's ships he was much shaken and deteriorated in body. His grant was paid with a fair amount of regularity until 1439[283] being reconfirmed by Henry VI at the same time as Soper's patent of 1416. Pyn or Patrick Hogkyn also employed as a carpenter may have been his son.

HOPPIER, Edward
Edward Hoppier was the master of the king's balinger *George*. He was rewarded for the successful naval operations of 1415–17 by the grant of a pension of 66s 8d per annum in August 1417. This was paid regularly until 1420.[284]

HONGARIS, Antony (Antonio Ungarini)
Part-buyer of the king's carrack the *George*, a Venetian merchant trading with England, he also appears in the records as Antony Ungaryn or Hungarin. It seems very likely that his carrack suffered arrest and served as a transport or a fighting vessel during Henry V's French campaigns as he was paid two hundred marks stated to be for, *'le bon service quel nous ad fait et ferra,'* in March 1420.[285] The following year he suffered the misfortune of losing his carrack to pirates from Dartmouth and mobilised the combined forces of the merchants of Venice, Lombardy and Flanders in England, to petition for its return.

HUSKARD, Ralph
Ralph Huskard was one of the most important of the king's ships' captains. His principal command was that of the balinger *Ane*, a vessel which was frequently used for the conveyance of notables on diplomatic business and other private business of the king. She could give a good account of herself in a fight as well, being involved with the *Cracher* in the capture of the *Saint Jake* and *Saint Marie*.[286] He was also briefly in command of the *Grande Marie*. Later, in Henry VI's reign he continued in the royal service as master of the balinger *Petit Jesus* on a voyage to France with Cardinal Henry Beaufort and was also employed on a journey of the king himself to France in 1431.[287] His pension, granted in 1417, was paid at regular intervals until the death of Henry V.[288] When not employed in the royal service Huskard was a shipowner on his own account, buying with others the *Holigost of Spain* on the break up of the royal fleet. This ship is probably identical with the *Gost of Hampton* which was trading from Southampton in 1430.[289] In the Introduction the disastrous voyage made by this ship is mentioned when wool, seized by Huskard from a

carrack at sea, was taken from him by French raiders when on its way to the Staple at Calais.

JON, ION or JOHN, Jack or John

Jack John of Southampton was in command of the *Holigost of Spain* for a voyage to Bordeaux in 1422 in company with the *Cristofre de la Tour*, the *George*, the *Grande Marie* and the *Thomas de la Tour*. He was not among the group of ships' masters granted a pension by the Crown. However he bought the *Valentine* with John Emery and also went with Huskard on their eventful voyage to Portugal already described.

IUSTINYAN, Nicholas and IUSTINYAN, Prancato

The Giustiniani of Venice were a prominent family of merchants who were believed originally to have come from Constantinople; they are credited with the foundation of Giustinopoli (now Capo d'Istria) and are mentioned at Venice from 756 AD. The family grew and prospered to such an extent that 200 members of it were traditionally supposed to have sat on the Great Council of Venice at once. At this period several young men of the family bore the same Christian names, Niccolo (Nicholas) and Pancrazio (Pancrato) making identification difficult. However, these two were most probably Niccolo, son of Alviso, who was married in 1417; and Pancrazio, son of Marco, who married in 1424 Isabella Cornara daughter of a Venetian resident in Bruges.[290] In 1429 he wrote a letter to his father from Bruges containing a long description of the seige of Orleans including rumours of the part played by Jeanne d'Arc.[291] Further members of the family visited Southampton as patrons of carracks; Filippo in 1430, Francesco in 1435 and Marco in 1439.

JAMES, Peter

Peter James was another prominent Southampton merchant who was a close friend and business colleague of Soper's. He may originally have come from Weymouth in Dorset but, by 1414, he was well established in Southampton being elected steward of the town in that year. In the normal manner he became bailiff in 1416 and mayor in 1428, 1434, 1435, 1444 and 1447. He died some time before 1456 when his widow, Johanna, is noted as being married to one Walter Basyn.[292] He traded extensively with the foreign merchants visiting Southampton, buying iron and wine from the Spaniards (he shared the services of David Savage at Bilbao with Fetplace and Soper) and varied goods from the Italians. He may have made something of a speciality out of supplying innkeepers as he had trouble over money due from two of them. Some of the property he owned in the town was bought from Soper in March 1428[293] and he also acquired an estate at New Alresford the following year.[294] The inefficiency of the assessment methods used and the wiliness of the reluctant taxpayers are well illustrated by the fact that he avoided paying the Feudal Aid of 1431 altogether and was assessed as owning property worth only £10 in 1435.

The end of James' life was overshadowed by the litigation in which he became involved through his children. His daughter, Katherine, whose birth in 1416 had been followed by a christening at Holy Rood with Walter Fetplace as godfather, and Isabella, the first wife of Soper, and Katherine, the wife of William Nicholl, as godmothers, first married Andrew Payn. This young man soon died, leaving his property in Southampton to Katherine. James endeavoured to get control of it and was furious when she married John Searle, doing all in his power to keep the property out of his hands, even refusing to abide by the arbitration of John Flemyng, Walter Fetplace and Soper.[295] His reluctance to accept the good offices of Flemyng, at that time (1445–6) mayor of the town, may have been caused by the difficulties his son Andrew experienced in getting hold of some other property, rightly his after the death of his wife Johanna, Flemyng's daughter.[296] Andrew later married a daughter of John Payn and became closely involved with the anti-alien party in Southampton in the troubles of the 1460s after his father's death.[297] This marriage probably did little to promote family harmony as the brother-in-law of the young couple, the husband of another daughter of John Payn, Thomas White, had arrested (apparently with no justification) 25 butts of Rumney wine and 2 tuns of bastard shipped to Peter James from Spain by Martin Ochoa.[298]

LOCKIER, Peter

A Southampton smith who manufactured a considerable amount of ironwork for the royal ships. Soper bought particularly large quantities of nails of various types from him and it is probable that supplying the clerk of the king's ships formed a substantial part of Lockier's business.

MARKE, MARKES or MARCUS, Richard

One of the group of Southampton smiths working for Soper producing mainly nails but also other ironwork.

MERBURN or MERBURY, Nicholas

Nicholas Merbury, a king's esquire, came from Northamptonshire and married Margaret the widow of one Edward Latymer in 1411. He was master of the works of the king's engines and guns and other ordnance for war, and by 1414 was in charge of the royal ordnance in the Tower of London. In 1415 he was rewarded by the grant of £40 yearly from the farm of the manor of La Berton by Gloucester, and for 'le were' in the manor of Mynstreworth and half the proceeds of the 'were' of Dury.

MERSSH, John

John Merssh was first master of the *Katherine de la Tour*. He was then in charge of the carrack *Marie Sandwich* and finally the *George*. He was granted a pension of 10 marks per annum in 1417 which was paid more or less regularly until the death of Henry V.[299]

MEXTOWE, George

Master of the *Falcon*, Mextowe was not one of the group of captains rewarded by an Exchequer grant and may have been only temporarily employed (there is some evidence that he was master of Soper's own ship the *Julian*). He also seems to have become involved in some kind of illegal action as in October 1421 Soper was ordered to arrest him and keep him in custody until further notice. He probably came from Fowey in Cornwall where a John Mixstowe was in trouble for piracy in 1434.

MORELL, Paul

Paolo Morelli became the resident Florentine agent in Southampton, in succession to Bartolomeo Marmora, about the time of this account. A member of a well-known Florentine family,[300] he spent over thirty years in Southampton renting a large house called the West Hall in Bugle Street. His trade both on his own behalf and that of other Florentines was very varied, including the import of many luxury items produced in the Mediterranean area and the Levant and the export of wood, tin, lead, pewter and cloth. He died in 1448 leaving his sister as his heiress, his children having predeceased him.[301]

MORGAN, John, of Bristol

Morgan, the buyer of the carrack, *Christopher*, had earlier hired the vessel in 1419 with other merchants for a voyage to Bordeaux for wine.[302] Later, in 1422, he and William Tenderly, the master of the *Christopher*, were authorised to get a crew for a similar voyage when he was apparently employed on board as the clerk or purser.

NICHOLL, William

It has been suggested, most recently by Mr Platt,[303] that there were at least two men by the name of William Nicholl prominent as merchants and burgesses in Southampton during the first half of the fifteenth century. This confusion has largely arisen because of the number of ladies of differing names who are said, at approximately the same period, to be 'the wife of William Nicholl'. In 1396, the wife's name is given as 'Elena' and during the reign of Henry VI variously as 'Katerine', 'Alice' and 'Juliana'.[304] In the account given under oath of the Will, however, it is clear that William Nicholl was married to 'Juliana' at the time of his death and had no children or other relations except Alice the daughter of his brother Oliver. No other hint is given by the documents that two William Nicholls were active in Southampton at the same time, as for example, does happen in the case of the two John Williams, both men of much smaller importance than William Nicholl. It seems fairly certain that only one man of that name was active in Southampton at this period, perhaps married several times. Undertaking the usual civic offices of the successful citizen, Nicholl was bailiff of Southampton in 1401 and 1407 and mayor in 1411, 1417, 1422, 1427 and 1438.

From the amount of waynscot, cordage, tar, canvas and other things which Nicholl provided for Soper's ships it is clear that he had a considerable business in naval stores; he also bought iron and wine from the Mediterranean. He seems, however, to have spent a great deal of his time and energy speculating in land and property in Southampton and its suburbs. Far more than his associates he regarded land as a commodity to be manipulated to the best advantage rather than the basis of his social position or an inheritance for his family. One parcel of land at South Storeham was in and out of his ownership twice between 1427–30, perhaps to provide liquid funds for some other venture.[305] His investments were reasonably successful in that in 1431 he was assessed at £6 for the Feudal Aid and in 1435 for the subsidy at £16. He was, moreover, well respected in the town, hearing the plaint of the local tailors against the unfair competition of those from the Italian carracks in 1406. In 1417 also he took charge of 11 tuns of wine while William Soper and Richard Walsop endeavoured to sort out the correct ownership of the cargo of the Portuguese ship *La Trynyte* which had been captured by certain men of Bristol and brought into Southampton.[306] His death, however, some time between 1443–5 uncovered a situation which illustrates how the rigid nature of the common law often drove contemporaries to find somewhat dubious ways to circumvent it. Nicholl had commanded Thomas Pyrie his servant to write his Will leaving the greater part of his property, apart from pious bequests, in half shares to his wife Juliana and his kinsman Richard Thomas, his factor and purser of his ship the *Marie of Hampton*. As he lay on his deathbed his wife suddenly realised that the South Stoneham property was outside the limits of Southampton and could not therefore be left by Will and would therefore pass to his niece Alice who had disgraced the family by marrying a bondman from Twyford. A deed of feoffment would right the situation and although Nicholl was already in a coma Pyrie put the seal in his (Nicholl's) hand and sealed the deed, and seisin was delivered according to the deeds; nothing seems to have been said of this occurrence until well into the reign of Edward IV.[307] The executors themselves, however, had other troubles; a rascally Cornish so-called cousin of Nicholl's also produced a fictitious bond for £100 in the Common Pleas even though he had been turned out of the house by Nicholl himself some eight years before, when he tried to press his suit on Nicholl's step-daughter Katherine despite the fact that he had a wife and family in Bodmin.

OVEREY, William

William Overey was another prominent Southampton merchant. By 1418 he is described as an alderman when witnessing deeds enrolled in the Black Book. He was Southampton's senior Member of Parliament in 1425–6 with the very experienced Thomas Marleburgh. His wife Agnes was previously married to Bartolomeo Marmora, at one time the resident Florentine agent in Southampton. After her second marriage she remained on good terms with the visiting Italians; Luca di Maso degli Albizzi visited them during his stay in Southampton in 1430 and presented Agnes with a basket he had bought in Majorca. Overey left two children, John and Juliana, and another William Overey, perhaps a grandson, was also prominent in Southampton affairs.[308]

PAYN, William

William Payn was one of the most experienced of the group of royal sea captains. He was first appointed master of a royal ship in 1416 when he took command of the *Margaret*. In the following year he was the master of the captured carrack *Paul*, formerly the *Vivande*, and was among those granted a fee of ten marks yearly from the Exchequer.[309] Finally in 1418 he was commissioned to take a crew for the great ship *Gracedieu*. Evidently the supply of suitable seamen was running very low in Southampton because when the ship eventually put to sea in 1420 there were great problems in mustering the crew – indeed some of the crew mutinied and insisted on being put ashore on the Isle of Wight. Payn remained nominally in charge of the *Gracedieu* all through the long years of her decay and was in charge of laying her up on the mudflats at Bursledon.[310] He seems to have turned increasingly to a merchant career and after dealing in naval stores was Soper's partner in a voyage to Ireland exporting wine and salt and importing salmon and hides. He may possibly have been related to John Payne prominent in Southampton trade in the 1450s and 1460s.

REYNWELL or RENWELL, John

John Reynwell, a citizen of London and member of the Fishmongers' Company, was the son of William Reynwell and had two brothers, William and Thomas and one sister Christina.[311] He was an alderman continuously from 1416–45 and M.P. in 1410, 1415, 1433, 1445 and auditor in 1409–11,

1414, 1417 and 1419.[312] He was also sheriff and in February 1415 collector of the subsidy on land in the City and its suburbs. He was involved in the disastrous trading venture to Genoa promoted by Drew Barentyn and William Waldern in 1413 and also involved with Soper in the incident which led to the capture of the *Saint Clare of Spain* when freighted with the goods of John Martinez and Agostino Lomellino. Like other merchants of similar standing he was obliged to make loans to the Crown when the king's need of money was pressing. In 1430 he became Mayor of the Staple of Calais and was granted a house there, the former inn of the Earl of Hereford which had fallen into disrepair. He died about 1443 leaving the bulk of his property to the Corporation of London with annuities for William his son, Fridiswida his daughter and Christina his sister.[313]

RICHMAN, William
Richman or Richeman, a royal sea captain was first in command of the *Gabriel de la Tour*. Since this vessel is described as a ship, the clerks making up the Patent Rolls were probably referring to the *Grand Gabriel*. Although Richeman's petition to have command of the *St Gabriel de Heybon* (later refitted as the *Gabriel Harfleur*) is said to have been granted,[314] by late 1417 he was in command of the carrack *Marie Sandwich* and received a fee yearly at the Exchequer of 10 marks.[315] Finally, in 1422 he was master of the carrack *George*.

ROWE, Richard
Richard Rowe entered the service of the Crown as one of the group of mariners regularly employed as masters of the royal ships somewhat later than the others, not having his first command, the *Swan*, until 1418.[316] The following year he was given charge of the barge *Valentine* and was granted a fee of 5 marks yearly in 1421; unlike the others with earlier grants there is no evidence that he was ever paid this fee. Despite this, however, and the fact that according to his rather doleful petition, in 1423, neither he nor his crew had received any wages for voyages going back as far as 1418,[317] he remained in the royal service as late as 1435 when he was master of the rebuilt *Petit Jesus*.[318] He was also involved in the episode which resulted in Soper being required to arrest certain royal ships' masters; perhaps the attack on shipping in the harbour at St Peter Port.

SAVAGE, William
A master carpenter, the only one referred to as a 'carrack carpenter'. There is a possibility in these circumstances that his name has been anglicised and he was in fact Italian.

SCORTEFEGON, Thomas (Tommaso Squarciafico)
A Genoese, patron of a carrack, from a family connected for some time with the shipping of Genoa. 'Raphael Squortefig' was in Southampton in November 1402 trading wool, the property of Neri Vitturi.[319] Morosini mentions a carrack called *la Squarciafica* in 1409;[320] Thomas himself is recorded in the Southampton Port Book for 1427 and in 1433, he and Francesco Spinola were in charge of the Genoese fleet of ten ships sailing to Flanders; Squarciafico was instructed by the Signoria to unload certain goods at Cartagena and then to make straight for Southampton.[321] He was, again, in Southampton in 1439 when his name appears in the Port Book as 'Thomas Skoreffigo'.

SELDERE, John
John Seldere was a merchant and burgess of Southampton, of sufficient wealth to be assessed as owning property of an annual value of £5 both for the Feudal Aid of 1431 and the subsidy of 1435. He was senior bailiff of Southampton in 1419 and 1423 and was mayor in 1429. He lived in the parish of All Saints in Southampton.[322]

SHADDE, Robert
Robert Shadde first appears as the master of a royal ship in 1415 when he was master of the *Philip de la Tour*. By 1417 he was master of the balinger *Nicholas* and received a grant of a fee of 5 marks annually paid fairly regularly until the death of Henry V.[323] Detailed accounts and indentures of the voyages he made in the *Nicholas* survive, although he was forced to petition the king in an effort to obtain payment of his own wages and those of his crew.[324]

SMYTH, Robert
A Southampton smith who was the principal supplier of nails, spikes, bolts and similar items for the repair or construction of royal ships. He also dealt in iron in a more general way; on one occasion having purchased scrap iron from Robert Berd after the building of the *Gracedieu* he passed this same iron on to William Catton, at that time keeper of the king's ships.

SMYTH, Thomas
A smith supplying the royal ships on occasion. A labourer of the same name is also mentioned in the Phillipps MS.

SONDAY or SOUNDAY, John
A caulker who was almost continuously in the royal service, particularly with regard to the *Gracedieu*.

STACY, Nicholas
A carpenter clencher employed on both the *Petit Jesus* and the *Ane*.

SPYNELL, Jacob
Giacomo Spinola was a young clerk from the Spinola family merchant offices in Southampton. The Spinola family and the Cattanei were the leading Genoese merchants with large branch organisations in Southampton. They handled a considerable proportion of the town's trade with Italy, both as principals and agents and also had close connections with London and the Low Countries. At this time Andrea Spinola was the head of the Spinola family firm with Simone Spinola as well as Giacomo as assistants.[325] The anchor bought by Giacomo from Soper was probably intended as a replacement for a Genoese carrack visiting Southampton.

STAFFORD, John
John Stafford was one of the most distinguished churchmen and public servants of the first half of the fifteenth century. His parents, Humphrey Stafford and Elizabeth Dyrham, both came from Dorset. He went up to Oxford as a young man graduating in canon law in 1413. Thereafter, his career was almost uninterruptedly successful. His training as a canon lawyer was put to use first as dean of the Court of Arches and then as Archdeacon and later chancellor of the diocese of Salisbury. His first appointment in

the public service was as keeper of the privy seal in 1421. In 1422 he was treasurer and 1424 bishop of Bath and Wells. Although he resigned as treasurer when Cardinal Beaufort fell from favour he was again keeper of the privy seal by 1428 and by 1432 chancellor. His career reached its peak in 1443 when he became Archbishop of Canterbury. His political future was bound up with that of Suffolk but although he resigned the chancellorship in 1450 he was not himself personally unpopular and died at Maidstone peacefully in 1452.[326]

STEPHEN, John
A carpenter 'berder' employed on the *Petit Jesus* and the *Ane*. He may possibly be the John Steyven of Southampton who bought some old sails of the *Holyghost* in 1434.

STERLINGE, John
John Sterlinge was the master and also the purchaser of the *Katherine Breton*. It has been suggested that he is identical with John Starling the clerk of the king's ships for a brief period under Henry IV.[327] There is, however, no direct evidence to support the identification apart from the similarity of names.

TENDIRLEY, William
Although he is here described as master of the carrack *George,* Tendirley's most important command was that of the carrack *Pynele* or *Christopher*. He became her master after her capture in 1417, and remained in command at least until 1422 when he took her to Bordeaux on a voyage for wines. He received the grant of 10 marks per annum awarded to all the carrack captains and was paid fairly regularly.[328]

VICTOR, Neron (Vetturi, Neri)
Neri Vetturi was a Florentine, a member of a prominent Tuscan family.[329] He was the son of Andrea Vetturi and elected one of the Priori in August 1411.[330] He had a long standing trading connection with Southampton, exporting cloth in Genoese carracks as early as 1397. In the following reign, in the winter of 1402–3 he exported from Southampton 395 pokes of wool and imported sugar, almonds, raisins, wood and one bundle of 'croci' perhaps saffron.[331] Other members of the same family also came to northern Europe from time to time; one John Victor or Vetturi was granted letters of attorney in 1425 while a carrack belonging to Bulgaro Vetturi was wrecked off Flanders in the same year.[332]

WELLES, Stephen
Stephen Welles was master of the *Craccher* also known as the *Alice*, from at least 1417 onwards. Although the grant does not appear on the Patent Rolls he was awarded 5 marks per annum at the same time as the other captains.[333] His enrolled account for voyages said to be 'on the king's secret business' among other things survives among the Foreign Accounts of the Lord Treasurer's Remembrancer.[334]

WENT, Thomas
A carpenter 'holder' working on both the *Petit Jesus* and the *Ane*.

WILLIAM, John

A certain amount of caution must be exercised in dealing with references to John William in the Southampton Records as it is clear that there were two men of this name living in the town at the same time – John William, shipman and John William, cooper.[335] However, one can be certain about the early stages of the career of our John William. He came originally from Dartmouth in Devon where he was employed by John Hawley as master of the *Craccher*, and, ignoring the niceties of the law, took goods valued at £210 from a ship of Seville on a voyage to Flanders off the coast of Spain. Some eight years later he came into the royal service as master of the *Cog John* on a voyage to Bordeaux. Although his old ship *Craccher* was then given (forfeit?) by Hawley to the Crown he did not take command again but was given charge of the *Jesus*, at 1,000 tuns the largest royal ship save only for the *Gracedieu*.[336] He must also have built up his personal position as at this time he was also able to own half-shares with the Crown in the *Margaret* of 70 tuns, based in Beaumaris. Although he was awarded the standard fee of 10 marks in 1417 with the other royal captains of large vessels, in his case the grant was cancelled because he had earlier been granted twenty marks a year – at first from the customs of Dartmouth, later transferred, because of the lack of revenue at that port, to those of Southampton.[337] The Exchequer clerks evidently found this a very confusing situation as on occasion they wrote warrants for issue for the benefit of William along with the other royal ships' masters.[338]

On the disposal of the royal ships William seems to have seized the opportunity to go into business as a shipowner, perhaps building on the experience gained with the *Margaret*. Together with various partners he bought the old *Craccher* and the *Swan*. By 1436 he was trading in wine on a small scale on his own account, and by 1440 also had a vessel employed either on the coastal trade from Southampton or as a lighter to unload the Genoese carracks which drew too much water to tie up to the quay at Southampton. One cannot be absolutely certain though that the John William who was steward of Southampton in 1440, mayor in 1448, 1455 and 1456 and also M.P. for the borough in 1455 is our man. Certainly by this time he would have been elderly and the John William of the 1450s and 1460s may perhaps have been his son; the same is true of the John William who owned a large house, three cottages, a stable and a garden in Southampton according to the Terrier of 1454.[339] Nevertheless, it is clear that he made the transition from seaman to respectable burgess, more successfully than any other of the royal ships' masters and it is an indication of this success and of their long friendship that he or his son was one of the witnesses to William Soper's Will. Unfortunately no Will of his own exists that would help sort out this tangle.

WODOUSE, John

John Wodouse here named as an executor of Henry V's Will was a royal servant of long standing. In June 1413 he is described as a royal esquire when receiving a grant of the lands of an alien priory in East Anglia. In 1415 he received further estates at Bayford in Hertfordshire. From July of the same year he was one of the chamberlains of the Exchequer. Apart from Exchequer business, though, he was also frequently appointed to serve on commissions of array, of the peace and so on, usually for the county of Norfolk. His close connection with this county is further evidenced by his founding of a chantry in Norwich Cathedral in 1421, and his appointment as constable of Rysing castle. He died some time before February 1431 when Ralph Lord Cromwell became constable in his stead.

YAFFORD, John

Although described as Master of the *Roos* in the Phillipps MS he does not form part of the permanent group of ships' masters employed by the Crown and is not otherwise mentioned.

YALTON (ZALTON), William

Before becoming master of the *Trinity Royal* around 1420 Yalton was master of the ship *Christopher* (the *Christopher* of Spain). In this capacity he was granted a fee of 100s per annum although the grant does not appear on the Patent Rolls.[340] Later on during the declining years of the royal ships he helped with laying up of the *Gracedieu*.[341]

APPENDIX IV
VESSELS IN THE CHARGE OF THE OFFICE OF THE CLERK OF THE KING'S SHIPS DURING THE REIGNS OF HENRY V AND HENRY VI [342]

THE KING'S GREAT SHIPS

Gracedieu 1,400 tuns: clinker-built with at least three masts: built by Robert Berde under the general supervision of William Soper. The cost cannot be determined as the accounts only give the total amount spent on the making of the *Valentine, Falcon,* and *Gracedieu* with no sub-totals for individual ships. However, Berde received a total of £4,549 10s in cash not counting the value of materials supplied in kind. She was laid down in 1416 and completed some time after 1418 and was blessed by the Bishop of Bangor in July of that year.[343] After being employed in 1420 on the expedition of the Earl of Devon, under the mastership of William Payn, she was anchored in the Hamble River until laid up on the mud in 1433. She was struck by lightning and burnt to the waterline in 1439. Her remains are still visible at extreme low water during equinoctial spring tides.[344]

Holyghost de la Tour 740–760 tuns: rebuilt out of the *St Clair* or *Santa Clara* of Spain: apparently clinker-built although the *Santa Clara* may have had a carvel-built hull: 2-masted. Her master was Jordan Brownyng and she was employed on the expeditions led by the Earl of Dorset, the Duke of Bedford, the Earl of Huntingdon and the Earl of Devon. In 1429 she was laid up at Hamble where she gradually mouldered away on the mudflats.

Jesus 1,000 tuns: clinker-built, 2-masted; built under the supervision of William Goodey at Winchelsea; completed in November 1416 at a cost of £1,377 19s. Her master was John William and the king used her as his flagship in 1417. She was not laid up at Hamble with the other great ships but remained at Southampton and was finally granted to Christopher Barton and Richard Greneacres, servants of Cardinal Beaufort in 1446. She was in a very bad state of repair and soon became a wreck. It has been suggested that the remains of a ship found in Southampton Harbour in 1848 were those of the Jesus.[345]

Trinity Royal 540 tuns: clinker-built, probably 2-masted: rebuilt in 1413 from Henry IV's ship of the same name: acted as the king's flag ship in 1415, and also took part in the expeditions led by the Earl of Dorset, the Duke of Bedford and the Earl of Huntingdon. Her master was Stephen Thomas. She was laid up in 1429 at Hamble and eventually mouldered away on the mud there.

CARRACKS

Agase   No tunnage available; 2-masted; carvel-built by the Genoese, captured by Hugh Courtenay at St Edward Pole near Netley on 23 August 1417; almost immediately wrecked off Southampton; sold in 1420 to Richard Rowe and John Bolle, sailors, of Southampton for £6 13s 4d as a wreck sunk in 'le wose'.

Andrew   Tunnage 800 botte (Italian) approximately equivalent to 400 tuns (English)[346] 2-masted: carvel-built by the Genoese; captured on 24 August 1417 by the Earl of Huntingdon; originally named the *Galeas Negre*, patron Luigi de Negroni; sank during a storm at the anchorage at Hamble on 15 August 1420.

Christopher   600 tuns: 2-masted; carvel-built by the Genoese; captured by the Earl of Huntingdon on 24 August 1417. She was originally called *Pynele*, patron Luciano Pinelli and was employed on a voyage to Bordeaux for wine by John Morgan of Bristol and others at a fee of a third of the cargo. She was finally sold to the same Morgan for £166 13s 4d on 23 May 1423.

George   600 tuns: 2-masted; carvel-built by the Genoese: captured by the Duke of Bedford in 1416: used on voyages to Bayonne and Bordeaux for salt and wine. She was sold on 10 August 1425 to Antonio Ungarini, Pancrazio Iustiniani and Nicholas Iustiniani of Venice for £133 6s 8d. These merchants had hired her for the previous two years.

Marie Hampton   500 tuns: may have been single-masted: carvel-built by the Genoese. She was captured by the Duke of Bedford in 1416 and sank at Hamble on 13 July 1420.

Marie Sandwich   550 tuns; may have been single-masted; carvel-built by the Genoese; captured by the Duke of Bedford in 1416; employed on the expedition led by the Lord Castelhon. She was sold in poor condition with the carrack *Paul* for £26 to Richard Patyn and Richard Preste of Hamble and John Gladwyn and William Gladwyn of Shotteshalle on 10 September 1424.

Paul   Tunnage 1,200 botte (Italian) approximately 600 tuns (English); carvel-built by the Genoese; 2-masted: captured by the Earl of Huntingdon in 1417; originally the *Vivande*, patron Tonello de' Vivaldi. She was sold with the *Marie Sandwich* as above.

Peter   Tunnage 1,200 botte (Italian) approximately 600 tuns (English): carvel-built by the Genoese: 2-masted: captured by the Earl of Huntingdon in 1417. Her original patron was Gasparo Spinola and she was sold to Robert Morynge and William Tassyer of Southampton in bad condition for £13 6s 8d on 23 October 1424.

SHIPS (NAVES) ALL CLINKER-BUILT

i. COGSHIPS[347]

Cog John   220 tuns; single-masted. She may be identical with a ship that belonged to the Duke of Bedford – perhaps the Prussian ship given to him in 1407. She sank off the Breton coast while on a voyage to Bordeaux on 7 October 1414.

Rodcogge   120 tuns: probably a prize formerly known as the *Flaward de Geraint*; single-masted. She was sold to Robert Colbroke of London for £6 13s 4d in 1418 because of her poor condition.

ii. OTHERS

Christopher of Spain   No tunnage available; single-masted; a prize vessel taken by Stephen Welles and Ralph Huskard in 1417 during the Lord Castelhon's voyage. She was granted to John Seynt Pee, Knight, in August 1418.

Grand Gabriel   180 tuns: single-masted. Origin uncertain but she was employed on trading voyages mainly for wine to Bordeaux from 1416. She was granted to Catton on his retirement in 1419.

Grand Marie   126 tuns: single-masted. Origin uncertain but may date from Henry IV's time. She was employed continuously throughout Henry V's reign on various expeditions. She was granted to Richard Buckland in part payment of debts owed by the Crown on 3 July 1423 having been valued at £200.

Holighost of Spain   290 tuns: 2-masted: captured by Hugh Courtenay and Thomas Carrew on 1 August 1419; used on both trading and warlike voyages. She was sold for £200 to John Radcliff, Ralph Huskard, Henry Baron and John Wodefford of Southampton on 15 June 1423.

Katherine   210 tuns: single-masted; purchased in early 1415 or late 1414 for £440 and then employed on Lord Talbot's voyage. She was docked in a garden at Greenwich for repairs in 1421; and later sold for £5 to John Perse and others of Greenwich because of her bad condition on 6 March 1425.

Margaret   70 tuns: single-masted. She was owned by the king and John William in half shares and used on trading voyages with Beaumaris as her home port. She was sold for £8 3s 4d to Henry Lovell of Chichester in May 1421.

Marie Breton   Tunnage unknown; single-masted; entered royal ownership in 1415; used for trading voyages to Bordeaux and to Newcastle for coal. She was captured by the French off Le Crotey in August 1421.

Marie Spaniard   100 tuns: single-masted: captured by Stephen Welles and Ralph Huskard on 24 August 1417. She was granted to John Radcliff, constable of the castle of Bordeaux in September 1419.

Marie Hulke [348] Tunnage unknown: single-masted: captured by Sir William Clifford on a voyage to Bordeaux in June 1417. She was sold in 1417 for £5 to William Halyng of Hamble.

Nicholas 330 tuns: single-masted: bought in 1415 for £500. She was wrecked in May 1419 on the mudflats in the port of London, and then sold to John Reynold, shipwright, for £5 in May 1424, probably for the value of her timber.

Petit Marie 80 tuns: single-masted: origin uncertain: sank in a storm off Cornwall on 22 May 1416.

Petit Trinity 120 tuns: single-masted: dating from 1413; employed on voyages to Bordeaux and also on the expedition of the Lord Castelhon. She was sold to her master John Pers for £5 in 1418.

Philip 130 tuns: single-masted: dating from 1415: used for trading voyages and also for Lord Talbot's and the Agincourt expeditions. She was sold in October 1418 to Robert Purfote of London.

Thomas 180 tuns: single-masted; employed from 1413 on trading voyages and Lord Talbot's expedition. She was refitted in October 1418 at Wapping near Deptford and later sold in September 1422 for £133 6s 8d to John Church, mercer, of London.

BALLINGERS.   ALL CLINKER-BUILT

Ane 120 tuns: 2-masted: built in 1416 being completed in November when a total of £179 19s 1¼d had been spent. She was used among other things, as the king's own transport across the Channel and was sold for £30 to John Slogge of Saltash on 27 June 1424.

Craccher 56 tuns: single-masted. She was given to the king by John Hawley of Dartmouth in September 1416 and was sold to John Cole, Thomas Asshelden and John William of Dartmouth and Kingswear on 30 April 1423 for £26 13s 4d.

Falcon 80 tuns: single-masted. She was built by Berd at the same time as the *Gracedieu*, and completed by the summer of 1420. She was used for trading voyages and sold to Adam Forster of London for £50 on 1 June 1423.

Gabriel Harfleur 40 tuns; single-masted; originally the *St Gabriel de Heybon* (a port in Brittany) a prize taken by Lord Talbot. She was refitted by Soper at the same time as the *Holyghost* and was lost at sea some time in the early years of Henry VI's reign.

Gabriel de la Tour 30 tuns: single-masted. She was bought by Henry IV in 1410 for £10 7s 4¼d and used on fishery protection voyages and other expeditions. She was granted to Catton in June 1417.

George 120 tuns: two-masted: built at Small Hythe *ad modum unius galee*, between September 1416 and February 1420 at a cost of £229 11s 4½d. She was used on military voyages and royal passages across the Channel and was sold for £20 to William Bentley of Plymouth on 31 August 1423.

George 24 tuns: single-masted: briefly in royal ownership from 1412–13.

James Tunnage unknown: single-masted: originally the follower (small assistant vessel) of the *Holyghost* and renamed in March 1417. She was granted to Ralph Botiller for the defence of Dieppe in June 1422.

Katherine Breton Tunnage unknown: single-masted. She was captured in September 1417 by the Lord Castelhon and used extensively on both merchant and warlike voyages. She was sold for £20 to John Starling of Greenwich on 5 March 1423.

Little John Tunnage unknown: single-masted. She originally belonged to the Duke of Bedford, first appearing in the royal accounts in April 1416 and may possibly have been a follower of the *Cog John*. She was sold to men of Southampton in 1420 for £1 3s 6d because of her bad repair.

Nicholas 120 tuns: single-masted steered by two steering sculls: transferred from the custody of the clerk of the Duke of Bedford in March 1417 and then rebuilt at Redcliff. She was used extensively on military voyages and sold for £66 13s 4d to John More, William Strange, Richard Rowe and others of Dartmouth on 11 September 1422.

Paul 24 tuns: single-masted: dating from 1413 and disposed of some time before 1416.

Peter 24 tuns: single-masted: dating from 1413 and given to Gilbert Umfraville in October 1414.

Petit Jesus Tunnage unknown: originally single-masted and the follower of the *Jesus*, refitted as a ballinger in 1422. She was completely rebuilt in 1435 as a three-masted vessel. She was placed in the custody of her master Richard Rowe and her ultimate fate is uncertain.

Roose 30 tuns: 2-masted: forfeit to the king at Bayonne in February 1419 and bought to England by Ralph Huskard and Stephen Welles. She was sold to William Castle of Southampton for £1 6s 8d because of her bad condition on 17 February 1425.

Swan 20 tuns: single-masted; originally the follower of the *Trinity Royal*. She was renamed at the same time as the *James* in 1417 and sold for £18 to John William, Thomas Downing and Nicholas Stephens of Kingswear on 1 April 1423.

BARGES. ALL CLINKER-BUILT

Marie Britton Tunnage unknown; single-masted: owned by the king and Richard Rowe in half-shares for two years between 1420–2. She was used for merchant voyages and victualling and sold for £40 because of her bad condition to John Tendryng of Dartmouth in July 1422.

Valentine   100 tuns; single-masted; built by Berde and finished by August 1420. She was used on merchant voyages and sold for £80 to John Jon and John Emery of Southampton on 1 March 1424.

OTHER

Galley – also known as *Jesus* or *Jesus and Maria*; tunnage unknown: single-masted; came into royal ownership in 1409, sunk in the mud in the Thames by July 1415. She was sold to William Foundart of London for £13 6s 8d in 1417.

APPENDIX V
GLOSSARY OF TECHNICAL TERMS

The terms included in the glossary are those which are in English in the original manuscript. They are indicated in the body of the work by being printed in italics. Unfamiliar Latin or Latinised words in the MS have been translated without comment.

Where quotations have been made from the seventeenth-century dictionaries listed below the spelling has been modernised when necessary.

The following dictionaries and works of reference have been used in the compilation of this glossary:

Henry Manwayring, *Seaman's Dictionary*. London, 1644.

John Smith, *The Seaman's Grammar*. London, 1653.

Falconer's Marine Dictionary improved and enlarged by Dr. William Burney. London, 1815.

A. Jal, *Glossaire Nautique*. Paris, 1848.

Admiral W. H. Smyth, *The Sailor's Word Book*. London, 1867.

B. Sandahl, *Middle English Sea Terms*. Vols. I and II. Uppsala, 1951, 1958.

M. Oppenheim (ed.), *Accounts and Inventories of Henry VII*. Navy Records Society. London, 1896.

New English Dictionary, ed. Murray. Oxford, 1933. (abbreviated to *N.E.D.*)

For entries marked * I am indebted to Dr Sandahl for information very kindly sent to me by letter.

Aftir Kegge More usually known as the skeg; the after part of the keel, the small triangular extension projecting aft under the heel of the stern post.

Annede or Annend An alternative term for a rove, or burr, that is to say the rivet which is clenched on to the end of a clench-nail in clinker-built ships.

Bakstay Standing rigging leading aft.

Balinger or Ballinger A type of vessel common from the fourteenth to the beginning of the sixteenth century. From the lists of equipment which exist for various royal ballingers and from the tasks which they carried out, it seems that they were small or medium sized ships from approximately 30–120 tuns, propelled both by oars and sails according to circumstances, suitable for swift reconnaissance, the rapid conveying of important messages or passengers and piracy. The amount of space for cargo was probably fairly limited.

Barge A word of very loose meaning covering vessels of many different sizes and uses; varying from a river boat or ferry to a medium sized cargo carrying ship.

Bark A general term for small boats.

Basnett A small light steel headpiece somewhat globular in shape terminating in a point raised slightly above the head; usually closed in front with a ventaill or visor.

Bast Probably connected with bastard – a boltrope of soft-laid, rot-proofed hemp.

Bechys Beech trees.

Bedew Made of iron. A note in W. T. Riley's *Memorials of London Life* mentioned by Alan Moore in *The Mariner's Mirror*, Vol. VI, 1920, p. 229, gives the meaning 'Boring-bit', and Dr Sandahl suggests that it may have resembled a bill-hook.

Bemes Beams, strong thick pieces of timber stretched across the ship from side to side to support the decks and retain the sides at their proper distance.

Bensenges May be connected with the dialect word 'bensel' which has the meanings of 'bending' or 'tension'.

Berders Ship's carpenters.

Berlinges A pole or spar; can be a long pole used for bearing off a ship from a wharf, another ship's side, etc., or just a general term for small spars. M. W. Prynne suggested that they might have been used in conjunction with a canvas cover to a hold or temporary structure on deck.

Billet A thick piece of wood cut to a suitable length for fuel.

Bitbeme One of the beams forming the bits; a frame composed of two strong pieces of timber fixed perpendicularly to the forepart of the ship whereon to fasten cables when riding at anchor. They are bolted to the ship's beams through the deck.

Bittackle *See* Bytakyll.

Bolt Cylindrical piece of iron used as a permanent method of fixing or securing some moveable object temporarily; sometimes having an eye with a ring.

Boltrope A rope sewn right round the edges of a sail to strengthen it and to which the ropes controlling the sail are attached. Manwayring adds 'three stranded rope made gentle and not twisted so had to be more pliant to the sail and easier to sew to it.'

Bolts with Forelocks Bolts with eyes and rings which are hammered right through some piece of timber and secured with a forelock hammered in a hole at the small end of the bolt over a washer.

Bondes Small iron plates or clamps used to increase the strength of a joint.

Bord Board – all timber sawn to a thickness of less than one inch.

Bordnaill A spike or large brad.

Bordstokkes Perhaps connected with stocks – a frame erected on the shore on which to build a ship.

Botomshyde Bottom-side. Keel.

Bowlyn Bowline – line used to keep the weather edge of the sail tight and steady when the ship is close hauled to the wind.

Bowspret Bowsprit – a spar extending forward from the bows of the ship for extending the bowlines or catting (i.e. suspending above the water) the anchor.

Boyes Buoys.

Boyrope A rope attaching a buoy to an anchor, the anchor usually being taken up in a dinghy at this date.

Brails, Braill-Pulleys The ropes and the pulleys, or blocks through which they pass, on either side of the ties a little further along the yards which come down in front of the sail and are fastened to the bottom lower corners of the courses so that the sails may be furled more easily and quickly.

Bredecotes Possibly a form of meat safe for the sailors' food, particularly bread.

Bremynge, Breaming The process of clearing the filth off the bottom of a ship by holding burning furze to the bottom melting the pitch and tar so that the grass, ooze, sea shells, barnacles, weeds, etc. may be scraped off. The bottom is then painted with tallow and re-pitched.

Brewesbord Has not been identified as yet.

Buckler A small round shield.

Bursar Naval officer with duties approximating to those of a purser, quartermaster or treasurer.

Bylwes Bellows; used in this case in the forge.

Bytakyll Binnacle. Manwayring's definition is very clear: 'a close cupboard placed in the steerage before the whip or tiller whereon the compass doth stand which is fastened together not with iron nails but wooden pins because that iron would draw the compass so that it could never stand true.'

Cabilhokes Probably hooks used in the making of cables to suspend the spun hemp while being twisted by the winch.

Cable Rope usually over 10″ in diameter for use with anchors, etc.

Calfatenaill Nail possibly used to fasten canvas or a strip of wood over caulked seams.

Calfatyng Caulking; i.e. the process of ramming moss or oakum between the overlapping timbers forming the hull of a clinker built ship and then covering the seams with pitch and bitumen.

Capstan Mechanical contrivance for lifting great weights on board ships.

Carlynges Carlings; pieces of timber (usually oak) about 8 ft long and 8 inches square ranging fore and aft from one of the deck beams to another to sustain and fortify the smaller beams of the ship. By connecting the deck beams they strengthened the rigidity of the hull.

Carrack Possibly – according to Jal – from the Latin *carricare* = to load. A great ship of Mediterranean origin with a large amount of cargo space but also equipped to fight, carvel-built usually with two masts at this date, much used by Genoese seamen.

Celynge Lining of planks on the inside of the ship's frame.

Clasplyn Probably a rope attached to a clasp either (*N.E.D.*) a grappling iron or a clasp hook, an iron clasp in two parts moving on the same pivot and overlapping one another.

Clencher A carpenter engaged in clenching, a necessary part of 'clinker-building' in which the planks forming the sides of the vessel overlap and are fastened with nails which are secured with rivets or clenches on the end hammered through the timber.

Close-Brestes The *N.E.D.* gives as one of the meanings of 'close' 'fitting tightly'. It, therefore, seems likely that some form of armour for the chest is intended here.

Clove-Bord Timber which had been split, not sawn into planks.

Coffre Coffer. Small chest.

Compasses Jal could not find a reference for compass = a magnetic device for discovering the north before 1532; the earliest reference to the meaning in the *N.E.D.* is 1515. Naish found a reference as early as 1410 and it seems clear that in the text the magnetic compass is generally intended although the entry 'compasses gross' may refer to dividers used for measuring distances on charts, etc.

Cook Boat, Cok Boat   A small boat used in harbour for ferrying passengers and goods to a ship not tied up to a quay.

Cork   The bark of the cork oak tree.

Cotes   Sandahl (Vol. 1) relates the word to its usual meaning of 'small house' and defines it as an erection for shelter or protection on board ship.

Crane Lyne   In the *Naval Accounts of Henry VII* (p. 40) this is defined as a piece of rigging going 'from the sprit mast to the fore stay to steady the former.' At this earlier date, however, it was part of the tackle used to haul up the iron darts to the top castle whence they were thrown down on to the decks of an enemy ship in battle.

Cross Braces   From the entry in the MS these are evidently made of bronze; they may possibly be connected with cross-bars, round bars of iron bent at each end used to turn the shank of an anchor.

Dele, deal   A ¼ inch thick plank of soft wood timber, principally fir, coming from the Baltic.

Dioll   From the article by G. P. B. Naish in the *Journal of the Institute of Navigation*, Vol. VII, No. 2, April 1954, pp. 205–8, it is quite clear that the dioll was a sand glass or hour glass used to time the ship's passage.

Dobbles   The usual terms for buoys made of wood rather than cork. (See *Accounts and Inventories of Henry VII*, p. 50).

Dregge   A device consisting of an iron-framed triangle with a net to remove large samples from the sea bed.

Englysh Bord   Sawn timber less than 1 inch thick of English origin, of hard wood.

Fane Cloth   *N.E.D.* gives two meanings of fane: either a flag or banner or a weather-cock. Thus a fane cloth could equally be a flag or a cloth to show the direction of the wind, rather in the manner of the modern wind sock at airports. A quotation from 1483 from the *Catholicon Anglicum*, 'A fane of a ship – ubi a weather-cock', makes this latter possibility more attractive.

Fillace   Jal gives the meaning 'fil de caret', that is to say rope-yarn.

Firestaff   As it appears in an entry with several pairs of tongs perhaps a poker or other fire iron.

Flaill   Described in the MS as – a piece of ironwork for the windlass. Normally a windlass is a piece of machinery very similar in its purpose to a capstan; however, maybe a 'Spanish' windlass is intended here. This was a simple mechanism consisting of an iron bolt (the flaill?) acting as a lever in a block to stretch small rigging. The *N.E.D.* gives a general definition of flaill as something that swings on a pivot. Dr Sandahl tells me that it was a pawl for the windlass.*

Forestay   Standing rigging leading forward.

Gaddes of Iron   These were iron missiles used for throwing from the tops of vessels in battle shaped rather like darts.

Garnettes   In the entry 'garnettes for making bredecotes'. Perhaps the meaning of garnette = a kind of hinge, is intended here.

Gemelett   *See* Gymlette.

Gire   This can probably be identified with IEERE described by Maynwayring as a 'piece of a hawse which is made fast to the mainyard and foreyards close to the ties of great ships and so is reeved through a block which is seased close to the top and so comes down and is reeved through another block at the bottom of the mast close by the deck.' They were used to help hoist the yard and as a precaution against the breaking of the ties.

Gittons Small flags. (*Acts and Inventories*, p. 40).

Gondell A small ship's boat.*

Grapnell A grappling iron or a large hook used to fasten together two ships of opposing sides in battle to facilitate the boarding of the enemy.

Gymlete, Gemelett Gimlet; a wood-boring tool.

Hacches Hatches; nowadays coverings to seal the hold but at this date decks or deck planks. Sandahl says the modern meaning does not occur before the seventeenth century (Sandahl I, p. 190).

Hacchnail Nails used in the fastening of the 'hatches' or deck planks with somewhat larger heads than usual.

Haliers Ropes used to hoist or lower the sail on its yard.

Hand Ropes Possibly a 'fall' – a rope to be hauled upon.*

Haspyng Lynes From the meaning of to hasp in the *N.E.D.* probably a rope used to fasten one thing to another.

Hauncer Hawser; large ropes or middle sized cable; despite its name it was usually 'cable laid', that is to say the strands twisted to form the hawser usually nine in number had themselves been twisted together in groups of three.

Hedropes The shrouds or standing rigging supporting the mast, usually referred to in couples.

Helme The tiller or steering mechanism including the rudder.

Herches A measure of quantity used for tar.

Hoke Ropes Perhaps for use with the hooks on scaling ladders or when fishing the anchor.*

Holders Carpenters engaged in shipbuilding.

Isynge Rope This may be a synonym for halier. Jal mentions the Italian verb 'issare' with the French translation 'hisser'. This has the English meaning of to hoist, to haul out sails or to sway up yards.*

Jakkes A kind of sleeveless tunic or jacket formerly worn by foot soldiers and others usually of quilted leather but occasionally plated with iron.

Kele Rope, Kyle Rope Manwayring explains: 'Limber holes are little square holes cut in the bottom of all the ground timbers and hooks next to the keel, about 3 or 4 inches square, the use whereof is to let the water pass to the pump well which else would lie betwixt the timbers; into these there is put the keel rope' – (for the purpose of keeping a clear passage through the holes).

Kelyn Said to be used in making sails.

Kne, Knowe Knee; a piece of timber so shaped that it has two arms at an angle to secure, for example, the deck beams to the side of the ship.

Laskes Scarf or fish piece. (Sandahl I, p. 73).

Lernail Probably nails for securing lerynges.

Lerynges Stout blocks of wood acting as mast partners; that is to say to support the mast.

Lyfftynges Ropes rigged between the masthead and each end of the yard to support the same.

Mappolde Sheepskin mops for laying on pitch, rosin and tallow.

Mast Parrail Bands of rope, threaded through beads by which the centre of a yard is fastened at the slings to the mast so as to slide up and down when necessary.

Mekhoke Geoffrey Callender in an article in the *Mariner's Mirror*, Vol. V,

p. 34, identifies the mekhoke with the 'miche' of a canon; a fitting which prevents the gun leaving its carriage on being fired; but in one instance in this MS a mekhoke is stated to be 'for the sail'. It would then probably = MIKE a support to hold up spare spares or a lowered mast.*

Merlyng Line   Perhaps identical with mar-line, a type of small line composed of two strands of rope yarn slightly twisted.

Mesan-Maste, Mesan Sail, Mesan Sailyerd   Archaic spelling of mizzen. The development of the mizzen mast is fully discussed in Sandahl, II, pp. 73–8. He concludes that despite the French use of 'misaine' for fore-mast, the mizzen mast was the aftermost mast of the ship.

Morynge-Rope   Rope used for mooring at the quayside or to a buoy.

Nawger   Auger – a tool for boring holes in wood.

Pavis, Pavys   The usual meaning of this term is simply a shield; however in a naval context it may mean also the shields fixed along the waist and sometimes also the forecastle and poop of the ship bearing the coats of arms of distinguished persons on board. By the reign of Henry VII at least they had become purely ornamental wooden shields. (*Accounts and Inventories*, p. 51, note.)

Pendantz   A short rope made fast at one end to the head of the mast or the yard or to the clew of a sail with a block with sheaves at the other end for receiving running tackle.

Persandes   Made of canvas: use not clear.

Peynt Anchor   Ropes or chains with which the shank and flutes of the anchor are confined when carried at the cathead. Painter is the modern term: shank painter is a short length of rope or chain used to secure an anchor to the ship's side.

Peyntyng Hokes   Hooks to which the above chains are attached.

Picchynge   Pitching, i.e. covering with pitch to discourage rot and improve the waterproof qualities of the hull.

Pikoys   Pikes.

Pile   A beam of wood driven into the ground to form a solid foundation for building upon.

Pollances, Pollancre Ropes, Pollantz   A special kind of block and tackle used for hoisting heavy articles.

Pollaxes   A kind of hatchet used to cut away the rigging of an adversary when attempting to board her in battle.

Pompe, Pompe Boxes, Pompe Naills, Pompe Yerde   Pump – a long wooden tube, the lower end of which rested on the ship's bottom between the timbers in an apartment called the well, near the middle of the ship's length. The pump was managed by the brake i.e. the pump yerde, the hand or lever of the pump and two boxes or pistons. Pump nails were used in its construction.

Portleux, Portloofs   Wooden supports for the loof i.e. a spar used in mediaeval times to boom out the tack of the big square sail when sailing on a wind.

Priall Ropes   Possibly a group of three ropes for some as yet unknown purpose: prial being a corruption of 'pair-royal'.

Quarell   The bolt fired from a cross-bow.

Ransakynge   A general term for the overhaul of a ship.

Rerbraces   Armour for protecting the back of the arm.

Revesynge   Identical with the modern 'rising', a strake supporting the thwarts.

Roll Teldes   Roll of awning.*

Rood Safe-riding at anchor, in the roads.*

Rooff Naills Nails used in building clinker-built ships which are hammered through the timber and then clenched to the rove – a little iron plate or rivet.

Rosyn Rosin; the solidified sap of pine trees.

Rothir Rudder.

Saill Box Either the box in which spare sails were stored or another term for a binnacle box.

Sailneld Sailneedle for use in making sails (F.39r.). From the context it cannot be a compass needle, as suggested by G. P. B. Naish in the article cited above under 'Dioll'.

Sailyerd The yard supporting the top of a sail.

Sarpler A large canvas sack used for wool or other merchandise.

Saye A fine woollen cloth, resembling serge.

Scaltrowe Shaltree. A pole used for propelling a vessel. M. W. Prynne has suggested another possible meaning – spars used to build temporary structures on deck.

Scalyng Ladders Scaling ladders used to get on board a taller ship when boarding her.

Scepnail Scupper nail; nails with broad heads used to nail the flaps of scuppers.

Sherroke, Sheer Hoke A sickle apparently fixed to the yards for cutting the rigging of an opposing vessel when running up to board her.

Shetes Ropes fixed to the lower corner of the course to leeward to assist the vessel in tacking to windward, leading aft.

Shives Little wheels on which the rope works in a block.

Shores Props fixed under a ship's side or bottom to support her when aground or on the stocks.

Shroud, Shrowde The standing rigging supporting the mast; more usually called hedropes at this date.

Siropes Should probably read 'stiropes' i.e. 'stirrup' meaning either a 'U' shape clamp or support, or an iron or copper plate that turns upwards on each side of a ship's keel and deadwood at the fore-foot. (*N.E.D.*)*

Skegge The after-keg or after part of the keel.

Skettfates Alan Moore in the *Mariner's Mirror,* Vol. VI, 1920, p. 229, prints the inventory of a barge of Edward III from *Memorials of London Life* edited by H. T. Riley in 1868. Riley in a note gives the meaning of skettfates as 'vats for necessary purposes'.

Somercastell, Somerhuche At this date these terms were both used to describe a light superstructure erected on the deck usually on the after-castle to act either as cabins or as some sort of protection to soldiers and gunners in battle. By the time of Henry VII, Oppenheim feels that a somercastell was really a poop carrying many guns. (*Accounts and Inventories,* p. 176).

Sondyngled Sounding-lead. A piece of lead smeared with grease let down over the side of a vessel on a rope marked off in fathoms to ascertain the depth of the water and obtain a sample of the sea-bed – a vital aid to navigation in coastal waters.

Sondynglyn Sounding-line. The rope mentioned above.

Spikes Nails with snug heads made in a diamond form about 4–12″ long.

Sporcatenaill, Sporcanaill Nails for fastening the spurkets – the most probable mediaeval meaning of this term being 'rider', but see Sandahl, I, pp. 93–5.

Spornwater The channel left above the ends of a deck to prevent the water coming any further.

Stempne The bows.

Stempne Peces Stem piece – the foremost pieces of timber uniting the bows of the ship with the lower end scarphed into the keel and the bowsprit resting on the upper end.

Stern Post The large timber scarphed into the keel from which the rudder is suspended.

Sterynge Sculles Large sculls on either side of the after part of the hull, a steering mechanism used before the introduction of the rudder.

Stetyng *Accounts and Inventories*, p. 48, has 'studynges' but defines them only as 'some sort of rope gear'.

Stodel Perhaps a variant name for 'stocks', a frame erected on the shore whereon to build a ship.

Strike Ropes Probably ropes for lowering sails and their yards. *Accounts and Inventories*, p. 37, suggests they are connected with the main sail (at this date in most cases the only one).

Stroppes Pieces of rope spliced in a circle and then put round a block, used about the mast and rigging or for fitting tackle to a rope.

Susternes Connected with the parrel; perhaps a special kind of double block or pair of thimbles lashed together. See Sandahl, II, pp. 101–2.

Takkes Ropes used to confine the foremost lower corner of a course in a fixed position when the wind crosses the ship's course obliquely, leading forward.

Talwynge Tallowing, covering the seams in the ship's planking with tallow to make them more waterproof.

Tilate Legges These seem to have been the supports for the clinker-built horizontal planking on the ship's upper works which resembled shingles on a roof. (See Sandahl, I, p. 165.)

Tongges Fire-tongs.

Topp Abbreviation of top-castle, the fighting platform at the top of a mast.

Touches Made of iron, for use in firing the cannon?

Towe Fibre of flax or hemp used for caulking or for packing in pump-boxes.

Transyng Tymbre Transom timber; the cross beam in the frame of a ship.

Trenaill Nails made of wood: used extensively in shipbuilding.

Tre Pitch Pitch derived from boiling the resin of pine trees.

Trevett Trivet – a three-legged stand of iron usually intended for supporting a pot or kettle over a fire.

Trice Hokes, Trice Pulley Maynwayring gives the meaning of the verb 'to trice' as to haul up anything 'by the immediate and only force of hands'. These hooks and pulleys would therefore be the tackle for achieving this.

Trisynge Rope Trussing rope. Truss.

Truss Pulleys, Truss, Truss Parraill, Trussel Parraill These all refer to the rope and pulleys used to haul back the yard to the mast and to heave it down when necessary.

Upties The ropes by which a yard is suspended from the mast head.

Vambraces Defensive armour for the forearm.

Ventaill Vizor (see basnett).

Vletynes Perhaps gaskets.*

Walees Wales were continuous lengths of planking three or four in number nailed on outside the planking proper acting as fenders. They may have been on occasion tree trunks split with the bark left on.

Warschetes Perhaps identical with sheets-ropes fixed to the lower corner of the sail to leeward to assist the vessel in tacking to windward. *Accounts and Inventories,* p. 71, mentions Warre Takkes, apparently tacks knotted in a particular way.

Watir Baill, Watir Scope Bails.

Watir Dales Long wooden spouts made of elm timber running across the ship and through the side to discharge water raised by the pumps without wetting the deck.

Waynscot A log or plank of oak of superior quality imported from Russia, Germany or Holland.

Walslell Not yet identified.

Wegges Wedges.

Wellinges A variant of woolding – strong binding for a mast.

Wose Mudflats.

Wronges Floor or ground timbers.

Wynches (For making cable). Small winches with fly wheels used in the making of ropes.

Wyndlasse Windlass. A mechanism for raising heavy weights.

Wyndyng Rope, Wyndyng Polley Rope and block used in conjunction with it taken to the windlass.*

Wynelynge or Wyveling This seems to have been a kind of caulking material; see Sandahl, I, pp. 180–1.

Wynkes, Wynwes The meaning of this term has been much discussed; see Sandahl, II, pp. 130–5. From the context it is quite clear that in this instance the meaning of WYNWES is: bands strengthening the sails.

NOTES

1 These particulars are P.R.O. Exchequer Accounts Various (E101) 53/5 and 53/6. All surviving particulars from which enrolled accounts were later made up can be found in this class.
2 Will of William Soper *Blk. Bk.* Vol. II, p. 99.
3 B. Carpenter-Turner, 'Southampton as a Naval Centre 1414–18', in *Collected Essays on Southampton* ed. J. B. Morgan and Philip Peberdy, p. 40.
4 Lambeth Palace Library: register Stafford f. 173 r. Will of Walter Fetplace, burgess of Southampton dated 18 July 1449. Details of Fetplace's career can be found in Appendix III – Select Biographies.
5 Will *Blk. Bk.* Vol. II, p. 141: details in Appendix III.
6 Will *Blk. Bk.* Vol. II, p. 153.
7 Details of Robert Aylward's career in Appendix III.
8 Details of William Nicholl's career in Appendix III.
9 For commercial relations between England and Italy at this period see A. A. Ruddock, *Italian Merchants and Shipping in Southampton*.
10 Davies, p. 154. H. W. Gidden (ed.), *The Stewards Books of Southampton*, S.R. Soc. Vol. II, p. vi.
11 Southampton City Record Office S.C. 4/2 210,212.
12 Davies, pp. 202–3.
13 *C.P.R. 1413–22*, p. 14.
14 *C.P.R. 1413–22*, p. 4.
15 B. Carpenter-Turner, *op. cit.*, p. 42.
16 Southampton City Record Office. SC4/2/223.
17 P. Studer (ed.), *Port Books of Southampton 1427–30*, S.R. Soc.
18 Details of Peter James's career in Appendix III.
19 B. Bunyard (ed.), *The Brokage Book of Southampton 1439–40*, S.R. Soc., p. 111. The Dean of Salisbury at this date was Nicholas Billesdon, or Bildeston. J. Le Neve, *Fasti Ecclesiae Anglicanae*, Vol. II, p. 616.
20 MS Port Book for 1441–2 in the Southampton City Record Office. The MS is unfoliated.
21 O. Coleman (ed.), *Brokage Book of Southampton 1443–4*, S.R. Ser., p. 28.
22 Southampton City Record Office MS. Brokage Book for 1447–8 (unfoliated): entry for 17 October.
23 P.R.O. Chancery. C76/98 membrane 7.
24 *C.P.R. 1416–22*, p. 295.
25 P.R.O. Exchequer. Enrolled Customs Accounts E356/17, E356/18.
26 Details of these mariners' careers will be found in Appendix III.
27 British Museum Cotton MSS. Vespasian F XIII.51. The date is given as 'le xx jour doctobre le v' without saying whether Henry V or Henry VI is intended. If the date were 5 Henry V (1417) this licence could be a duplicate of the first one mentioned although the amount of wool is slightly different.
28 P.R.O. Chancery. C76/119 membrane 10. *C.P.R. 1436–41*, p. 36.
29 P.R.O. Early Chancery Proceedings C1/9/403.
30 Details of these protections and licences can be found in *Deputy Keeper of the Public Records 48th Report*, Calendar of French Rolls, pp. 232, 263, 275, 286, 287.
31 P.R.O. Early Chancery Proceedings C1/9/403.

32 *C.P.R. 1422–9*, p. 329.
33 P.R.O. Exchequer Accounts Various E101/49/25.
34 P. Studer, *op. cit.*, pp. 4, 33, 75.
35 G. R. Elton, 'Informing for profit, a sidelight on Tudor methods of law enforcement', *Cambridge Historical Journal*, Vol. XI (1953–5), pp. 149–166.
36 Southampton City Record Office S.C. 4/3/4.
37 Southampton City Record Office S.C. 4/3/6 and 7.
38 The Hosting Act is 18 Henry VI cap. 4. Statutes of the Realm Vol. II 1377–1509, pp. 303–5. There were earlier acts on similar lines for example, 5 Henry IV cap. 9 but there is little evidence to show attempts to enforce them. A. A. Ruddock, 'Alien Hosting in Southampton in the fifteenth century', *Economic History Review*, Vol. XVI (1946), pp. 30–37.
39 P.R.O. Exchequer. Accounts Various E101/128/31. View of Nicholas Bylot. View of John Emory.
40 P.R.O. Exchequer. Accounts Various E101/128/31. View of John Bentham for 20 Henry VI and for 21–22 Henry VI.
41 The diary has been edited by M. E. Mallett in *The Florentine Galleys in the Fifteenth Century*.
42 'Aure' is misidentified by Mallett, *op. cit.*, p. 255 with Soper. For the correct identification and the wife's first marriage see A. A. Ruddock, *Italian Studies*, 1968, p. 166.
43 This was probably the property 'Le Wose' or 'Osiers' in the parish of Dibden which Soper and his first wife bought in 1426. *C.C.R. 1422–9*, p. 319.
44 M. E. Mallett, *op. cit.*, p. 256–60.
45 M. E. Mallett, *op. cit.*, p. 196.
46 M. E. Mallett, *op. cit.*, p. 50.
47 P.R.O. Exchequer. Accounts Various E101/28/31: view taken by Peter James, Michaelmas 21 Henry VI to Easter following and E179/173/107, a view of hosts erroneously listed as an alien subsidy return.
48 Southampton City Record Office. Terrier of 1454, f. 8r.
49 Terrier, f. 3r.
50 Terrier, f. 4v.
51 P. Studer (ed.), *The Port Books of Southampton 1427–30*, S. R. Soc., p. 86.
52 H. W. Gidden (ed.), *The Stewards Books of Southampton*, S. R. Soc., Vol. 1, p. 10.
53 Southampton City Record Office, MS Port Book for 1433–4 f. 49v.
54 H. W. Gidden, *op. cit.*, Vol. 1, p. 114.
55 B. Foster (ed.), *Port Book of Southampton for 1435–6*, S. R. Ser. Indenture B, pp. 124–5.
56 Southampton City Record Office. MS. Steward's Book for 1441–2, f. 6v.
57 *Calendar of the Plea and Memoranda Rolls of the City of London*. Roll A49. 12 August 1420, pp. 105–6.
58 P.R.O. Early Chancery Proceedings C1/16/301 a.b.
59 *Davies*, p. 173.
60 *Davies*, p. 202.
61 *C.P.R. 1413–16*, p. 192.
62 *C.C.R. 1413–19*, p. 166–7.
63 *C.P.R. 1413–16*, p. 178. B. Carpenter-Turner, 'The building of the *Holy Ghost of the Tower* and her subsequent history', *M.M.*, Vol. XLI (1954), pp. 270–281.
64 The embarrassment would have been caused by the suspicion of piracy in the original capture of the ship.
65 *C.P.R. 1416–22*, pp. 38, 84. B. Carpenter-Turner, 'The building of the *Gracedieu, Valentine* and *Falconer* at Southampton', *M.M.*, Vol. XLI (1954), pp. 55–72.
66 *C.P.R. 1416–22*, pp. 169, 256.
67 P.R.O. Exchequer. Foreign Accounts E364/81 Membrane G.
68 *C.P.R. 1422–9* p. 460.
69 *C.C.R. 1441–7*, p. 259.

70 P.R.O. French Rolls. C64/17 Membrane 20 dorse.
71 B. Carpenter-Turner, 'Southampton as a naval centre' in *Collected Essays on Southampton*, (ed.) J. B. Morgan and Philip Peberdy, p. 45.
72 British Museum Add. MSS. no. 23938: *Bulletin of the John Rylands Library*, Vol. XI (1957-8), p. 79.
73 T. Rymer, *Foedera Conventiones Literae et cuiuscunque generis acta publica* etc. Hague Edition, 1740, Tom. 4 Part 4, p. 81.
74 A case which illustrates the problem of jurisdiction is *C.P.R. 1436–41*, p. 535. This case is also unique at this period because the result of the commission of inquiry or inquisition survives in the class of Chancery Inquisitions in the P.R.O. (C145/310 no. 11). This states that the act of piracy did indeed take place in territorial waters between 'Geynore' (Gurnard I.O.W.) and Lepe (Hants.) and therefore came within the jurisdiction of the English courts.
75 *C.P.R. 1422–9*, p. 221: *C.P.R. 1436–41*, pp. 84, 506.
76 A further example of Beaulieu being used in this manner will be found in *C.P.R. 1441–6* p. 49; in this instance 70 tuns of wine stolen from a Breton barge in 1441 were unloaded from the ship when moored at Beaulieu.
77 *C.P.R. 1446–52*, p. 442. Carracks were attacked on several other occasions when they were vulnerable, for example when sheltering from a storm (*C.P.R. 1436–41*, p. 575: *ibid. 1441–6*, p. 247) and when off the Isle of Wight (*C.P.R. 1422–9*, pp. 221, 548).
78 *C.P.R. 1422–9*, p. 324.
79 P.R.O. Ancient Petitions. S.C.8. file 118 nos. 5863 and 5504. One document seems to be a copy of the other in different handwriting.
80 *Calendar of entries in the Papal Registers relating to Great Britain and Ireland. Papal Letters* Vol. VII (1417–31), p. 337.
81 *Blk. Bk.* Vol. 11, pp. 57-8.
82 *Papal Letters* Vol. VIII (1427–47), p. 579. The mandate to grant the dispensation is directed to the Bishop of London. Soper may well have felt it was better to be away from Southampton while his affairs were put in order.
83 P.R.O. Chancery. Inquisitions Post Mortem. C39/120 No. 43 for April 1445.
84 *Feudal Aids* Vol. 11, pp. 359–60.
85 P.R.O. Exchequer Lay Subsidy Roll E179/173/92.
86 P.R.O. Ancient Deeds. Exchequer E326 no. 11804.
87 Southampton City Record Office. SC4/3 no. 7.
88 This document, in the Southampton City Record Office, is known as the Terrier of Southampton of 1454.
89 Bargent Deed no. D/LY7/25 transcribed in *Report on the work of the Civic Record Office Southampton*, 1963, pp. 6–9.
90 P.R.O. Ancient Deeds Chancery C146 no. 6772.
91 *V.C.H. Hampshire*, Vol. IV, pp. 510–11.
92 *Calendar of Inquisitions Post Mortem Henry VII*, Vol. 1, p. 174.
93 *C.C.R. 1422–9*, p. 319.
94 *C.P.R. 1436–41*, p. 130. Fine of 6s 8d paid into the hanaper for entry without licence to the lands at South Langley.
95 Papworth Index at the Society of Antiquaries of London. Starkey's Roll circa 1460 no. 1121.
96 Indenture of August 30th 1455. *Blk. Bk.*, Vol. II, p. 123.
97 P.R.O. Early Chancery Proceedings. C1/29/31. Dating from between 38 Henry VI and 5 Edward IV.
98 P.R.O. Chancery. Inquisitions Post Mortem. C145/15 no. 71.
99 *C.P.R. 1476–85*, p. 317.
100 P.R.O. Early Chancery Proceedings C1/202/250–263.
101 For further details of the Ludlow/Fletcher litigation see P.R.O. Early Chancery Proceedings C1/54/205, C1/634/54, and C1/504/56 and K.R. Memorandum Roll E159/276 15 Henry VII (1499–1500) Easter Term

membrane 16 dorse, Trinity Term membrane 3 dorse. Newton Bery, Chamberleyn's and Osiers (as the properties came to be named) were finally sold to William Compton for £60. P.R.O. Exchequer Inquisitions Post Mortem. Series II E150/986 no. 3.

102 Hampshire County Record Office. Clarke-Jervoise Collection No. 18 m. 64.

103 J. T. Tinniswood, 'English Galleys 1272–1377', *M.M.*, Vol. XXXV, 1949. For the inventory of the *Paul* of London see Alan Moore, *M.M.*, Vol. VI, 1920.

104 John Chamberlain's enrolled accounts are to be found in P.R.O. Exchequer L.T.R. E364/39 and E364/43. The particulars from which these accounts were made up, consisting of indentures, more detailed accounts etc. are to be found in P.R.O. Exchequer, Accounts Various, E101/42/39, E101/43/2 and E101/43/6.

105 P.R.O. Exchequer, Accounts Various E101/42/39. The timber for building the ship cost £9 2s 9d and the iron nails and fittings a total of £7 18s 3d. The letter commanding Chamberlain to deliver the *Ane* to the Archbishop of Canterbury is item 6 in P.R.O. Exchequer Accounts Various E101/32/2.

106 P.R.O. Exchequer, Warrants for Issue. E404/15/32: the *Katherine* was originally bought for use in northern waters.

107 The letter and indenture, including an inventory, concerning this delivery are items 7 and 8 in E101/43/2.

108 Details of the building of this ship are in P.R.O. Exchequer, Accounts Various. E101/43/6. Timber cost a total of £101 15s and ironwork £38 12s 9d.

109 P.R.O. Exchequer. Warrants for Issue. E404/24/303–305.

110 P.R.O. Exchequer. Warrants for Issue. E404/24/288–290.

111 P.R.O. Exchequer. Warrants for Issue. E404/21/50.

112 P.R.O. Exchequer. Warrants for Issue. E404/16/414, E404/17/375. Similarly Thomas Sperman was paid for timber supplied for the *Godesgrace* after a delay of eight years. E404/28/204–5.

113 P.R.O. Exchequer. Accounts Various E101/44/20.

114 P.R.O. Exchequer. Accounts Various E101/43/2. Item 9.

115 *C.P.R. 1405–8*, p. 189.

116 P.R.O. Exchequer. Warrants for Issue E404/15/421. Also F. Devon *Issues of the Exchequer*, p. 277.

117 John Elmeton's Accounts for 7–11 Henry IV are P.R.O. Exchequer L.T.R. E364/46. Writs subsidiary to his accounts will be found in Accounts Various E101/44/12.

118 The enrolled accounts of John Starling are noted in P.R.O. Lists and Indexes No. XI as being on roll E364/45. I have been unable to trace them on this or adjacent rolls in the series. Fortunately the particulars of his accounts survive in Exchequer Accounts Various E101/44/17. These consist of a) Starling's patent of appointment; b) the indenture between Starling and Elmyng Leget at the end of the former's term of office; c) the particulars of Starling's accounts from 19 November 11 Henry IV to 22 June 12 Henry IV. Extracts have been printed by Alan Moore in *M.M.* Vol. IV 1914.

119 The *Bernard* was apparently larger than 135 tuns capacity. She took on a cargo of this size at Bordeaux in 1412. J. Bernard, *Navires et gens de mer à Bordeaux vers 1400-vers 1550*, p. 295.

120 P.R.O. Exchequer. Warrants for Issue. E404/25/208. It has been suggested that Starling, the mariner and Starling, the clerk are identical but this does not seem likely. See Starling (Sterling) in Appendix III. This ship was a Genoese carrack which had been attacked in Milford Haven, by pirates believed to be Bristol men. *C.P.R. 1408–13*, pp. 175, 178, 179, 182, 310.

121 P.R.O. Exchequer. Accounts Various. E101/44/23. There may have been some connection between Leget and Loveney as they were involved together

in a dispute over the wardship of a manor in Essex. *C.P.R. 1408–13*, pp. 231, 240.

122 Catton's first enrolled accounts cover the period from July, 1 Henry V (1413) – 4 Henry V (1416) and are to be found in P.R.O. Exchequer L.T.R. E364/54. The relevant particulars are P.R.O. Exchequer, Accounts Various. E101/44/24 which are mainly concerned with trading voyages on the king's behalf. His second set of accounts is P.R.O. Exchequer L.T.R. E364/59.

123 P.R.O. Exchequer. Warrants for issue. E404/37/426.

124 *C.P.R. 1405–8*, p. 362.

125 P.R.O. Exchequer. Treasury of Receipt. Council and Privy Seal. E28/31.

126 P.R.O. Exchequer. L.T.R. E364/59.

127 Purchase of the *Katherine*. P.R.O. Exchequer. Pell Rolls. E403/619. Purchase of the *Nicholas*. P.R.O. Exchequer. Pell Rolls. E403/621.

128 P.R.O. Exchequer L.T.R. E364/61. This roll contains two distinct accounts referring to Soper's activities. One, on the dorse of membrane G refers only to the building of the *Holigost* and the repair of the *Gabriel* undertaken at a time when Soper did not hold a patent of appointment as clerk of the king's ships. The other, beginning on membrane D is the record of Soper's first accounting period from 1418–22 including details from before his appointment as well as his accounts as clerk of the king's ships. The accounts of the building of the *Ane* are here. The particulars exist as P.R.O. Exchequer. Accounts Various E101/49/29 but are badly damaged.

129 Robert Berd's accounts for the building of the *Gracedieu*, two ballingers, two batells and three cock boats are P.R.O. Exchequer L.T.R. E364/57. His patent to 'survey the works of a new ship' at Southampton, with Soper, is *C.P.R. 1416–22*, p. 84.

130 P.R.O. Chancery Miscellanea. C47/2/49 item 14.

131 C47/2/49 items 27 and 28. Richard Spicer received a total of £63 14s to pay his men for three months duty. P.R.O. Exchequer. Warrants for Issue. E404/33/202.

132 Preamble to Soper's accounts: E364/61. His salary was paid fairly regularly until 1436.

133 The *Petit Marie* was returning from Bordeaux laden with wine when she was lost. P.R.O. Exchequer. L.T.R. E364/59.

134 Details of the careers of these and other royal ships mentioned can be found in Appendix IV. It should be noted that there were two ships in royal ownership called *Marie Breton*, this one and another captured off Le Crotoy in 1421.

135 British Museum. Cotton Collection. Titus A 26: discussed by R. C. Anderson in *M.M.*, Vol. XI, 1925. Another treatise, the MS. Fabrica de Galere is dated by Anderson not earlier than 1500 though it may refer to earlier conditions. *M.M.*, Vol. XXXI, 1945, p. 160.

136 J. Bernard, *Navires et gens de mer à Bordeaux vers 1400–vers 1550*, Vol. I, pp. 238–241. J. Bernard fully discusses the problems raised by the loose use of the names of ship types as well as those raised by the untechnical nature of most contemporary pictures. A very good collection of pictures of seals is included in the *Descriptive Catalogue* of the Nederlandsch Historisch Scheepvaart Museum of Amsterdam.

137 The expedition is described in the *Journal of the British Archaeological Association*, Vol. XXXII, p. 70.

138 R. C. Anderson, 'The Bursledon Ship', *M.M.*, Vol. XX, 1934, p. 158; discussed also in M. W. Prynne, 'Henry V's *Gracedieu*', *M.M.*, Vol. LIV, 1968, p. 115.

139 F. T. O'Brien, note p. 323 in *M.M.*, Vol. LVII, 1971.

140 M. W. Prynne, *op. cit.*, p. 123. The phrase 'per estimationem' occurs quite frequently in the Phillipps MS.

141 P.R.O. Exchequer. Accounts Various E101/44/24.

142 P.R.O. Exchequer. L.T.R. E364/54.

143 P.R.O. Exchequer. Accounts Various E101/49/28. Details are provided by the clerk's enrolled accounts or the subsidiary particulars.
144 J. Bernard, op. cit., p. 249.
145 P.R.O. Exchequer L.T.R. E364/59. Expenses and inventory under ship's name.
146 P.R.O. Exchequer. Accounts Various. E101/53/5.
147 J. Bernard, op. cit., p. 250, feels that it is unwise to use the number of men carried as the basis of any argument concerning the handling of ballingers because of the mixing of sailors with soldiers and other non-naval personnel. However, the English accounts used here carefully distinguish between the crew of the vessel and any soldiers etc. on board.
148 P.R.O. Exchequer. L.T.R. E364/54. Memb. B. Account of Ralph Huskard master of the Ane. Falaise is not nowadays on a navigable river. The Ane may have come up the Orne as far as possible and then the supplies she was carrying may have been landed and carried overland.
149 P.R.O. Exchequer. L.T.R. E364/54. Memb. B. Account of Stephen Weller, master of the Craccher.
150 P.R.O. Exchequer. Accounts Various. E101/49/10: E101/49/16. Accounts and indentures of Robert Shadde, master of the Nicholas.
151 G. Callender, 'The ships of Maso Finiguerra', M.M., Vol. IV, 1912, p. 294.
152 R. Morton-Nance, 'The ship of the Renaissance', Maritime Miscellany No. 10. Articles reprinted by the Society for Nautical Research from M.M., Vol. XLI, 1955. An illustration of WA's Craek appears on p. 288.
153 Carvel-built hulls obviously presented some problems to English shipwrights. At one stage, Soper petitioned the Council for permission to employ foreign carpenters because, 'en cestes pays ne trouvons que poy de gentz qui savont nye nief nies le carrakes renoveller.' P.R.O. Exchequer. Treasury of Receipt. Council and Privy Seal. E28/38. Carvel building was not common at Bordeaux until the very end of the fifteenth century. J. Bernard, op. cit., pp. 334-5. In Brittany, H. Touchard does not find any local carvel-built ships before 1460. H. Touchard, Le commerce maritime Breton à la fin du Moyen Age. pp. 316-7.
154 The Bayonne ship is mentioned in a letter written by John Alcestre published in Sir H. Ellis (ed.), Letters illustrative of English History, 2nd Series, Vol. I, No. XXI. The figures for Italian botte should be approximately halved to get comparable English tunnage figures. F. C. Lane in Appendix VII p. 266 of his Italian Ships and Shipbuilders of the Renaissance mentions two round ships built by the Venetian government (ordered in 1451, completed about 1457), both of 2,000-2,500 botte.
155 T. Glasgow, 'The Hulk', M.M., Vol. LVIII, 1972, pp. 103-4.
156 R. Morton-Nance, op. cit., p. 180.
157 Sir A. Moore, 'Rig in Northern Europe', Maritime Miscellany No. 11. Articles reprinted from M.M., Vol. XLII, 1956, p. 9.
158 P.R.O. Exchequer. Accounts Various. E101/48/14. Muster of Thomas Carrew's retinue.
159 P.R.O. Exchequer. Accounts Various. E101/51/6.
160 P.R.O. Exchequer. Accounts Various. E101/44/24.
161 P.R.O. Exchequer. L.T.R. E364/54.
162 P.R.O. Exchequer. L.T.R. E364/54. The ships' return to London was not because of their masters' 'cautious timidity' (M. K. James, Studies in the Medieval Wine Trade, p. 120) but because they were needed for keeping the seas.
163 A. Guistiniani, Annali della Repubblica di Genova, p. 277.
164 B. Williams (ed.), Gesta Henrici Quinti, p. 79.
165 L. A. Muratori (ed.), Rerum Italicarum Scriptores, Vol. 17. G. Stella, 'Annales Genuenses', p. 1268. A. Giustiniani, op. cit., p. 277.
166 A. Giustiniani, loc. cit.
167 B. Williams, op. cit., p. 85.
168 P.R.O. Exchequer. L.T.R. E364/59.

169 A. Giustiniani, *op. cit.*, pp. 278–9.
170 B. Williams, *op. cit.*, p. 97.
171 The *Paul*, the *Christopher* and the *Andrew* were known in Genoese hands as the *Vivande*, the *Pynall*, and the *Galeas Negra*. *C.P.R. 1416–22*, p. 142. Titus Livius Forojuliensis in his *Vita Henrici Quinti* describes how the carracks were bigger than any ships seen before and how the battle raged all through a summer's day. T. Hearne (ed.), *Vita Henrici Quinti*, p. 30.
172 P.R.O. Exchequer. L.T.R. E364/59.
173 P.R.O. Exchequer. L.T.R. E364/61.
174 *C.P.R. 1416–22*, p. 169.
175 P.R.O. Exchequer. Accounts Various. E101/49/33. A full translation of this document has been published in *M.M.*, Vol. LXIII, 1977, pp. 3–6.
176 P.R.O. Exchequer. Accounts Various. E101/49/10. E101/49/16.
177 E101/49/27 and 28.
178 P.R.O. Exchequer. L.T.R. E364/54. Membrane B. Account of Stephen Welles.
179 Loc. cit. Account of Ralph Huskard.
180 The patent ordering Soper to sell the ships is *C.P.R. 1422–9* p. 57 dated February 26, 1423. Henry V had died on 31 August 1422.
181 C. F. Richmond in 'The keeping of the seas during the Hundred Years War 1422–1440', *History*, Vol. XLIX, 1964, pp. 283–98 discusses the sale of the royal ships in detail. It should be noted that the table on pp. 286–7 and his comments (p. 289) giving the fate of Henry V's ships are not accurate in several respects supposing that some ships sold earlier were still in royal hands. See Appendix IV.
182 P.R.O. Exchequer. L.T.R. E364/65: Soper's enrolled accounts for 1422–7.
183 P.R.O. Exchequer. Accounts Various. E101/53/37.
184 His patent of office was issued a few days after the order for sale. *C.P.R. 1422–9*, p. 64 dated 5 March 1423.
185 Foxholes had shared the work involved in the collection of customs with Soper in Southampton from 1417. *C.F.R. 1412–22*, pp. 203–4. He was reappointed on the accession of Henry VI. *C.F.R. 1422–9* pp. 19, 22, 23, 24, 25, 107, 151. Banastre was appointed later, in 1426. *C.F.R. 1422–9* pp. 139–40, 150.
186 C. F. Richmond, *op. cit.*, p. 288.
187 P.R.O. Exchequer. L.T.R. E364/65.
188 P.R.O. Exchequer. Accounts Various. E101/51/20. Account of Roger atte Gate lately mayor of Winchelsea.
189 P.R.O. Exchequer. L.T.R. E364/69. Soper's accounts for the years 1427–32.
190 The enrolled account for this period is P.R.O. Exchequer L.T.R. E364/71. The book of particulars – similar to the Phillipps MS – is P.R.O. Exchequer. Accounts Various. E101/53/5; the account book of Nicholas Banastre as controller is E101/53/6. B. Carpenter-Turner's article, 'The *Little Jesus of the Tower*. A Burlesdon ship of the early fifteenth century', *Proc. H.F.C.*, Vol. XVIII, 1953, states the *Petit Jesus* was a new ship. It was however, the result of the re-building of the old vessel.
191 P.R.O. Exchequer. L.T.R. E364/76. This is Soper's last account.
192 P.R.O. Exchequer. L.T.R. E364/73. Soper's account for 15–17 Henry VI.
193 P.R.O. Exchequer. L.T.R. E364/76.
194 The indenture certifying the transfer of office is P.R.O. Exchequer. Accounts Various. E101/53/37. Clyvedon held the appointment on the same terms as Catton with a wage of 12d per day. His account as clerk of the New Forest is P.R.O. Exchequer, L.T.R. E364/72.
195 P.R.O. Exchequer L.T.R. E364/81.
196 P.R.O. Exchequer L.T.R. E364/86.
197 Shotteshall: part of the estates of the Abbey of Netley in the Parish of Hound. *V.C.H. Hampshire*, Vol. IV(2), p. 555.
198 Godshouse or the Hospital of St Julian: founded in 1185 by Gervase le Riche: in 1343 placed in the custody of the Queen's College, Oxford: cared

for old men and women under the custody of a warden. (Davies, pp. 450–63). The warden at this date may have been either Walter Belle or Rowland Bires (*op. cit.*, p. 463). The chapel still survives heavily restored.

199 The storehouse was built in 1417: P.R.O. Exchequer L.T.R. E364/61.

200 Folio 5v. is blank in the MS.

201 A village on the further side of the River Itchen from Southampton.

202 The next-door village to Weston: there is still woodland shown on a modern map of the district now a suburb of Southampton.

203 The whole of this folio 30 v. has been crossed through in the MS. with the note in the left hand margin, 'iste parcelle allocata per consilium Baronum' – these particulars have been allowed by advice of the Barons (of the Exchequer).

204 This paragraph and the two following have been crossed through in the MS with the addition of the note, 'que alibi hominibus allocata' – allowed elsewhere to these men.

205 In the MS, this section appears to be in a different hand and has been crossed through with the note 'cancellate quia sine warranto' – cancelled no authority.

206 The Abbey of Titchfield was a house of Premonstratensian Canons founded in 1222 by Bishop Peter des Roches, a colony of the house at Halesowen in Shropshire. The Abbey lands included property at Swanwick, Porchester, Walswork, Cosham, the manor of Cadlands and holdings in Hythe, Stanswood, Woodcote and Felde in the parish of Fawley. The Abbot referred to here is most probably Richard Aubrey elected the twelfth abbot in 1420. After the Dissolution, Wriothesley, the Earl of Southampton acquired the whole property and built a house on the Abbey site (now the ruined Palace House). *V.C.H. Hampshire*, Vol. II, p. 181, Vol. III, p. 220.

207 Olonnes: canvas made originally in Lower Poitou using flax grown locally or imported by the Loire from Anjou: by the fifteenth century the term was a generic one for canvas cloth. A. Rebillon, *Histoire de Bretagne*, p. 93. Y. Abbé, 'Les débuts d'une ville bretonne. Vitré au xvᵉ et xviᵉ siècle': in *Mémoires de la societé d'histoire et d'archéologie de Bretagne*, 1944, p. 67 et seq: and H. Touchard, *Commerce Maritime Breton à la fin du moyen âge*, pp. 25, 66.

208 The whole of the following paragraph has been cancelled in the MS with the marginal note, 'Because this has been allowed elsewhere, in his account in the fifth roll of royal accounts of King Henry VI.'

209 This paragraph has also been cancelled in the MS with the note 'Bonus (regardium) of the controller disallowed because without authority.'

210 A note at the foot of the page states, 'Total expenses of the said keeper, controller and other expenses up to here £748 7s 3¼d.'

211 The Tower of London, the storehouse of the Master of the Ordnance.

212 The Arabic numerals on the left hand side of the text refer back to the entries in the Table of Contents and are present in the MS.

213 The arrangement of some of the entries in the inventory section of the original does present some difficulties. In the MS the entries for each ship are indicated by a sub-heading in the left hand margin. All the entries concerning a particular ship are enclosed in a form of wide bracket on the right. Then, in certain cases, a further bracket on the right includes notes relating to items which have been disposed of in various ways. Sometimes the notes are so extensive that the folios of the MS almost resemble a maze of brackets and connecting lines. In the translation the names of ships are printed as sub-headings and the bracketed notes follow the items to which they refer.

214 These chains were intended as a means of defence against raids by the French for the ships anchored in the Hamble River. Their installation was ordered in 1418, *C.P.R. 1416–22*, p. 201.

215 Lynn – King's Lynn. The cordage concerned would have been imported

from the Baltic area. 'Black' cordage had been tarred – 'white' had not been treated in this way.

216   The area of Upper Normandy in the vicinity of St Valery-en-Caux.

217   A single ostrich feather was one of the personal badges of Henry IV and Henry V as also earlier of Edward III. Henry VI preferred a more elaborate design: an ostrich feather in bend argent surmounted by another in bend sinister or. As the equipment of the *Nicholas* was supplied in the reign of Henry V, one would imagine that the simpler version is implied here. W. H. Humphreys, *A short account of the Armorial bearings of the Sovereigns of England.* National Council of Social Service for the standing conference for Local History, p. 18 et seq.

218   The familiar cross of St George: a red cross on a white background.

219   This may be a reference to the two, 'lyme kylnes . . . scituat in Templstrete'. Bristol Archive Office AC/M21/7. I am indebted to Mrs J. Vanes for this reference.

220   Baltic cordage exported to England via Zealand in the Low Countries.

221   In the MS this section has been crossed out with the note 'these remain after the audit'.

222   The smithy adjoining the storehouse at Southampton sold at this time to the Warden of Godshouse (see above).

223   Berd had been in charge of the building of the *Gracedieu, Valentine* and *Falcon* and this timber was surplus to his requirements for that purpose.

224   This item has been crossed through in the MS with the note, 'because not among the purchases'.

225   The arms attributed to St Nicholas were: ermine a chief quarterly or and gules. W. Berry *Encyclopaedia Heraldica* Vol. 2, Dictionary of arms.

226   The arms of Edward the Confessor (St Edward) were traditionally: azure a cross flory between five doves or. *Boutell's Heraldry* revised by C. W. Scott-Giles, pp. 205, 208. They were marshalled with the Royal Arms by Richard II.

227   The badge of the Holy Spirit was the dove. C. Norton Elvin, *A Dictionary of Heraldry*, plate 22 F.4.

228   The royal arms of England between 1405 and 1603 were as follows: first and fourth quarters: Azure 3 fleur de lys or; second and third quarters: Gules three leopards or. W. H. Humphreys, *A short account of the Armorial Bearings of England*, p. 7.

229   A chained antelope was one of the personal badges of Henry V; and a silver antelope of Henry IV. W. H. Humphreys, *op. cit.*, p. 18.

230   The royal leopard of England.

231   Fleur de lys or badge of the French royal family; adopted by the English kings after their claim to the throne of France at the beginning of the Hundred Years War.

232   The badge of St Mary the Virgin was: azure a lily of nature argent.

233   A complicated design representing the Trinity on an azure ground, also used as the ensign of the monastery of Greyfriars in the City of London: for an illustration see C. Norton Elvin, *A Dictionary of Heraldry*, Plate 22 f. 1.

234   Appendix I consists of a fragmentary account dating from the last years of the reign of Henry V: it is bound in at the front of the volume containing the accounts. The folios are numbered from 17 in a contemporary hand but as this numbering could be confusing it has been omitted.

235   At this point in the MS several words are illegible because of its poor condition: there is also a small hole in the folio.

236   The weighhouse in Southampton housed the king's Weigh Beams where goods were weighed for assessment to customs duties. It stood in French Street and was unfortunately heavily damaged in the war. (R. Douch, *Collected Essays on Southampton* ed J. B. Morgan and P. Peberdy, p. 9.)

237   Sevenokeskey: possibly the quay belonging to William Sevenoke, a merchant of London. *C.P.R. 1422–9*, p. 319.

238 The Pool of London.
239 A 'craier' was one of the most common types of medieval merchant ship and is usually thought to have been a small 'round' square rigged vessel with one mast.
240 Middelburgh is on the island of Walcheren near Flushing. It is no longer a port.
241 The MS has been damaged at this point and this is only the last figure of the sum of money.
242 The folio has been cut off at this point.
243 The bottom of the folio has been cut off at this point.
244 Probably a mistake for Walter Fetplace, Soper's friend and business associate.
245 A word is missing here through damage to the MS.
246 The folio has been cut off at this point and a blank folio intervenes before the start of the accounts proper.
247 Appendix II consists of some further fragmentary accounts which have been bound in at the end of the Soper account book. They are concerned with repairs and alterations to ships which went on the Duke of Bedford's expedition in 1416. The folio numbering (which is not contemporary) continues from the Soper accounts to the end of the volume in one sequence: (as already noted Appendix I is not numbered in this way). Folio 115v., however, is blank and these accounts begin abruptly on folio 116r. They have all been cancelled with a line drawn down each folio and most page and marginal headings and the totals of expenditure have been erased.
248 Netley – a village on the east side of Southampton Water, south of Southampton itself.
249 Winsor – a manor in the parish of Eling of which a third part belonged to the Abbot of Netley (*V.C.H. Hampshire*, Vol. IV (2), p. 555).
250 Totton – a village situated where the River Test enters Southampton Water.
251 The Abbey of Netley was consecrated to the Virgin and Edward the Confessor. It was founded for the Cistercians by Henry III in 1239 as a colony of Beaulieu Abbey. Its land lay in Netley, Hound, Wellow, Totton, the New Forest and also Surrey. The Abbot at this date could have been either John de Gloucester or Richard de Midleton, both of whom held office after 1396. The existing ruins of the Abbey are quite extensive. *V.C.H. Hampshire*, Vol. II, p. 146; Vol. III p. 472.
252 The Manor of Allington in the parish of South Stoneham: *V.C.H. Hampshire*, Vol. I, p. 498a. Vol. III, p. 485.
253 Langley – a village near Fawley in the New Forest where Soper himself had property.
254 There is a hole in the MS at this point so the number of needles is lacking.
255 The MS comes to an end at the bottom of folio 123v. and a note has been added in a more modern hand. 'Misplaced in binding: see the beginning'.
256 Southampton City Record Office, Terrier of 1454, ff. 6r. 9v. 12r. 13r.
257 Royal Commission on Historical MSS., 11th Rep. Appendix III, p. 83.
258 E. C. Williams, *My Lord of Bedford*, p. 232.
259 *Feudal Aids* Vol. II, pp. 359–60; P.R.O. Lay Subsidy Return E179/173/92.
260 Details of Blount's career can be found in J. H. Wylie's *Henry IV* Vol. III and *Henry V* Vols. I, II and III.
261 P.R.O. Exchequer Warrants for Issue. E404/34/149, E404/35/196, E404/36/129, E404/37/175.
262 E404/48/147.
263 P.R.O. Exchequer. Accounts Various. E101/53/5 ff. 7v. 8r.
264 P.R.O. Exchequer. L.T.R. E364/57, Account of Robert Berd.
265 *Calendar of Letter Books of the City of London* Letter Book K pp. 43, 63. He is also described as an alderman here, (p. 280) though not listed in Beaven's *Aldermen of the City of London*.

266 P.R.O. Customs Account E122/161/1, 1423.
267 For import of corn: Southampton City Record Office MS Port Book for 1430: import of iron, steel, nails and carpets; P.R.O. K.R. Memoranda Roll E159/208: Trinity recorda, membrane 7. Import of oil; P.R.O. E.C.P. C1/11/204.
268 His factor was called Janetto Salvagge. P.R.O. E.C.P. C1/11/204.
269 P.R.O. Exchequer. Accounts Various, E101/128/31.
270 loc. cit. and A. A. Ruddock, 'Alien Hosting in Southampton', *Economic History Review*, Vol. XVI, 1946, pp. 32–3.
271 P.R.O. E.C.P. C1/16/656.
272 Wardens' Accounts of the Mercers' Company, ff. xxxiv v. lxxi r. He was also master in 1425, 1429, 1434, 1441. Beaven, *Aldermen of the City of London*, Vol. II, p. 6.
273 *Calendar of Wills preserved and enrolled in the Court of Husting, London*, Part II, Section II, pp. 609–11. *Calendar of London Letter Books*, Letter Book K, pp. 231–2.
274 J. R. Dunlop, *The Family of Fettiplace*, p. 3.
275 Lambeth Palace Library: Stafford Folio, f. 173r.
276 P.R.O. Exchequer. Accounts Various, E101/128/31; K.R. Memoranda Roll, E159/208, Trinity Recorda m.7.
277 Fetplace's prominent position in inland trade from Southampton is discussed in B. Carpenter-Turner, 'The Brokage Books of Southampton. A Hampshire Merchant and some aspects of Medieval Transport'. *Proc. H.F.C.*, Vol. XVI, 1944–7, pp. 173–7.
278 P.R.O. Exchequer L.T.R. Memoranda Roll E368/231. m.135.
279 P.R.O. Common Pleas, Feet of Fines. C.P. 25/207/31, no. 25; C.P. 25/207/32, no. 41.
280 Southampton City Record Office, Terrier of 1454, f. 4v.
281 P.R.O. Chancery Inquisitions, Post Mortem, C140/48. The estate became embroiled in a law suit between the Ludlows and Ringwoods. C1/57/99–100.
282 P.R.O. Exchequer Warrants for issue, E404/34/196, E404/35/145, E404/36/127.
283 P.R.O. Exchequer Warrants for Issue, E404/56/64.
284 P.R.O. Exchequer Warrants for Issue, E404/34/194, E404/35/242, E404/36/244, E404/37/126.
285 P.R.O. Exchequer Warrants for Issue, E404/36/272.
286 Ralph Huskard's accounts for the *Ane* are P.R.O. Exchequer L.T.R. E364/54 memb. B. The capture of the *Saint Jake and Saint Marie* is referred to in E364/57, Berd's account.
287 P.R.O. Exchequer Warrants for Issue, E404/47/297, E404/48/147.
288 E404/33/250, E404/34/154, E404/35/147, E404/36/131.
289 Southampton City Record Office, MS Port Book 1429–30, f. 46r. Huskard also took pilgrims to Compostella.
290 Pompeo Litta, *Famiglie Celebri Italiane*, XLVIII Tables V and VI.
291 Morosini, *Chronique: extraits relatifs à l'histoire de France* (ed. G. Lefèvre-Pontalis), Vol. I, p. 53.
292 Southampton City Record Office, MS Stewards' Book for 1456–7. Robert Bellous Book, f.11.
293 P.R.O. Ancient Deeds Exchequer E326/11804.
294 P.R.O. Common Pleas, C.P.25/207/32 no. 25.
295 PR.O. E.C.P. C1/15/184, C1/73/144–5.
296 C1/16/277.
297 A. A. Ruddock, *Italian Merchants and Shipping in Southampton*, pp. 176–8.
298 P.R.O. E.C.P. C1/17/235.
299 P.R.O. Exchequer Warrants for Issue, E404/33/245, E404/34/155, E404/35/151, E404/36/134.
300 Paolo's genealogy may be found in Ildefonso di San Luigi, *Delizia degli erudite Toscani*, Vol. XIX, p. xciii. He was a member of the Arte della Lana and had two children. The family traditionally supported the Guelf faction

and came originally from the Mugello. Gamurrini, *Istoria Genealogica delle Famiglie Nobile, Toscane et Umbre*, Vol. II, pp. 319–28. Coat of arms, Vol. III, p. 22.

301   A. A. Ruddock, *op. cit.*, pp. 98, 105, 122–3, 131.

302   P.R.O. L.T.R. E364/61.

303   C. Platt, *Medieval Southampton, the port and trading community, A.D. 1000–1600*, App. I, pp. 252–3.

304   *Royal Commission on Historical MSS. 11th Report*, Appendix III p. 74, p. 80. *Blk. Bk.* Vol. II p. 159.

305   *Royal Commission on Historical MSS*, loc. cit., pp. 78–82.

306   *Calendar of Inquisitions Miscellaneous*, 1399–1422, p. 310.

307   *Royal Commission on Historical MSS*, loc. cit., p. 88.

308   Hampshire County Record Office, H.R.O. 18 M 64.

309   P.R.O. Exchequer Warrants for Issue. E404/33/120, E404/34/156, E404/35/152.

310   P.R.O. Exchequer, Accounts Various, E101/53/5 f. 5r.

311   S. Thrupp, *The Merchant Class of Medieval London*, p. 363; *Calendar of London Letter Books*, letter book I, p. 81.

312   Beaven, *Aldermen of the City of London*, Vol. II, p. 5.

313   *Calendar of Wills preserved in the Court of Husting, London*, Part II, Section II, pp. 576–7.

314   P.R.O. Exchequer, Council and Privy Seal, E28/31.

315   P.R.O. Exchequer, Warrants for Issue. E404/33/246, E404/34/157, E404/36/135.

316   P.R.O. Exchequer, Council and Privy Seal, E28/57.

317   E28/57. His accounts for these voyages are P.R.O. Exchequer Accounts Various, E101/49/27, and L.T.R. E364/57.

318   P.R.O. Exchequer Accounts Various, E101/53/11.

319   P.R.O. Exchequer K.R. Customs Accounts, E122/139/4.

320   Morosini, *Chronique: extraits relatifs à l'histoire de France* (ed.) G. Lefèvre-Pontalis, Vol. I, p. 250.

321   C. Desimoni and L. T. Belgrano (eds.), *Documenti sulle Relazioni di Genova colle Flandre*, pp. 396–7.

322   Southampton City Record Office MS Terrier of 1454, f. 1r.

323   P.R.O. Exchequer Warrants for Issue, E404/35/167, E404/36/136, E404/37/129.

324   P.R.O. Exchequer Accounts Various. E101/49/16, E101/49/10. L.T.R. E364/63. Council and Privy Seal, E28/41.

325   A. A. Ruddock, *op. cit.*, pp. 88, 107, 120, 124–5.

326   *Dictionary of National Biography*, Vol. 53, p. 454.

327   The relevant clerk's accounts are E101/44/17. The suggestion has been made by C. F. Richmond in 'The keeping of the seas during the Hundred Years War 1422–40', *History*, Vol. XLIX 1964, p. 287. At the beginning of the reign of Henry V a John Sterlyng was collector of the subsidy of tunnage and poundage at Great Yarmouth. P.R.O. Exchequer Enrolled Customs Accounts. E356/15.

328   P.R.O. Exchequer Warrants for Issue, E404/34/158, E404/35/153, E404/36/132, E404/37/131.

329   E. Gamurrini, *Istoria Genealogica delle Famiglie Nobile Toscane et Umbre*. The family of Vetturi is not treated in detail but is frequently mentioned as marrying into the more prominent families.

330   Ildefonso de San Luigi, *Delizie degli Erudite Toscane*, Vol. XIX, p. 19.

331   P.R.O. K.R. Customs Accounts E122/138/24, E122/139/4, E122/139/11.

332   Morosini, *op. cit.*, Vol. II, p 270.

333   P.R.O. Exchequer. Warrants for Issue, E404/33/251, E404/34/19, E404/34/161, E404/35/155, E404/36/128.

334   P.R.O. Exchequer L.T.R. E364/54.

335   The two John Williams will be found together in P.R.O. Exchequer, Accounts Various, E101/53/5 ff. 6 v. (sailor) and 7r. (cooper).

336 His accounts as master of the *Jesus* are P.R.O. Exchequer. Accounts Various E101/48/26; and L.T.R. E364/61.
337 In the original patent, this grant is stated to be in lieu of lands in Anglesey – perhaps William's place of origin *C.P.R. 1416–22*, pp. 120–1.
338 P.R.O. Exchequer, Warrants for Issue E404/34/162.
339 Southampton City Record Office, Terrier of 1454, ff. 10v., 11r., 11v.
340 P.R.O. Exchequer, Warrants for Issue E404/34/163, E404/35/156.
341 P.R.O. Exchequer, Accounts Various E101/53/5, f. 5r.
342 Evidence for the number of masts carried by a vessel and other equipment, e.g. sails, running and standing rigging, etc. comes from the inventory sections of the enrolled accounts of the clerk of the king's ships under the name of the ship concerned. These accounts are found in the Exchequer L.T.R. Foreign Accounts class at the Public Record Office. Similar evidence is provided by the inventory section of this account book also. It must be borne in mind that it is not possible to ascertain whether these lists are complete or not: each consists of what was on board at a particular date not what should have been aboard. Details of the voyages undertaken by a vessel come from the same source (expenditure section) and also the particulars of accounts of various expeditions in the Exchequer Accounts Various class also in the Public Record Office.
343 Devon, *Issues of the Exchequer*, p. 356.
344 R. C. Anderson, 'The Bursledon Ship', *M.M.*, Vol. XV, 1934.
345 F. T. O'Brien, note in *M.M.*, Vol. LVII 1971, p. 325. R. C. Anderson feels that this identification is unlikely. *M.M.*, Vol. LXIX, 1973, p. 48.
346 Lefèvre-Pontalis (ed.) Morosini. *Chronique, extraits relatifs à l'histoire de France*, Vol. II, p. 138. The Italian botta is a wine measure from Crete – the butt of malmsey which contained between 140–126 gallons. F. C. Lane, *Venetian Ships and Shipbuilders of the Renaissance*, Appendix on Weights and Measures. By 1483 it had stabilised at the latter figure. The English tun of Bordeaux wine by a series of statutes beginning with 18 Henry VI Cap. 8 was defined as containing 252 gallons. A botta was, therefore, approximately of the capacity of half a tun.
347 Cogs as a ship type are discussed by P. Heinsius, 'Dimensions et caractéristiques des "Koggen" hanseatiques dans le commerce baltique,' in M. Mollat (ed.) *Le Navire et l'économie Maritime du Nord de l'Europe du Moyenâge au XVIIIe siècle*.
348 In view of her name this ship may be an early example of the ship type 'hulk' which is fully discussed in two notes in the *M.M.*, Vol. LVIII, 1972, by T. Glasgow Jr. pp. 103–4 and by D. A. Kirby pp. 344–7.

INDEX

This is mainly an index of proper names and places with a few subject entries. References to royal ships will be found under the heading, 'Ships' names – in royal ownership'; as several vessels had the same name they are distinguished by date or type as applicable. Other ships are referred to under 'Ships' names – trading vessels.' Unusual items of ships' equipment are listed under 'naval stores' or 'timber, types of'. Common items occur so frequently in the inventory section that they are not included in the index.

The names of the many workmen mentioned are listed under the following headings: carpenters – *berders*, carpenters, caulkers, clenchers, fellers, holders, master-carpenters and sawyers; workmen – carters, labourers and porters, and smiths. The names of sailors are listed under 'mariners' divided into masters of royal ships, masters of trading vessels, and shipkeepers.

Navy Records Society

(FOUNDED 1893)

THE Navy Records Society was established for the purpose of printing rare or unpublished works of naval interest. The Society is open to all who are interested in naval history and any person wishing to become a member should apply to the Hon. Secretary, c/o The Royal Naval College, Greenwich, London, SE10 9NN. The annual subscription for individuals is £5.50, the payment of which entitles the member to receive one copy of each work issued by the Society for that year. For Libraries and Institutions the annual subscription is £7.

The prices to members and non-members respectively are given after each volume, and orders should be sent, enclosing no money, to the Hon. Secretary. Those volumes against which the letters 'A & U' are set after the price to non-members are available to them only through bookshops or, in case of difficulty, direct from George Allen & Unwin (Publishers) Ltd, PO Box 18, Park Lane, Hemel Hempstead, Herts HP2 4TE. Prices are correct at the time of going to press.

The Society has already issued:

Vol. 40. *The Naval Miscellany* (Vol. II.). Edited by Sir J. K. Laughton. (*Out of Print.*)

Vol. 41. *Papers relating to the First Dutch War*, 1652–54 (Vol. V.). Edited by Mr. C. T. Atkinson. (*£6.50/£12.00*).

Vol. 42. *Papers relating to the Loss of Minorca in* 1756. Edited by Capt. H. W. Richmond, R.N. (*£6.50/£12.00.*)

Vol. 43. *The Naval Tracts of Sir William Monson* (Vol. III.). Edited by Mr. M. Oppenheim. (*Out of Print.*)

Vol. 44. *The Old Scots Navy*, 1689–1710. Edited by Mr. James Grant. (*Out of Print.*)

Vol. 45. *The Naval Tracts of Sir William Monson* (Vol. IV.). Edited by Mr. M. Oppenheim. (*£6.50/£12.00.*)

Vol. 46. *The Private Papers of George, second Earl Spencer* (Vol. I.). Edited by Mr. Julian S. Corbett. (*£6.50/£12.00.*)

Vol. 47. *The Naval Tracts of Sir William Monson* (Vol. V.). Edited by Mr. M. Oppenheim. (*£6.50/£12.00.*)

Vol. 48. *The Private Papers of George, second Earl Spencer* (Vol. II.). Edited by Mr. Julian S. Corbett. (*Out of Print.*)

Vol. 49. *Documents relating to Law and Custom of the Sea* (Vol. I.). Edited by Mr. R. G. Marsden (*£6.50/£12.00.*)

Vol. 50. *Documents relating to Law and Custom of the Sea* (Vol. II.). Edited by Mr. R. G. Marsden. (*£6.50/£12.00.*)

Vol. 51. *Autobiography of Phineas Pett*. Edited by Mr. W. G. Perrin. (*£6.50/£12.00.*)

Vol. 52. *The Life of Admiral Sir John Leake* (Vol. I.). Edited by Mr. G. A. R. Callender. (*£6.50/£12.00.*)

Vol. 53. *The Life of Admiral Sir John Leake* (Vol. II.). Edited by Mr. G. A. R. Callender. (*£6.50/£12.00.*)

Vol. 54. *The Life and Works of Sir Henry Mainwaring* (Vol. I.). Edited by Mr. G. E. Manwaring. (*£6.50/£12.00.*)

Vol. 55. *The Letters of Lord St. Vincent*, 1801–1804 (Vol. I.). Edited by Mr. D. B. Smith. (*Out of Print.*)

Vol. 56. *The Life and Works of Sir Henry Mainwaring* (Vol. II.). Edited by Mr. G. E. Manwaring and Mr. W. G. Perrin. (*Out of Print.*)

Vol. 57. *A Descriptive Catalogue of the Naval MSS in the Pepysian Library* (Vol. IV.). Edited by Dr. J. R. Tanner. (*Out of Print.*)

Vol. 58. *The Private Papers of George, second Earl Spencer* (Vol. III.). Edited by Rear-Admiral H. W. Richmond. (*Out of Print.*)

Vol. 59. *The Private Papers of George, second Earl Spencer* (Vol. IV.). Edited by Rear-Admiral H. W. Richmond. (*Out of Print.*)

Vol. 60. *Samuel Pepys's Naval Minutes*. Edited by Dr. J. R. Tanner. (*Out of Print.*)

Vol. 61. *The Letters of Lord St. Vincent*, 1801–1804 (Vol. II). Edited by Mr. D. B. Smith (*Out of Print.*)

Vol. 62. *Letters and Papers of Admiral Viscount Keith* (Vol. I.). Edited by Mr. W. G. Perrin. (*Out of Print.*)

Vol. 63. *The Naval Miscellany* (Vol. III.). Edited by Mr. W. G. Perrin. (*Out of Print.*)

Vol. 64. *The Journal of the First Earl of Sandwich*. Edited by Mr. R. C. Anderson. (*£6.50/£12.00.*)

Vol. 65. *Boteler's Dialogues*. Edited by Mr. W. G. Perrin. (*£6.50/£12.00.*)

Vol. 66. *Papers relating to the First Dutch War*, 1652–54 (Vol. VI.; with index). Edited by Mr. C. T. Atkinson. (*£6.50/£12.00.*)

Vol. 67. *The Byng Papers* (Vol. I.). Edited by Mr. W. C. B. Tunstall. (*£6.50/£12.00.*)

Vol. 68. *The Byng Papers* (Vol. II.). Edited by Mr. W. C. B. Tunstall. (*£6.50/£12.00.*)

Vol. 69. *The Private Papers of John, Earl of Sandwich* (Vol. I.). Edited by Mr. G. R. Barnes and Lieut.-Commander J. H Owen, RN. (*£6.50/£12.00.*)

Corregenda to *Papers relating to the First Dutch War,* 1652–54 (Vols. I. to VI.). Edited by Captain A. C. Dewar, R.N. (*£6.50/£12.00.*)

Vol. 70. *The Byng Papers* (Vol. III.). Edited by Mr. W. C. B. Tunstall. (*£6.50/£12.00.*)

Vol. 71. *The Private Papers of John, Earl of Sandwich* (Vol. II.). Edited by Mr. G. R. Barnes and Lieut.-Commander J. H. Owen, R.N. (*£6.50/£12.00.*)

Vol. 72. *Piracy in the Levant,* 1827–8. Edited by Lieut.-Commander C. G. Pitcairn Jones, R.N. (*£6.50/£12.00.*)

Vol. 73. *The Tangier Papers of Samuel Pepys.* Edited by Mr. Edwin Chappell. (*Out of Print.*)

Vol. 74. *The Tomlinson Papers.* Edited by Mr. J. G. Bullocke. (*£6.50/£12.00.*)

Vol. 75. *The Private Papers of John, Earl of Sandwich* (Vol. III.). Edited by Mr. G. R. Barnes and Commander J. H. Owen, R.N. (*£6.50/£12.00.*)

Vol. 76. *The Letters of Robert Blake.* Edited by the Rev. J. R. Powell. (*£6.50/£12.00.*)

Vol. 77. *Letters and Papers of Admiral the Hon. Samuel Barrington* (Vol. I.). Edited by Mr. D. Bonner-Smith. (*£6.50/£12.00.*)

Vol. 78. *The Private Papers of John, Earl of Sandwich* (Vol. IV.). Edited by Mr. G. R. Barnes and Commander J. H. Owen, R.N. (*£6.50/£12.00.*)

Vol. 79. *The Journals of Sir Thomas Allin,* 1660–1678 (Vol. I. 1660–66). Edited by Mr. R. C. Anderson. (*£6.50/£12.00.*)

Vol. 80. *The Journals of Sir Thomas Allin,* 1660–1678 (Vol. II. 1667–78). Edited by Mr. R. C. Anderson. (*£6.50/£12.00.*)

Vol. 81. *Letters and Papers of Admiral the Hon. Samuel Barrington* (Vol. II.). Edited by Mr. D. Bonner-Smith. (*Out of Print.*)

Vol. 82. *Captain Boteler's Recollections* (1808 to 1830). Edited by Mr. D. Bonner-Smith. (*Out of Print.*)

Vol. 83. *Russian War,* 1854. *Baltic and Black Sea: Official Correspondence.* Edited by Mr. D. Bonner-Smith and Captain A. C. Dewar, R.N. (*Out of Print.*)

Vol. 84. *Russian War,* 1855. *Baltic: Official Correspondence.* Edited by Mr. D. Bonner-Smith. (*Out of Print.*)

Vol. 85. *Russian War,* 1855. *Black Sea: Official Correspondence.* Edited by Captain A. C. Dewar, R. N. (*Out of Print.*)

Vol. 86. *Journals and Narratives of the Third Dutch War.* Edited by Mr. R. C. Anderson. (*Out of Print.*)

Vol. 87. *The Naval Brigades in the Indian Mutiny,* 1857–58. Edited by Commander W. B. Rowbotham, R.N. (*Out of Print.*)

Vol. 88. *Patee Byng's Journal.* Edited by Mr. J. L. Cranmer-Byng. (*Out of Print.*)

Vol. 89. *The Sergison Papers* (1688–1702). Edited by Commander R. D. Merriman, R.I.N. (*£6.50/£12.00.*)

Vol. 90. *The Keith Papers* (Vol. II.). Edited by Mr. C. C. Lloyd. (*£6.50/£12.00.*)

Vol. 91. *Five Naval Journals,* 1789–1817. Edited by Rear-Admiral H. G. Thursfield. (*£6.50/£12.00.*)

Vol. 92. *The Naval Miscellany* (Vol. IV.). Edited by Mr. C. C. Lloyd. *(£6.50/£12.00.)*

Vol. 93. *Sir William Dillon's Narrative of Professional Adventures (1790–1839)* (Vol. I. 1790–1802). Edited by Professor Michael A. Lewis *(Out of Print.)*

Vol. 94. *The Walker Expedition to Quebec. 1711.* Edited by Professor Gerald S. Graham. *(Out of Print.)*

Vol. 95. *The Second China War,* 1856–60. Edited by Mr. D. Bonner-Smith and Mr. E. W. R. Lumby. *(Out of Print.)*

Vol. 96. *The Keith Papers,* 1803–1815 (Vol. III). Edited by Professor C. C. Lloyd. *(£6.50/£12.00.)*

Vol. 97. *Sir William Dillon's Narrative of Professional Adventures (1790–1839)* (Vol. II. 1802–1839). Edited by Professor Michael A. Lewis. *(Out of Print.)*

Vol. 98. *The Private Correspondence of Admiral Lord Collingwood.* Edited by Professor Edward Hughes. *(Out of Print.)*

Vol. 99. *The Vernon Papers (1739–1745).* Edited by Mr. B. McL. Ranft. *(Out of Print.)*

Vol. 100. *Nelson's Letters to his Wife and Other Documents.* Edited by Lieut.-Commander G. P. B. Naish, R.N.V.R. *(£6.50/£12.00.)*

Vol. 101. *A Memoir of James Trevenen (1760–1790).* Edited by Professor C. C. Lloyd and Dr. R. C. Anderson. *(£6.50/£12.00.)*

Vol. 102. *The Papers of Admiral Sir John Fisher* (Vol. I.). Edited by Lieut.-Commander P. K. Kemp, R.N. *(Out of Print.)*

Vol. 103. *Queen Anne's Navy.* Edited by Commander R. D. Merriman, R.I.N. *(Out of Print.)*

Vol. 104. *The Navy and South America,* 1807–1823. Edited by Professor G. S. Graham and Professor R. A. Humphreys. *(£6.50/£12.00.)*

Vol. 105. *Documents relating to the Civil War,* 1642–1648. Edited by the Rev. J. R. Powell and Mr. E. K. Timings. *(Out of Print.)*

Vol. 106. *The Papers of Admiral Sir John Fisher* (Vol. II.). Edited by Lieut.-Commander P. K. Kemp, R.N. *(£6.50/£12.00.)*

Vol. 107. *The Health of Seamen.* Edited by Professor C. C. Lloyd. *(£6.50/£12.00.)*

Vol. 108. *The Jellicoe Papers* (Vol. I: 1893–1916). Edited by Mr. A. Temple Patterson. *(£6.50/£12.00.)*

Vol. 109. *Documents relating to Anson's Voyage round the World,* 1740–1744. Edited by Dr. Glyndwr Williams. *(£6.50/£12.00.)*

Vol. 110. *The Saumarez Papers: The Baltic,* 1808–1812. Edited by Mr. A. N. Ryan. *(£6.50/£12.00.)*

Vol. 111. *The Jellicoe Papers* (Vol. II: 1916–1935). Edited by Professor A. Temple Patterson. *(£6.50/£12.00.)*

Vol. 112. *The Rupert and Monck Letterbook,* 1666. Edited by the Rev. J. R. Powell and Mr. E. K. Timings. *(£6.50/£12.00.)*

Vol. 113. *Documents relating to the Royal Naval Air Service* (Vol. I: 1908–1918). Edited by Captain S. W. Roskill, R.N. *(£6.50/£12.00.)*

Vol. 114. *The Siege and Capture of Havana: 1762.* Edited by Assistant-Professor David Syrett. *(£6.50/£12.00.)*

Vol. 115. *Policy and Operations in the Mediterranean: 1912–14.* Edited by Mr. E. W. R. Lumby. *(£6.50/£12.00.)*

Vol. 116. *The Jacobean Commissions of Enquiry: 1608 and 1618.* Edited by Dr. A. P. McGowan. *(£6.50/£12.00.)*

Vol. 117. *The Keyes Papers.* (Vol. I: 1914–1918). Edited by Dr. Paul G. Halpern. *(£7.50/£12.00—A & U.)*